WOODWORK

ONE

DAVID WILLACY BED DLC

Head of Art Studies, St Albans School, St Albans
Moderator and Chief Examiner in Woodwork, GCE and CSE Boards

Illustrated with photographs
and with line drawings by
NORMA CROCKFORD

THIRD EDITION

Nelson

By the same author
WOODWORK TWO

Thomas Nelson and Sons Ltd
Nelson House Mayfield Road
Walton-on-Thames Surrey
KT12 5PL UK

51 York Place
Edinburgh
EH1 3JD UK

Thomas Nelson (Hong Kong) Ltd
Toppan Building 10/F
22A Westlands Road
Quarry Bay Hong Kong

Distributed in Australia by

Thomas Nelson Australia
480 La Trobe Street
Melbourne Victoria 3000
and in Sydney, Brisbane, Adelaide and Perth

First published in Great Britain by Hamish Hamilton Ltd 1970
Second edition (metricated and revised)
published by Thomas Nelson and Sons Ltd 1971
Reprinted 1973, 1974, 1975, 1977
Third Edition 1979
Reprinted 1980, 1981, 1982, 1983, 1984, 1986

ISBN 0-17-431025-0
NCN 28-KPR-3174-03

Map on page 19 by H. J. Blackman

Printed and bound in Hong Kong

CONTENTS

SPECIAL TOOLS

DRAWING

DESIGN

(Each section contains data for the job, problems to answer, appearance, proportion, design features, use of new ideas, decoration, construction, final adjustments, the working drawing.)

TABLES

PREFACE

The basic content of this book remains the same as previous editions although many of the original photographs have been replaced and twenty new ones have been added. I have pursued a policy of featuring new tools where their performance appears to justify inclusion—many of which are designed for the DIY market—and disregarding those which are no longer made.

Writing about timber is a precarious task—for surely no one could have foreseen the changes in the world market which have occurred in the last five years. It is with caution that I have withdrawn details of three timbers and included seven new ones—my guide being those that are available to schools now and in the foreseeable future.

The principles and techniques outlined in the Design section still seem valid and remain unaltered, but additional examination questions have been added at the end of this and other sections.

In the first editions of *'Woodwork 1'* I recorded my debt to my wife Joan for 'preparing the typescript'. In *'Woodwork 2'* I thanked her 'for her constant encouragement to write well and for keeping Karen and Laura out of the study'.

The girls are now at school and it is my son Gavin who persistently enquires the reasons why I need to borrow his scissors to cut a seemingly wholesome book! I hope that you will appreciate, more than he does, the need for the changes I have made.

I am very grateful for the help given in compiling this book by the following firms and organisations:

Aaronson Brothers, Aeropreen, 'Alwayse' Castor Co., Armstrong Patents Co., Berman Brothers, The British Standards Institution, Carborundum Co., Carver & Co., Ciba-Geigy (UK), Cintride, James Collins, Copydex, Crompton Nettlefold Stenman, Cuprinol, Denford Machine Tools, Dunlop, English Abrasives Corporation, English Sewing, Evode, The Fibre Building Board Development Organisation, Firth Brown Tools, Fitchett and Woollacott, Formica, Furniglas, Gliksten Hardwoods, Guest Keen & Nettlefold, Hadfields (Merton), L. G. Harris & Co., T. S. Harrison & Sons, W. W. Hill Son & Wallace, Imperial Chemical Industries, F. Leiner and Co., Isaac Lord, The 3M Co., Record Ridgway Marples, James Neill and Co. (Eclipse), Nettlefold Stenman, Norton Abrasives, F. Parramore & Sons, E. Parsons & Sons, Power Tools, Pirelli, Plywood Manufacturers Association of British Columbia, Rabone Chesterman, The Rawlplug Co., Rentokil, Rexel, Wm. Ridgway & Sons, Rustins, Rylands Brothers, Safety Products, Selectus, Spear and Jackson, Stanley-Bridges, Stanley Tools, Storey Brothers and Co., Sterling Roncraft, Timber Research & Development Association, UAC Timber, Alec Tiranti, Thor Hammer Co., Tower Manufacturing Co., Unibond, Wadkin, Wolf Electric Tools, E. C. Young.

My thanks go also to Mr. D. J. Gothard and Mr. S. F. Robertson who took the photographs in the design section and those of the tools in workshop use.

D.M.W.

General Acknowledgements

The author and publishers are grateful to the following companies and individuals for permission to reproduce copyright photographs in this book, page nos. as follows:
Carborundum Co., 81
Ciba-Geigy (UK), 33, 36 (top, middle R, bottom R), 92, 184 (bottom L)
Denford Machine Tools, 78 (middle, bottom)
D. J. Gothard, 110, 155 (bottom), 156, 164, 166, 171, 177 (all), 182 (bottom), 183 (bottom)
G.K.N., 97 (all)
H.M.S.O., The Controller, photographs originally published in Forest Research Laboratory Leaflet No. 39 'Timber Decay and its Control' (H.M.S.O. 1962), 22 (bottom L, bottom R), 23 (top, middle, bottom), 25 (D, E, F)
John Laing and Son, 104
Lervad (UK), 76
Parramore, 84 (bottom R)
Rentokil Laboratories, 25 (A, B)
Record Ridgway, 55 (all), 69, 71 (top L, bottom L), 85, 88 (top, middle L, middle R), 116, 117, 125
S. F. Robertson, 18 (bottom L), 49 (top L, top R, bottom R), 71 (middle), 87 (middle), 132, 144 (top, bottom), 150, 155 (top), 163 (top, bottom)
Sterling Roncraft, 101 (top)
Gordon Russel, 148
Spear & Jackson, 41, 58 (top), 60
Stanley Works (GB), 40, 42, 49 (bottom L), 50 (R), 52, 54 (all), 56 (R), 58 (bottom R), 63, 64, 66, 67, 68 (R), 71 (top R), 82 (top L), 86 (all), 95, 111, 113 (all), 114, 115, 124, 185
Timber Research and Development Association, 14, 16
Thames Plywood Manufacturers, 36 (middle L, bottom L)
United Africa Company (Timber), 28 (all), 31
Victoria and Albert Museum, 18 (bottom R)
Kenneth Wood, ARIBA, AMISE, 18 (top)
Woodworker, 181
Wouldham Manufacturing Co., 78 (top)
The following photographs were taken by the author: 49 (top L & R, bottom R), 50 (L), 54 (all), 58 (bottom L), 62 (all), 68 (L), 82 (top R, middle L & R, bottom L & R), 83, 84 (middle L, bottom L), 88 (bottom), 90 (all), 98, 100, 101 (all), 118, 130, 134 (all), 144 (middle), 147, 160 (all), 161 (all), 182 (top L), 183 (top L), 184 (R), 186 (all).

The author and publishers are grateful also to the following G.C.E. and C.S.E. Regional Boards for permission to reprint questions from their examination papers. Initial letters are used in the text as follows to indicate the Board concerned:

Associated Examining Board for the G.C.E.	AEB
East Midland Regional Examinations Board	EM
Joint Matriculation Board	JMB
Metropolitan Regional Examinations Board	MET
North Western Secondary Schools Examinations Board	NW
Southern Regional Examinations Board	S
The South-East Regional Examinations Board	SE
Welsh Joint Education Committee	W
West Midlands Examinations Board	WM

WORKSHOP SAFETY

Clothing

Loose clothing such as pullovers and ties can cause serious accidents. You should remove your jacket, tuck in your tie, and wear an apron. Girls and boys with long hair should tie it back or wear a cap.

Hand Tools

1. Carry dangerous tools in a safe manner
2. Place tools down safely when not immediately needed
3. Pass tools safely to one another, handle first
4. Make use of holding devices to reduce danger

Machinery

1. Do not use a machine tool unless you are familiar with the correct method of use and the safety precautions for that machine
2. Make sure that guards for belts, pulleys and gears are properly in position before starting work
3. The floor near the machine must be free from obstruction
4. *Read and obey warning notices* displayed for your benefit

Electrical

1. Familiarize yourself with emergency stops and starter switches as well as the normal method of stopping a machine

Lathes

1. Only one person at a time should operate the lathe
2. Do not brake a moving faceplate or chuck by hand to reduce the speed after switching the drive off
3. Swarf (waste) must never be removed by hand
4. In poor light do not hesitate to use the light provided
5. Wear goggles at all times
6. Avoid conversations with other students. The work that you are doing requires your full attention

Power Drills

1. Thin materials must be held in a clamp when drilling
2. Chuck keys must not be left in the drill chuck as these can fly a considerable distance if the machine is started

Saws

1. Circular saws must always have the guard and riving knife in position and must only be used by the teacher. After use the isolator switch must be turned off as well as the machine switch

Band Saw

1. Safety precautions are similar to those for the circular saw, but in addition you must never attempt to make any adjustments to the blade guides whilst the saw is moving

Portable Tools

1. If you have portable power tools in the workshop use them only where they are safe (e.g. long leads can be dangerous) and only when the machine is designed to do the job you require it to do
2. If in doubt about the safety of a tool consult your teacher

First Aid

1. All accidents, which will occasionally happen in spite of taking all reasonable precautions, must be reported and it is important for each of you to know the whereabouts of the first aid kit and fire extinguisher

INTRODUCTION

TO THE TEACHER

The syllabuses of the CSE Regional Boards and the GCE Examining Boards cover a multiplicity of subjects from carving and veneering, boat-building and group activities to the safe use of portable electric tools. The examination papers fully reflect these variations.

Most of the information asked of students will be found in this book and in *Woodwork* Two which are planned in a series of 60 sections—each representing one week's consideration up to the holiday preceding the examination term. The sections are not intended to inhibit the originality of the work being done in a particular school but to make the facts available in an adaptable way for your use.

Book One deals with Timber, Tools, Equipment, Special Tools, Drawing and Design.

Book Two has chapters on Joints, Methods of Construction, Machine and Portable Electric Tools, Turning, Laminating and Bending, Upholstery, Woodcarving and Sculpture, Hardware and New Materials, Tools and Processes. There is an additional section of Designs and advice is given on the writing of a Personal Study or Project.

Although the book frequently mentions ways in which tools should be used this is not its main function. It is assumed that most teachers would prefer to give demonstrations of practical work and use the text as a source of reference.

Sufficient questions will be found after each section for both homework and examination requirements.

TO THE STUDENT

The basic information needed for your written examinations will be found in the clearly set out sections which will also make revision easy to plan. The use of authentic questions after each part of the book will also help you in this way.

The chapter on drawing is designed so that you can work through it yourself to develop the skill of producing simple but effective drawings. These will be used when designing jobs or answering questions which invariably include the words 'sketch, draw or illustrate'!

1 TIMBER

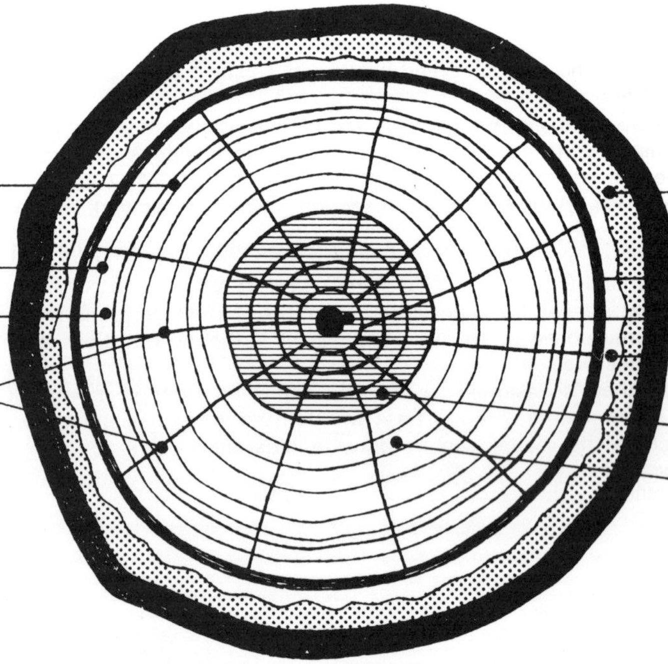

1 THE TREE

Trees are highly developed plants that grow taller and increase in girth each year. This yearly addition of new cells is called an *annual ring* or *growth ring* and, because the ring may be in two distinguishable bands, it is often possible to calculate the age of a tree that has been felled. This is particularly true of softwoods such as Red Deal.

The lighter coloured soft band of wood *(spring growth)* is wider than the ring of darker, harder wood *(summer* and *autumn growth)*.

GROWTH

The amount of growth depends upon:

1. *The kind of tree*—softwoods grow quicker than most hardwoods.
2. *The type of soil*—its depth, drainage and chemical properties.
3. *The position of the tree*—the amount of sun or shelter from strong winds it receives.
4. *The climate and weather*—trees grow quickly in Tropical countries because the climate is usually hot and wet. Trees in this country grow little during a cool or dry summer.

STRUCTURE

The young tree consists of cells made of cellulose which have thin walls that absorb the moisture from the roots and begin to grow. They eventually become old (lignified), the walls thicken and harden, and the cell 'dies'.

This part of the tree is called the *heartwood (duramen)* as distinct from the *sapwood (alburnum)* which consists of the younger living wood cells.

1. The *heartwood* contains resins and is more durable than the softer *sapwood.* It resists decay, attack by insects and fungi, and is the most useful part of the tree from which to make furniture.

When trees are very young most of the trunk is sapwood, but as the tree matures a greater proportion becomes heartwood.

2. The centre of the trunk is called the *pith (medulla)* and is often soft. It is the remains of the original *sapling.*

3. Completely surrounding the sapwood is the *cambium layer* which is sometimes referred to as the *growth layer* because the cells are very active. On the inside most of them become new sapwood whilst some of the outside become the new *bast.*

4. The *bast* is a thin green tissue and is most important as its tube-like cells are the main supply lines of the sapwood for elaborated sap (manufactured from crude sap in the *leaves*).

5. *Waste products* such as resin, which is stored in the heartwood, are transported there by paper-thin *medullary rays* that extend like the spokes of the wheel from the cambium layer to the pith (medulla).

On some timbers they are hardly visible but on others, such as oak, they produce the attractive, characteristic, silvery 'figure' seen on boards cut radially (section 8).

All these parts are covered with a protective *bark.* The inside of the bark is soft and expands with the tree's growth, whilst the outside becomes harder and often cracks. The bark protects the growth layers of the tree from excessive heat and cold and attack from insects and animals, and also prevents moisture inside the tree from escaping (which is called *transpiration*).

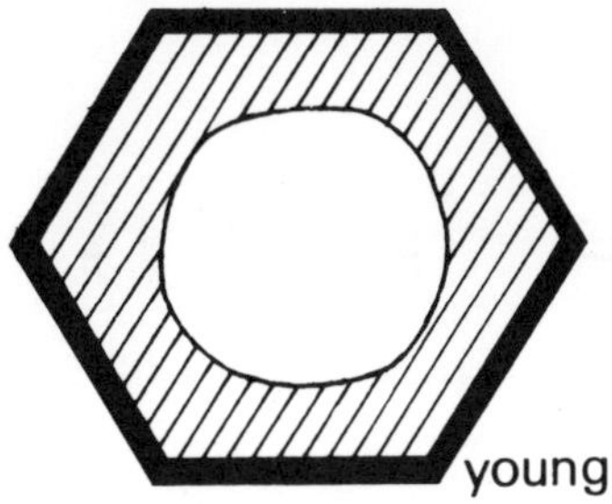

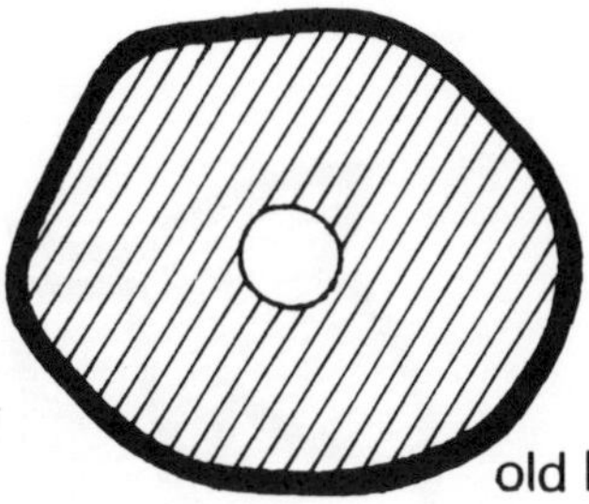

Hardwood and softwood trees are usually easy to distinguish from each other.

The deciduous oak tree loses its broad leaves each year and grows into the familiar 'mushroom' shape.

The coniferous spruce (white wood) keeps its needle-like leaves throughout the year and grows tall and slender.

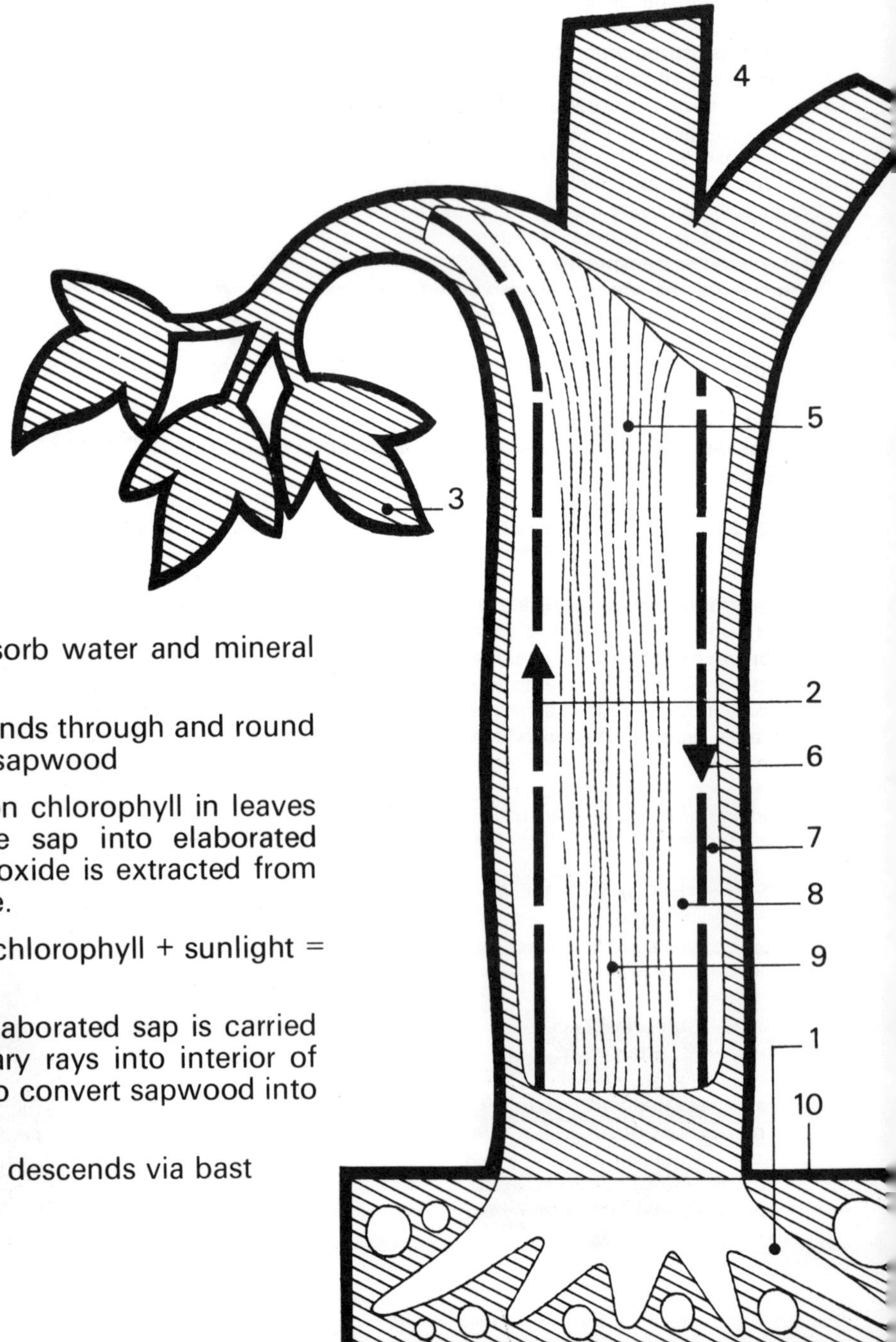

1 Root fibres absorb water and mineral salts
2 Crude sap ascends through and round the outside of sapwood
3 Sunlight acts on chlorophyll in leaves changing crude sap into elaborated sap. Carbon dioxide is extracted from the atmosphere.
4 CO_2 + H_2O + chlorophyll + sunlight = sugar
5 Some of the elaborated sap is carried by the medullary rays into interior of trunk helping to convert sapwood into heartwood
6 Elaborated sap descends via bast
7 Bast
8 Sapwood
9 Heartwood
10 Ground level

2 TIMBER—SOFTWOOD

TIMBER

The terms 'Hardwood' and 'Softwood' can be very misleading because some 'hard' woods are softer than many Softwoods and vice versa.

The distinction between them is a *botanical* one based on the arrangement of the *cells* (or *fibres*).

SOFTWOOD

Softwood cells are small, independent compartments called *Tracheids*. They are usually less than 6 mm long and are narrow and elongated. *Crude sap* from the roots is transported to the leaves by these cells through small apertures called *pits*. Their other main function is to support the tree.

These cells are the *'grain'* of the wood and what we refer to as the 'Direction of Grain' depends upon the way in which the cells form.

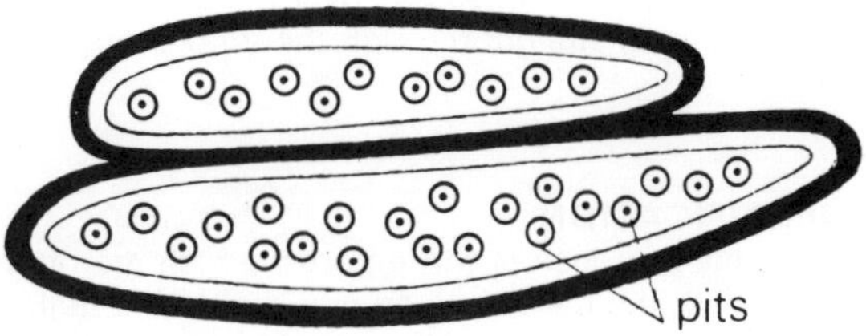

IDENTIFICATION

Softwoods come from *coniferous trees* and are quite easy to identify because of:

1. The distinct growth rings.
2. The relative proportions of the early-wood (Spring) and late-wood (Summer and Autumn) zones.
3. The presence of resin ducts—deposits of medullary rays.

In addition softwoods are usually lighter in weight (exceptions are Yew, Larch and Pitch-Pine), lighter in colour and are more easily worked than the majority of hardwoods.

EXAMPLES

Pine (Scots Pine or Red Deal)

Yellow-white sapwood, pale reddish brown heartwood, distinct growth rings, moderately resinous, fairly straight grain, frequently knotty.

Parana Pine

Light sapwood, heartwood variable—generally pale brown but often with vivid red streaks, indistinct growth rings, very straight grain, few knots, fairly heavy and available in wide boards.

Western Red Cedar

Sapwood is narrow, reddish-brown heartwood, narrow growth rings, straight grain, wide boards, few knots, light in weight with a distinct smell when fresh-cut, no resin ducts.

Spruce

(Whitewood or White Deal)—heartwood and sapwood a similar pale colour, growth rings visible, slightly resinous, no distinct smell, light in weight, resin ducts.

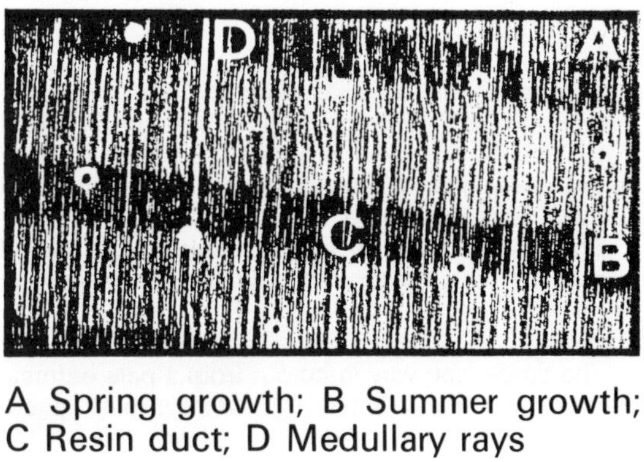

A Spring growth; B Summer growth; C Resin duct; D Medullary rays

3 TIMBER—HARDWOOD

HARDWOOD

The bulk of hardwood consists of *fibres* which correspond to the tracheids in softwoods (except that they are very much smaller) in that they give support to the tree.

They *do not* transport crude sap from the tree roots to the leaves.

This function is performed by the *pores* or *vessels* which are formed one over the other making a *tube* running straight through the whole length of the tree.

fibres

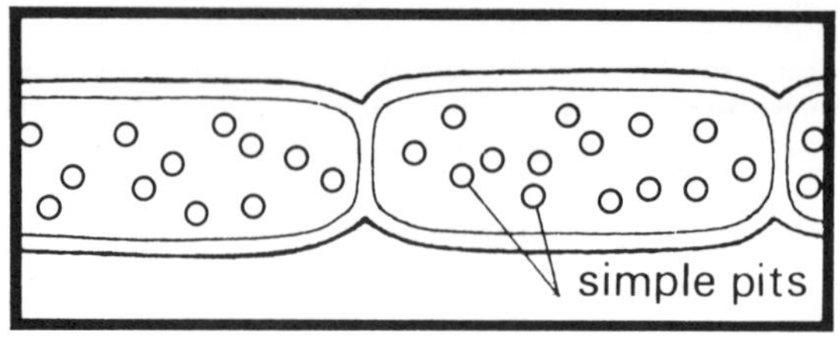

pores or vessels

IDENTIFICATION

It is the presence of these pores, which are often visible with the naked eye on end grain, that makes the distinction between hardwoods and softwoods relatively obvious. In addition, hardwoods are usually heavier in weight (Balsa wood is a famous exception), darker and more varied in colour and more difficult to work with than softwoods.

Hardwoods are themselves divided into two main groups:

1. *diffuse porous*
2. *ring porous*

The pores of timbers such as Beech, Birch and Lime are fairly evenly spread throughout the tree (diffuse porous) while those of Oak, Elm and Ash, for example, are formed in rings (ring porous). The pores of these timbers appear quite large in the early spring growth and are very much smaller, although still present in good number, in the later summer growth.

EXAMPLES

Elm

The yellow sapwood is distinct from the brown heartwood, and the large pores in the spring wood ring make the grain very prominent on the surface of boards. The grain is variable but often coarse and uneven, making planed surfaces dull.

The ring structure is easily visible to the naked eye as are the rays on end-grain which are few in number.

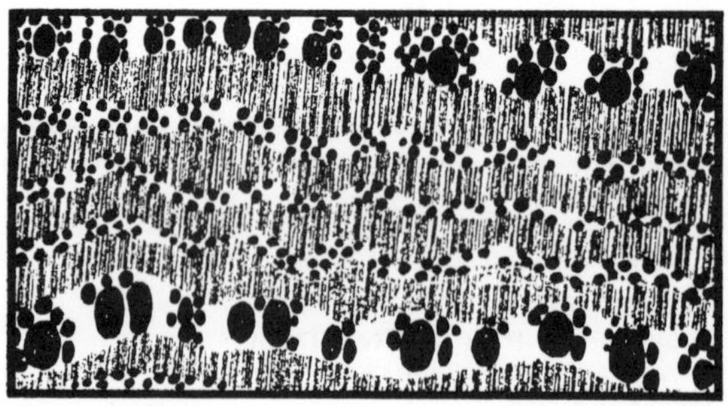
ring porous elm

Beech

The timber can vary in colour from a pale oatmeal to a strong 'pink' when it has been kiln dried. The crowded pores are diffuse and are only visible with a lens, and the annual rings are no more conspicuous. The rays are, however, a distinguishing feature, and though small in size are numerous. The denseness of the grain results in a silky surface being readily obtained.

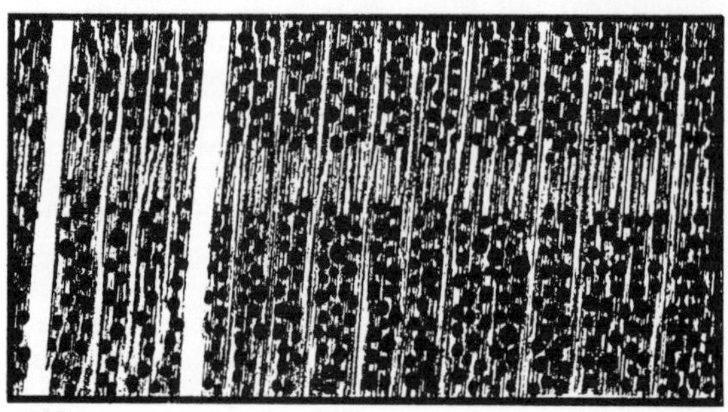
diffuse porous beech

GRAIN AND FIGURE

We can now tell the difference between hardwoods and softwoods when seen under a microscope; but in the workshop we need to be able to recognise different kinds of timber within the main groups, and choose 'like' pieces of wood for a particular job.

Looking at a labelled sample you should notice its colour, the coarseness of its texture and the straightness or irregularity of its grain. It is the *nature* of this *grain* which gives us the information we require to recognise a particular piece of wood. You should remember, though, that trees are individual plants with peculiar characteristics and care should be taken, say, when selecting timber for a cabinet, that the colour and grain patterns of the different boards are similar. With frequent handling in your workshop timbers will become familiar to you and their peculiarities of real interest.

Whilst some trees grow tall and straight-grained, such as Western Red Cedar, others are renowned for their special grain and figure.

1. *Oak* has the silvery figure mentioned earlier and some boards have almost the whole surface covered by a complex system of *medullary rays.*
2. Often in *Mahogany* and sometimes in *Sycamore* a pattern known as *fiddle-back* occurs when uneven growth produces a rippled effect which is frequently seen on the backs of violins.
3. A striped effect with alternate strips of grain running in opposite directions is caused by *spiral growth* which makes the fibres interlock. It is difficult to plane but can look extremely attractive and is a distinguishing feature of the West African wood, *Sapele.*
4. The unusual pattern on *Bird's Eye Maple* may be seen on veneers and is attractive enough to have been photographed and reproduced as a plastic lamination. The unique mottled effect is believed to be caused by *bacteria* which thrive on the sweet sap of the tree.

Figured Oak. The medullary rays form an irregular pattern across the grain.

Fiddleback Mahogany. Light is reflected from the grain in different ways to give a rippled effect.

4 COMMON TIMBERS

HARDWOODS

Of the many hundreds of different types of tree throughout the world only a *small* number are suitable for schools and the furniture industry to use. Many of the lovely trees that grow in our own country are not usable on a commercial scale because they grow in small quantities and are expensive. The finest examples of British timbers, often old oak or walnut trees, are usually cut for veneers. (section 10).

Early editions of this book mentioned timbers that are no longer available in the United Kingdom and in recent years we have had to learn the names and become familiar with the characteristics of new woods. For mainly economic and political reasons the supplies of timber from the Far East and South America, for example, Malaysia and Brazil, are now totally unreliable. In most instances substitutes have been found and, in the main, these grow on the African Continent.

From experience you should now be able to recognise some of the timbers in the workshop. Their characteristics and important uses are listed below.

EUROPEAN

Ash This open-grained wood is tough and flexible and is used for tool handles, ladders and hockey sticks.

Beech Mainly imported from Central Europe, it is close-grained and difficult to work. Used for making workshop equipment and tools such as jack planes, and extensively for childrens' toys and in chair manufacture.

Birch Not very attractive but wears well and is close-grained. Mainly used for plywood veneers.

Elm Renowned for its toughness and durability. Traditionally used for coffins, farm carts and water troughs.

Lime A pale, close-grained wood that cuts evenly and is well liked for carving and for piano parts. It is not durable and supplies are limited.

Oak Noted for its 'figure', its strength and durability. It is a hard wood which is not easily worked, yet is much in demand.

Sycamore A white close-grained wood grown in limited quantity. It is suited for bread boards, etc., and as a contrasting inlay on dark woods.

FAR-EASTERN

Elm (Japanese) Similar in colour to the British variety but straight-grained and easier to work. Used for furniture making.

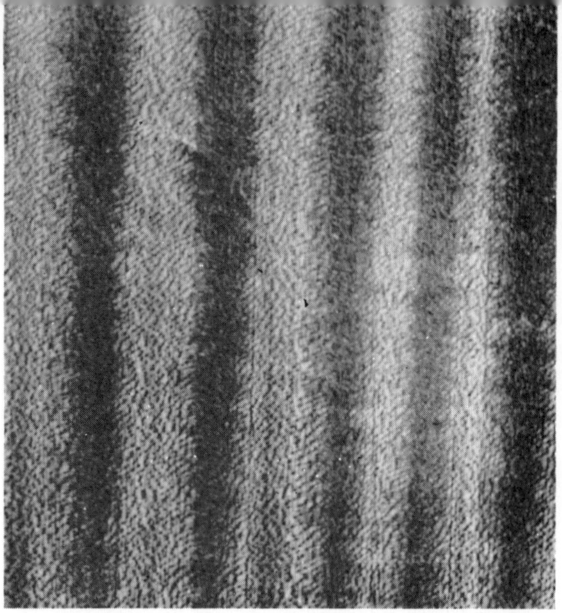

Striped Sapele. The light and dark striped effect caused by spiral growth is often a feature of veneered furniture.

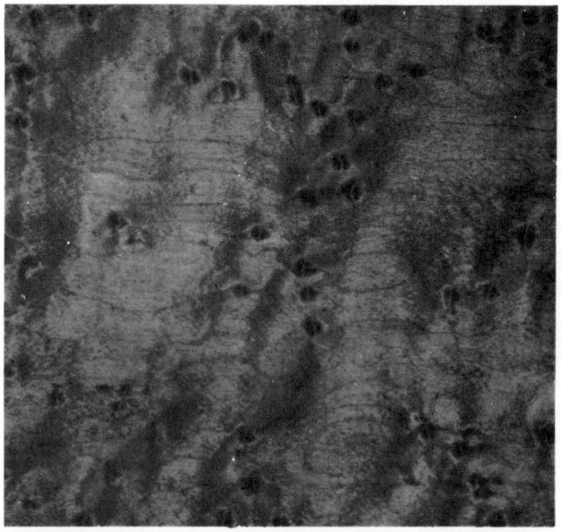

Birds Eye Maple. This unique timber lacks strength and is usually seen only as a decorative veneer.

Japanese Oak Milder to work than the English oak, free from knots but similar in all other respects. It is popular for cabinet work and high-class interior woodwork.

Burma Teak An expensive timber that has long been known for its resistance to decay and is used in ship-building and laboratory equipment. Its rich golden-brown colour and attractive grain have made it popular for furniture.

Jelutong A fine, even-textured, straw-coloured wood used for pattern making and carving. It is not very strong or durable.
Meranti (Lauan) The fairly wide boards of knot free wood are suitable for most work, the 'Dark Red' variety for furniture and the paler varieties in plywood manufacture.
Ramin A popular timber for kitchen cabinet framework, dowel rod, mouldings and picture frames. It is similar in colour and texture to Beech but, in small sections, keeps straighter.

AFRICAN

Abura An even-textured light-brown wood with fairly straight grain, often matched to more expensive woods. It is not strong but stains well.
Gaboon A reddish-brown wood, similar in appearance to many of the mahoganies (see below), but with little character and of light weight. It is used for drawer sides, etc., and in the manufacture of plywood.
Idigbo (Emeri) A straight-grained wood which is ideal for general joinery work. The yellow-brown heartwood is durable and stains well. Avoid sapwood.
Iroko (Odum) Sometimes called 'African Teak but it is lighter in colour than Teak—a golden-brown. The grain often interlocks which makes it difficult to obtain a good finish. High-class joinery.
Limba A relatively insignificant timber of a green-grey colour. It works easily, but, as it is perishable, is only used in indoor work.
Mahogany Trees that yield a red timber tend to come under this general heading and as a result the quality of the wood received is not of the highest order. At its best it is straight-grained, of a rich colour and works well. At its worst it is impossible to plane and tends to twist badly in storage. Generally the wood is in plentiful supply with a good proportion of wide boards.
Mansonia A smooth-textured, straight-grained, brown-purple timber that works and finishes well. The dust can be unpleasant and limited supplies prevent its extensive use as a substitute for black walnut.
Obeche A soft, fast-growing wood which is mostly used as a core for plywood. It is pale in colour and takes a variety of stains well.
Sapele Widely used as a veneer on bedroom furniture because of the attractive striped effect (above, left). It is best finished by machine sanding and polishes well.
Utile This wood is similar to sapele but is more stable and easier to work. Good supplies are available.

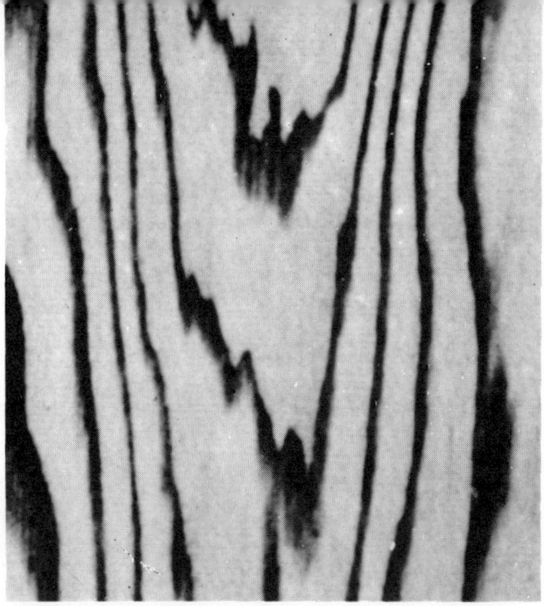

Douglas Fir. A Canadian softwood which has distinct spring and summer growth markings. It is extensively used in making prefabricated buildings and plywood.

Walnut Sometimes called 'golden' because of its colour, it has a similar grain to the mahoganies and often contains an attractive dark streak. It is not a true walnut but is available in good sizes and is used for interior fittings.

SOFTWOODS

With few exceptions most of our softwoods are imported from countries in Northern Latitudes and usually are in regular supply. There are some exceptions. Damar Minyak, a cream/light-brown wood, is one. It comes from the Far East, is easy to work with and is being used as a substitute for Parana Pine.

EUROPEAN

Pine (Red Deal) This is a common timber that works cleanly and finishes well with paint. Used in house-building for roofs and floorboarding. Our main supplies are from the USSR and Scandinavia.

AMERICAN

Parana Pine A hard timber from Brazil that is used for good joinery work. It is straight-grained and often contains streaks of red and grey.
Spruce (Whitewood) A plain timber used for interior fittings (kitchen furniture), and for packing cases as it has a high resistance to splitting.
Western Red Cedar Many of the buildings in Canada are made of this weather-resisting timber. Long straight-grained, knot-free boards are available which are used here as a decorative feature on the outside of buildings.

5 TIMBER—POSSIBLE USES

This section will help you to select timber for the jobs on which you are working. Whilst the outstanding properties of some timbers make them ideal for certain uses, such as close-grained sycamore for breadboards, the choice of wood for furniture is much wider.

You may have to match up the wood with older furniture in your home or you may be free to choose a specially attractive or fashionable timber such as teak.

Long lengths of straight-grained Western Red Cedar are used as an attractive design feature of this house. They require a minimum of maintenance.

OUTDOORS

Garden Shed The framework of strong resinous *Pitch Pine* clad with *Western Red Cedar* and suitably protected.

Garden Seat Made in oily *teak* it will require only an occasional coat of linseed oil to keep it fresh. An alternative, *English Oak,* will need regular varnishing.

Garden Gate *English Oak* is ideal but *Red Deal* or *Parana Pine* can be used if it is to be painted.

Decorative Plant Troughs *English Elm* resists rot and is attractive.

Wheelbarrows of wood are best in *English Elm* with the smooth springy handles of *Ash.*

Cricket Stumps and Bails are made on the lathe. *Ash* will turn well and not splinter in normal use. A straight-grained substitute would be *Japanese Oak.* Both would need a protective coat of varnish.

INDOORS

Coffee Table *Teak* is popular and has a high resistance to heat and stains, but any hardwood, suitably finished with polyurethane (section 36) is usable.

Music Stool The stool should match the piano, modern designs being finished in *Teak* and *Sapele.* The darker shades can be matched by careful staining of *Mahogany.*

Bookshelves As these tend to mark, a darker timber is best, such as *Mansonia.*

Kitchen Table If it is being painted a softwood underframe is ideal. The top could be of *veneered blockboard* or covered with a laminated plastic sheet, e.g. *'Formica'.*

Kitchen Stool *Beech* will withstand the hard wear and scuffs from shoes.

Pairs of Steps Used wholly indoors, *Parana Pine* is hard enough for the treads and sides.

Breadboards and Rolling Pins need to be close-grained and hygienic. *Sycamore* is most suitable with *Beech* as a good substitute.

Childrens' Toys A wood that will not splinter easily and will take both paint and polish well is *Beech.*

Drawing Boards These are usually of *Yellow Pine* but a good quality *plywood* or *blockboard* is suitable.

Decorative Carvings can be done with any wood, but *Lime* will cut most easily and *Yew* is colourful and has an attractive grain.

Table/Reading Lamps If it is to be turned *Walnut* is ideal, the American variety taking a high finish.

Effective use of contrasting timbers. Bowl—Sapele and French Walnut. Lamp base—Teak and Sycamore.

The smooth-cutting quality of lime enabled a 16th century craftsman to make this deeply-carved figure.

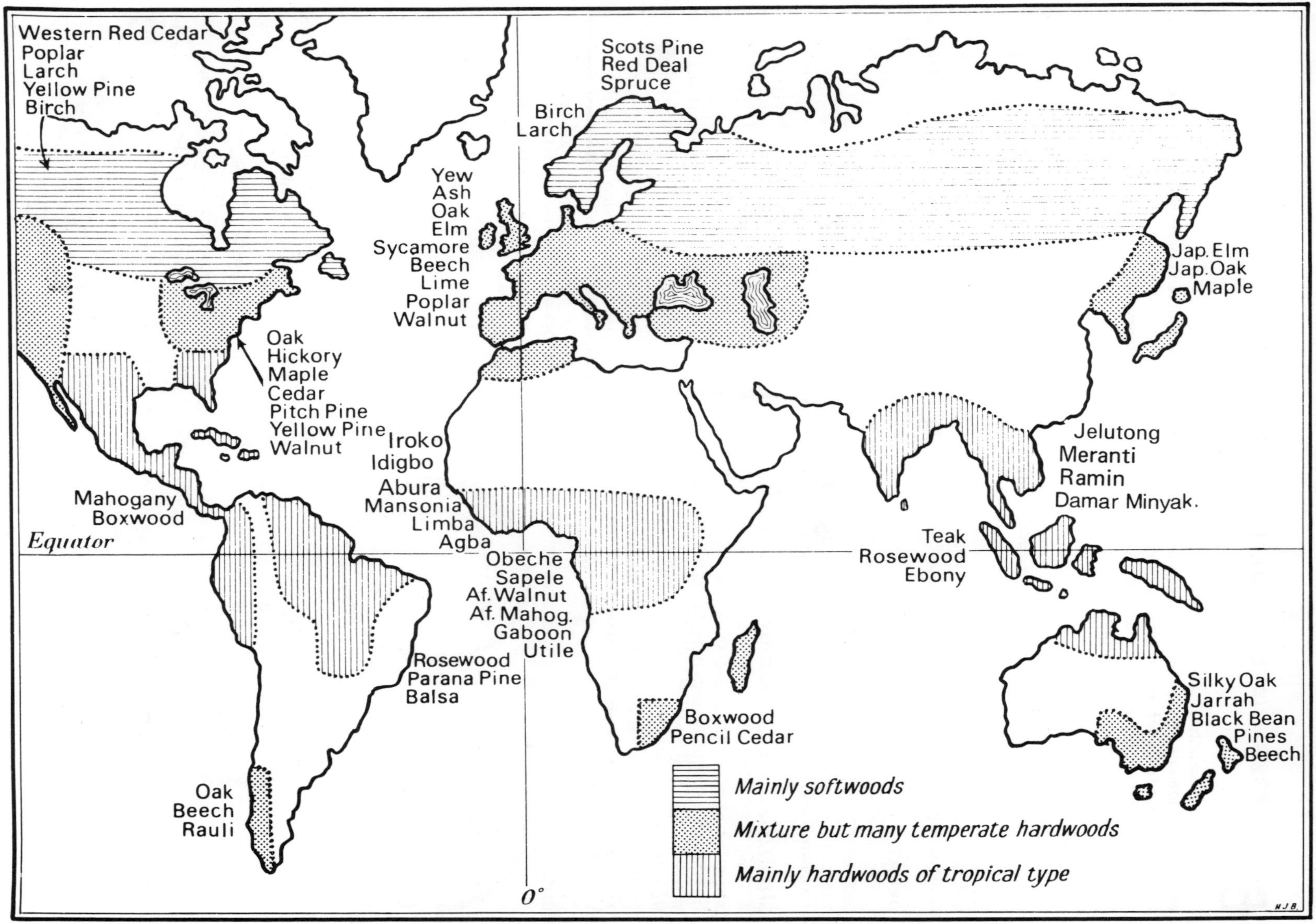
Western Red Cedar
Poplar
Larch
Yellow Pine
Birch
Oak
Hickory
Maple
Cedar
Pitch Pine
Yellow Pine
Walnut
Mahogany
Boxwood
Equator
Oak
Beech
Rauli
Rosewood
Parana Pine
Balsa
Yew
Ash
Oak
Elm
Sycamore
Beech
Lime
Poplar
Walnut
Iroko
Idigbo
Abura
Mansonia
Limba
Agba
Obeche
Sapele
Af. Walnut
Af. Mahog.
Gaboon
Utile
Birch
Larch
Scots Pine
Red Deal
Spruce
Boxwood
Pencil Cedar
Jap. Elm
Jap. Oak
Maple
Jelutong
Meranti
Ramin
Damar Minyak.
Teak
Rosewood
Ebony
Silky Oak
Jarrah
Black Bean
Pines
Beech
Mainly softwoods
Mixture but many temperate hardwoods
Mainly hardwoods of tropical type
0°
H.J.B.

6 TIMBER—NATURAL DEFECTS

Defects are structural faults within the timber which may impair its strength, resilience or durability, and should not be confused with surface blemishes. Features of some timbers, such as knots, may be called *natural defects,* whilst others, such as short-grain are termed *artificial defects* because they could have been avoided with more careful conversion (sawing of the log into useful sizes) and seasoning (the reduction of the moisture content in timber). Most of the wood that we use in the school workshop is free from serious defect such as decay, and many less serious faults have been eliminated in the sawing of the tree at the timber yard.

DECAY

The fibres of the tree usually rot and crumble because of the action of varying *fungi* that have attacked it (section 7). This is invariably noticed at the sawmill and the useless timber is cut out.

SHAKES

These are 'splits' along the length of the plank where the cells or fibres have separated.

1. Where the medullary rays have failed to hold the growth rings together, shrinkage causes a *cup shake* or a *ring shake.*
2. A *heart shake* is caused by shrinkage within the old heartwood and being in the centre of the tree it can spoil many boards.

cup shake

ring shake

heart shake

KNOTS

Knots are the remains of outgrowing branches of a tree. Their grain runs in the opposite direction to that of the main timber and where the knots are large or numerous the fibres are distorted and the strength of the timber is much reduced.

Knots that we call *'tight'* and those that are *'inter-grown'* do not fall out, but after seasoning *loose* knots do fall out and leave holes that need filling.

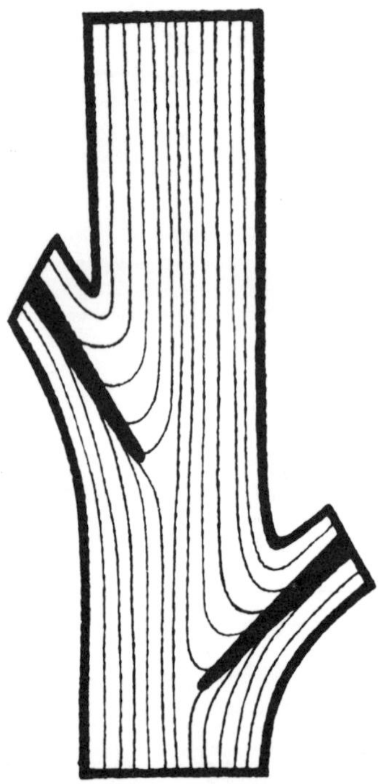

Section through trunk showing direction of branch growth

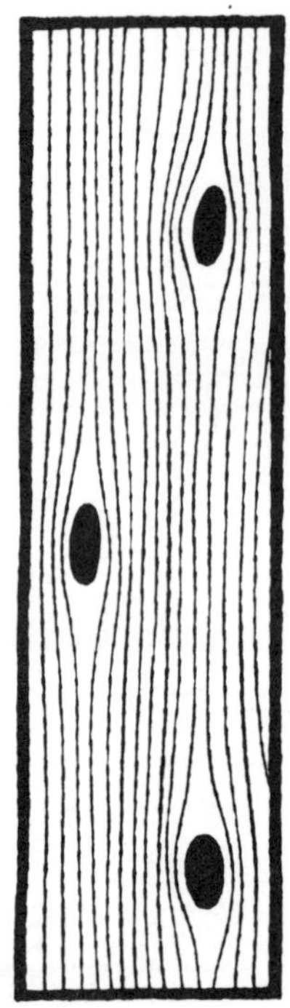

Knots in the board 'not severe'

WANEY EDGE

This name is given to a board that retains some of its bark after conversion. It reduces the usable width of the timber that has been bought and obviously means that sapwood is present.

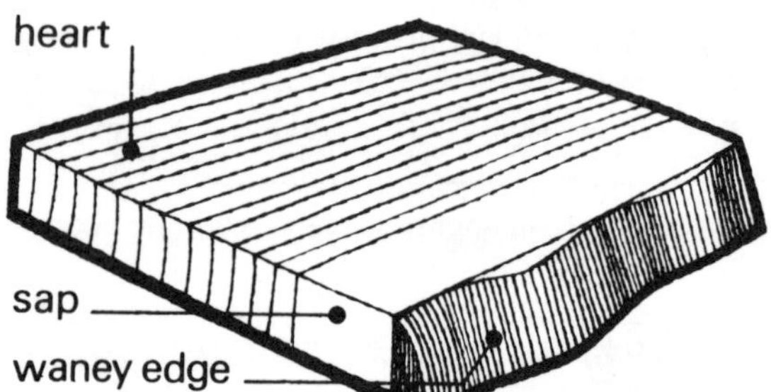

SAPWOOD

This is the living part of the tree and in itself is not a fault. Because it is soft and easily attacked by woodworm it should not be used in constructional work and should be removed during conversion.

SHORT GRAIN

The name *diagonal grain* is sometimes used for this fault which not only makes the planing against the 'direction' of the grain almost impossible but drastically reduces the strength of the wood. This fault is usually caused by careless conversion of the tree.

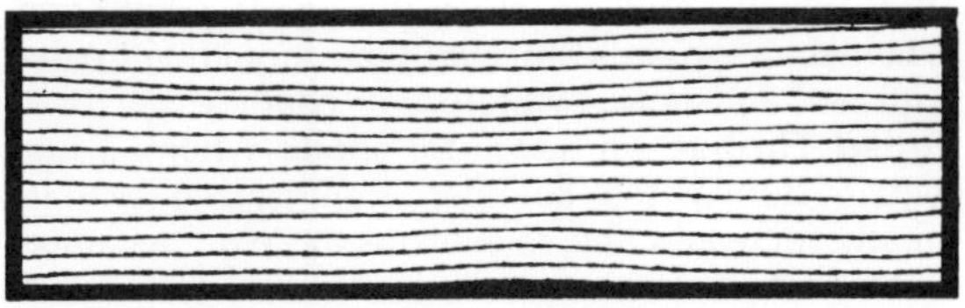

(a) straight-grained timber

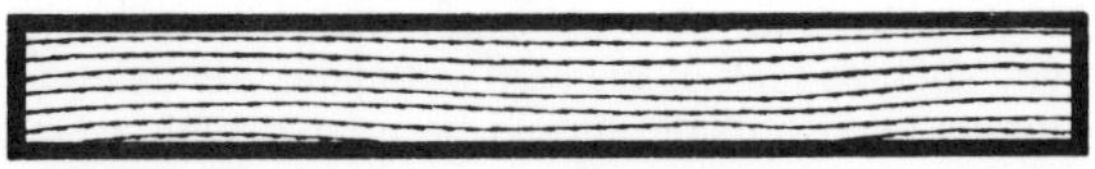

Similar effects on side grain

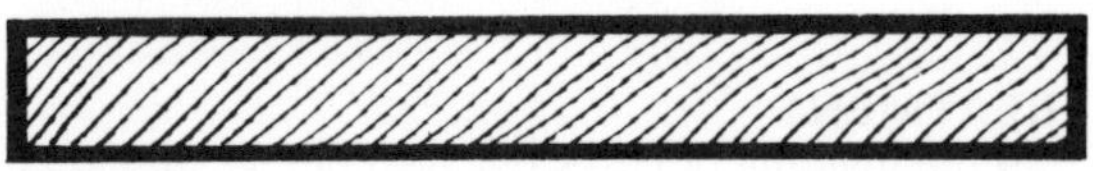

(b) short or diagonal-grained timber

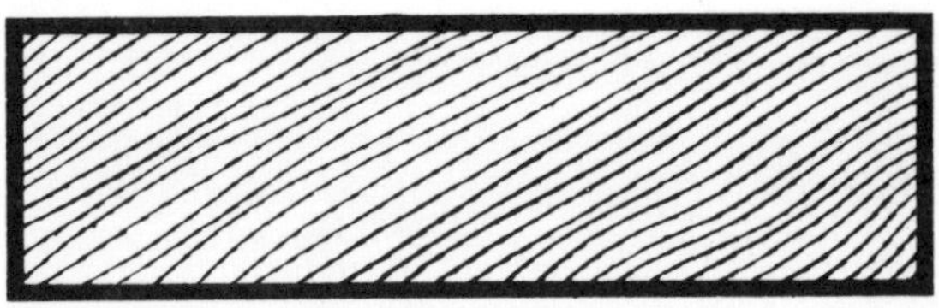

(a) straight-grained timber
(b) short or diagonal-grained timber
Example: The timber illustrated in drawing *(b)* will have only half the strength of the straight-grained timber *(a)*. This factor is particularly important where timbers are what we call 'load bearing'.
Example: roof and floor supports or a door or window lintel.

ARTIFICIAL DEFECTS

CHECKS - END SPLITS - STAR SHAKES

A *check* is a crack along the length of a board which may be very small and therefore not a serious weakness.

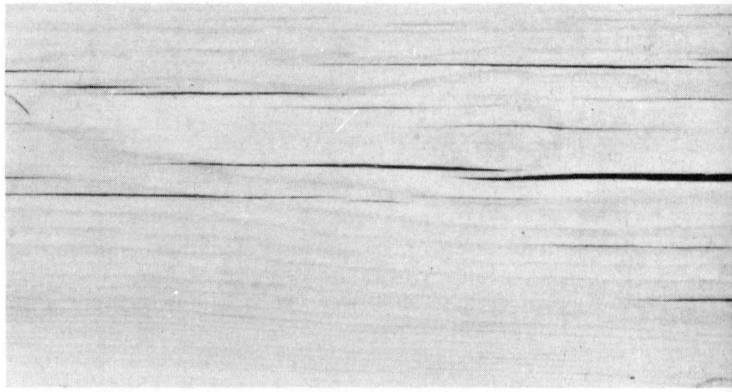

End splits are usually wider, thus spoiling wide boards and reducing much valuable timber in length.

Both of these faults are caused by incorrect *Kiln Seasoning* (section 9).

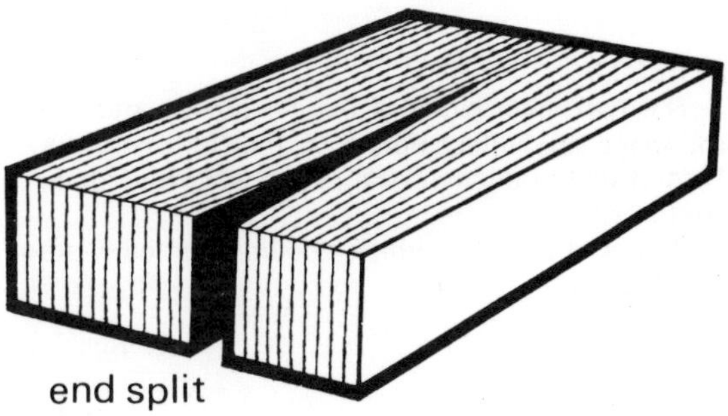

end split

Star shakes are a serious defect which often begins in the too-rapid drying of the newly-felled tree. If sufficient care is taken they can easily be avoided.

star shake

7 TIMBER—DECAY

Trees are living plants and as such provide a ready source of food for a variety of destructive *fungi.*

Fungus is a low form of plant life that thrives where there is:

1. A supply of air
2. A suitable food
3. Sufficient moisture
4. A suitable temperature.

Conditions in the forest are often ideal for growth (page 23) and could develop in the timber yard if waste and weeds were not regularly cleared. Fungal attack takes many forms and *spores* alighting on wood with a moisture content of more than 20% can develop a readily recognisable growth (fruit body) which in its turn can send out millions of similar spores to do damage elsewhere.

Such a fungus, *dry-rot,* is well known for its ability to spread not only through wood, but over brick surfaces, thus destroying whole house structures. It is called 'dry' because the timbers develop a cracked appearance, become brittle and have little strength.

EFFECTS

The two main kinds of decay, *brown* and *white rot* (page 25), affect boards in the following ways;

1. A discolouration of the wood showing dark or light streaks
2. A loss of strength which occurs in an early stage of infection
3. A loss in weight of up to 80% in the most serious cases
4. Absorbs moisture easily, like a sponge and will quickly ignite
5. Hardwoods are weakened and can then be more easily attacked by beetle.

PREVENTION

Standing Timber A broken branch may allow entry which could rot away the whole heartwood. When such wounds are seen they should be treated with an antiseptic, waterproof coating.

Felled Timber—a haven for spores where, if logs remain during the summer months, the warmth greatly increases the rate of decay, e.g., sycamore and beech must be removed immediately for conversion or treated with a suitable preservative.

Sawn Timber in Storage Correct stacking (below left) allowing a free flow of air is the best preventive measure.

Timber in use Unless particularly durable timbers, such as teak or western red cedar, are used, all timbers used outside should be treated with a preservative and sapwood avoided where possible.

TREATMENT

In the majority of cases decayed timber should be *cut out* and *destroyed.*

Bracket Fungus can cause heart-rot in timbers such as Beech, making the timber of no practical use.

Cap Fungi are flourishing on a log left lying in damp forest undergrowth.

Far left: Carefully stacked timber being air-seasoned. It is protected by a sloping roof and rests on brick piers set on a weed-free base. Under these conditions the free circulation of air is likely to prevent decay.

Left: This timber is not sheltered and is becoming overgrown with weeds. Piles of damp timber are an ideal breeding ground for fungi which cannot be easily located and destroyed.

Dry Rot Fungus at the base of stairs. This well-developed fruit body has a fluffy appearance and a musty smell.

TIMBER—INSECT ATTACK

The structural timbers of buildings in this country and the furniture within them are frequently weakened or destroyed by the boring activities or various beetle or woodworm, the most common of which are:

Common Furniture Beetle (Woodworm)

The larvae of this pest are responsible for 75% of all known damage.

Powder Post Beetle (Lyctus)

A larger beetle, with a life span of one year, it attacks the starchy sapwood of newly converted timber such as oak, ash and elm.

Death Watch Beetle

Unfortunately famous for its attack on the large beams of historic buildings such as churches.

WOODWORM—A LIFE CYCLE

Fully grown beetles will invade a house and the females lay eggs in cracks and crevices on the unpolished surfaces of woodwork and furniture such as the backs of wardrobes. The eggs hatch out in about three weeks and the small grubs *(woodworm)* bore into the wood where they continue their boring activities for two years or more. They then make small cavities near the surface where they *pupate* (become chrysalises). After two or three weeks the *pupae* become fully grown beetles and bite their way through the remaining fibres leaving *exit/flight holes* about 2 mm in diameter.

Note—It is only at this stage that the presence of the woodworm devastation is apparent. The beetles have flown away to do damage elsewhere.

PREVENTION—TREATMENT

Such attacks can be prevented by the application of preservatives to all timbers. Timbers that will remain outside, such as telegraph poles, are pressure-impregnated with *creosote,* whilst roof timbers and floor joists may be given *chemical* treatment applied in a spirit or water solution. Room furniture should be kept clean and given an occasional coat of wax —this gives adequate protection.

The treatment of badly affected timbers requires the skilful attention of a specialist although small outbreaks can be treated with insecticide bought from a do-it-yourself store.

Where possible the timber should be removed and destroyed, but where it is not, the wood must be treated with an insecticidal fluid capable of deep penetration. This can be applied by brush or spray, or injected. This strong chemical fluid attacks the woodworm in two ways:

1. It penetrates the *boreholes* and kills the larvae immediately
2. It prevents further attack from outside by leaving a protective layer on the wood's surface.

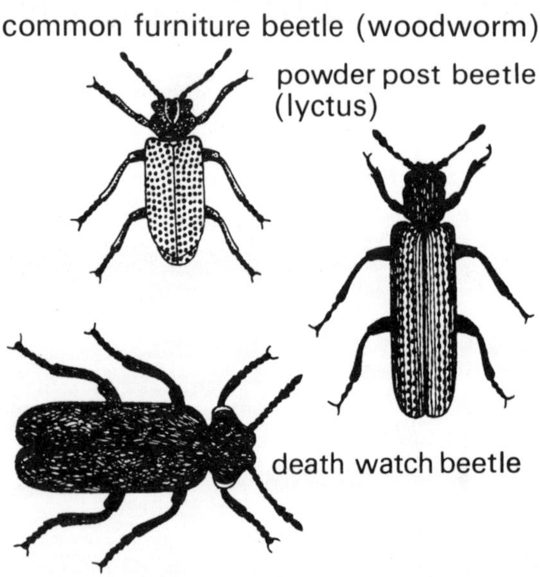

Actual length: Woodworm 3 mm, Lyctus 6 mm, Death Watch Beetle 6 mm

---

Opposite:

(a) The Death Watch Beetle often weakens Oak beams by boring away the centre.

(b) Flight holes of the Common Furniture Beetle from a softwood floorboard.

(c) The one flight hole of a Powder Post Beetle gives little indication of the severe damage below the covering veneer.

(d) Brown Rot in a board of Red Deal shown in an early stage of development.

(e) Brown Rot shown in an advanced stage—the board is devastated by the attack.

(f) White Rot usually attacks hardwoods and is recognisable by its white patches and dark streaks.

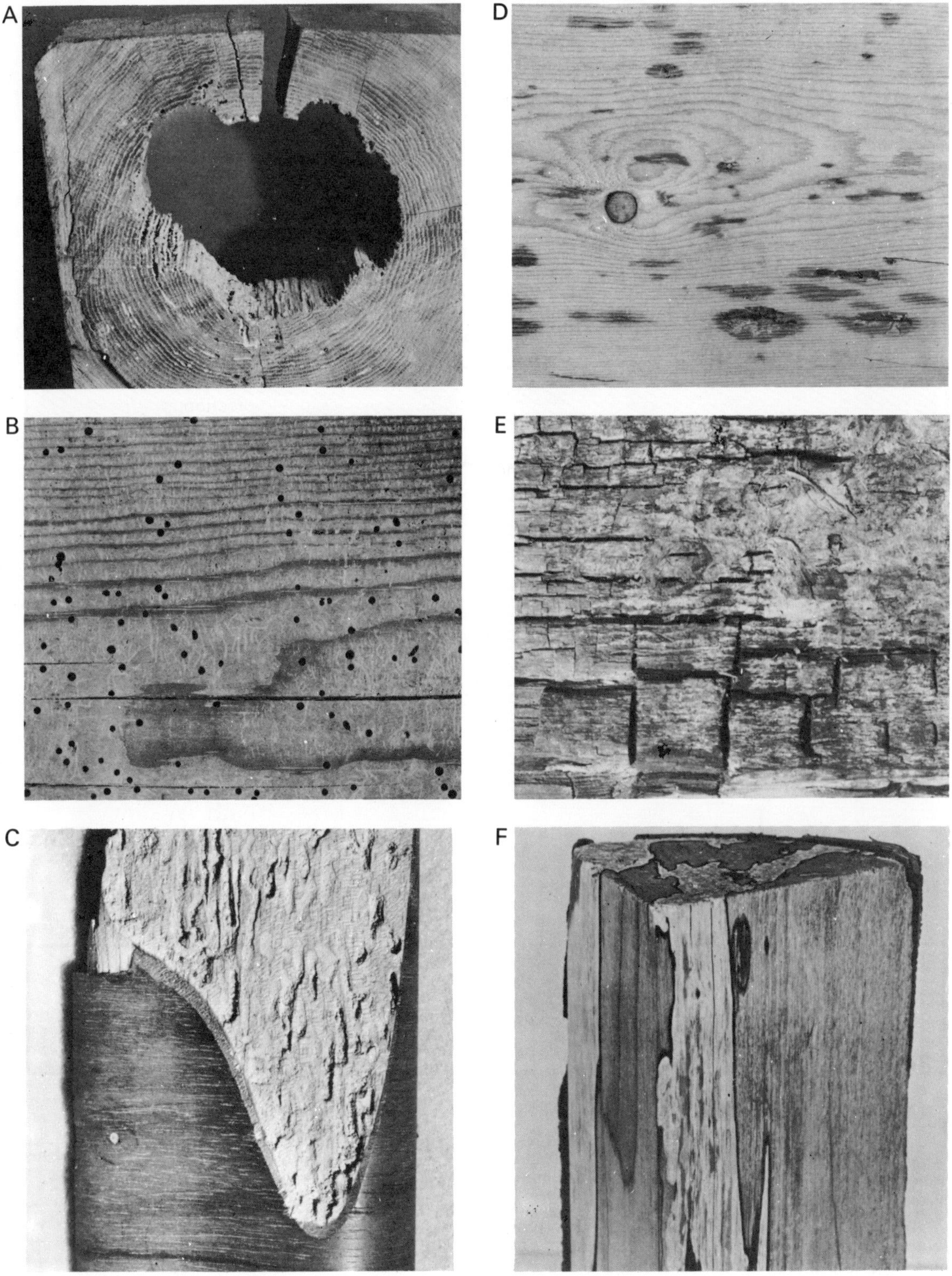
A
B
C
D
E
F

8 TIMBER—COMMON SIZES

Terminology

In the past various timber sections have been given names such as baulk, deal, batten etc.

We are concerned with giving accurate descriptions, i.e. the size of the timber. The full size sections below indicate some of the common planed sizes you are likely to work with.

Hardwood and Softwood

Boards are sold in units of square metres (m^2) and narrow sections in units of lineal metres (m). Normal lengths are from 1800 mm upwards. Hardwood widths from 150 mm and softwood widths from 75 mm upwards.

Available sawn thicknesses are 12, 16, 19, 22, 25, 32, 38, 44 and 50 mm. Boards which are planed on both sides (PBS) are 4 mm thinner than these.

Manufactured Board (e.g. plywood, blockboard and chipboard)

This is sold in units of 10 square metres (10 m^2 or 10 sq. m).

Sheet sizes and thicknesses are given in millimetres. The standard sheet measures 2440 × 1220 mm in thicknesses 3, 4, 5, 6, 9, 12, 15, 18, 22 and 25 mm.

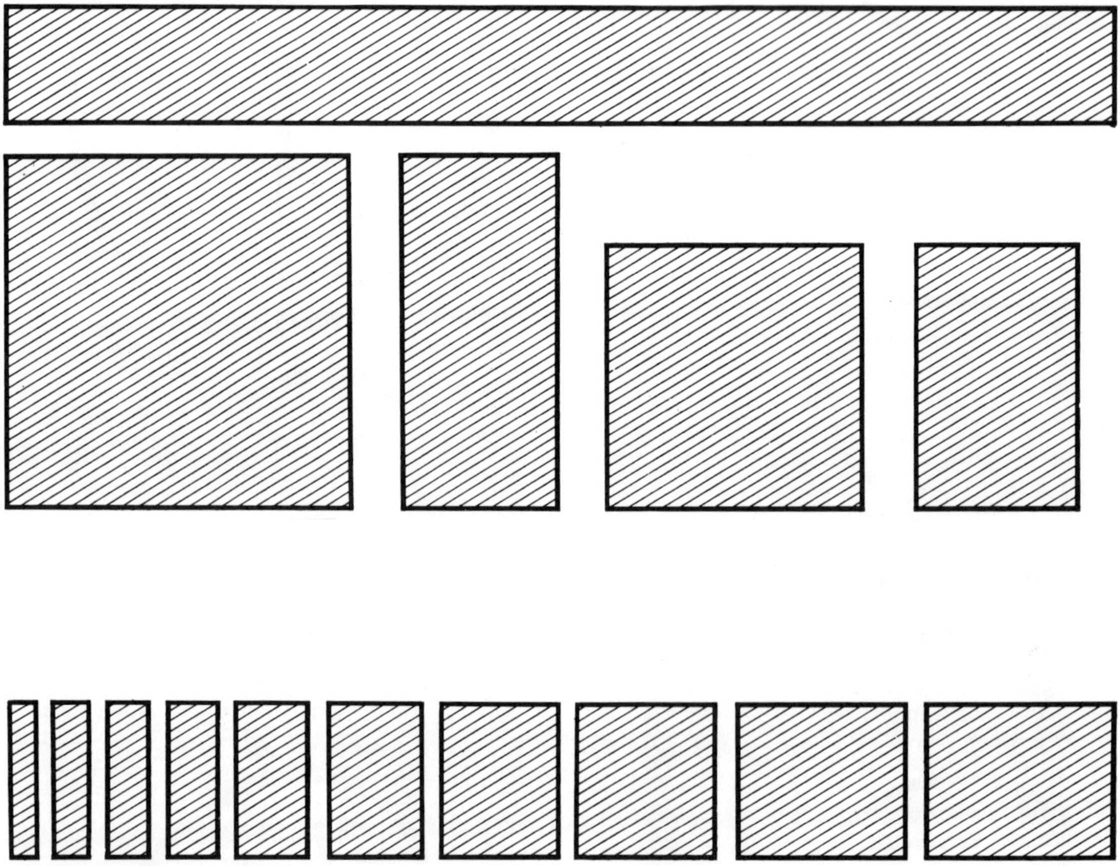

TIMBER CONVERSION

Conversion is the term used for the sawing of the log into timbers which are a useful shape and size for general use. The process of conversion takes place before seasoning (section 9).

Many varying factors will influence the sawyer when he chooses the method to be used in converting a log, including the following:

1. *Use of the Timber* Softwoods that are to be used for floor-boarding and the like are usually flat (or slab) sawn to common sizes, whereas expensive logs such as teak will be sawn for specific jobs.
2. *Presence of Defects* Decay must be removed as soon as possible and a bad star shake will make the production of valuable wide boards impossible.

Slabs cut from the log to form a *baulk* remove most of the unwanted sapwood.

3. *Kind of Timber* Distinguishing features of timbers are revealed by skilful cutting such as the silver figure of radially cut oak.

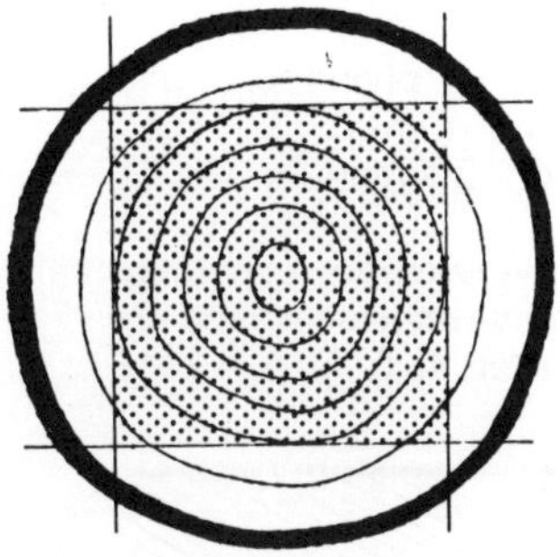

Methods of Conversion

The many known methods of converting logs can be confusing but all are variations on the two basic cuts.

1. *Radial cut.* Along the medullary rays
2. *Tangent cut.* At right-angles to the rays and, therefore, to the radial cut.

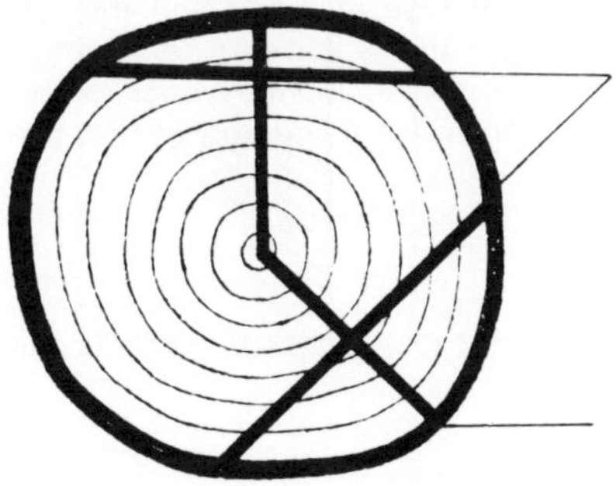

Flat (Slab)—Plain—Through and Through

Little thought is given to the use of the timber and consequently it is used mainly for softwoods. The method is cheap and some boards are wide, but the outer boards or planks tend to warp (or cup).

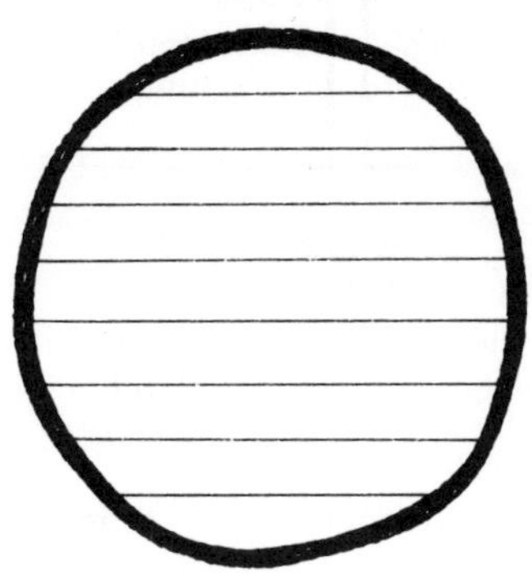

Quarter or Radial Sawing

Traditionally used for oak, this method shows medullary figuring to advantage, but when properly 'quartered', as in *(a)*, the wastage is excessive and the wood expensive to buy. Less perfect but more economic methods are shown at *(b)*, *(c)* and *(d)*. When cut on the 'quarter' each has the much-sought-after qualities of a *centre board.* They shrink evenly and very little, rarely warp and are therefore valuable in high-class cabinet making.

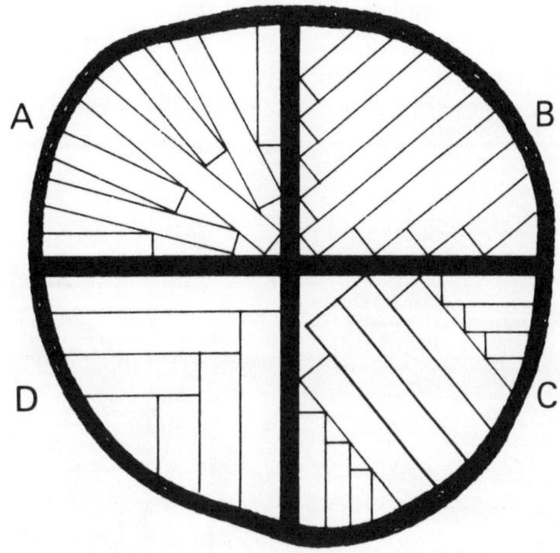

Tangential Sawing

Successive boards cut from a square baulk show off strongly grained woods, such as pitch pine, to good advantage.

Boards cut in this manner tend to warp but are frequently used in places where this is impossible, such as panelling.

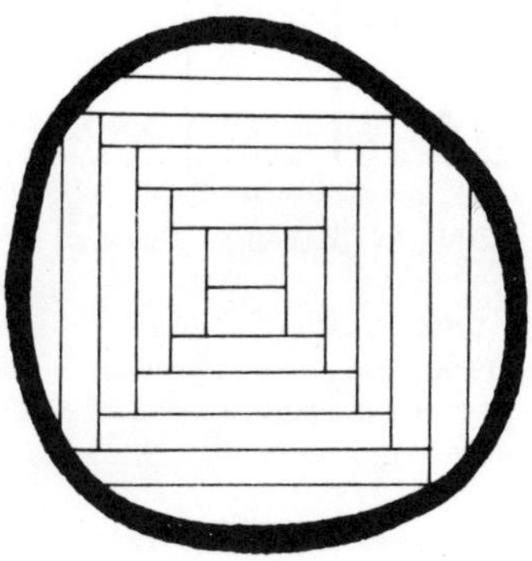

A West African forester using a modern chain saw to fell a giant hardwood.

Large cranes are needed to handle logs weighing several tons. Here they are sorted and crosscut to length.

A log is rolled on to the carriage, which feeds it through a large band-saw, converting it into boards.

9 TIMBER—MOISTURE CONTENT

The *moisture content* (M.C.) of timber is expressed as a percentage of its dry weight. This can be found by oven-drying a sample of timber after it has been weighed in its original *wet* or *green* condition and making the following calculation:

$$\frac{\text{Weight of moisture}}{\text{Weight of dry timber}} \times \frac{100}{1}$$

Example:	Weight of wet timber	6 kg
	Weight of dry timber	4 kg
	Moisture taken out	2 kg

$$\frac{2}{4} \times \frac{100}{1} = 50\% \text{ moisture content}$$

It is quite common for the M.C. of newly-felled hardwoods to be as high as 100% and some softwoods nearer to 200%. Timber in this condition is impossible to saw and plane properly, is likely to suffer from dry-rot, is not very strong and will shrink and split badly unless it is carefully dried out. This drying-out process we call *seasoning.*

The amount of moisture to be left in the timber varies according to the type of wood and the job it is going to do (where this is known). Ideally, the M.C. of a piece of timber should be equal to the humidity of the air into which it is going so that the wood remains stable.

Table showing the M.C. considered suitable for a variety of jobs:

16%	Garden tools and furniture.
15%	Timbers for most general joinery jobs.
14%	Furniture in cool rooms, e.g. bedrooms.
13 12 %	Wood in normally heated rooms—doors, furniture, musical instruments, toys.
11 10 %	Office and store furniture in premises that are centrally heated. New houses.
9%	Woodwork in any type of room that is close to heat—mantelpieces, radiator covers.
8%	Parquet tiles over underfloor heating.

TIMBER SEASONING

The sticks between boards must be of equal size (usually 20 to 25 mm square) and placed directly above each other. If this is not done accurately the timber will bend and distort under its own weight and will be useless.

Boards 25 mm thick need sticks no more than 450 mm apart and thicker material, say 63 mm, up to 900 mm apart.

Timber seasoned in this way takes a long time to dry (25 mm boards take about one year) and its M.C. can only be reduced to the humidity of the surrounding air (usually 16 to 20%). This can be measured with an hygrometer.

Most timber requires further drying and this can be done in a kiln.

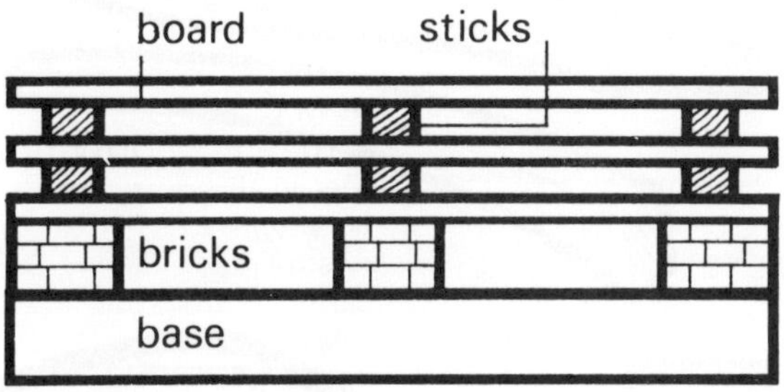

NATURAL SEASONING (AIR)

The necessary conditions are:

1. A flat, dry, weed-free base, e.g. concrete.
2. A free circulation of air.
3. Shelter from direct sunshine and rain.

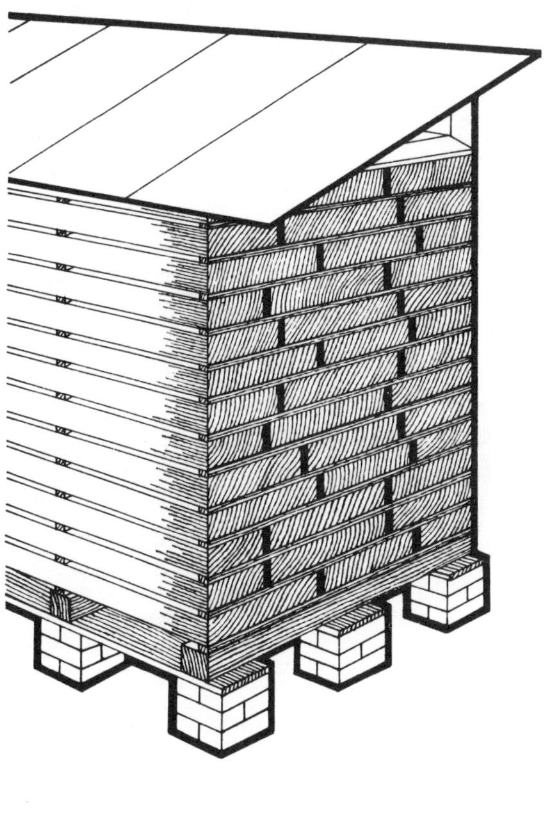

ARTIFICIAL SEASONING (KILN)

By this method seasoning time can be reduced to a matter of weeks instead of months. Controlled application of both *heat* and *humidity* enables the M.C. to be quickly and accurately reduced without spoiling the properties of the timber. Timber can be supplied to the furniture manufacturer at a given time—in fact, the kiln process becomes an important part of the production line.

As in natural seasoning the stacking of the timber on portable trolleys is important, and regularly tested samples are taken.

A stack of timber being taken from a kiln.

RADIO FREQUENCY SEASONING

Experiments continue to be made into ways of reducing the M.C. of timber in a short period of time so that money can be saved on storage and handling costs.

The radio frequency (RF) method involves putting wood onto a conveyor belt and passing it through a kind of 'oven'. In this way, for example, one tool manufacturer (Marples) managed to reduce the time taken to dry boxwood and jarrah to about half an hour.

The latest test results suggest that a combination of kiln and RF seasoning might work well. The subject is an interesting one and might make a good combined Science/Craft CSE study.

10 TIMBER—SHRINKAGE AND WARPING

After the tree has been felled the water within the log begins to evaporate and the wood cells contract. We call this *shrinkage*.

The newly-felled log loses most of its moisture through the porous *end grain* and if it is not quickly converted, rapid drying will result in wasteful shakes.

Timber felled in winter stands less risk of shakes because both the moisture content of the log and the air temperature are at their lowest.

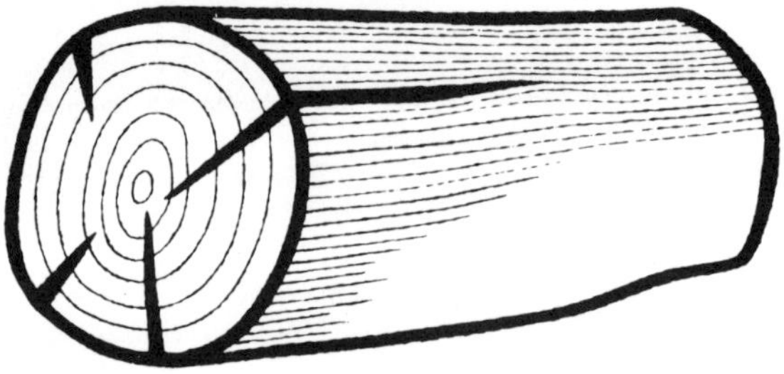

WARPING

The *tensions* which cause splitting in the log are released when the timber is converted. *Shrinkage* is then free to take place and the tendency is for boards to *cup* or *warp*. This can be prevented by correct stacking and, if necessary, weighting the wood down.

The greatest amount of shrinkage is *along* the *annual rings* and, when flat sawn, boards tend to curl outwards from the heart in varying degrees (B).

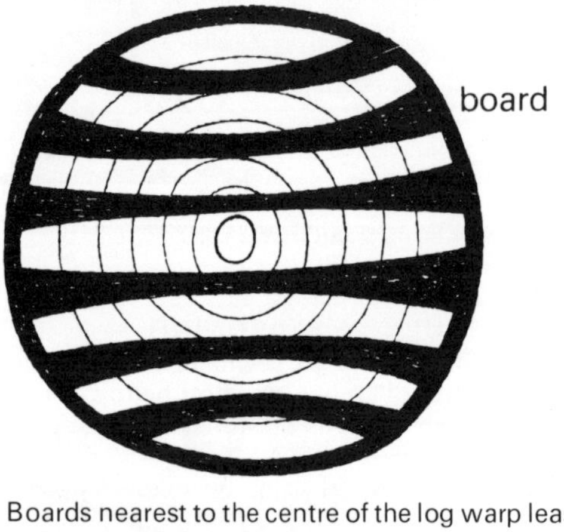

Boards nearest to the centre of the log warp least. (A).

Drawings C & D show the effect of excessive shrinkage on square timber cut from the centre of the tree (C) and towards the bark (D).

Outside boards with the *annual rings* running *across* the width shrink considerably in width (as much as 10%) whilst 'centre' boards reduce in thickness.

In all boards the amount of shrinkage that occurs in length is negligible and can safely be ignored in all constructions.

TWISTING AND BOWING

Although timber may be reasonably well seasoned it may have a tendency to twist (most noticeable in wide boards) or to bow (a common feature of scantlings). These faults may be caused by:

- bad storage
- a sudden change in moisture content
- sawing a board along its length

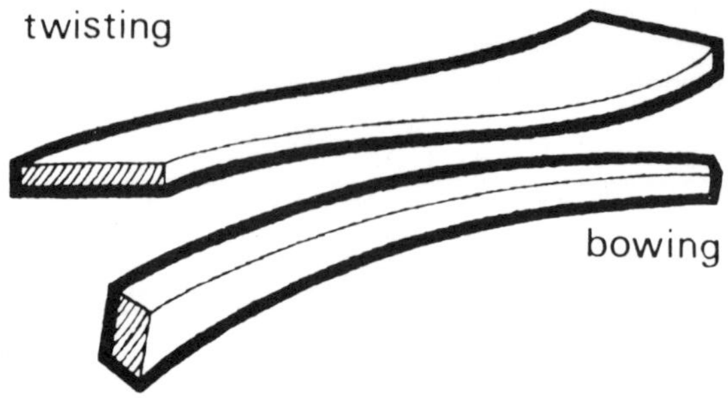

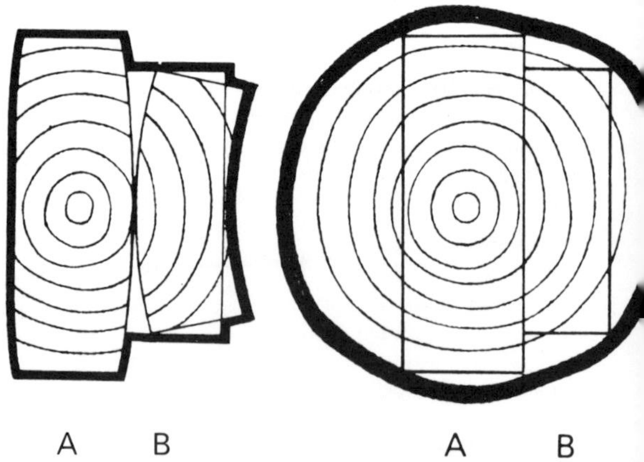

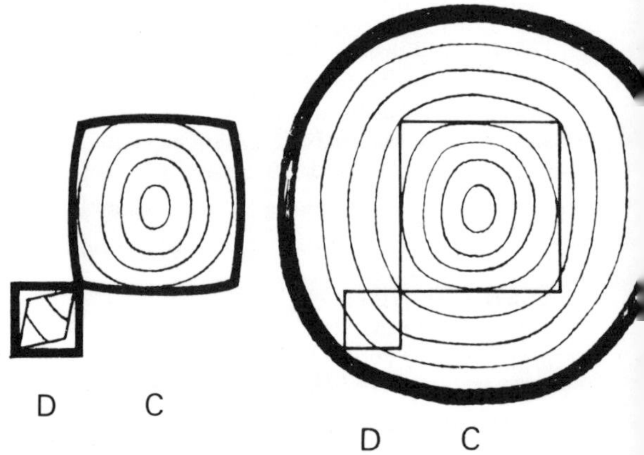

TIMBER—WOOD VENEERS

From the 17th century onwards exotic foreign timbers were sawn into thin slices (veneers) and glued on to less attractive timbers, such as yellow pine (an even-grained softwood now used for good quality drawing boards). These were made into furniture and sold to the rich tradesmen and gentry.

Unfortunately this excellent idea, which made furniture *stronger* as well as *better in appearance* fell into disrepute. Many 19th century manufacturers, seeing this as a means of making easy money, applied the veneers to timbers of the poorest quality. The word 'veneer' came to mean 'superficial' and such work was regarded as 'shoddy'.

African Hardwood being prepared for rotary cutting of veneers to be used in plywood manufacture.

VENEER IN THE HOME

Today nearly all mass-produced furniture has a veneer applied with the help of modern adhesives (section 31) to fault-free manufactured boarding such as plywood and chipboard. The result is furniture with *large flat surfaces* and much *simpler designs* that are easy to make and will take a *high standard of finish*.

Modern technology and mass-production methods have made it possible for examples of expensive timbers (teak), timbers with twisted fibres (sapele) and weak non-construction timbers (bird's eye maple) to be commonplace in many homes.

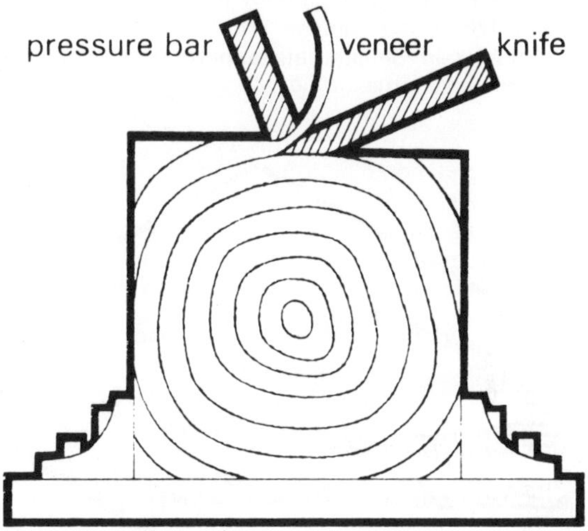

TYPES OF VENEER

1. *Knife cut veneer.* These veneers can be cut by slicing with a sharp knife. The baulk of timber is first boiled or steamed under pressure to soften the fibres before being mounted on a sliding bed. This is moved against a horizontal knife, the bed being raised the thickness of a veneer after each cut.
2. *Rotary cutting* is the cheapest method of veneer production. The soaked log is mounted between centres and rotated against a long knife which is fed towards the timber. The veneer peels away in a continuous width and cut to the size that is required.

Because the cut is around the annual rings the veneer has no character and is mainly used in the manufacture of plywood, etc.

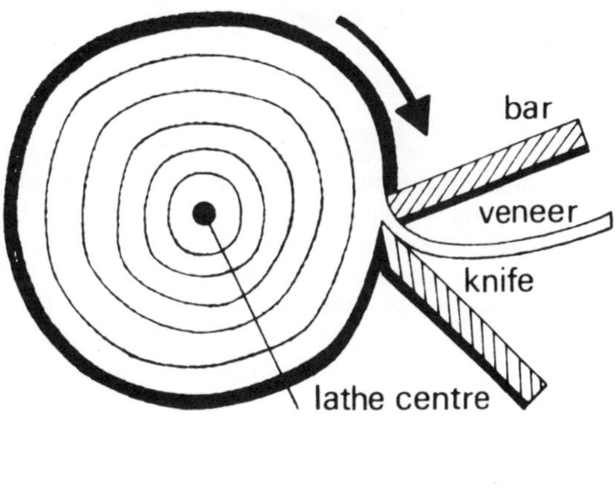

VENEER LAYING

Only small items, such as cigarette boxes, are occasionally veneered by hand in the workshop because pre-veneered boards of all types and sizes, in a variety of woods are now available at a reasonable cost.

11 TIMBER—PLYWOOD

The extensive use of plywood and other laminated boards during this century has revolutionised the building, boat and furniture industries. Hardly a day goes by without us coming into contact with plywood, be it sitting on a moulded chair, standing on a bus deck or opening a desk lid.

Although it has altered our way of life plywood is not a new invention. We have merely developed an art that was known to the Egyptians nearly 4,000 years ago. The invention of the rotary cutting machine in 1890 really set the pace and early uses ranged from tea-chests to grand piano frames. Today it is produced in a wide range of sheet sizes (up to 15 m for boat building) and thicknesses, constructed in as many ways as there are jobs for it to do. It is an adaptable material, with a very wide range of uses.

WHAT IS PLYWOOD?

It is a manufactured board made up of an odd number of wood veneers (not less than three) with the grain of alternate veneers crossing each other at right angles.

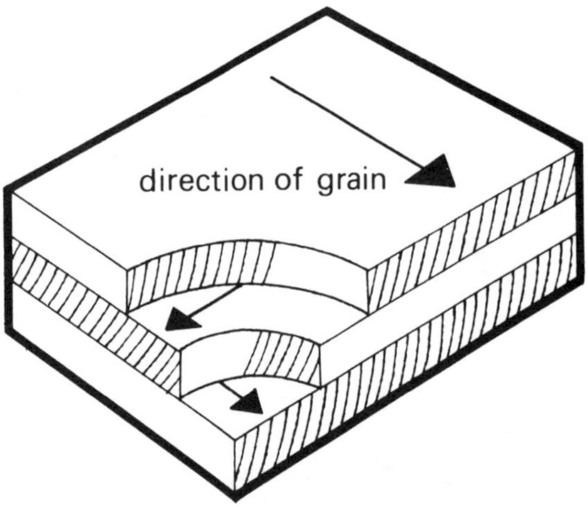

It is this construction, combined with the use of large areas of adhesive, that gives it its tremendous strength and stability.

Multiply. This name is given to plywood with more than three layers of veneer.

Stout-heart. So called when the middle veneer *(core)* is thicker than the outer *(face)* veneers.

These face veneers are normally cut 1·5 mm thick.

MANUFACTURE

After the veneers have been cut (section 10) they are dried, inspected for defects (mainly small knots) and given a grade, the better veneers being used for facings.

Large rollers are used to apply adhesive to the veneers which are then put under pressure—usually in an electrically heated press. Setting may take only a matter of seconds if radio-frequency heating is used. The sheets are finished by being trimmed to size (standard sheet 2440 × 1220 mm), sanded, inspected and given a final grading. British Standard grading 1; 2; 3; more or less corresponds to the imported grades A; B; BB.

MATERIALS USED

Plywood not faced with a decorative veneer is usually one of two colours.

White. This is often imported from the U.S.S.R. or Finland and is made of Birch. It is used mainly in 'whitewood' furniture which is to be painted.

Red. Mainly made of Gaboon although less well-known hardwoods such as Lauan are frequently used. Drawer bottoms and cabinet backs are its main uses.

ADHESIVES

Interior grade plywood is usually made with animal glue or *casein* adhesive. Exterior grade plywood that is moisture resistant (MR) is often made with *Aerolite* and that which is weather and boil proof (WBP) with *Aerodux*. This latter quality is mainly used in boat building.

multiply

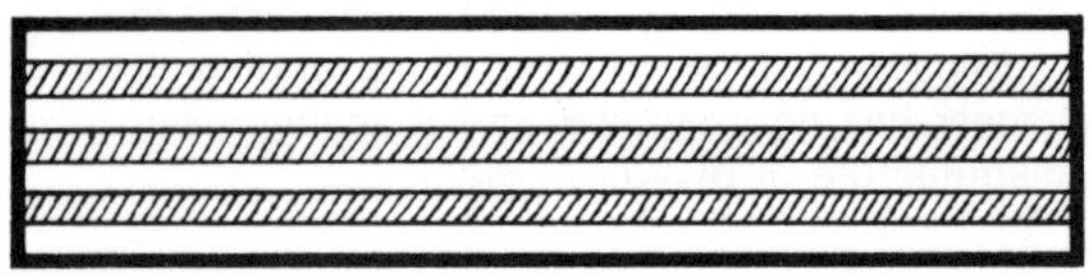

stout heart

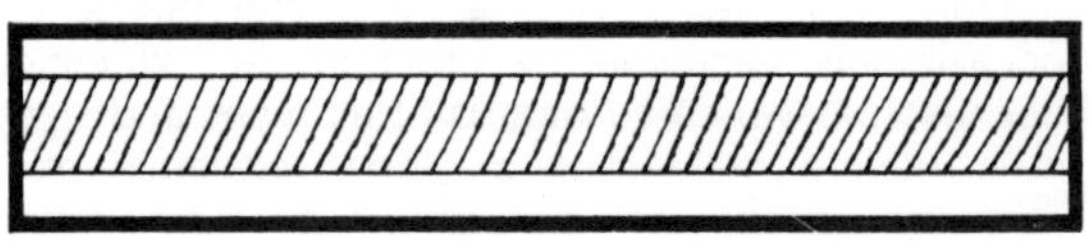

MAIN USES

Outside

Exterior grade plywood. Building industry including concrete shuttering and temporary walling.

Marine work of all kinds from canoe building to luxury cabin cruisers.

Portable buildings such as school classrooms and caravans.

Plywood, manufactured with waterproof adhesive, is used in aircraft construction.

Inside

Interior grade plywood. The general furniture trade uses most of the Birch veneers in the manufacture of kitchen fittings.

The specially veneered boards are used in carcase constructions such as sideboards and large flat surfaces such as table tops, T.V. cabinets.

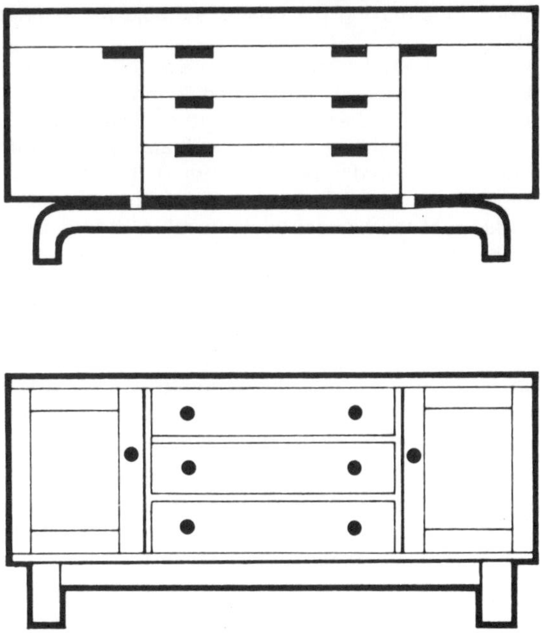

These drawings show how stable, smooth-surfaced, flexible plywood enabled designers, by eliminating many of the joints necessary with solid timber, to produce sideboards of simple appearance which are easy to keep clean.

TEN ADVANTAGES OVER SOLID TIMBER

1. Available in *large sizes,* thus much less jointing is required.
2. The board is *stable*—changes in temperature and humidity have very little effect on size.
3. If the boards are stored properly they *will not twist or warp.*
4. *Perfect surfaces* that will take a high-class finish are easily obtained, even with 'difficult' veneers.
5. The boards *can be faced* with veneers of exceptional beauty at relatively little cost.
6. It is far *stronger* than solid wood of similar size and has the same strength in all directions.
7. The grading of boards ensures that there is a *reliable standard* in timber that is purchased.
8. For these reasons much *simpler constructions* are possible.
9. The material is *flexible*—the thinner sheets in particular can be easily formed (bent).
10. Adhesives can give a *high resistance to decay* and attack by woodworm and marine life.

12 TIMBER—MANUFACTURED BOARDS

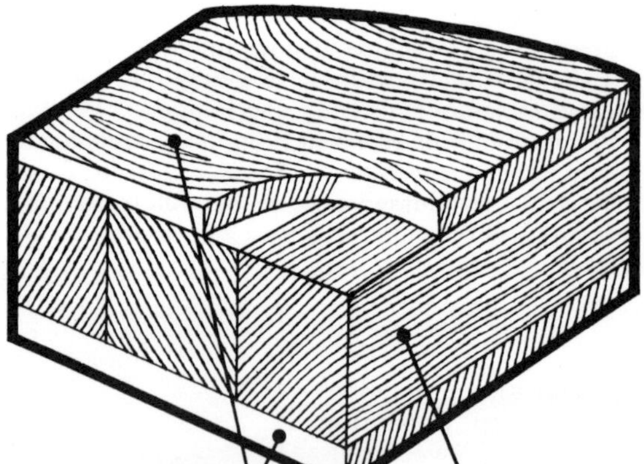

LAMINATED BOARD

Plywood is a remarkable material but the processes involved in its manufacture make it expensive, particularly in the thicker sizes (say over 12 mm). There are three types of *laminated board* that are occasionally used as a substitute for multiply.

They are all made by gluing a number of strips of solid timber side by side to form a core, which is then sandwiched between two facings (about 3mm thick) whose grain runs at right-angles to that of the core.

Many *timbers* are used in their manufacture but the core is usually of Pine or Spruce and the facing veneers of Birch or Gaboon. The *adhesive* used is mainly moisture resistant or weather and boil-proof, thus making the boards suitable for exterior use.

1. **Laminboard.** The narrowness of the core strips (which must not exceed 7 mm) make this very stable board an *ideal ground for veneering.*

Veneers of the same thickness are laid on both sides of the board to prevent bowing. It is not cheap and is used in the furniture industry only for large surfaces of the highest quality such as board-room table tops.

2. **Blockboard.** The wider core strips (up to 25 mm) make this a cheaper board, but there is a tendency for the surface to show a slight 'ripple'. It is not used for high-class veneered work but where *strength and stability* are required at reasonable cost, e.g. bottoms of carcases, leather-covered desk tops and knock-down furniture.

laminboard

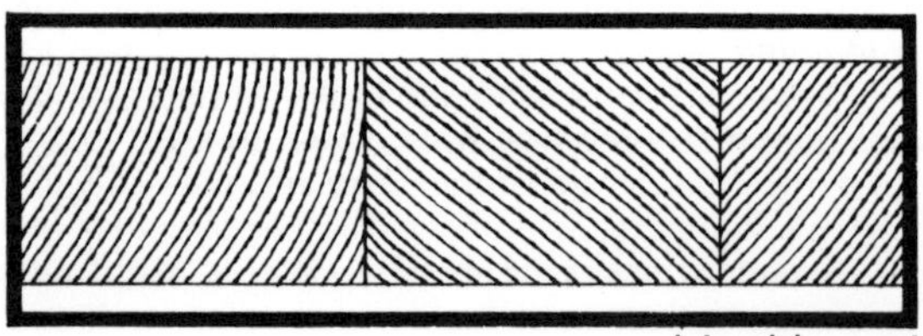

blockboard

CHIPBOARD

This is a comparatively new material which is being extensively used for cabinet making in mass-produced furniture.

It consists of *fine wood particles* made from forest thinnings and other offcuts of both hardwoods and softwoods, compressed and bonded together with a synthetic resin adhesive (Aerolite is commonly used).

There are two main kinds of board:

1. **Single layer.** The particles are of similar size and gain their strength from being bonded in a haphazard way (interlocked).
2. **Sandwich construction.** Coarser chips are sandwiched between outer layers of finer material. This adds some strength and also gives a finer surface finish.

The boards can be made durable in outside conditions but used in large areas they require considerable support.

They veneer extremely well with both wood and plastic and being poor conductors of sound can be used for wall panelling. Veneers are laid on both sides of the board to prevent bowing.

Jointing

Is not possible by traditional methods, e.g., dovetails and mortice and tenons, and as with plywood and laminated boards the edges require covering (see *Woodwork* 2).

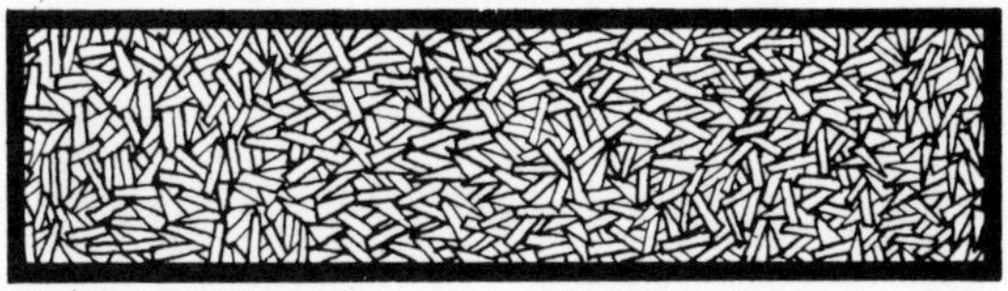

single layer

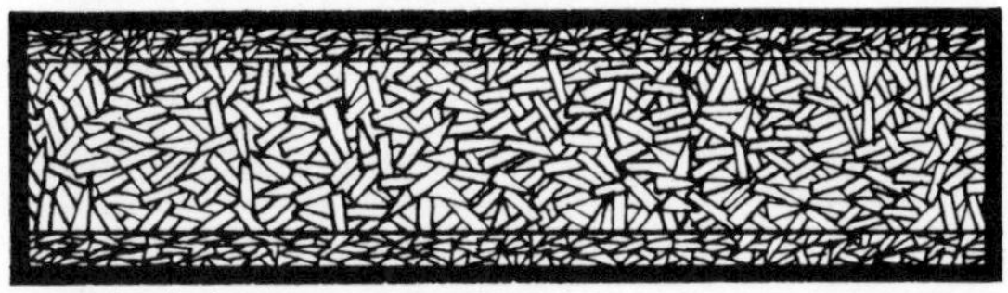

sandwich construction

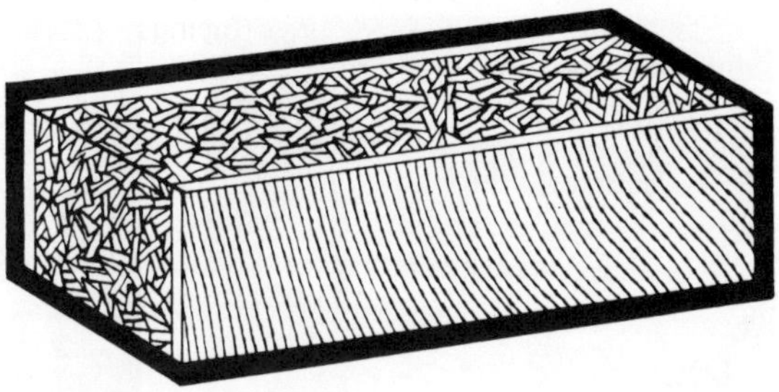

veneered chipboard

HARDBOARD

This is a light material used as a comparatively cheap substitute for plywood where *space filling* and not strength is required.

It is made by subjecting a mixture of *wood pulp* and *resins* to heat and enormous pressure in a large press. The result is a board of good quality that has one very smooth surface that can be veneered with wood or plastic (as in the case of kitchen cabinets). A *'superboard'* is made by increasing the pressure in manufacture and treating the smooth surface with oil, thus making it suitable to take paint. The surface of the standard grade is very absorbent and painting it is both time-wasting and expensive.

In its raw state this grade is useful for the unseen backs of cheap cabinets and as a support for foam-upholstered loose seats. It is used in a variety of thicknesses to suit the job, ranging from 2/3 mm to 6 mm and has the advantage over plywood of not splitting when nailed and of being easy to glue.

INSULATING BOARD

This is made of similar materials as hardboard but is not so compressed. Its *low density* makes it both *light and weak* for its thickness (12 to 25 mm) but used as an interior wall surfacing it is a good insulator of both heat and sound. *Acoustic tiles* are made in *slotted* and *perforated* form to improve sound absorption.

COMMON SIZES

All these boards are readily available in a wide variety of standard sizes.

New and exciting forms of building are possible using laminated timbers.
The beams on this swimming pool are glued with Aerodux.

Far left: Sapele faced Marine grade plywood used to deck a 'Flying Dutchman' yacht (Thames Plywood Manufacturers Ltd).

Left: A stacking chair for use in schools has laminated frames quickly set by radio frequency heating and a plywood seat and back.

A single sheet of 'Thames-Chassiply' used between decks on a double-decker bus (Thames Plywood Manufacturers Ltd).

Finely veneered grand piano rims are being laminated with Aerolite adhesive at normal workshop temperature.

EXAMINATION QUESTIONS

At the end of each section in the book you will find a selection of questions which may be used for *homework*—to practise sketching and to select the information asked for, and for *revision*—as these are the kind of questions that you will be asked in your own CSE and GCE Examinations.

The answers to most questions will be found in your textbook but in some instances you will have to do some research into more specialised books.

There is a mixture of long and short questions and you may notice that similar questions are asked in different ways. This is because the 'style' of paper differs from region to region.

QUESTIONS

1 . 2 . 3 GROWTH AND STRUCTURE

1. What can you tell about the cross-section of a tree from seeing its stump?

2. Draw a cross-section of a tree indicating clearly the following: *(a)* Sapwood, *(b)* Heartwood, *(c)* Bark, *(d)* Cambium, *(e)* Medullary Rays.

Add notes to explain the function of each in the growing tree.

3. Timber is usually divided into two basic types. Name these two types and under each heading, sketch the appearance of:
(a) the outline of the tree
(b) a typical leaf formation.

4. Make a sketch, 75 mm across, showing a cross-section of a tree trunk. Label 5 main parts. Compare the end grain of Beech with that of Red Deal (pine). (JMB).

5. Name two softwoods which have distinct annual rings and two hardwoods with distinct medullary rays.

6. A highly figured wood such as Bird's Eye Maple is usually cut to make veneers.

If such a wood were cut into boards to make a table top, what would the probable result be, and why?

7. What is meant by grain in timber? How does it vary in hard- and softwoods?

4 & 5 USES OF TIMBER

1. Name four different timbers used in making woodworkers' tools and equipment, saying for what purpose they are used and giving reasons for using them. (WM)

2. List the following and opposite each name the timber from which it would best be made:

1. Garden fence post
2. Jack plane
3. Painted bedroom door
4. Folding rule
5. Chair with a curved back
6. Cooking spoon
7. Rowing oar
8. Greenhouse frame
9. Shoe-cleaning box
10. Bookcase
11. Canoe
12. Clothes airer
13. Axe shaft
14. Rabbit hutch
15. Bowling skittle
16. Salad bowl
17. Cricket bat
18. Black chessman
19. Archery bow
20. Barrel

3. Write out a list of all the processes homegrown hardwood would pass through from the time a tree is felled to its appearance as a planed board in the school timber store. Explain each process very briefly. (JMB).

4. Each of the timbers in list (B) is used in making one article in list (A). Pair off each timber with the appropriate article.

(A)	(B)
Workbench top	Walnut
Garden seat	Scots pine
Gunstock	Teak
Fencepost	Mahogany
Painted bathroom cabinet	Oak
Coffee table	Beech

(S)

6 DEFECTS

1. These drawings show two defects in timber:

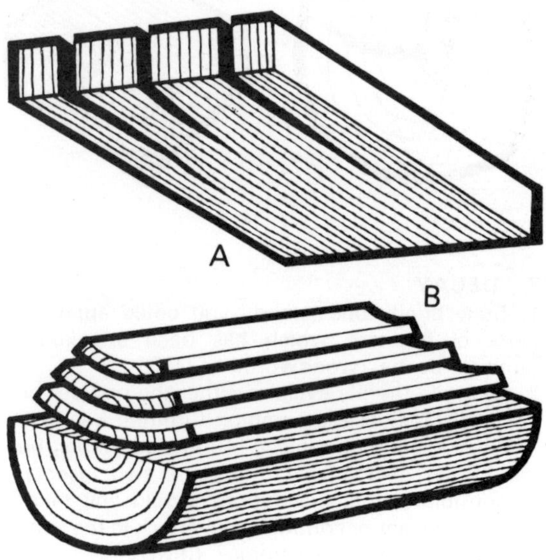

In each case state how they have been caused and how they might have been prevented. (W)

2. Name four defects to avoid when buying timber.
3. Make labelled sketches showing the ends of logs or planks to illustrate each of the following:

(*a*) a cup shake
(*b*) a heart shake
(*c*) warping
(*d*) plain oak
(*e*) figured oak.

4. What is a knot? How may the presence of a knot affect the quality of the timber? Use sketches to illustrate your answer.
5. The sketches show some of the defects which are liable to occur in timber.

State the name of each one and briefly suggest how the fault may have been caused.

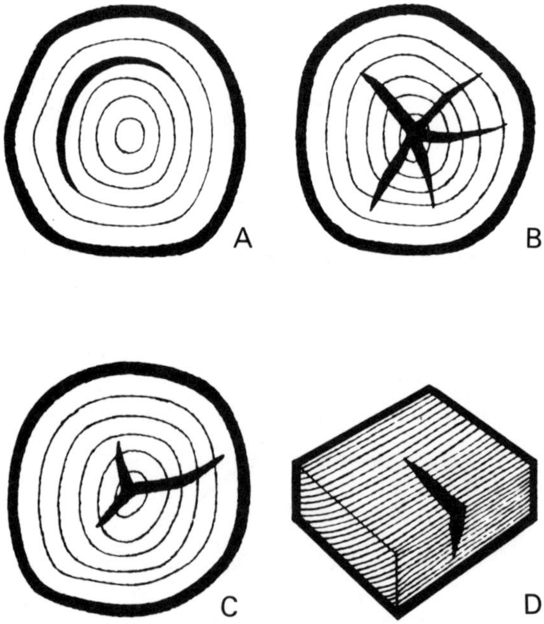

7 DECAY

1. State briefly one remedy you could apply to a piece of furniture which has been attacked by furniture beetle (woodworm). (JMB)
2. Describe the life cycle of either the powder post beetle (lyctus) or the common furniture beetle.

When examining a piece of infected timber, how would you decide which of these two insects is responsible? What precautions would you take in order to prevent or control insect attack in the school wood store and in your home? (JMB)
3. What part of the tree which produces timber is most likely to be attacked by woodworm?

8 CONVERSION

1. Describe briefly what is meant by conversion.

State which methods of conversion would be best for timber required for the following purposes:

(*a*) softwood packing cases
(*b*) to show annual ring figuring
(*c*) to show medullary ray figuring.

2. By means of notes and sketches show how boards should be cut from:

(*a*) a log of softwood
(*b*) a log of hardwood to give in each case the best natural markings. (JMB)

3. Draw a circle approximately 75 mm in diameter. Then draw in this circle the cross sections to show two methods of converting an oak log to provide the maximum number of figured boards. (SE)

9 SEASONING

1. Why must timber be seasoned before it is used in constructional work? Explain clearly the methods of seasoning timber by

(*a*) natural *and*
(*b*) artificial means. (JMB)

2. Some planks of 25 mm thick softwood have been purchased to be used for shelving at a later date.

Write a sentence and make a drawing to show how this timber could be successfully stored for six months or more.

Write sentences to state what would happen if:

(*a*) the wood were stored in a damp cellar
(*b*) the wood were left leaning against a wall. (MET)

3. Why should timber be seasoned before being used for indoor or jointed woodwork?

Name and sketch two faults which are likely to occur if unseasoned timber is used for furniture making.

10 SHRINKAGE—WARPING

1. Even when timber has been carefully seasoned it continues to shrink and swell according to the moisture content of the atmosphere. Explain some of the difficulties caused by this movement when articles are made from wood.

Show how the movement is allowed for in the following articles:

(*a*) a drawing board
(*b*) the top of a coffee table
(*c*) a framed door with a solid wood panel. (MET)

2. The sketches below show the end view of two boards which have been cut from a log.

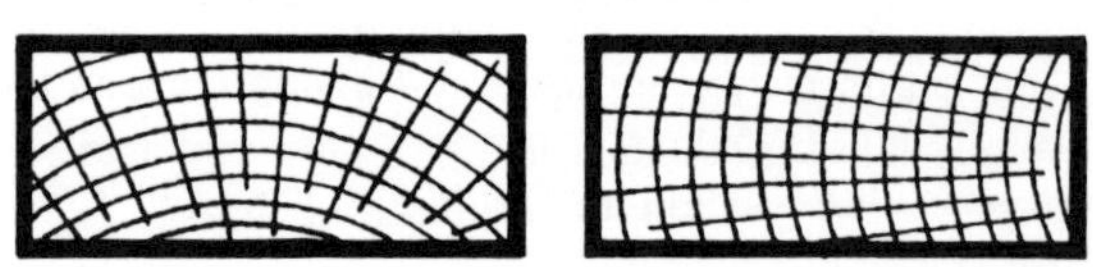

Show how you would expect these boards to change shape if they were left to dry freely, and explain how their shapes will differ. What precautions would you take when storing timber to reduce the possibility of it warping? (AEB)
3. In what direction does the maximum shrinkage in timber occur?
4. Shrinkage takes place during the process of drying or seasoning timber. The sketch shows the cross-section of a tree-trunk with outlines of various shaped pieces.

Make good-sized sketches of the shape these pieces would adopt in drying out.

VENEERS
1. What is veneer? (S)
2. Give a list of reasons why veneered furniture, basically a good idea, fell into disrepute. If you were to buy modern furniture, which items would you expect to be of solid wood and not veneered?

11 PLYWOOD
1. If you were asked to make a table-tennis table top say why you would use plywood rather than solid timber. Make a sketch to show how plywood is built up.

State one disadvantage of plywood as compared with solid timber when used in joinery or cabinet making, and explain how this disadvantage may be overcome.
2. Make sketches of 'stout-heart' and 'multiply' and label each of them. What does the term 'WBP' stand for? Explain as fully as you can.
3. Write what you know about the type of timber and adhesive used in the manufacture of plywoods.
4. Describe the stages in the manufacture of plywood from the log to the finished board. Which timbers are commonly used for this purpose and why do you think that they are most suitable? (JMB)
5. Show by means of sketches the differences between plywood and blockboard. Give an example of the use of each.
6. Make a sketch, with notes, of the corner of a piece of three-ply wood. (WM)
7. Plywood is shown in the photograph to be flexible. What are its other characteristics which make it a good structural material?

12 MANUFACTURED BOARD
1. What is chipboard? (S)
2. Write down an advantage of manufactured board compared with solid wood.

Write the name and draw a section through a manufactured board suitable for the back of a first-aid cabinet.

Write the name and draw a section through a manufactured board suitable for a 19 mm thick table-tennis table.

By what measurements are the thicknesses of manufactured boards generally quoted? (MET)
3. Name four common types of manufactured board.
4. Draw a section through a sheet of blockboard. (MET)
5. Describe, using freehand drawings, the difference between plywood and laminated board.

Explain how you would make a small flush door in teak-faced laminated board for a teak bedside table. (MET)
6. What is hardboard?

The structure of hardboard makes it necessary to be treated before being used out of doors.

Make a list of the precautions that you would take to prevent it from deteriorating and use sketches where necessary.
7. Plywood, blockboard and hardboard are often used instead of solid wood. Describe and sketch each of these 'manufactured' boards, explaining the differences between them and any advantages and disadvantages they may have compared with solid wood. Give a good example of where each could be used. (JMB)

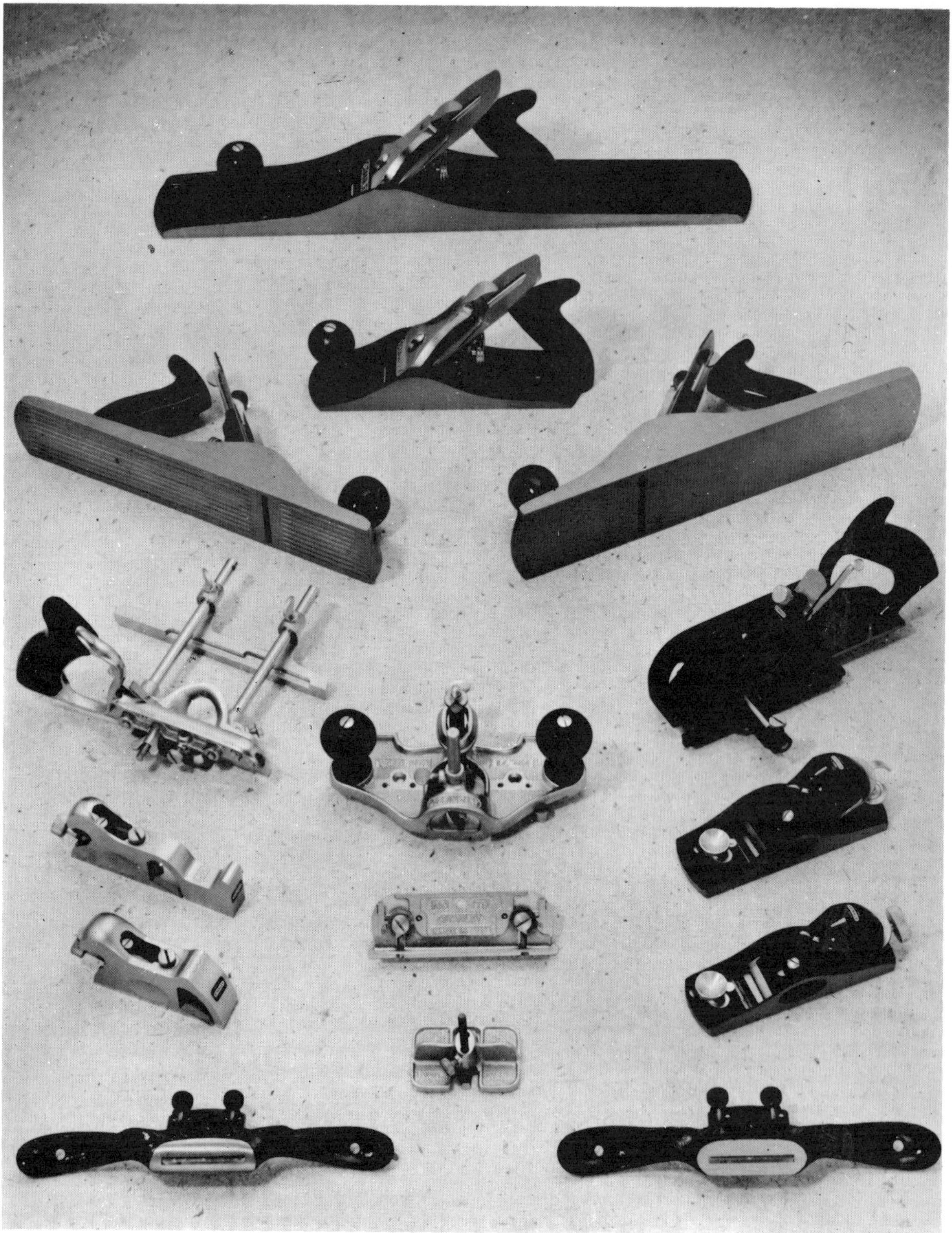

STANLEY TOOLS LTD

TOOLS 2

The quality of steel used in tool manufacture varies according to the job that tool is required to do.

The steel for a screwdriver blade must have high tensile qualities (be capable of twisting and bending without breaking) whereas a wood chisel demands a hard finely-grained steel that will sharpen to and maintain a good cutting edge.

Neither steel could be used for the other job—a brittle screwdriver would snap and a soft chisel would not sharpen properly.

MANUFACTURE

Steel is made from raw iron to which is added certain ingredients such as charcoal *(carbon)*, with *tungsten* or *vanadium* or *magnesium* which convert the iron into steel. The carbon content varies from 0·5% in soft steels to a maximum of 1·4% in the hardest steel.

High quality chisels which must be hard enough to take a good edge but not too brittle in use have a carbon content of 1·10% to 1·15%

HARDENING

The physical properties of tool steels are determined by their carefully controlled heat treatments.

When steel cools slowly from being red-hot the metal is *annealed* i.e. it is soft and could not be used as a cutting tool.

Quenching red-hot metal in water makes the steel 'dead hard'—a state in which it would cut very well but would be brittle and dangerous.

TEMPERING

This extreme hardness is removed by re-heating to a lesser degree (the oxides on the surface go from a pale straw colour to a dark purple blue, before beginning to glow red) and being allowed to cool.

Of the other ingredients in tool steel *tungsten* is the most used. A small quantity will enable the tool to hold a cutting edge for a much longer period and less sharpening means a longer life for plane and chisel blades.

High quality steel for saw blades being poured from a five ton furnace.

CLASSIFICATION OF TOOLS

Measuring	Steel tape, folding rule and steel rule.
Marking	Pencil, chalked line, marking knives, compasses, dividers, Marking, cutting and mortise gauges.
Testing	Try square, mitre square, sliding bevel, straight edge, winding strips and squaring rod.
Cutting	Paring: Chisels, gouges, planes, routers, spokeshaves, scraper. Boring: Joiners' brace and bits, hand drill and bradawls. Rasping: Hand, back and frame saws, files, rasps.
Driving	Screwdrivers, hammers, mallets and punch.
Holding	Vice, sash cramps, G-cramps and holdfast.

13 TOOLS—MEASURING

The accurate measuring of given distances is necessary if your work is to be of a good standard. Three main types of rule are in general use in the workshop, each with a different job to do.

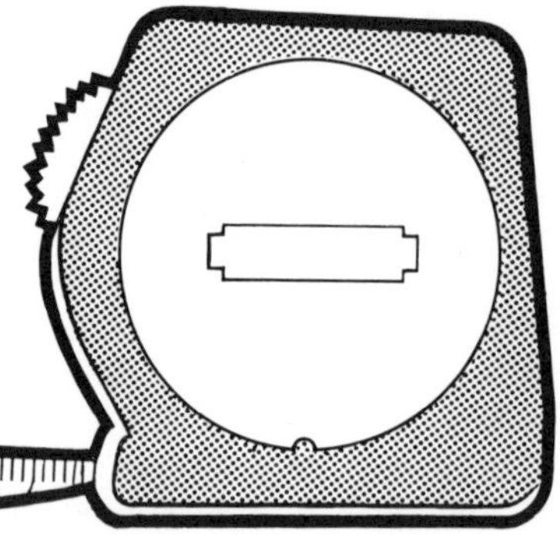

STEEL TAPE

This is mainly used for longer measurements, such as marking out on boards and checking the overall dimensions of work. They are from 2 m to 3 m in length and because of their flexibility are particularly useful for curved work.

Good quality tapes are covered with a new *polyester* finish that will not rust, will not crack and make the accurate markings permanent. On many models the blade can be locked in position and when released will spring back into its compact metal case.

To make internal measurements, such as those inside box constructions or between table rails, the Stanley Top-sight rule is useful. The measurements can be read through a window in the case.

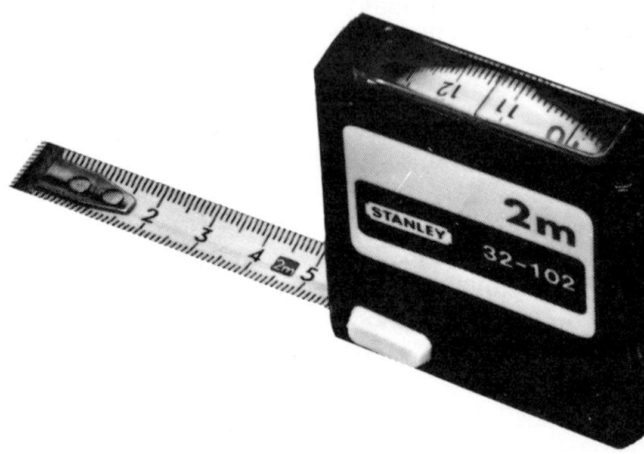

FOLDING RULE

The four-fold rules of one metre (extended length) are convenient for the woodworker to carry in his apron pocket. The best quality rules are made from *boxwood* with *brass hinges* and end-plates which are designed to prevent excessive wear. Boxwood rules are being superseded by a shock-proof plastic type with stainless steel fittings.

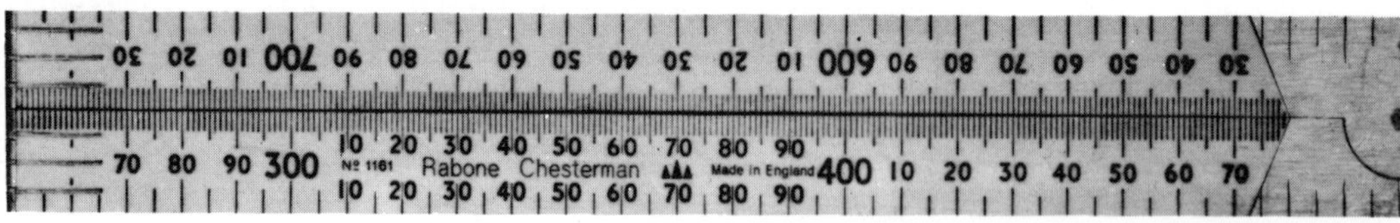

STEEL RULE

This is an essential part of the tool kit for *accurate marking out* and the square zero end, which must not be misused, makes gauge setting and the measuring of internal dimensions easy.

It may also be used as a straight edge and squaring rod on small work such as jewel boxes.

Note—Most rules and tapes can be purchased with metric divisions on one edge—in readiness for metrication.

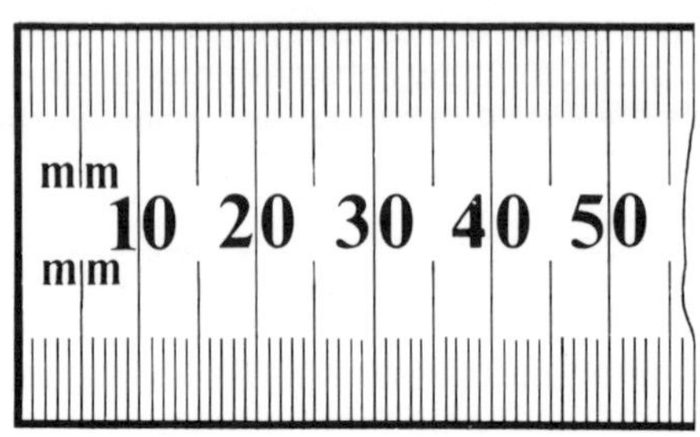

14 TOOLS—MARKING

PENCILS

Carpenters pencils which are oval in section and have a heavy lead, are longer-lasting than 'normal' pencils when marking out boards for sawing. A normal round or hexagonal HB pencil is most useful for marking out chamfers and temporary guide lines and cross-hatching or shading waste wood.

CHALKED LINE

Straight lines can normally be gauged parallel to the edge of boards with a rule and pencil, but when the edge is uneven or waney a chalked line is useful. A chalked line is knotted and trapped in a saw cut at one end of the board. It is pulled tight to the other mark and 'plucked'. The method is an ancient but effective one.

MARKING KNIVES

Marking knives are traditionally made of *steel* with *hardwood handles* (rosewood) riveted on. They are hard wearing but because of their wide blade are not convenient for work in small spaces, e.g. marking out dovetail pins from tails. This can more easily be done with a *Stanley 'Slimknife'* which has a variety of interchangeable blades to suit many jobs.

The *retractable blade* of the *trimming knife* is useful when working with harder materials such as plastic laminates, is shaped to fit the hand and can be safely carried in the pocket.

COMPASSES

A pair of simple compasses is useful in the preparation of timber for lathework, marking small curves, felt discs for table mats, etc.

DIVIDERS

Dividers are less frequently used in the workshop but are invaluable where repeated even spaces or distances are required.

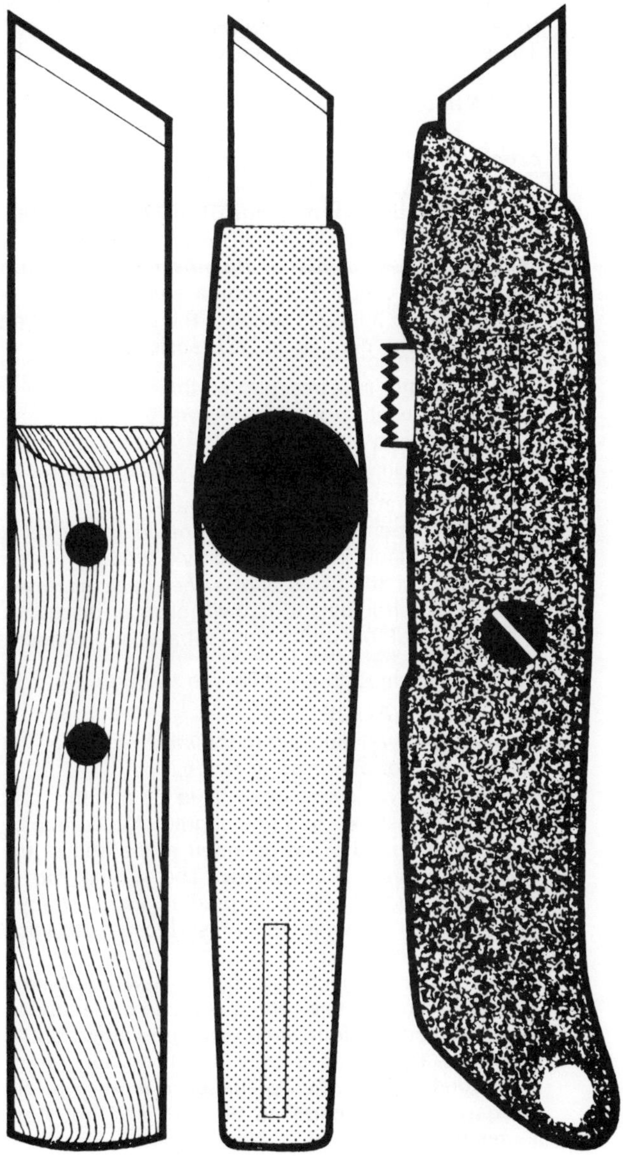

Traditional | Stanley 'Slimknife' | Trimming knife

TOOLS—GAUGES

Gauges are used for marking lines parallel to the edge or squared end of a board.

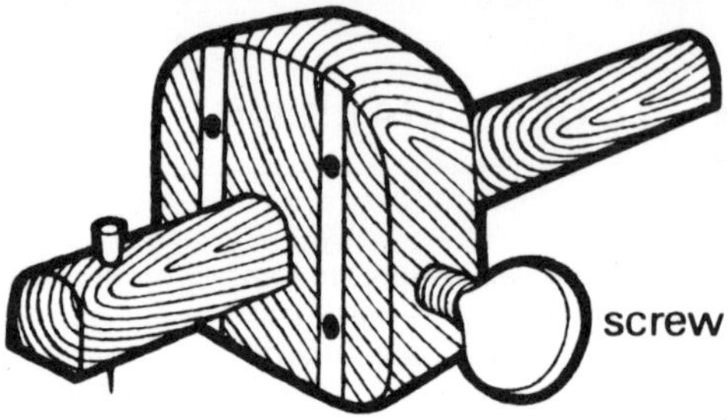

MARKING GAUGE

The hardened *steel spur* protruding from the *beech stem* marks lines *down the grain*—as when gauging to width or thickness.

The distance from the edge of the wood is determined by the position of the *beech stock* which is held in place by a *plastic thumbscrew* (boxwood was formerly used). The modern shape of stock is comfortable to hold and because the spur is set at an angle, to avoid 'digging-in', it is easier to use.

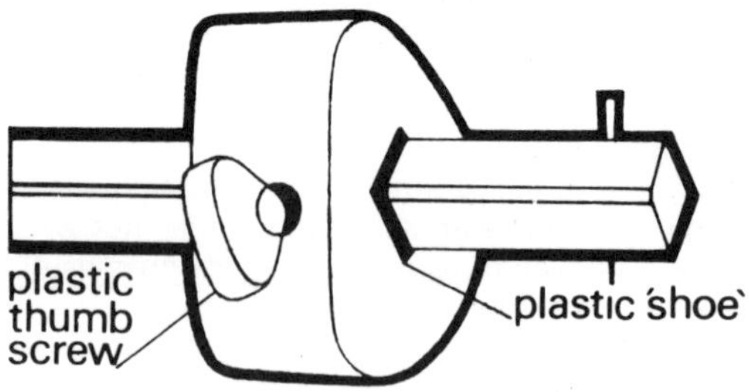

plastic 'shoe' prevents the screw from damaging the pentagonal stem

CUTTING GAUGE

With the exception of its cutter the design is identical to that of the marking gauge.

A small tapered mortise is prepared to accept a small sharp blade (held in place by a wedge) which is used *to cut* the fibres *across the grain,* as when marking the shoulders of lapped joints or dovetails. It is also useful for cutting small rebates and veneers.

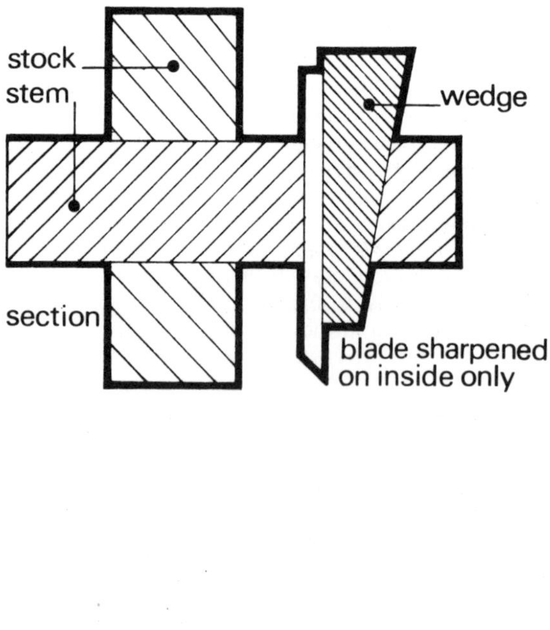

MORTISE GAUGE

This is an invaluable aid to the *marking out* of the parallel sides of a *mortise or tenon.*

There are two spurs—one fixed by a screw and the other adjustable, to a fine degree of accuracy by means of a threaded rod operated at the end of the stock by a brass thumbscrew. The *sliding rod* in which the spur is set is secured in its *⊥-shaped groove* by a screw in the brass-faced *rosewood stock.*

1. The minimum gauge setting on new equipment is about 5 mm but this can be reduced by removing the slides and carefully filing away unwanted brass.
2. As the actual size of, say 6 mm chisels varies, it is sound advice when preparing a mortise to set the gauge on the chisel to be used and not from a steel rule.

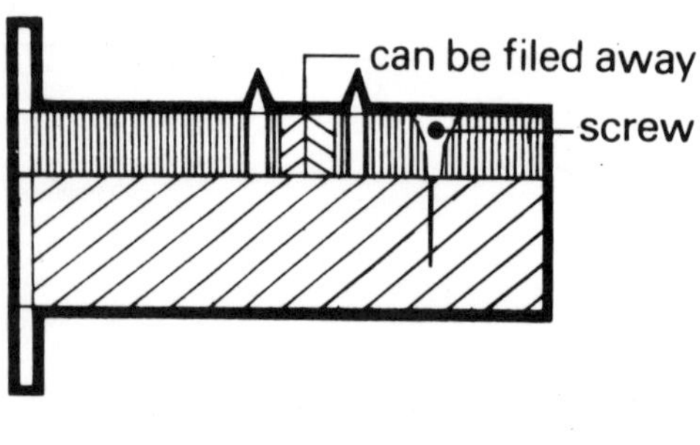

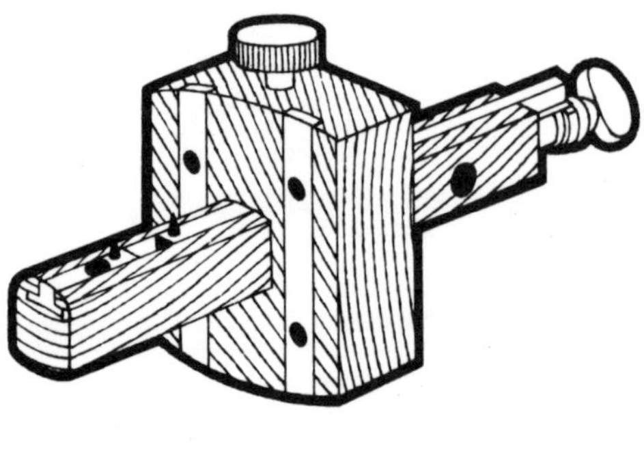

15 TOOLS—SQUARES

TRY SQUARE

The try square, mitre square and sliding bevel are traditionally made from similar materials. They are dual-purpose in that they are used in marking out joints and, at a later stage in the work, for testing squareness and a variety of angles.

The hardened and tempered *steel blade* is held in the *brass-faced hardwood stock* (usually rosewood) by means of *steel rivets* and *brass washers*.

Its chief use is for *testing* external and internal *right-angles,* marking out tenon shoulders, etc., and it is a short but convenient straight edge.

The blade lengths available are 150, 225 and 300 mm.

If the square becomes distorted or inaccurate (wear can often be noticed near the stock) no attempt should be made to adjust the blade, but it can be filed true. Marples produce an 'ever-true' square that has an L-shaped blade running through the length of the stock which will withstand the roughest use.

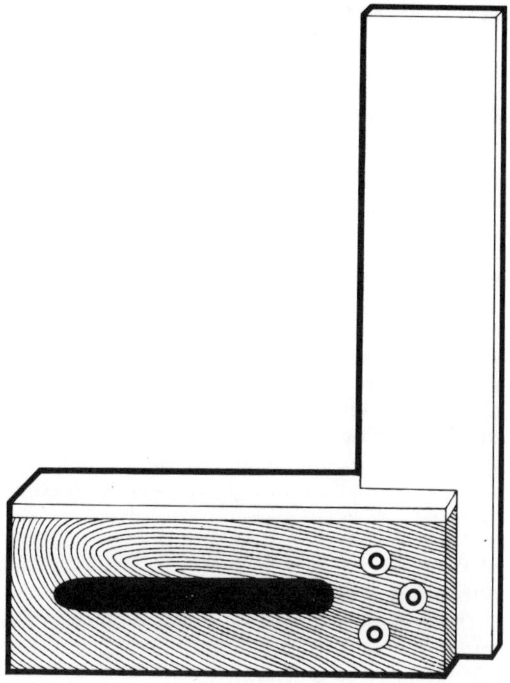

MITRE SQUARE

Made in a similar manner to the try square, its 250 mm blade is set in the stock at the acute angle of 45 deg. and the obtuse angle of 135 degrees. The stock is protected against wear and damage by inlaid brass plates. Its workshop use is limited to marking out and testing the set angles, particularly mitred joints at the corners of frames. Metal jigs, which make the cutting of mitres easy, have reduced its general use.

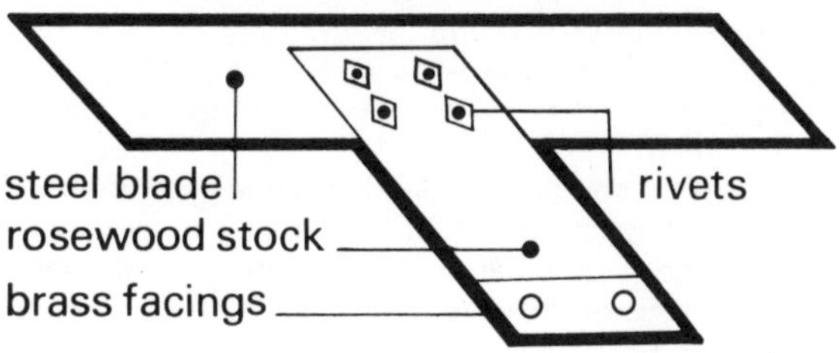

SLIDING BEVEL

The steel blade has a 45 deg. bevel point at one end and is slotted into a plastic stock. The offset slot enables lines to be drawn along its full length, clear of the stock. A finger-tight locking lever is used to fix the blade and to release it for adjustment.

Its value is its adaptability and lines can be marked or surfaces tested at any angle.

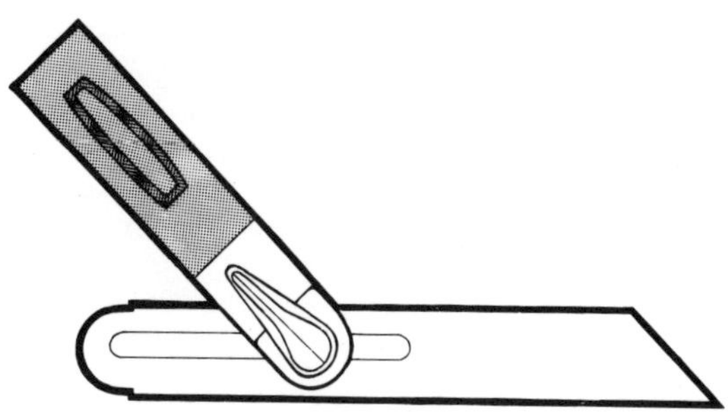

TOOLS—TESTING

STRAIGHT EDGE

The *testing* of *wood surfaces for flatness* and *trueness* is done with a straight edge. Short lengths can easily be tested with the edge of a try square or steel rule but longer surfaces require a longer edge. For this purpose metal edges can be bought, but at a useful 600 to 750 mm long they are heavy and difficult to handle.

One can be made in the workshop using a well-seasoned hardwood (750×75×12 mm) which, if well varnished and hung up when not in use, will give good service.

Regular checking of the edge is necessary and can be done by reversing it on its own line so that any fault is exaggerated. Winding strips can be tested in the same way and if necessary, trued with a try plane.

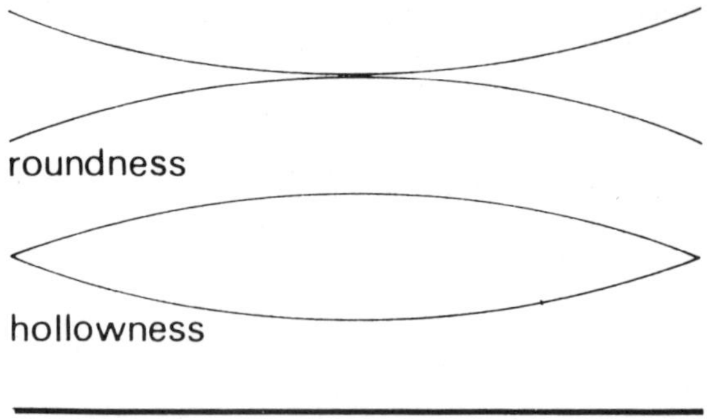

WINDING STRIPS

These can also be made in the workshop from a hardwood such as Honduras Mahogany, which is unlikely to twist or warp.

They must have parallel sides and are used in pairs for *testing surfaces and frames* to see if they are *twisted* or *in-winding*.

Placed at opposite ends of the work the edges are sighted from a few feet away and the degree of twist noted.

It helps if one edge is painted white and the other black or they can be inlaid with a strip of sycamore or blackbean or other suitably contrasting timbers. These too should be regularly tested for accuracy and hung up when not in use.

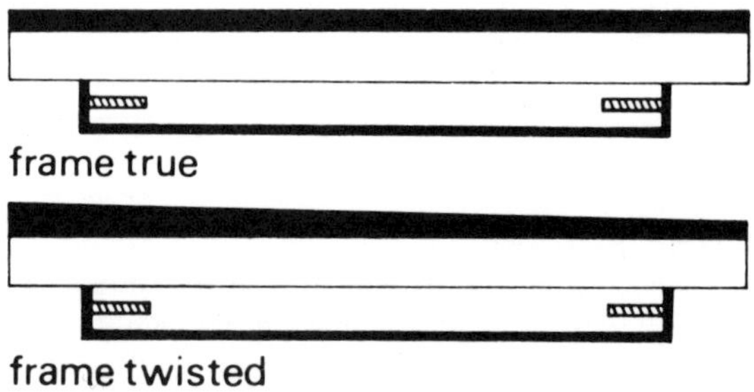

SQUARING RODS

Made from straight pieces of hardwood or soft-wood they are made to fit into the corner of frames and carcases to *test for squareness* i.e. that the internal diagonals are equal. Testing with a square is not accurate as the pressure of the cramps tends to distort the sides. The rod is marked with a pencil and if the frame or box is not square the true measurement is midway between the two marks.

A set of rods, three or four in number and varying in length from 600 to 1800 mm, will suit most purposes.

16 TOOLS—CHISELS

The best chisels are made of high-quality carbon steel that will maintain a sharp cutting edge throughout their length.

They are fairly brittle and can be dangerous if not used properly. It is important to have the right type and size of chisel for each job.

FIRMER CHISEL

This square-edged chisel is used in work where a certain amount of robustness is needed. Like most chisels it is made in a dozen blade sizes from 3 mm to 50 mm wide and can be fitted to a variety of handles. The boxwood handle has been in use for many hundreds of years and is most reliable. It rarely splits if used properly and is superior to the cheaper ash handle.

The use of the more expensive plastic handles will make the manufacture of wood handles a thing of the past. The newest material, cellulose acetate butyrate, can be moulded to any shape and is virtually indestructable. This material is used in the Stanley range of chisels.

These are made in the following millimetre widths: 3, 6, 9, 12, 13, 16, 18, 19, 25, 31 and 38.

boxwood 'carving' type

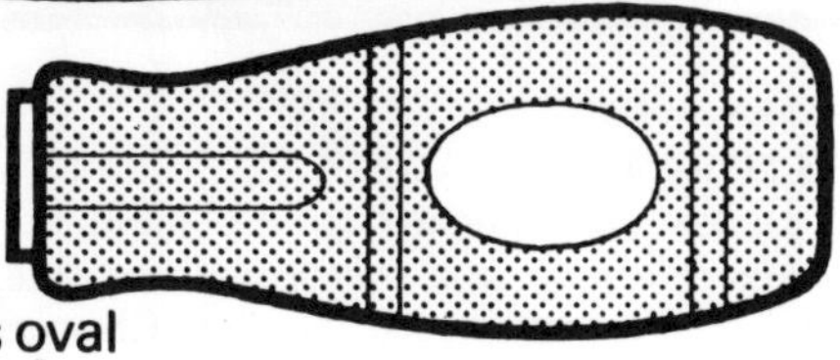

Marples oval splitproof

FIRMER CHISEL

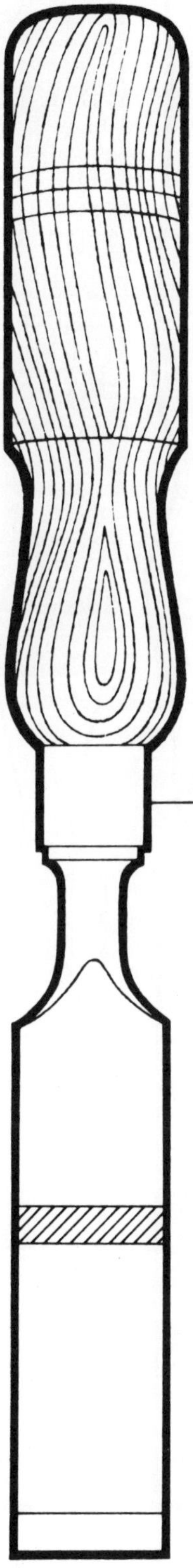

MORTISE CHISELS

There are three main types available:

1. heavy-duty
2. sash
3. registered

It is the registered type that you probably use more than any other, particularly for cutting mortises under about 9 mm wide.

chisels over ▶

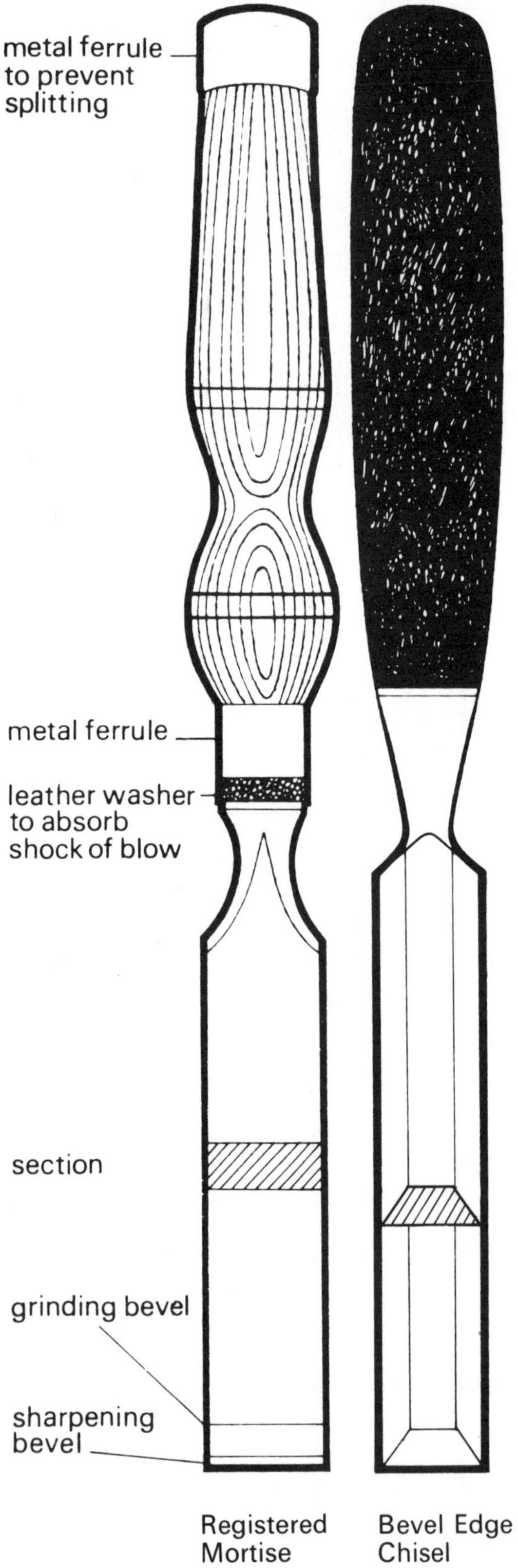

The traditional ash handle is bound at the striking end by a strong steel hoop or *ferrule* to prevent splitting. To resist shock, a *leather washer* is fitted between the shoulder and the usual brass or steel ferrule. This effective but complicated construction will gradually be replaced by the splitproof plastic handles.

The blades of these chisels differ from the firmer type in that they have a thicker section and a stronger neck, a source of weakness in other chisels if they are struck with a mallet.

1. Leverage can be applied to remove waste-wood from the mortise.
2. The thicker blade has less tendency to twist when hit, therefore the cut is more accurate.

BEVEL EDGE CHISEL

In its narrower sizes this chisel is very weak and must only be used by hand.

Similar in construction to the firmer chisel its edges are bevelled to allow access to difficult corners e.g. the pin spaces between dovetails, where the firmer blade would be too thick to reach.

The blades vary considerably in length, the longest being the paring chisel (250 mm). It is twice the length of a normal chisel and is difficult to control.

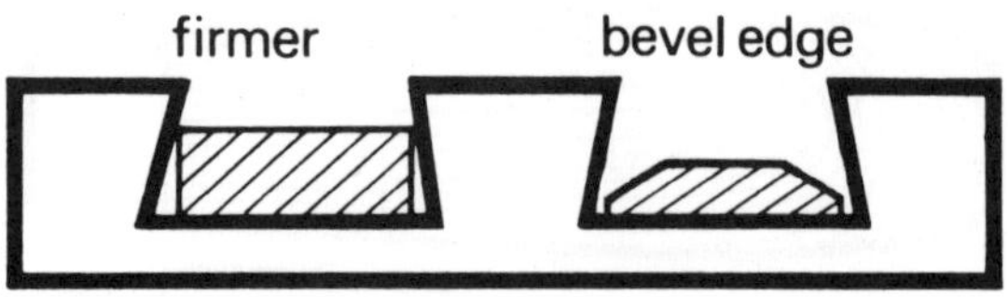

FITTING THE BLADE

Blades are attached to the handles either by means of a *tang* or a *socket* and both methods are used in the new plastic handles. Chisels that look best are usually the most comfortable to hold.

Examples are the Stanley 5001/4 and the Marples 'Blue Chip' ranges of firmer, bevel edged and mortise chisels whose blades fit into a virtually unbreakable solid plastic handle that has both the shape and 'feel' of the traditional boxwood.

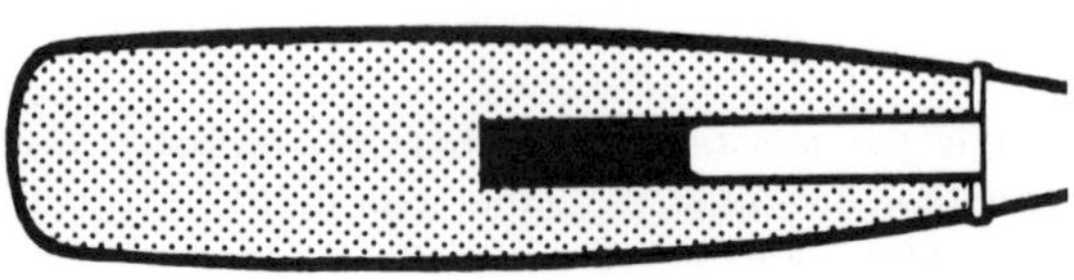

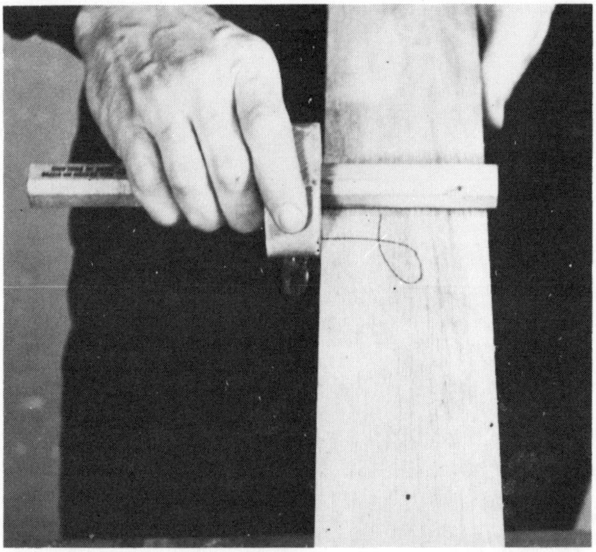

The Marking Gauge is pushed away from the user.

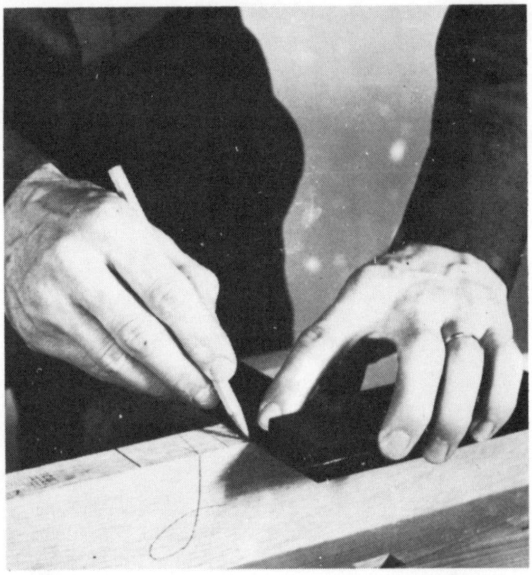

The Try-square is held against a face-side when squaring shoulders across an edge.

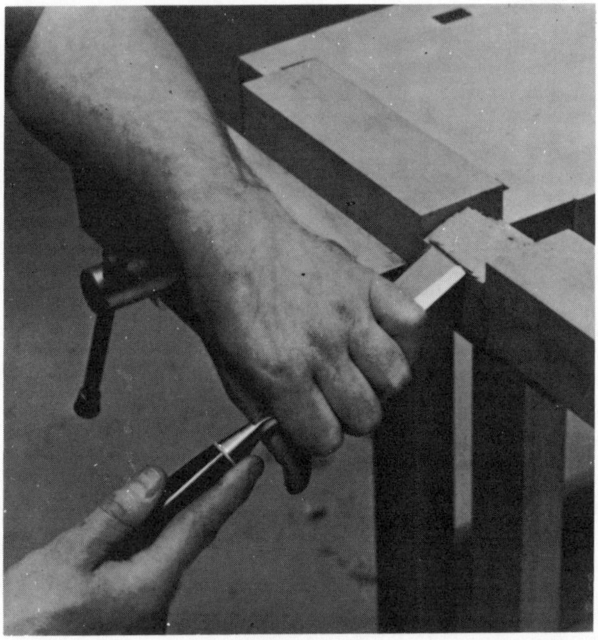

A plastic-handled bevel-edge chisel being used to remove waste from a halving joint.

A plastic-handled firmer chisel being used vertically to remove waste from an open mortise. Note the protective chiselling board.

SECTION THROUGH A SMOOTHING PLANE

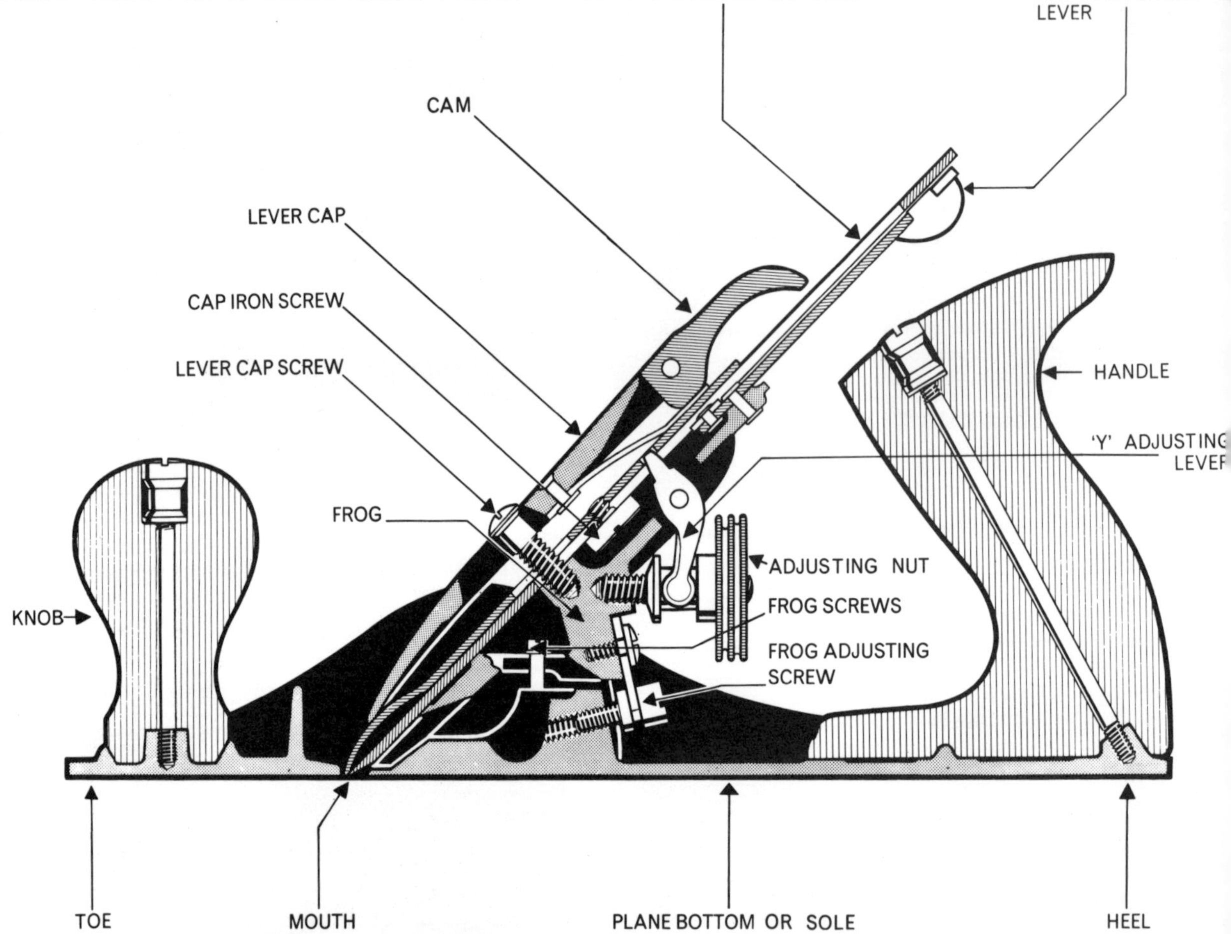

Planing a face edge. The fingers on the sole of the plane help to keep it straight.

Planing end grain. One method is to cramp a piece of waste to your wood to prevent splitting at the corner.

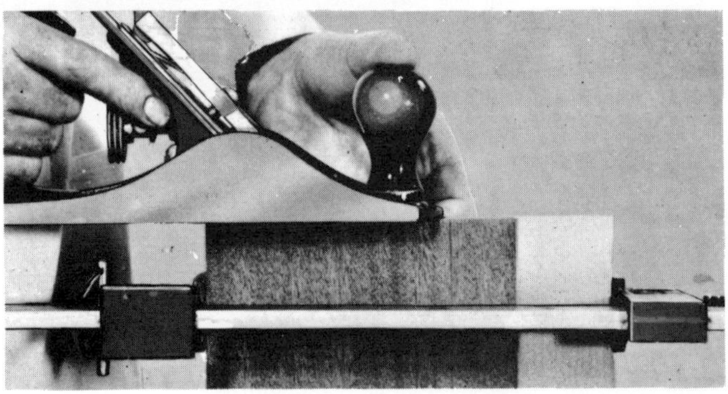

17 TOOLS—PLANES

Leaving aside the many special planes used in the workshop, there are three in regular use:

1. the *try* plane
2. the *jack* plane
3. the *smoothing* plane

The scale drawings below show how they vary in both length and width and it is important to remember that they are made from either *wood* (the traditional material) or from *cast iron.*

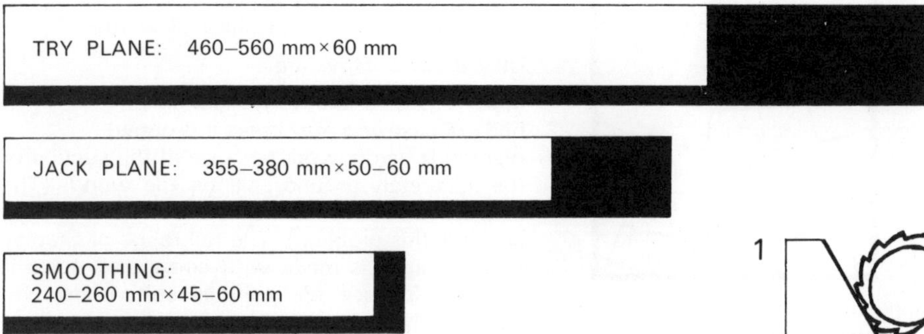

CUTTING ACTION

The principles behind the cutting action design are similar in all three planes.

(1) The *single cutting iron* breaks the wood fibres and tears the surface leaving it rough.

(2) The use of a *cap iron* improves this cutting action in two ways:

a. The blade is stiffened and this prevents 'chattering'.

b. The shaving is lifted soon after it has been cut and this prevents tearing.

The setting of the cap-iron affects the quality of the cut. The jack plane iron is set at about 1·5 mm from the cutting edge and the try and smoothing planes much less, thus lifting the shaving earlier. This cap-iron must be a good fit or 'clogging' of the mouth will soon occur. A *close mouth* will also improve the cut (4) preventing splitting ahead of the cutting edge (3).

As wooden planes wear this is a common fault and re-mouthing is the only cure (4). One of the main advantages of the metal planes is that the size of the mouth can be easily adjusted.

AWKWARD GRAIN

To obtain a good finish on wood that has an awkward grain you must:

1. have a keenly sharpened blade
2. have a closely set and well-fitted back-iron
3. set a small mouth
4. set the protruding blade as finely as possible.

1

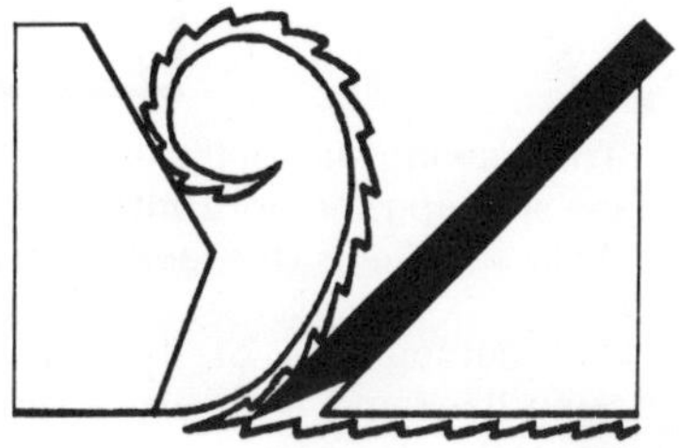

2

3

4

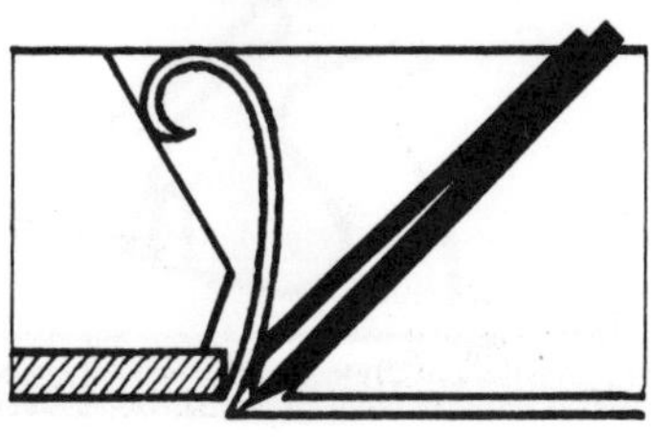

WOOD PLANES

These are made from close-grained beech which wears smooth in use and lasts well. It requires considerable maintenance such as re-mouthing, re-truing the sole, re-newing damaged handles, and it is not easy to adjust the depth of cut accurately.

Probably you are familiar with the wooden jack plane which has 'survived' the introduction of metal planes because it is relatively light to handle and does its jobs well (1) planing 'rough-sawn' wood (2) preparing timber quickly to size.

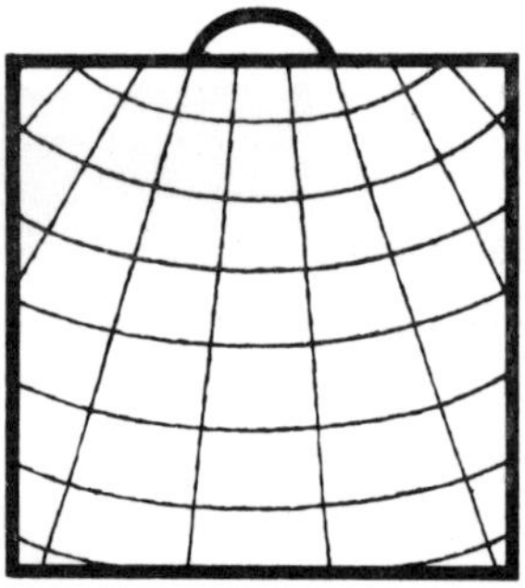

The drawing shows the end view of a good wood plane showing the horizontal annual rings resulting in even shrinkage (for faults see chapter 1 section 10).

The cutting iron of the jack plane is curved, making the removal of waste wood a quicker and easier task.

The try and smoothing plane blades are sharpened square across and have the corners taken off to prevent them 'scoring' the work.

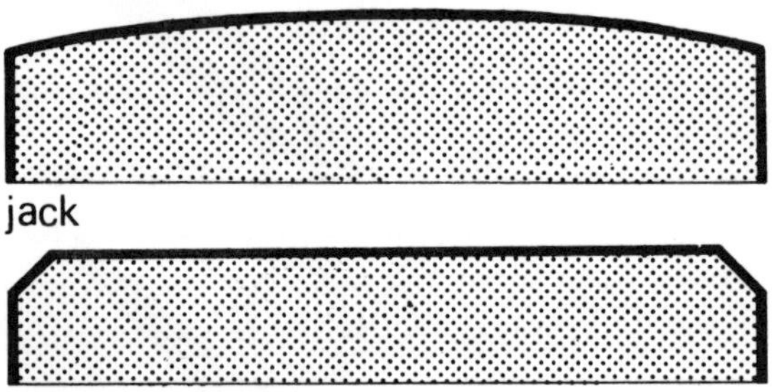

jack

try & smoothing

METAL PLANES

If a plane is set to finish awkward grain it will still give perfect results on more normal surfaces. Because the fine mouth and blade settings are most easily achieved on metal planes they are mostly used for truing edges for jointing and smoothing to a finished surface.

The *advantages* of metal planes over their wood counterparts are:

1. quick and accurate lateral adjustment of blade
2. similar depth of cut adjustment
3. width of mouth can be altered to suit type of work
4. thinner blade is easily kept sharp
5. convenient lever cap in place of wedge

Their *disadvantages* are:

1. initial outlay is relatively expensive
2. body of cast-iron may break if dropped
3. planing is harder work because of the suction of the accurately-ground sole on the wood. (The occasional use of an oil-pad or candle wax answers this problem). The full range of Stanley bench planes is made with corrugated soles if required for use on resinous softwoods. Not surprisingly they are used by all boys in Scandinavian schools.

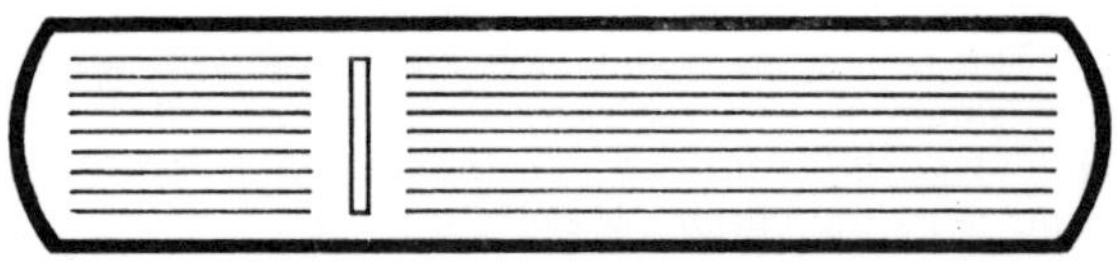

bench plane corrugated bottom

The try-plane is used to level surfaces and for truing edges, as when edge-jointing boards together to make a solid table-top. Its long true sole removes the tops of 'bumps' whereas the 'smoother' is likely to follow any undulations. Thus the job of the smoothing plane is mainly to finish off surfaces prior to glasspapering and polishing etc.

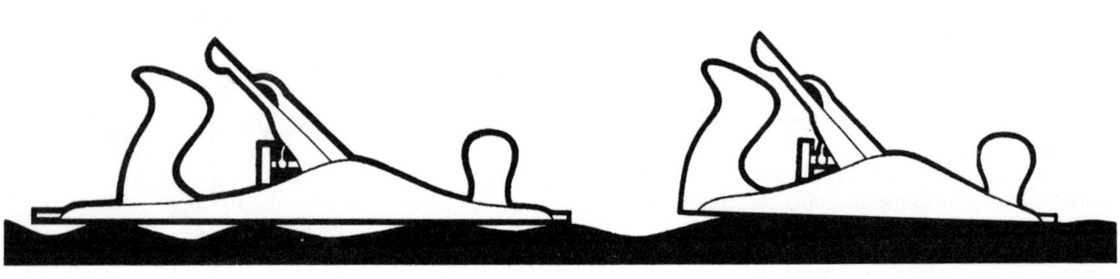

18 TOOLS—BORING

BRADAWL

This small but useful tool has two jobs to do:
1. 'boring' small holes in softwood for large nails or small gauge screws (say no. 4's.)
2. marking centres in wood prior to drilling.

The cast steel blade is sharpened to a flat 'point' and inserted into the work across the grain, to avoid splitting, and is then twisted. This twisting action requires a flat *tang* which can be strengthened by being pinned into the handle.

The handle is usually of the round ash or 'peg-top' boxwood type and the blade lengths, from 25 to 75 mm also vary in thickness from 5 to 18 wire gauge.

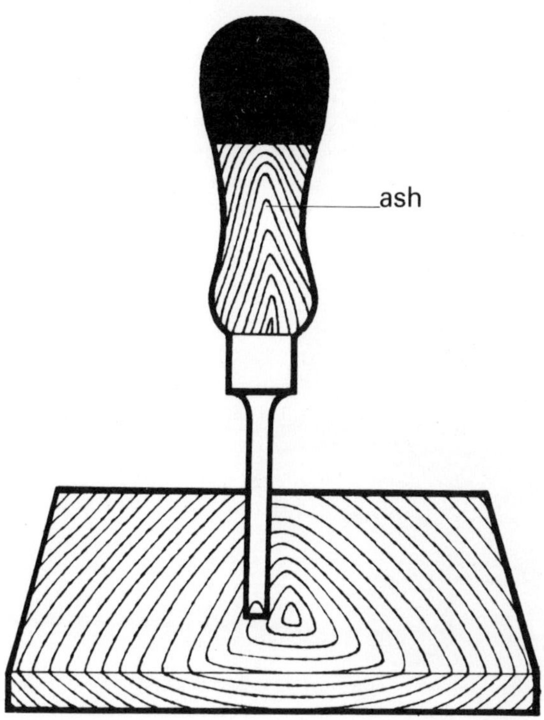

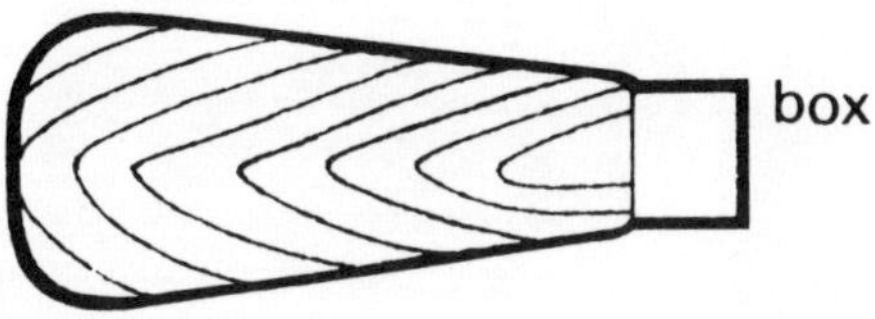

JOINER'S BRACE

Although it is still available in its plain form, the need to drill holes in restricted spaces has made the *ratchet brace* more useful. The *pawl and ratchet* gear enables the brace also to be used as a plain brace or in reverse.

The inside of the *chuck case* is threaded so that by rotating it the two alligator-type *jaws* will tighten on to or release the square shank of the bit.

The *arm* usually has a *sweep* of either 200 or 250 mm and is easily rotated because of the ball-bearings in the *head.*

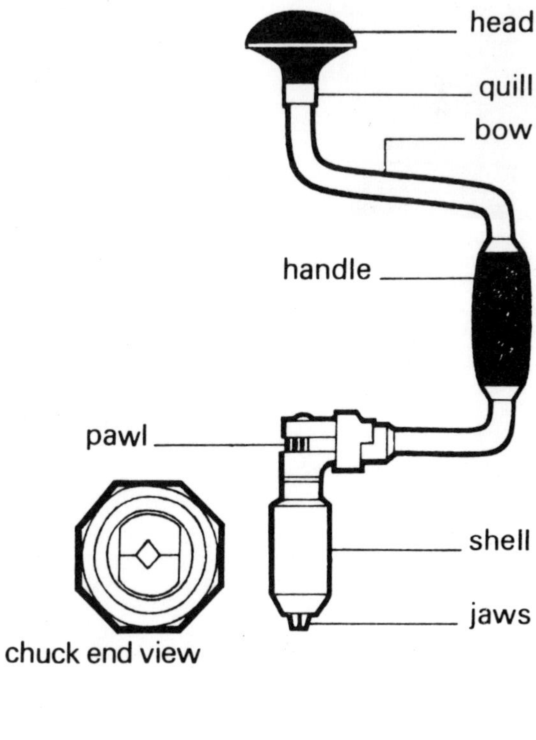

Horizontal Boring. The work is held in the vice; it is helpful to have an assistant to check that the bit is level. To obtain a clean finish the work is reversed when the point comes through the side of the wood.

Vertical Boring. The work is held firmly on the bench with a G-cramp.

Right: Great skill is needed to ensure that the twists on large diameter Auger bits are accurately ground.

TOOLS BORING—DRILLS

BITS

A wide variety of bits is available to fit the brace but their main use is that of boring holes of a large diameter or depth.

CENTRE BITS

Large shallow holes are bored with a centre bit, the old type being rather crude. It has a simple *centre point*, one *scriber* and one *cutter*.

The new pattern has a threaded centre point which gives a much better 'lead-in' to the wood and has two cutters. Sizes from 5 to 50 mm are available.

TWIST BIT

The centre bit is not suitable for boring into end grain nor *for boring deep holes*—this job being done by a *twist bit or auger bit*.

Of the many types made the *Jennings pattern* is perhaps the most common. It has two scribers and two *cutters* which speeds the cutting action; the twist removes the waste and its accurately ground parallel sides keep the hole straight.

Available in sizes from 5 to 38 mm, they are expensive to buy and should be kept in an enclosed rack or a suitable canvas roll.

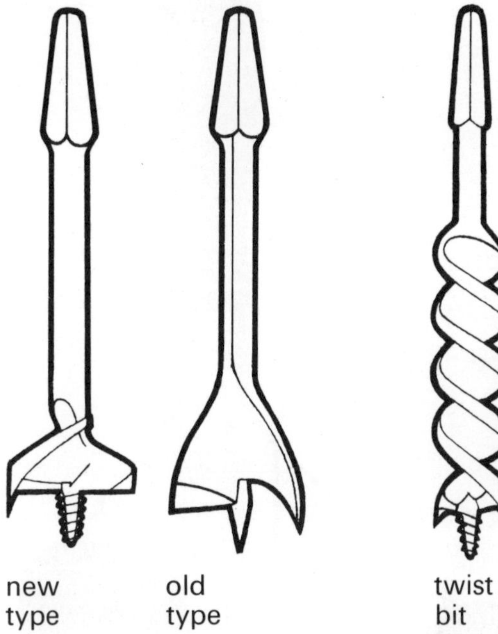

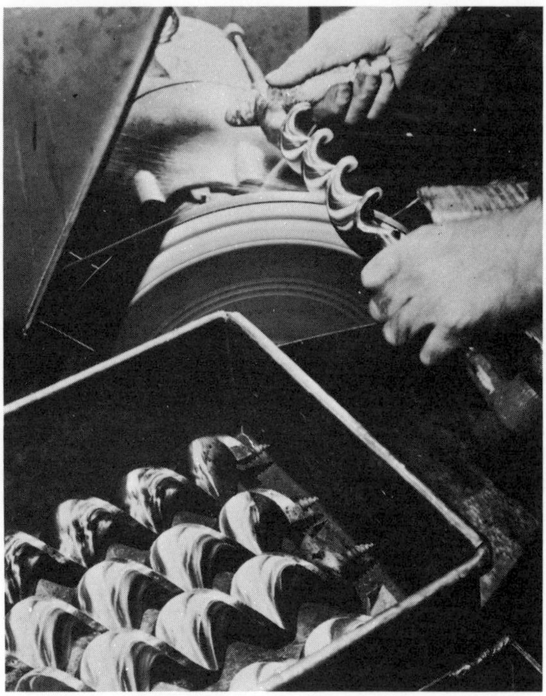

Precision tools, such as these twist bits, are well protected in a lined canvas roll.

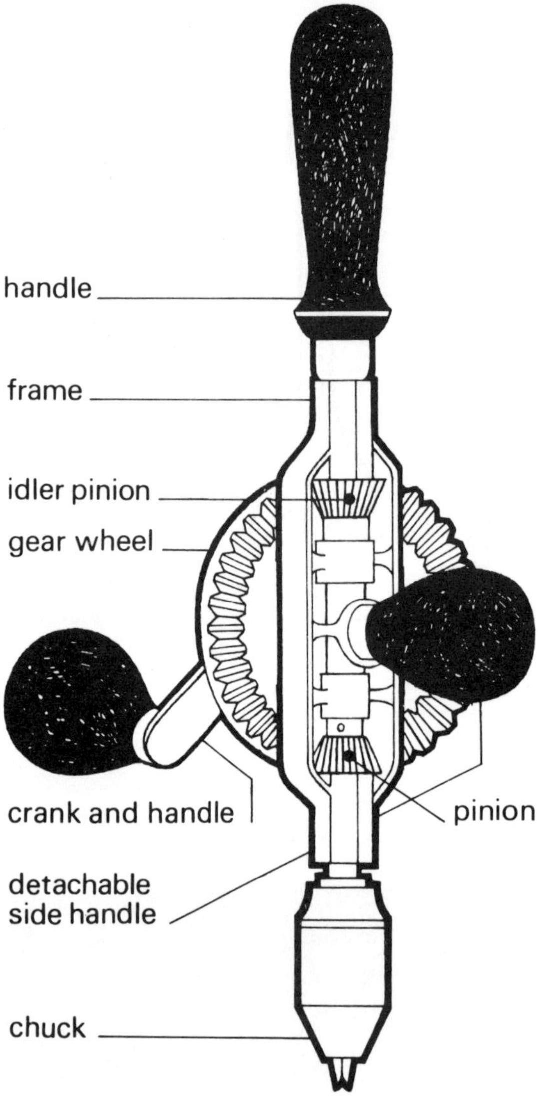

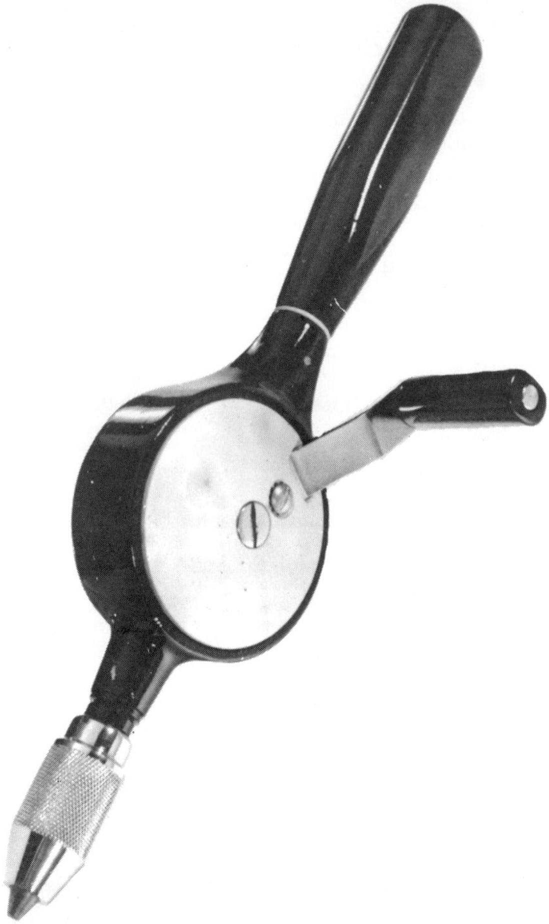

The Stanley 5803 Drill with enclosed gear wheel.

HAND DRILL (WHEELBRACE)

Originally designed as a metalworkers tool, the woodworker finds it most useful *for boring small holes* (with twist drills) to accommodate screws or small diameter dowelling.

The spring-loaded *three jaw chuck* has a drill capacity of 8 mm although the heavier breast drill can cope with a diameter of 13 mm. The iron or alloy *frame* has a side handle which is detachable for work in confined spaces and supports the two *pinions*. These are sintered with copper as is the gear wheel that drives them.

This gives added strength and to some extent makes them self-lubricating. This is particularly useful where the gears are enclosed as in the 'Stanley 5803 drill' which incorporates the new black cellulose-acetate handles.

TWIST DRILLS

These are parallel-sided drills and can be made for drilling wood only or of high-speed steel for drilling metal. Graduated in 0·1 mm, drills from 1·50 to 13 mm are common sizes. A 'rosehead countersink' is used to complete the preparation of screw holes where this is necessary.

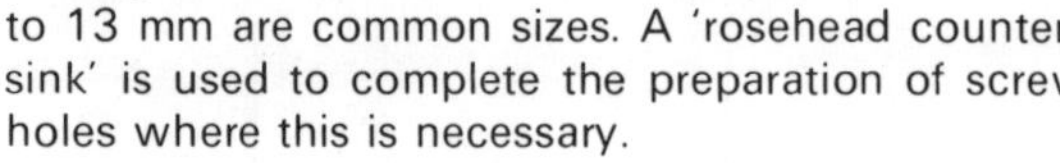

19 TOOLS—SAWS

There are three main types of saw:
1. hand saws
2. back saws
3. frame saws

Within each group, as with other tools we have both read about and used, there are several kinds of saw, each with a different job that it has been specially designed to do.

HAND SAWS

These are of two kinds:
1. the rip saw
2. the cross-cut and panel saws

RIP SAW

The saw blade is 660 mm long and there are 4 teeth to each 25 mm of blade. The severe set of these teeth produces a wide saw cut (kerf).

The teeth are sharpened to form a square cutting edge so that the saw's cutting action is similar to that of a large number of small chisels passing through the surface of the wood and is suitable only *for sawing down the grain* i.e. ripping.

This wide kerf prevents *binding* and allows easier movement of the saw in use. Binding is lessened in good quality saws because the blade is *taper-ground* from the cutting edge to the *skew back*.

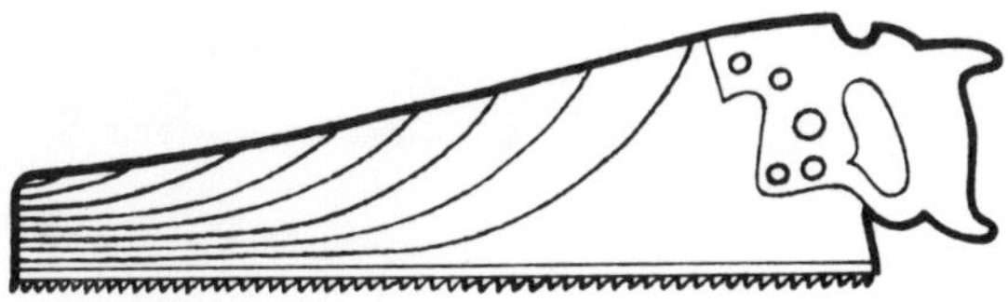

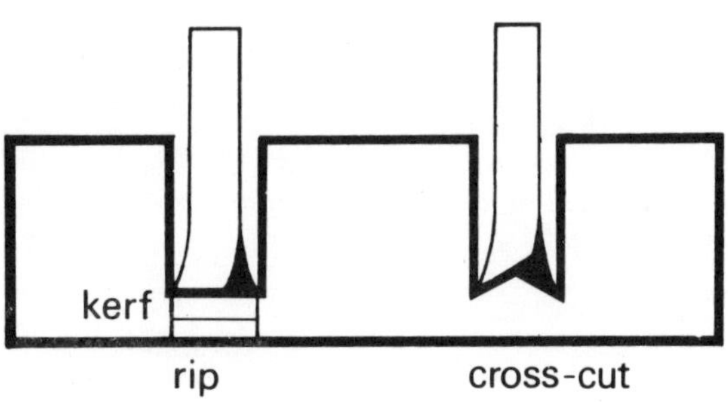

CROSS-CUT AND PANEL SAWS

Although similar in appearance to the ripsaw the teeth of these saws are specially designed to cut timber *across the grain*.

The cross-cut blade is 560 to 610 mm long and has 6 or 7 teeth to each 25 mm of blade. The panel saw blade is 510 mm long and has 9 or 10 teeth to each 25 mm of blade.

The teeth of these saws are sharpened at an angle to produce inside bevels and outside points which sever the wood fibres cleanly. The pitch of the teeth, i.e. the angle at which the leading edge of the tooth leans forward, is less than that of the rip saw. Thus it is possible to saw down the grain with a cross-cut saw; but the rip saw cannot be used across the grain as it will tear the fibres.

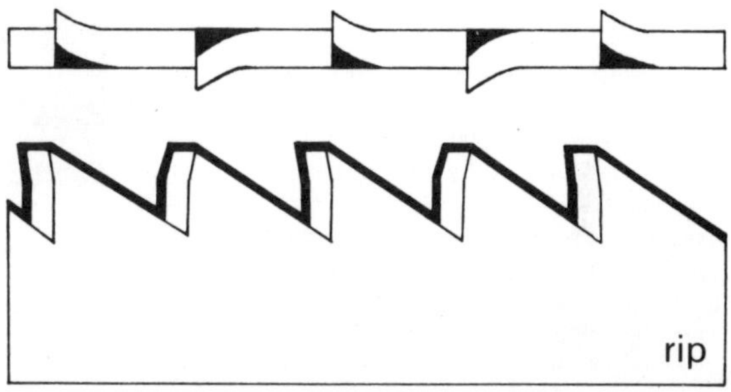

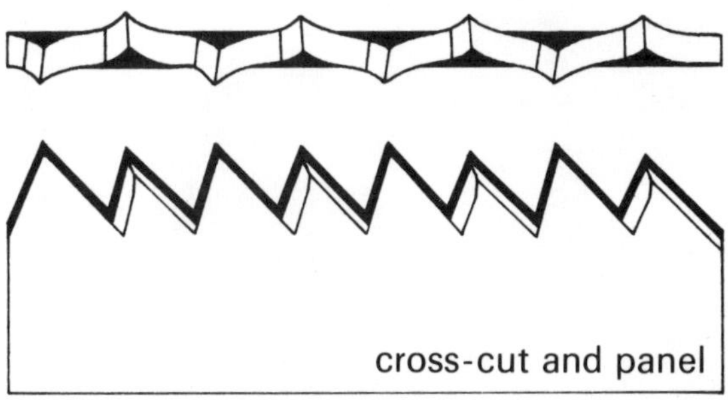

THE FLEAM TOOTH

Fleam teeth are symmetrical in shape and are sharpened in a similar manner to a traditional cross-cut saw. The teeth are most effective for cross-cutting solid timber but the teeth design tends to tear the fibres of plywood or veneered chipboard.

Fleam-tooth saws, with hardened tips, cannot be re-sharpened but they have four times the cutting life of normal teeth.

The 'set' of a saw (the amount that alternate teeth are bent outwards) is still done by skilled craftsmen on the best quality saws.

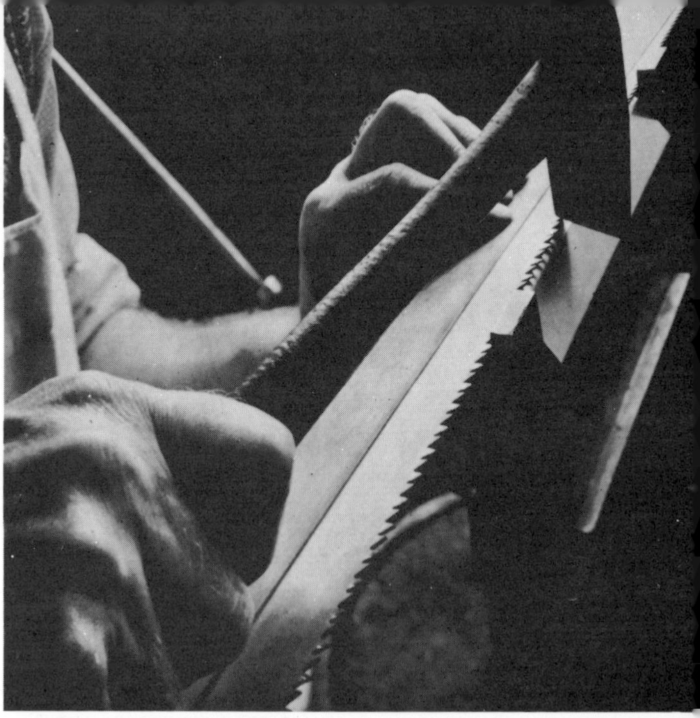

Below: Cross-cut sawing. The wood is held over the end of a trestle (it can be G-cramped in place) and a thumb guides the saw at the start of the cut.

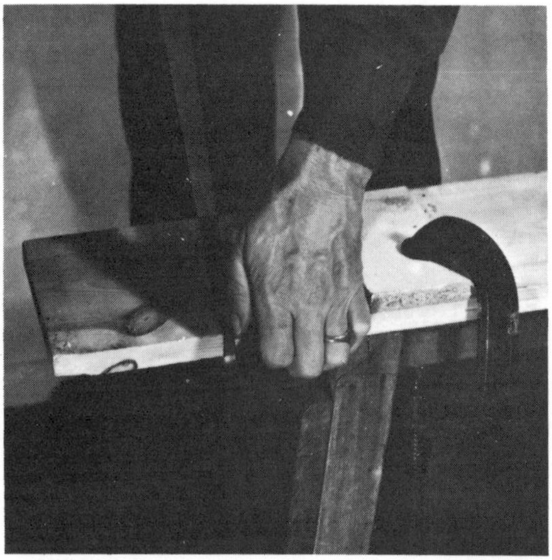

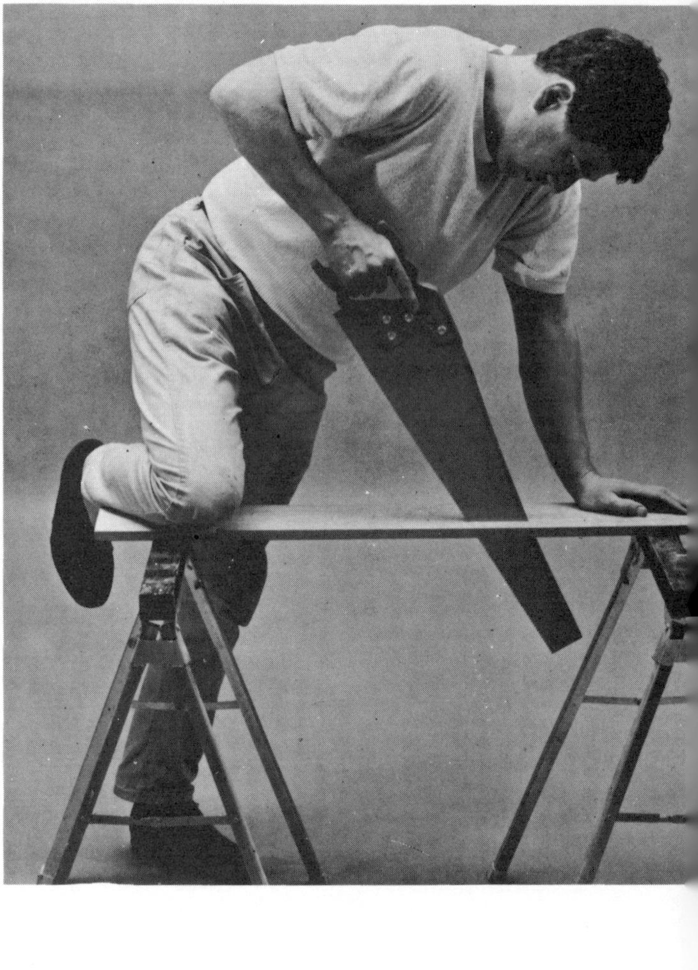

Right: Rip Sawing. The wood is supported between two trestles and the worker puts his weight over the saw to make effective cuts. The forefinger down the handle helps to keep the saw straight.

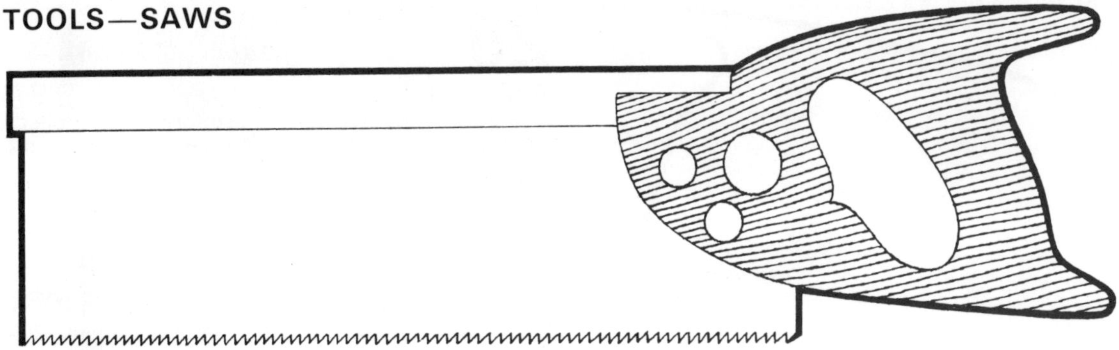

BACKSAWS

These are of two kinds:

1. the tenon saw
2. the dovetail saw

They are very much alike in most respects, both of them having teeth shaped like those of the cross-cut saw only on a smaller scale. They are both suitable for *accurate work both down and across the grain* and differ mainly in their length of blade and size of teeth.

The tenon saw is 250 to 300 mm long and has 12 to 14 teeth to each 25 mm of blade.

What you may call your 'bench saw' is likely to be the smaller of these and not the dovetail saw which is only 200 mm long and has as many as 19 teeth to each 25 mm of blade.

In spite of their names you must choose the saw most suited to the work that has to be done—you may cut a large dovetail with a tenon saw or a small tenon with a so-called dovetail saw!

The Back

Used in the cutting of joints, these saws must be able to cut accurately. This is achieved by having a thin carefully ground blade held firmly along its straight back by a 'fold' of brass or mild steel. As well as rigidity this back also gives weight to the cut, thus making sawing easier.

HANDLES

Although dovetail saw handles are occasionally 'open', most are 'closed' and are made of close-grained, knot-free beech.

The more expensive saws have the short grain of the handle reinforced by a length of beech dowel.

The handle is usually set low on the blade to produce an economic thrust halfway along its cutting edge.

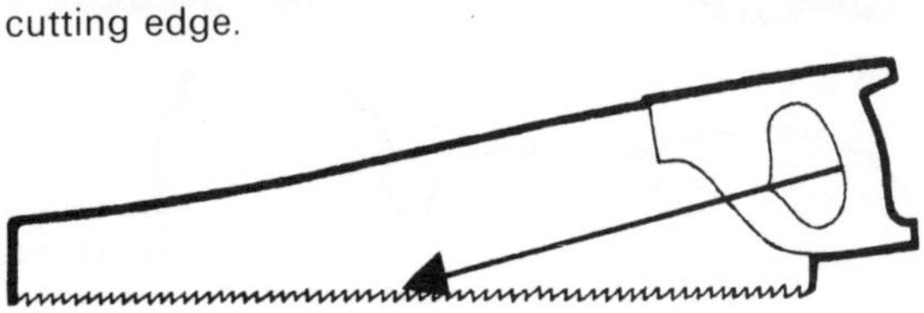

When buying a saw check that the back is in line with blade A not as in B

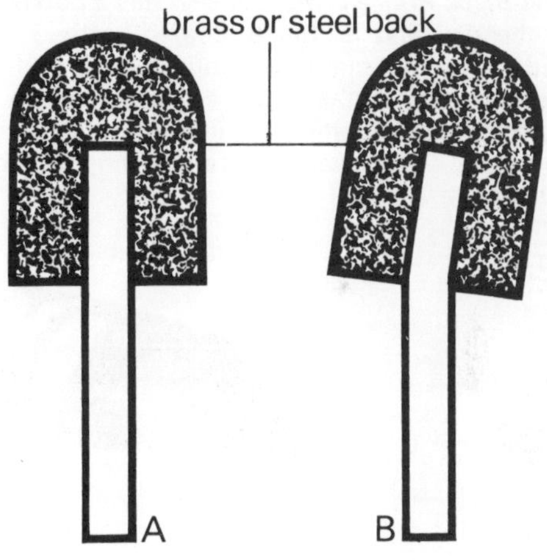

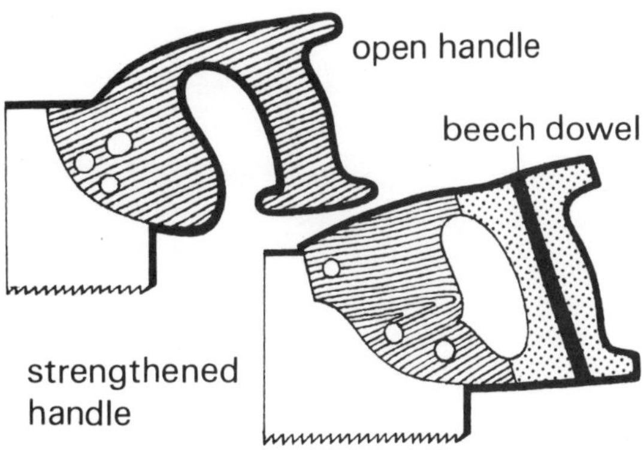

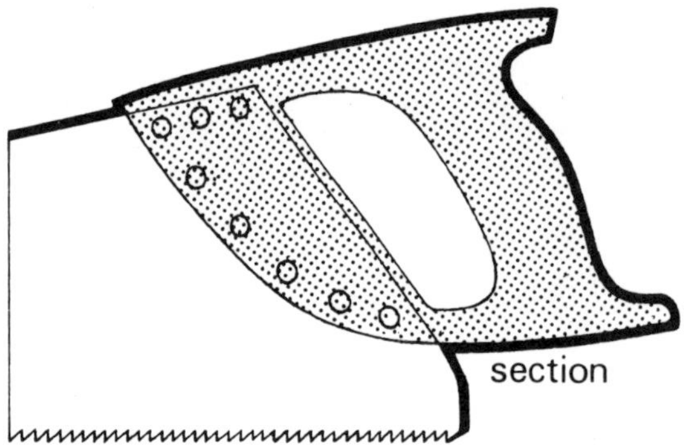

The blade is firmly fixed by a number of screws—depending on the type and size of the saw.

Not surprisingly, *plastic handles* are now available and are most successful where they do not try to imitate the traditional wood handle.

Such is Spear and Jackson's latest range in which the comfortable streamlined handle made of ICI 'Propathene' is immovably moulded on to the blade.

PROTECTED SAW BLADES

The *Black Prince* cross-cut saw has a polypropylene handle and a blade coated with P.T.F.E. (Teflon S), a material commonly used in non-stick cooking pans. The thin black coating helps to stop the blade sticking, particularly in resinous softwoods, thus making sawing easier and also giving protection against rust.

20 TOOLS—SAWS

FRAME SAWS

Frame saws have been in use for many hundreds of years. Two kinds are now in common use in the workshop:

1. Bow saw
2. Coping saw

BOW SAW

Although the shape of this saw has changed little over many centuries it is still efficient when *large curves* require cutting in fairly *heavy timber* e.g. a stool top in 19 mm elm.

The saws vary considerably in size, from blade lengths of 200 to 600 mm. A 300 mm blade is useful for most purposes and the size of the teeth varies accordingly—as does the throat size, which determines the possible depth of cut.

The H-shaped frame is made of beech wood and consists of two shaped sides connected

1. at the top by a taut cord.
2. in the middle by a rail or beam (fixed by a dry mortice and tenon joint).
3. at the bottom by the blade inserted in the handles.

The cord is tightened by being twisted with a wood key which, in turn, is held in place by the middle rail.

The dry mortice and tenon joints act as a fulcrum so that the blade is constantly held in tension, thus making the saw cut more accurate.

The tool-steel blade has teeth similar in shape and size to those of the cross-cut saw. It is fastened to the handles by means of steel locking pins and can easily be removed, if necessary.

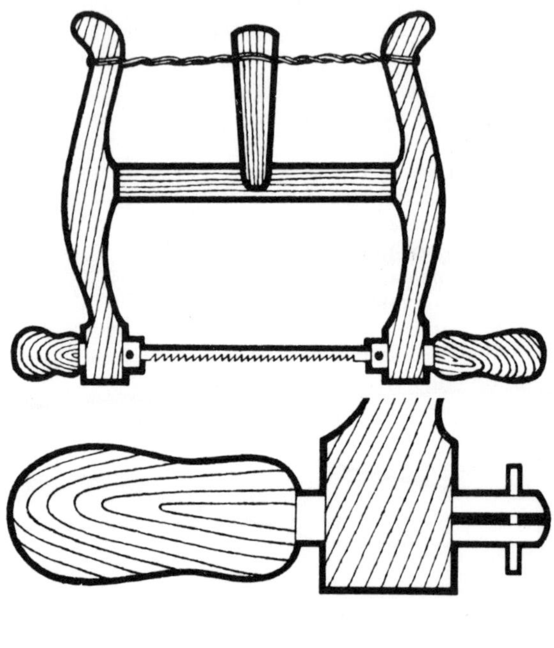

COPING SAW

This is a lighter modern frame saw working on the bow saw principle of a tensioned blade.

Making use of a light sprung-steel frame which keeps the blade taut it is easy to use for sawing both internal and external curves *in thinner material*—say timber under 12 mm thick or plywood and hardboard. It is also useful for removing waste from joints, for example, between dovetails and pins.

The blade is thin, hard and brittle so that, although it cuts effectively, it is easily snapped. Fortunately it is both cheap and easy to replace. It has pins at each end which hold it in the slotted pins attached to the frame at one end and threaded into the painted beech handle at the other.

By twisting the handle on this thread the blade is tightened. The pins are checked to see that they are in line and that the blade is not twisted, before the saw is used.

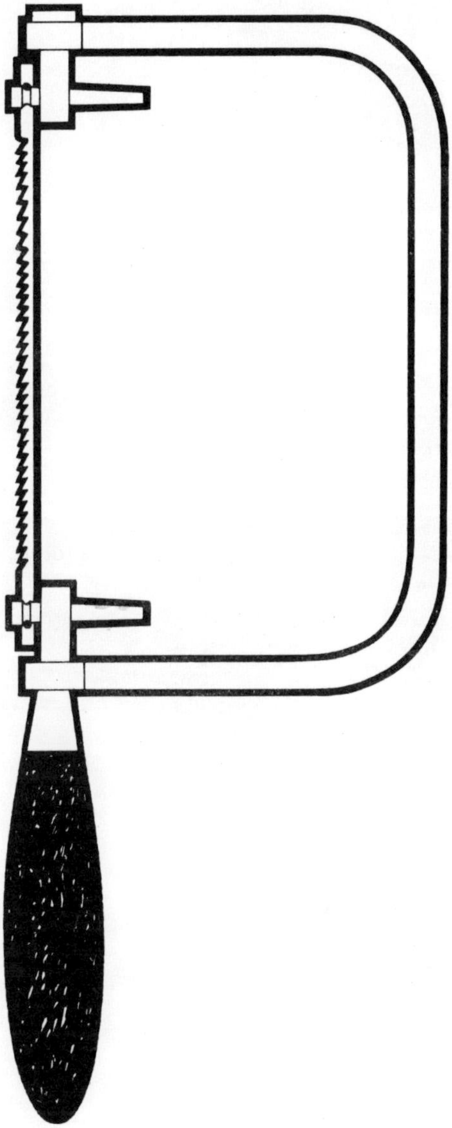

setting the levers

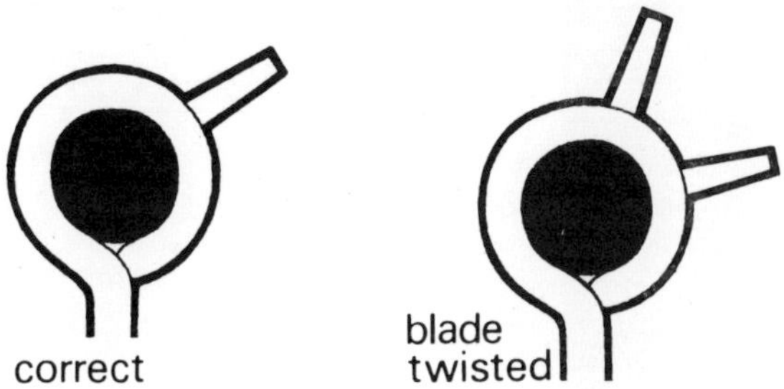

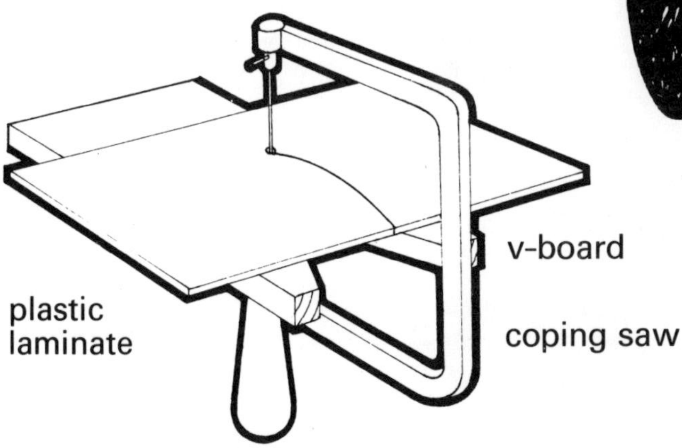

Curves cut in thin material such as plastic laminate are best cut on a V-board. The coping saw cuts on the downward stroke and the board prevents vibration and cracking.

The tenon saw being used to cut a through housing.

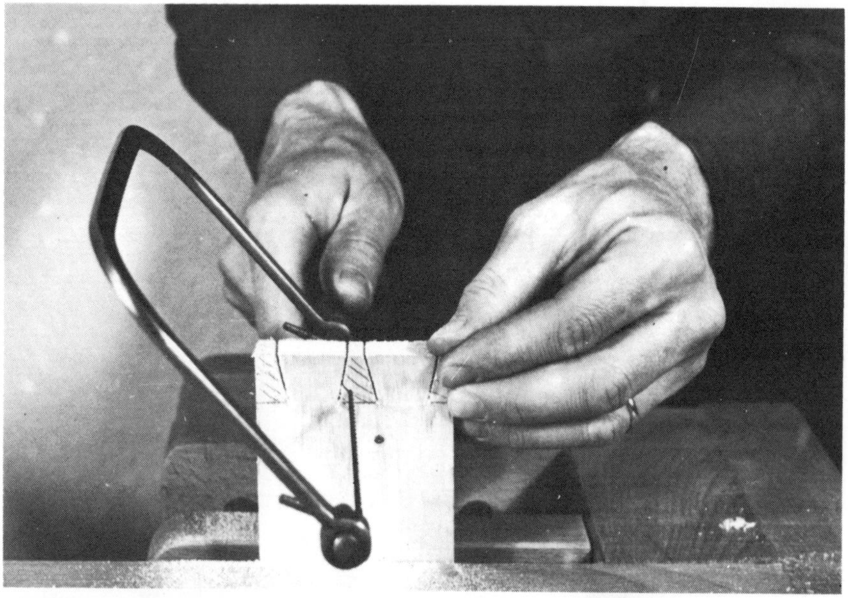

The coping saw is commonly used to remove the bulk of waste from between dovetails.

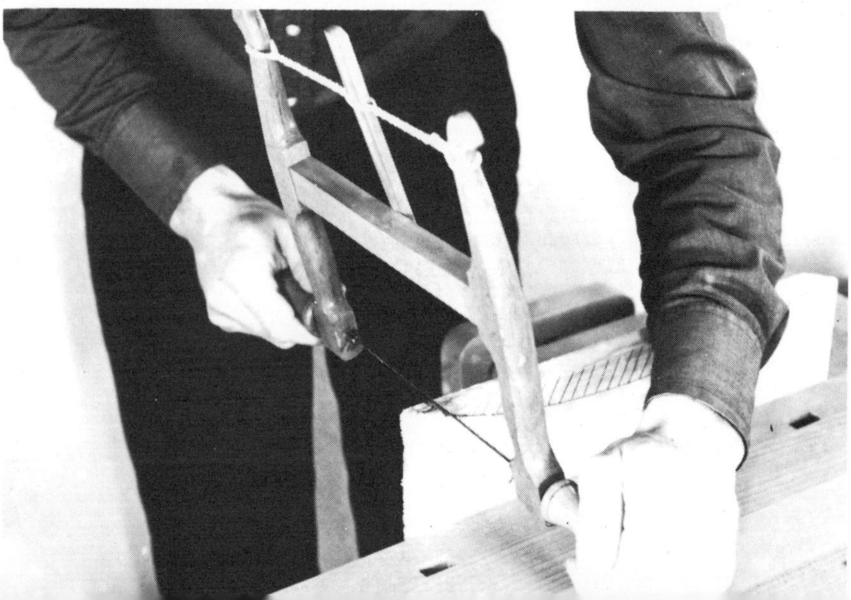

The bow saw being used to cut a curved rail. After the cut has been started (holding both handles) the left hand holds the frame above the larger handle.

21 TOOLS—FILES AND RASPS

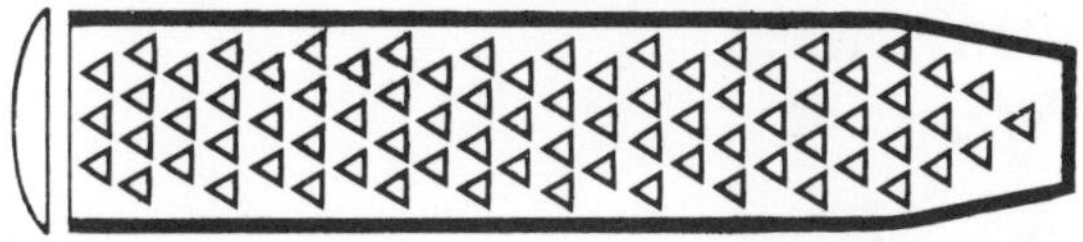

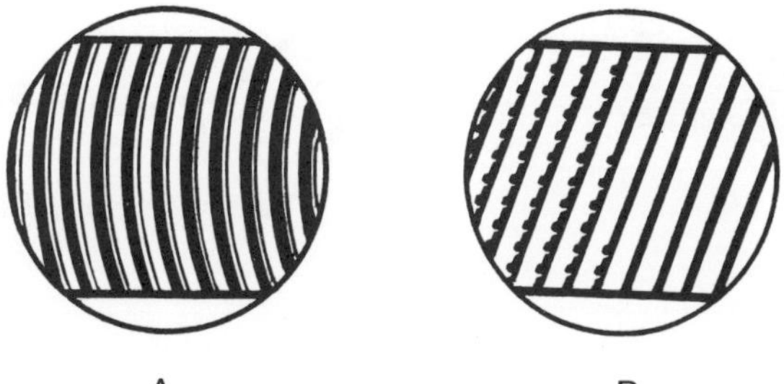

FILES

Files are used in the workshop for:
1. sharpening tools e.g. saws and bits
2. shaping in awkward corners.

Both square and half-round files have their uses, as does the rat-tail file for enlarging holes, whilst triangular files are used mainly for sharpening saws.

Their lengths vary between 200 and 300 mm and they are cleaned with a wire brush to maintain an effective cutting action.

The Aven 'Filemaster' is an unusual design with a variety of uses. The specially milled teeth prevent clogging as it has been designed as a cutting rather than an abrasive tool. The curved teeth (A) and the more orthodox teeth (B) both give a good finish on wood. The half round version has curved teeth and is used for removing material quickly.

In addition the blade is hard enough to cope with plastics, cast iron and steel.

RASPS

These coarse cutting tools have individually *raised teeth* that are most useful for *roughly shaping to size.* They must be used carefully to avoid splitting the grain.

The half-round and rat-tail are generally used and these vary in length from 150 to 350 mm. There are three sizes of teeth—coarse, medium and fine—and a simple round hardwood handle is used for all types.

A sculptor, Michael Smith, finds the round file useful for internal curves.

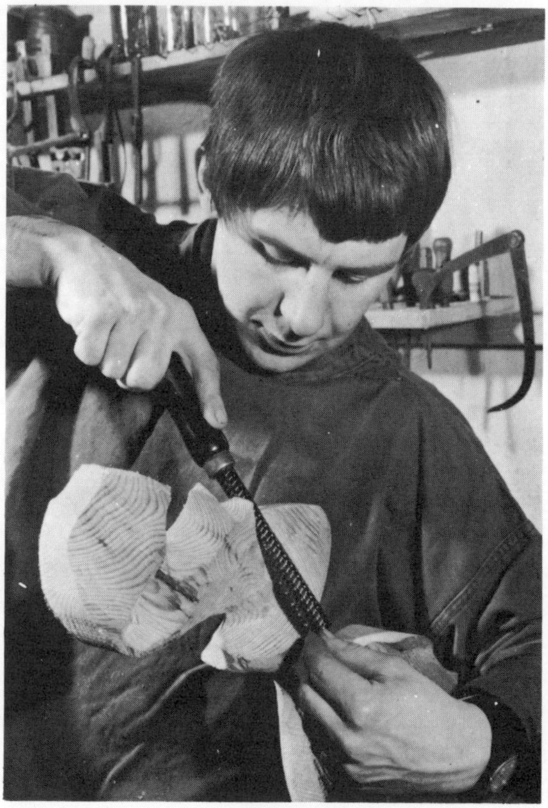

SURFORM

Stanley Surform tools are ideal for shaping wood, metals, plastic laminates, lino, glass fibre, nylon, rubber and cork.

The range of blades (four are 250 mm long) is:
1. A general purpose blade.
2. A 140 mm fine cut blade fits the blockplane.
3. A half-round general purpose blade.
4. A round blade rather like a rat-tailed rasp.
5. A heavy duty blade with a scraping action.

(See over)

The advantages over the rasp are that the *open blade resists clogging* and that, whether designed as a plane or file, the metal frames and well designed plastic handles makes them easier to hold and control.

The 'Planerfile', by simply changing the position of the handle, can be adapted to do both jobs.
(See over)

SURFORMS

'Planerfile'

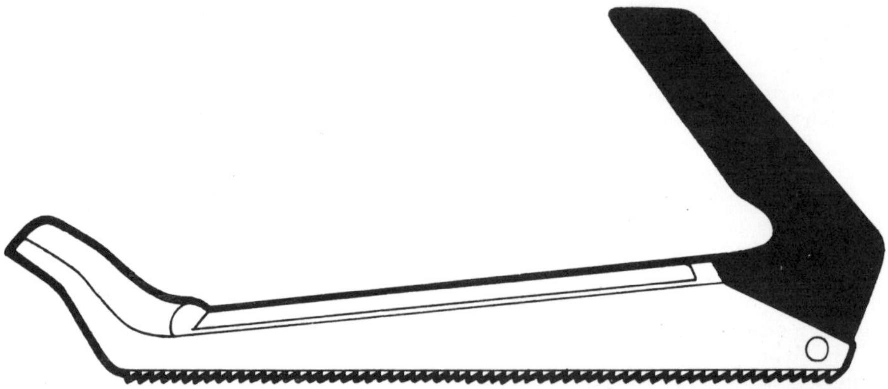

Surform blades (see previous page)

(see previous page)

TOOLS—SCREWDRIVERS

SCREWDRIVERS

Tool catalogues frequently produce a list of nearly 200 types and sizes of screwdrivers—one for every conceivable type of job. Apart from screwdriver bits designed for the joiner's brace and for the portable electric drill, three types are commonly used in the workshop. These are the

1. Cabinet
2. London pattern
3. Ratchet

CABINET TYPE (see over)

A good quality 'driver' has a *tempered alloy steel blade* to withstand the tremendous twist exerted on it in use. To resist this force the round blade is flattened towards the handle to form a *tang.*

The oval beech-wood handles are prevented from splitting by the use of a *steel ferrule.* This is not required in the new splitproof plastic handles.

Blade lengths are from 35 to 250 mm and tip widths are made to suit most screw sizes.

LONDON PATTERN

The strong flat sectioned blade of this wide-tipped screwdriver makes it ideal *for large screws* and it is often to be found on the sharpening bench as it is useful *for unscrewing plane irons.*

SCREWDRIVER TIP

The tip should be *cross-ground square,* have a *slight taper* to fit the screw slot and have the *corners removed* to prevent possible damage to work.

Common faults are:

1. Blade too narrow—excessive leverage needed will damage head
2. Blade too wide—will cause damage to surrounding timber

RATCHET TYPE

Altering a small button on the side of a ratchet mechanism enables the tool to be used for either inserting or withdrawing screws or as a normal fixed screwdriver. It is convenient that these operations can be carried out without releasing the grip on the handle, but the thin parallel-sided blade is *unsuitable for large screws.*

LONDON PATTERN

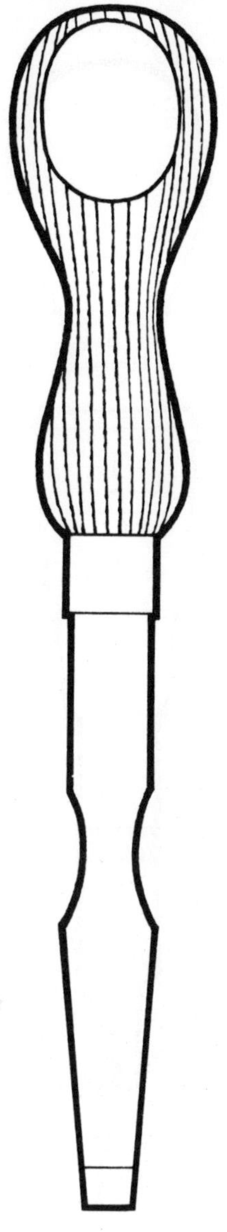

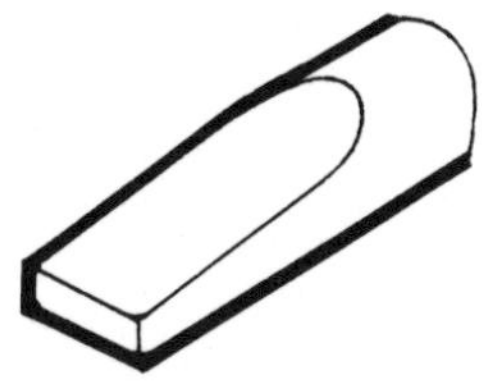

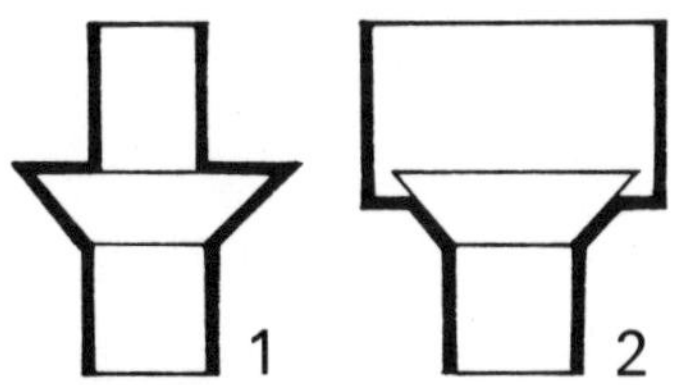

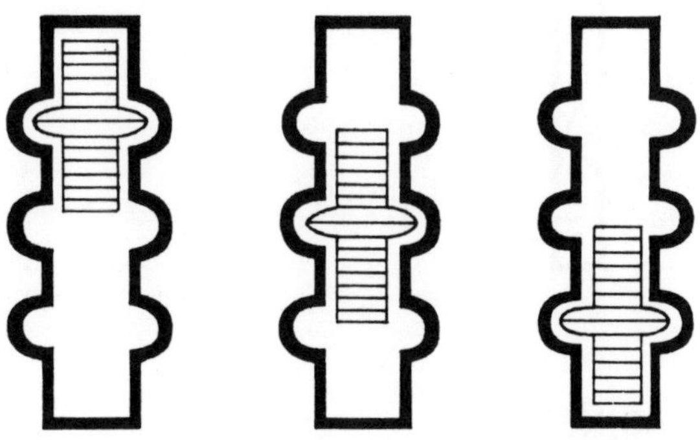

driving screw   blade locked   withdrawing screw

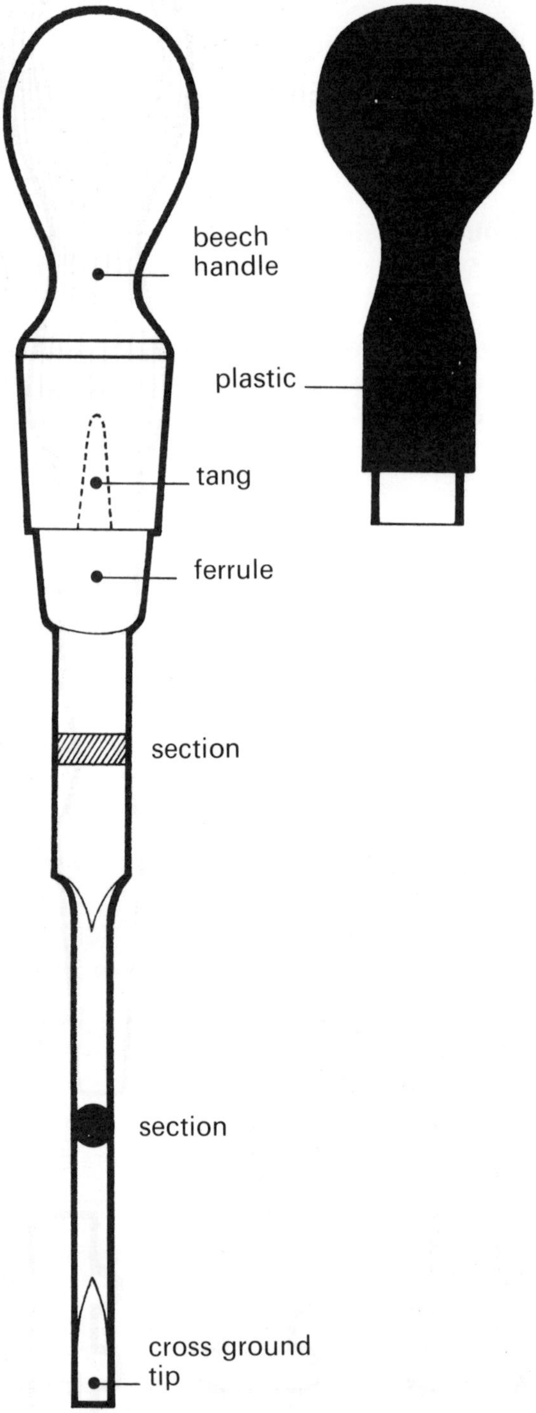

CABINET TYPE

22 TOOLS—HAMMERS

Hammer heads are usually made from a high grade alloy steel which has been forged to one of two shapes:

1. cross-pein
2. claw

CROSS PEIN TYPE

The cross pein of the 'Warrington' hammer is most useful *for positioning small nails* before driving them in with the opposite *face*.

The secureness of the head in high quality tools is ensured by using a pre-shrunk handle that can only expand in use and is further tightened in its tapered hole by two or three wedges. At least one of these will be an *iron wedge* which is barbed, rather like a fish hook.

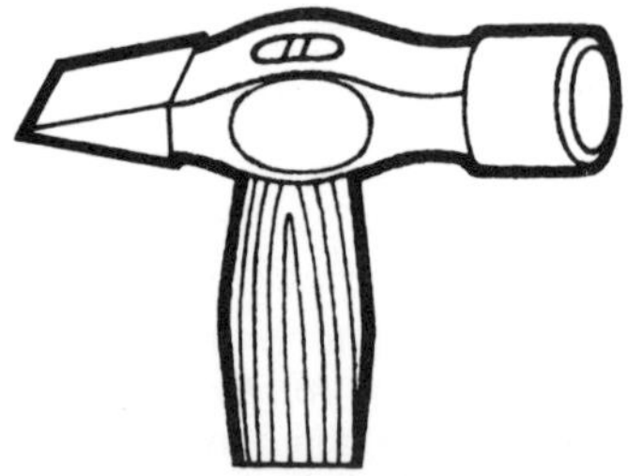

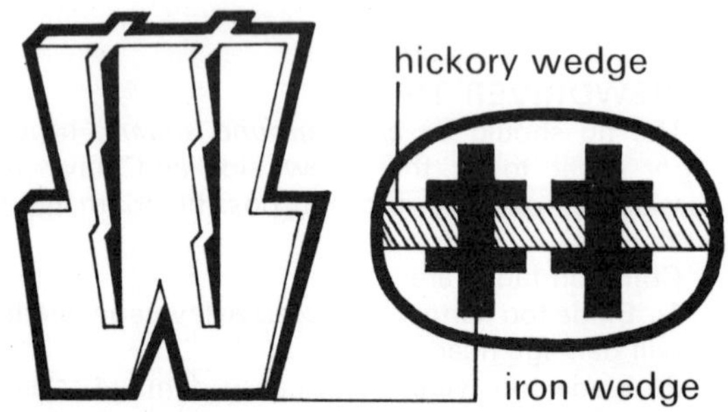

CLAW TYPE

The claw is effective in *removing fairly large nails* and is mainly used for outside work by joiners and carpenters.

The *Stanley 'Steelmaster'* head is drilled and reamed to ensure a perfect fit for the oval-sectioned solid-drawn handle. The tube is carefully heat-treated to withstand impact and is 'insured' by means of 'Araldite' adhesive.

The Claw Hammer being used to withdraw a large round nail.

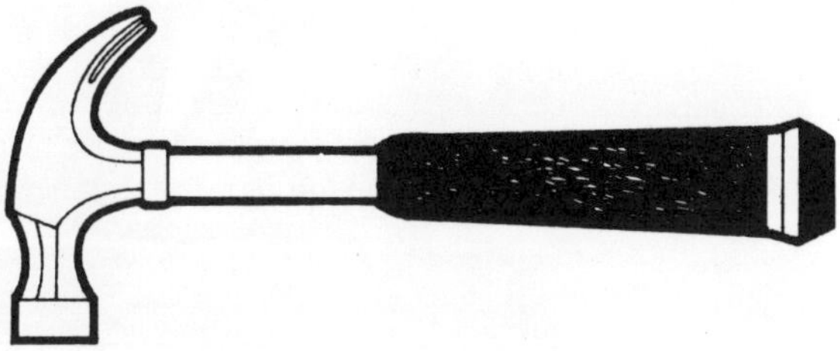

HANDLES

The Steelmaster handle is sealed to prevent it from cutting through the *natural rubber grip* which is fixed by a strong rubber adhesive.

Traditional handles are made from well-seasoned straight-grained knot-free *ash or hickory*.

SOFT-FACED TYPE

The *'Thor' rubber hammers* have the advantages of inter-changeable faces and are most useful *for fitting joints.* The red-faced head, which is a screw-fit into the diecast *aluminium head* will transmit a powerful blow to softwood without marking the surface in any way.

The oval ash handle is fitted into the tapered socket of the head, and is secured by a wooden wedge.

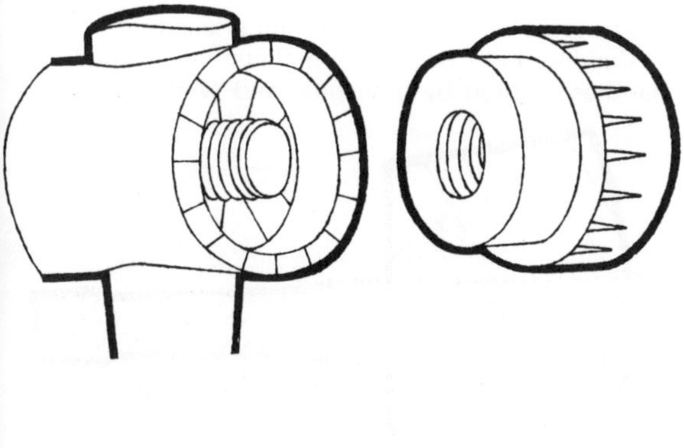

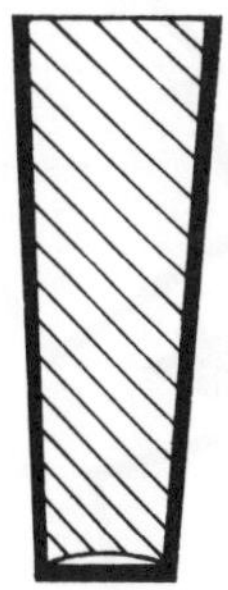

NAIL PUNCH (SET)

The nail punch or set, as it is sometimes called, is used with a hammer *to drive the heads of nails below the surface* of the wood. The resulting small hole is then filled and the surface cleaned off.

The punch is usually round in section, measures about 110 mm long, has a knurled shank to assist grip and a blunt 'point'. This varies in size from 1·5 to 4 mm in diameter to suit most nail heads.

Right: The cross pein of a Warrington Hammer being used to position a panel pin.

Below: A soft-faced hammer will not damage the surface of the wood.

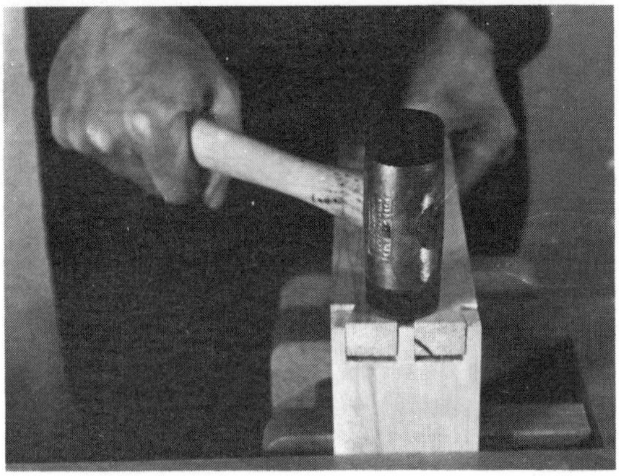

MALLETS

The common bench mallet is designed *to strike wood-handled chisels* where the use of a metal hammer would cause damage. The large face of the mallet is a great advantage as even with a soft-faced hammer it would be difficult to strike a true blow and, at the same time, concentrate on the cutting edge.

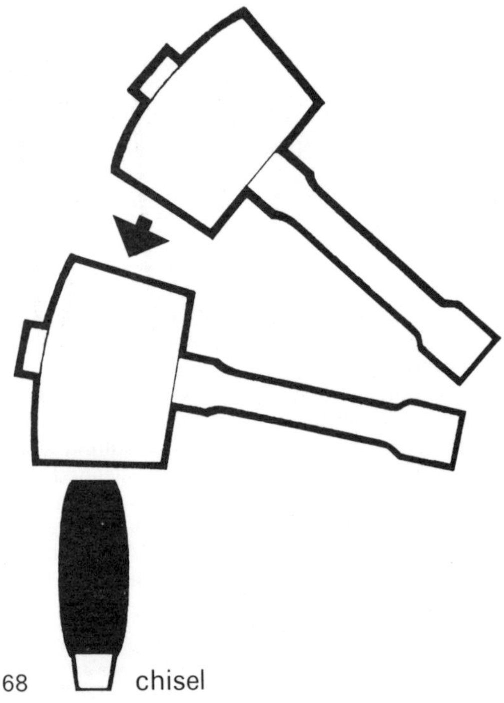

The Head

The rectangular head is made of well-seasoned beech. It keeps its shape best if the annual rings run across the head at right-angles to the sides, as any shrinkage that may occur will be even.

The striking surfaces are tapered towards the user so that a firm square blow may be struck.

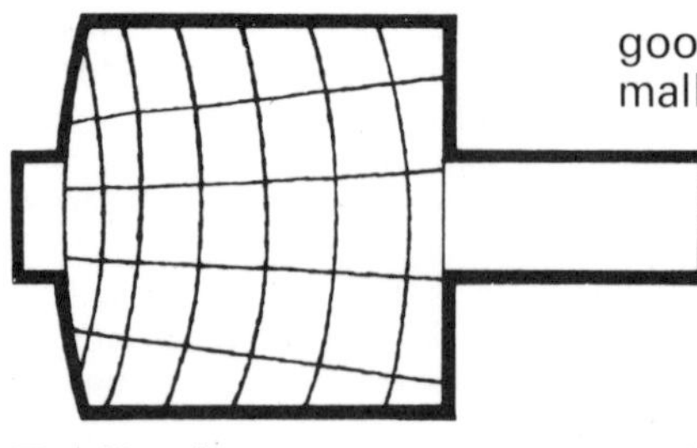

The Handle

Also made from beech, the handle fits into a *tapered mortise* which tends to tighten itself when the mallet is struck.

The joint is a dry one, no glue is used.

Carving and Continental mallets have turned ash handles secured by both glue and wedges.

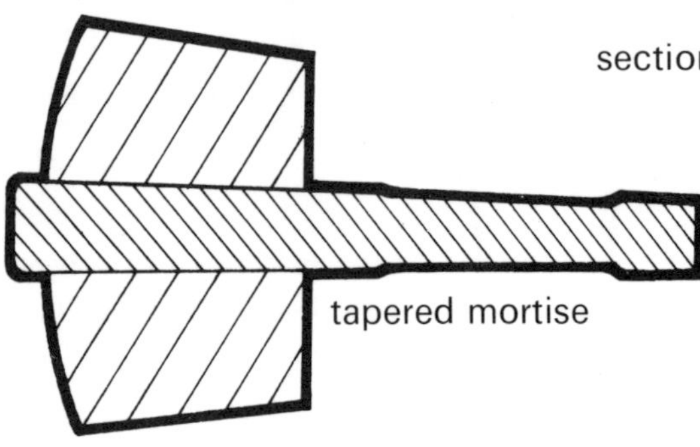

23 TOOLS—HOLDING

THE BENCH VICE

Do not under-estimate the usefulness of this holding tool. It has a large capacity for holding work and *is both strong and easily adjusted.* The vices are of two kinds:

1. plain screw
2. quick grip

Both vices have the same holding power, but the quick-grip allows a speedy alteration in the position of the sliding jaw by depressing the trigger near the handle. Alternatively, the plain screw action may be used if required.

The *cast iron jaws* vary in width from 175 to 260 mm and these have an opening capacity of 200 to 380 mm. The larger vices generally give the best service and the extra large jaws do less damage to work. The metal jaws are faced with hardwood or plywood cheeks of about 12 mm thickness.

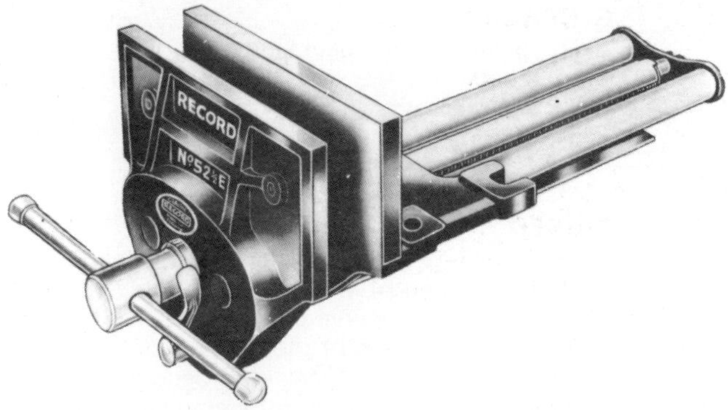

SASH CRAMPS

Sash cramps are generally *used in pairs in gluing-up* operations but their uses include *holding narrow material* for shaping and rebating etc., free from the bench side. They are of two kinds:

1. plain bar
2. T-bar

Both are available in the sections shown where it is obvious that the T bar cramps are heavy and have the increased rigidity necessary for cramping large and heavy work. The large slides also present a larger pressure area on to the cramping blocks.

The materials used are:

1. bar—cold drawn mild steel
2. head and slides—malleable iron
3. screw and handle—high quality steel

The rail slide is generally held by a *'peg and chain'*. In use this is too easily detached and lost so that the *Deacon tail slide* on 'Record' cramps is superior. It operates by means of a spring-loaded catch, the pin automatically selecting the next stop when released.

Cramp lengths are from 600 to 1500 mm long in multiples of 150 mm, the capacity between shoes being 150 mm less than the bar length. *Extension bars* of the same length can be obtained for use when assembling:

1. a large carcase e.g. sideboard
2. a heavy framework e.g. stage scenery

plain

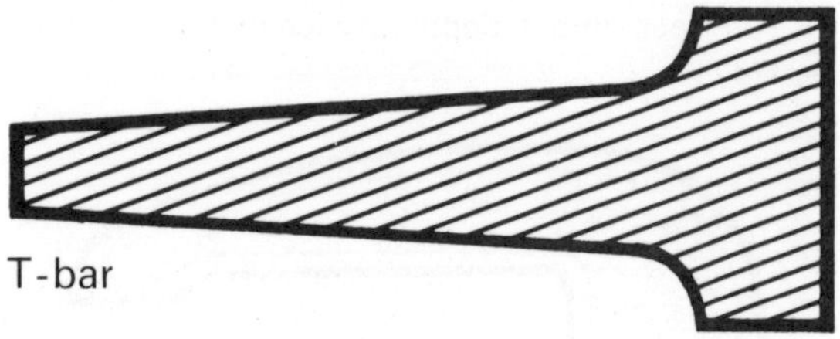

T-bar

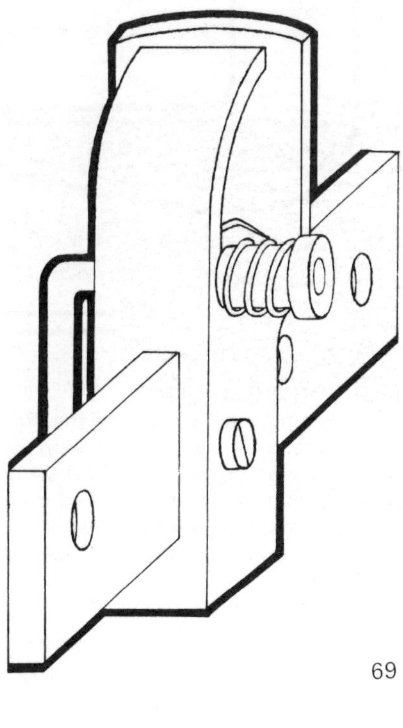

Deacon tail-slide

G-CRAMPS

These are of three main kinds:

1. ribbed
2. 'deep throat'
3. 'Spingrip'

RIBBED

The ribbed G-cramp is made of malleable iron (ribbed for strength) with an *Acme thread* of high quality steel. The opening capacity varies from 50 to 350 mm. The sizes of thread, area of the swivel shoes and depth of throat vary accordingly.

Although it can be used for cramping small work when glueing up, it tends to pull to one side and its main use remains that of *cramping work down onto the bench top*. The *swivel shoe* allows angled work to be effectively fixed.

'DEEP THROAT'

The throat capacity of cramps up to 100 mm is very limited and deep throat cramps *are designed to give greater reach* without having to use large traditional cramps which are cumbersome.

The 'deep-throat' depth is twice that of the ribbed G-cramp.

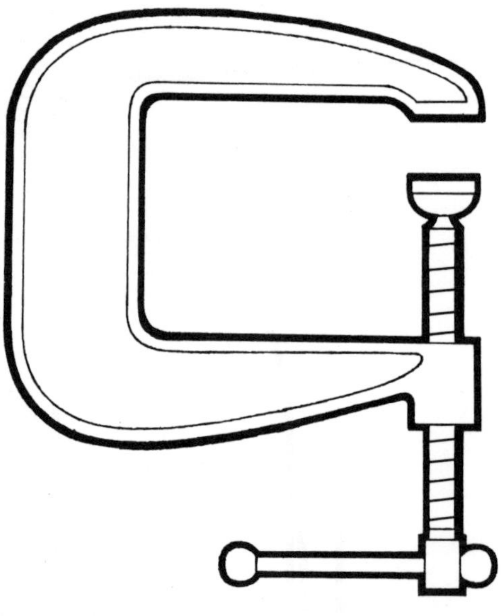

THE EDGING CRAMP

An edging cramp such as the *Record* 129 has swivel shoes for adapting to sloping faces and a two-way cramping action. It has been specially designed to make the fixing of edges and lips easier without the use of nails or screws. It is most valuable where sash cramps cannot be used, e.g. for round tables etc.

Size: Mouth opening: 70 mm, depth of throat: 32 mm.

'SPINGRIP'

The Record 'Spingrip' is an adaptation of the ribbed G-cramp and is made in 50, 75 and 100 mm openings. By means of rotating a *'spinner' wheel* it is possible to operate the cramp with the fore-finger of one hand whilst holding the work with the other. This is most useful as *no assistance is required* for small cramping operations.

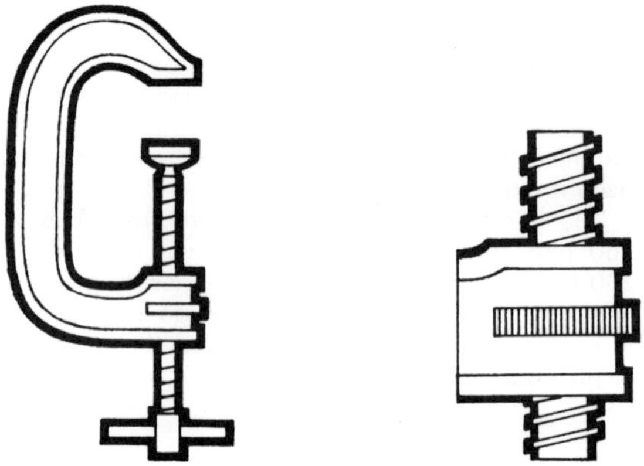

HOLDFAST

This cramp works on the *lever principle* to hold work flat on the bench top. It is easily altered to a wide range of thicknesses and has an extensive reach useful for securing wood to be grooved, etc., without interfering with the working tools.

The holdfast may be removed from its *collar* (recessed into the bench top), leaving the bench surface free from obstruction. There are three sizes, the largest having a reach of 215 mm and an 'opening' of 225 mm.

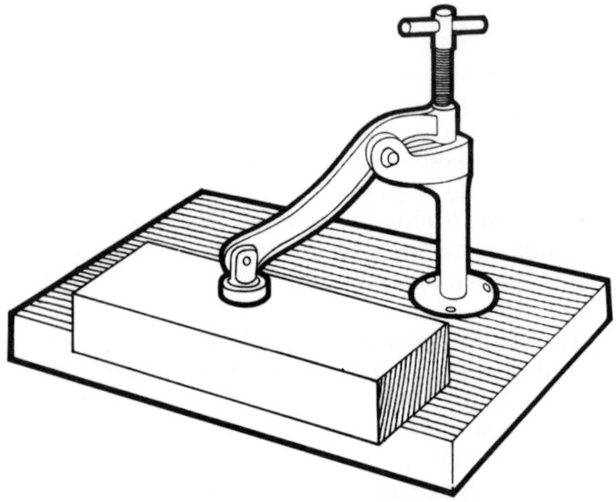

CRAMPING BLOCKS

When using these metal cramps protective wooden blocks should be used to prevent damage to the surface of the work. A variety of shapes and sizes should be kept to suit the work being done.

Left: The Record 'Springrip' G-cramp can be conveniently used with one hand.

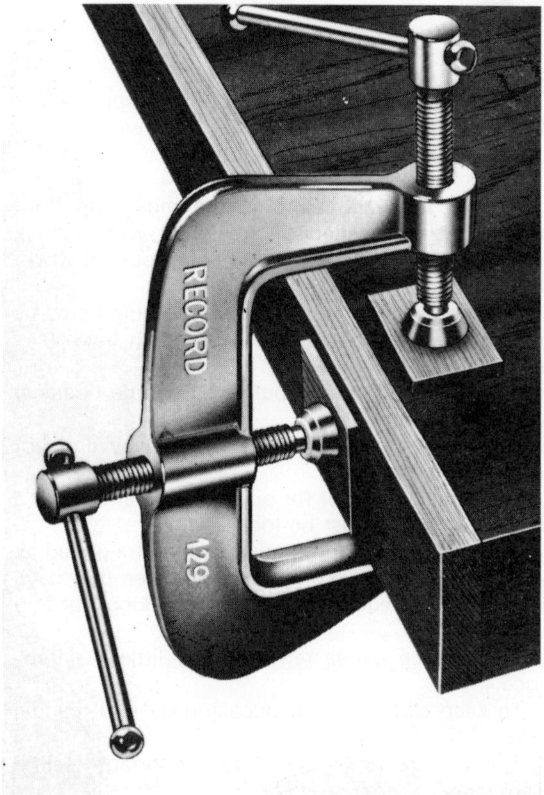

Above right: The edging cramp is used with thin plywood blocks to prevent surface damage.

Left: Bowing, when assembling work, can be avoided by using cramping blocks of the correct size.

Below: Cramp Heads can easily be fitted to a prepared hardwood bar of any length. They are economic if long cramps would only be used occasionally.

24 TOOLS—CARE AND STORAGE

Tools are the woodworker's basic equipment and they will serve us best if we treat them well.

A solid working bench is the most important 'tool' of all. It is specially designed with a thick hardwood surface to withstand the rigours of workshop practice.
1. It must be protected from saw and chisel cuts by using protective boards, e.g., the bench hook (see section 28) and,
2. From paint, stain and polish by a large board or sheets of newsprint.
3. Tools not in use should be put away and not left on the bench.

The *steel rule* is not for opening tins and its zero end in particular must be looked after.

Use only for measuring or as a small straight edge.

Marking knives are only valuable when they have a keen cutting edge; use only for marking out and trimming.

The *mortice gauge* requires very little maintenance.

To keep slide free rub occasionally with candle wax.

The *try-square* is our most important testing instrument.

Put away when not in use.

The *sliding bevel* is adjusted by an easily damaged screw.

Use only a screwdriver of the correct size.

Winding strips, being usually of wood, are liable to 'move'.

Check regularly and correct any faults, i.e., re-true with a try-plane.

The *squaring rod* is used when work has been glued-up.

To ensure accuracy keep the pointed end free from adhesive.

Most *chisels* still have handles made from ash or boxwood. Strike them with a wood mallet and not a metal hammer.

Both wood and metal *planes* are easily misused and can quickly become ineffective.
1. Store them on a felt or soft base to prevent damage to the blade.
2. Rest them on the lip of the bench well.
3. Check the surface to be planed for protruding pins, etc.

The plane, even when used properly, may become 'choked' and must be dismantled to free the blockage and determine the fault.
1. Do not try to poke shavings out.
2. Use a wide screwdriver to release the back iron.

The *joiner's brace* is a sturdy tool requiring little maintenance.

Lubricate moving parts occasionally.

The bits, however, are easily damaged and must not be sharpened too often.
1. Keep them in a rack, tray or protective leather or fabric roll.
2. Drills should also be kept in a labelled rack.

Saws will not need sharpening often unless damaged on metal.
1. Always use the bench hook or sawing trestle.
2. Protect the teeth with a cover of wood, plastic or material.
3. When not in regular use, lightly coat with oil to prevent rust.

Coping saw blades too often break before they become blunt.

Help to avoid this by checking that blades are not twisted.

Rasps and files are usually kept in a rack.

Keep the cutting edges free by brushing with a wire brush.

Hammers are potentially dangerous as both heads and shafts come under severe stress in use.
1. Do not strike faces together as they may chip.
2. Keep faces clean to prevent slipping and damage to work.
3. Regularly inspect the shaft and wedges.

The vice is in constant use and must be checked frequently.
1. Lubricate moving parts, e.g., thread and trigger.
2. Check wood jaws for cleanliness and accuracy.
3. Do not strain the vice with excessive downward pressure.

Sash cramps have a tendency to become very dirty.
1. Keep the bars and slides free from adhesives.
2. Oil the screw lightly.
3. Store in racks.

You have read of the quality of the steel from which your woodworking tools are made. It has been specially made to maintain a good cutting edge for a considerable length of time and so give, often literally, 'a lifetime's use'.

Tools need regular sharpening, but regrinding, as in the case of a chisel that has been chipped, considerably reduces its effective life. This can nearly always be avoided by taking care of the tools in your possession. The damaged blade, the 'smooth' saw and the blunt marking knife are nearly always the result of carelessness and not of poor materials or manufacture.

EXAMINATION QUESTIONS

13 MEASURING

1. Which measuring instrument would you find most useful to carry in your apron pocket?

   State the materials from which it is made and give reasons for your choice

2. Which is the most accurate rule in the workshop?

   Give a list of reasons for your choice and sketch (twice full size) the divisions of the first 30 mm.

14 MARKING

1. What tools would you use for the following operations: *(a)* to test a face side to see that it is flat, *(b)* to mark two lines parallel to the face edge, *(c)* to set out a rebate across the end of a piece of timber, *(d)* to set out a number of lines at 50 deg. to the face edge, *(e)* to test the angle of a 45 deg. chamfer or bevel? (S)
2. Although it is usual to use a sharp knife when marking out, there are occasions when a sharp pencil should be used. Give examples of the use of each—not more than five altogether. (WM)
3. Draw a section along the stem of a mortise gauge to show how the rods may be adapted for marking out a 4 mm mortise
4. Make a full-size sketch of a cutting gauge. Take particular care to show clearly the cutting edge of the blade

15 TESTING

1. Describe briefly how a large flat frame such as a mirror frame or a fire screen could be tested after being glued and cramped: *(a)* to see if it was twisted and *(b)* for squareness. How would you correct any error? (S)
2. Draw a good-sized sketch of a try square and show the place where excessive wear may occur.

   Suggest reasons for this and say how it could be re-trued.

3. With the aid of clear sketches describe how a try square can be tested for accuracy.

16 CHISELS

1. Make a good-sized sketch of a bevel-edge chisel naming its parts and the material from which each part is made.

   List the types of work for which this chisel is most suited.

2. Draw full size cross-sections to show two ways in which the chisel blade may be fitted to the handle.
3. Sketch a cross section of the blade of two types of wood chisel. Name each of them.
4. Sketch one wood and one plastic chisel or handle. Which of them do you consider to be the most comfortable to use? Make a list of reasons for choosing these particular designs.
5. Name the chisel most suitable for cleaning up the corners of a dovetail. (S)

17 PLANES

1. Why does a plane have a narrow mouth? How would you reduce the size of the mouth on a metal smoothing plane? Illustrate your answer with sketches.
2. The jack plane or general purpose plane is about 400 mm long and has a blade and cap iron about 55 mm wide pitched at 45 degrees to the sole; the blade, the cutting edge of which is very slightly curved, is not the full width of the stock (or body) of the plane. Name four other types of plane used in the workshop; say how each differs from the jack plane and give reasons for one of these differences in each case. (WM)
3. The mouth of your wooden jack plane is well worn and needs re-mouthing. Make sketches to show how you could do this.
4. The front of the wooden jack plane is not easy to hold when planing a face side. Make sketches to show how you would improve its design.
5. Name a plane which is used to plane long edges and large surfaces flat and true.
6. What is the flat underside of the plane that comes in contact with the wood called?
7. Name the plane that would be ideal to true the edges of two boards before joining them together. Give reasons for your choice.
8. It is often necessary to plane the end grain of a wide board and in such cases certain precautions are taken. Give an account of the procedure under the following headings: *(a)* choice of plane and other equipment, *(b)* special adjustment of the plane, *(c)* method of working; make clear sketches to illustrate two satisfactory methods.

18 BORING TOOLS

1. Make a list of the advantages, and disadvantages of the joiner's brace over the hand drill.
2. What does the term 'sweep' applied to a carpenter's brace mean?
3. Name the bit used for boring a hole of 30 mm diameter through timber 12 mm thick.
4. By means of sections or sketches show two ways that can be used to prevent splitting as a twist bit makes its exit through a piece of softwood.

5. Name the bits illustrated and state the special purpose for which each is intended.

List the precautions you would take when using these bits to ensure that work is accurate and clean. (JMB)

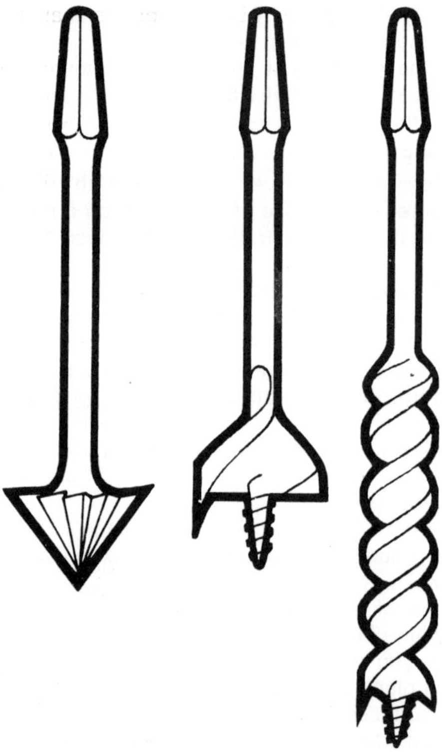

6. These are end views of the chucks of a joiner's brace and a hand drill with the jaws removed.

Make a copy of these and put in the jaws of each one. (W)

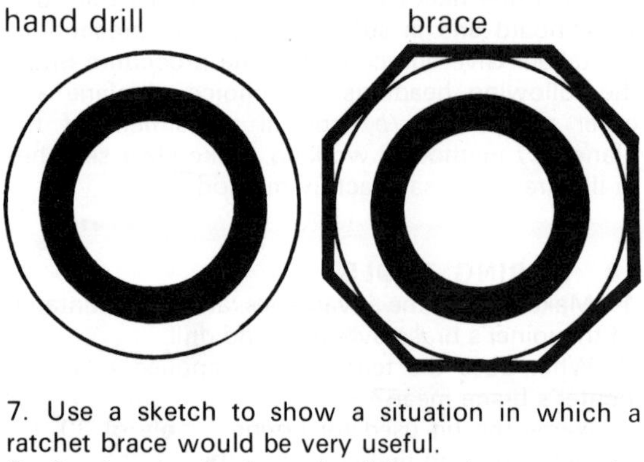

7. Use a sketch to show a situation in which a ratchet brace would be very useful.

8. On the shank of a twist drill you have seen the letters H.S.S. *(a)* What do these letters mean? *(b)* What advantage would you expect compared with a drill that is marked with the letters C.S.?

19 SAWS

1. Explain how the cutting action of a cross-cut saw differs from that of a rip saw. Use sketches.

2. Make enlarged sketches of five or six teeth of a rip saw and a cross-cut saw.

Explain in detail their essential differences and how they are designed to fulfil their different uses. (S)

3. Which saw is generally used for benchwork?

4. The photograph shows a saw being 'set'. What does this mean?

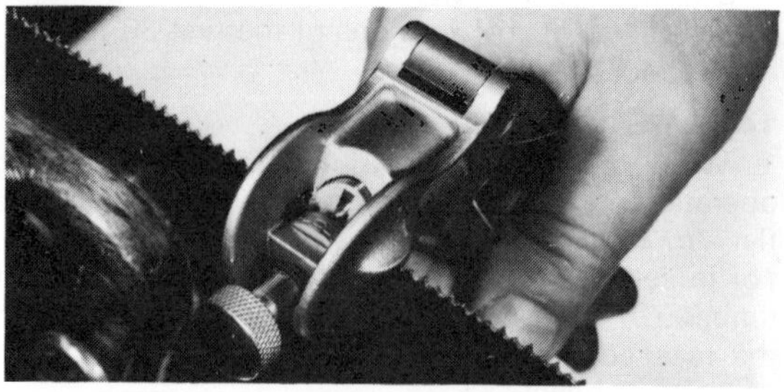

5. Which saw would you choose for cutting along the length of a plank?

6. Why is a back saw so-called?

7. For what purpose would you use a panel saw? (S)

8. If you could only afford one handsaw and one back saw for your own tool kit which would you choose? State the length, size of teeth and the material from which the handle is made.

In each instance give reasons for your choice.

20 FRAME SAWS

1. Some saws have very narrow blades. Name them and explain their uses.

Why do some saws have to be 'set'? (S)

2. Sketch the side view of a coping saw. (MET)

3. State, with reasons, when you should use a coping saw rather than a bow saw. (S)

4. Name two points to bear in mind when using a coping saw so as to prevent the blade from breaking. Give two examples where you would use this saw. (W)

5. What saws are best used for the following purposes:

(a) Sawing along the length of the 25 mm thick board shown. *(b)* Cutting across the board. *(c)* Cutting the curved shape?

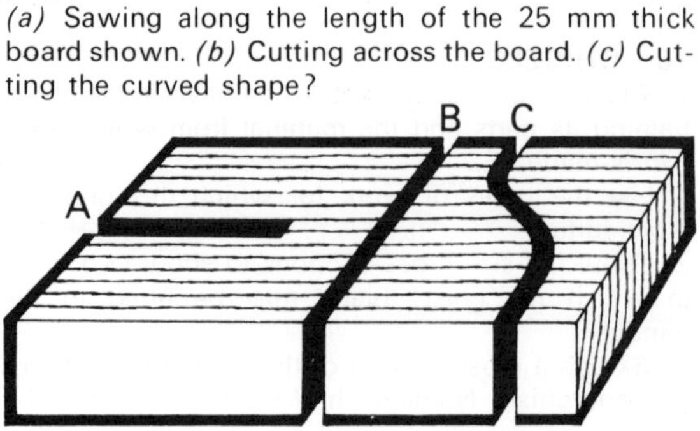

6. The sketches below show saw handles made *(a)* from beech and *(b)* from plastic.

Say which you prefer and give a list of good reasons for your choice.

A

B

21 FILES AND SCREWDRIVERS

1. Copy the screws below. On your copy put into the slots the views of the end of the screwdriver that suits the screw. (W)

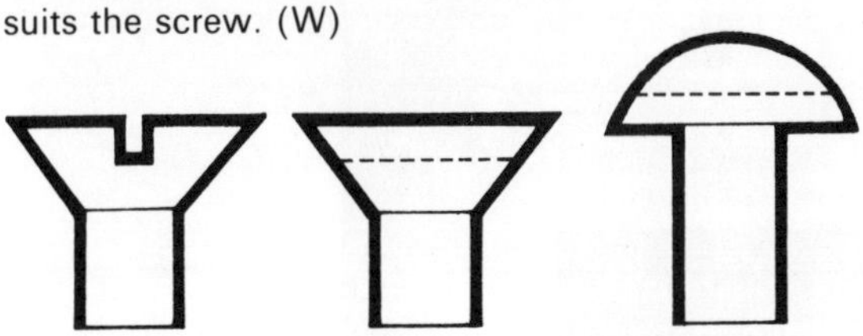

2. Make clear drawings of the tang belonging to *(a)* the screwdriver *(b)* the file.

Give the reasons why they are different in shape.

3. Sketch the end of a bradawl blade and the end of a small screwdriver blade showing quite clearly the difference between them. (WM)

4. The illustration shows the end of a screwdriver which has become badly worn and damaged through misuse.

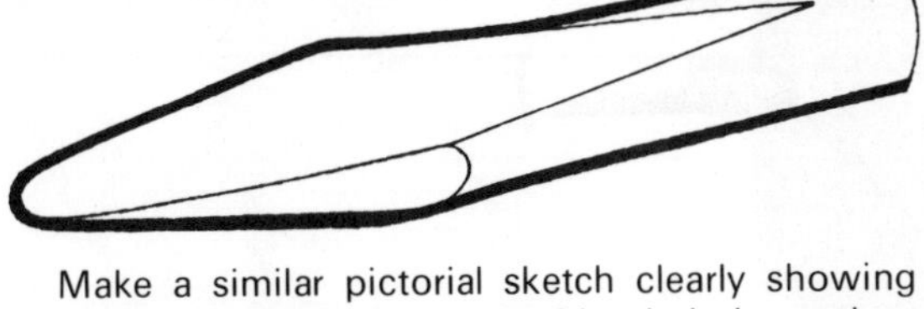

Make a similar pictorial sketch clearly showing the shape to which you would grind the end to make it serviceable again. (S)

22 DRIVING TOOLS

1. Describe with sketches and notes the method of fixing the heads on to the handle of:

(a) The hammer
(b) The bench mallet
(c) The carvers' mallet.

Can you give reasons why the carvers' mallet differs in shape and size from the bench mallet? (WM)

2. Name the type of wood suitable for making a woodworker's mallet and with the aid of a sketch clearly show how the head is held in position.

3. For what particular job would you choose each of the following tools: *(a)* 'Warrington' hammer *(b)* Claw hammer *(c)* Soft-faced hammer *(d)* Joiners mallet? In each instance give reasons for your choice.

23 HOLDING DEVICES

1. Describe with the aid of sketches three different types of holding or gripping equipment which you have used or seen used in your workshop.

Give an example of the use of each device.

2. Name a cramp for holding wood flat on the bench when cutting a mortise. (MET)

3. Name a tool which you would use to hold your work together when gluing-up a small stool. (S)

4. What should you use to protect the work when cramping up and gluing a small stool?

5. Write one advantage the quick release vice has over the plain type.

24 CARE OF TOOLS

1. Plane blades are made of tungsten steel and should not need grinding very often.

List all the precautions you can take to protect the blade from damage.

2. How was the screw of this sliding bevel damaged? How could it have been avoided?

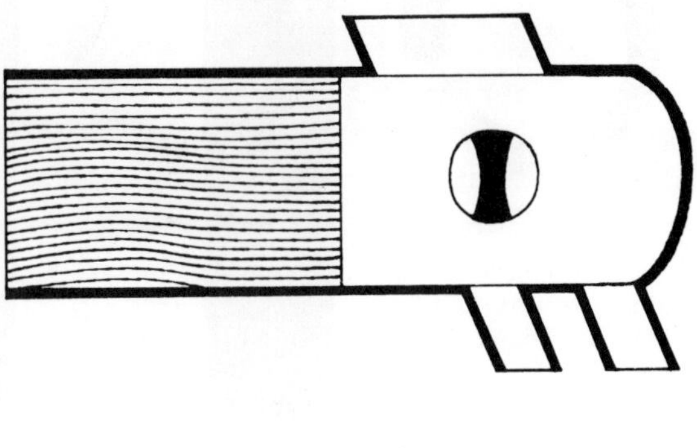

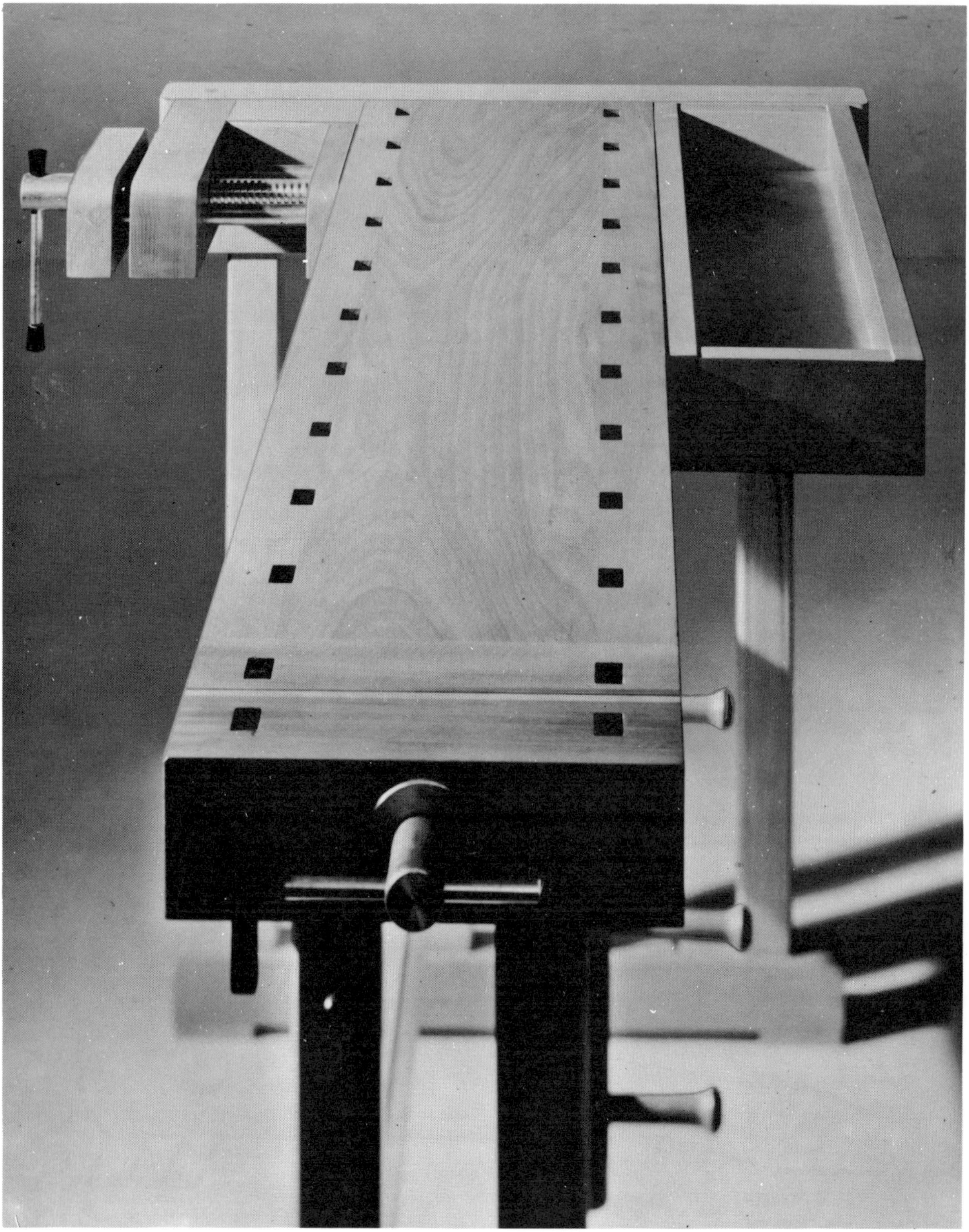

LERVAD (UK) LTD.

EQUIPMENT 3

Although we may take every precaution to keep our equipment in good condition, saws and boring bits, as well as plane blades and chisels, eventually become blunted by their cutting action on timber.

As you acquire more skill you will be able to sharpen and maintain all the tools you use with the possible exception of the saw, which can be done quickly and expertly by a saw 'doctor'. The main items of equipment you require are:

1. A grindstone
2. Oilstones of varying shapes and sizes
3. A small set of files

25 SHARPENING

GRINDSTONES

Plane and chisel blades usually have a *grinding angle* of *between* 20 *and* 30 *degrees* and the blade will need re-grinding if it has been chipped or when, after many sharpenings, the cutting angle has become too steep.

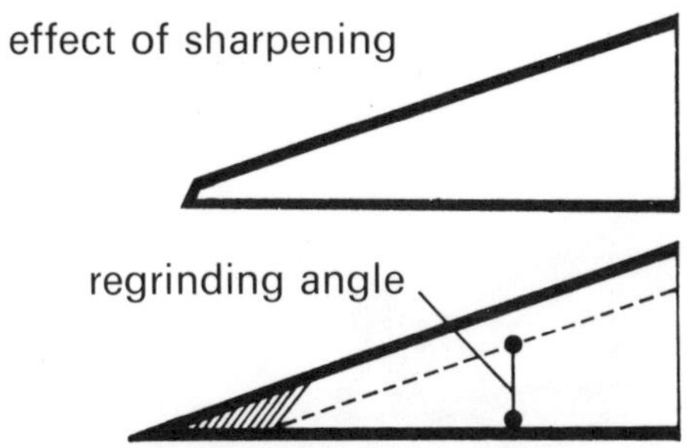

Traditionally, grindstones are made from, and named after, a naturally quarried stone such as *'Bilston'* from Staffordshire. A common size is 450 mm in diameter and 75 mm in width.

Although hand- or treadle-driven grindstones are still in use, motor-driven stones are now more common.

Water is the lubricant used for carrying away the particles of grit and steel and for cooling the edge of the blade, and is 'tapped' from a canister situated above the stone.

After grinding, the residue is drained from the bottom of the trough by opening a plug. If this is not done the stone soaks in the water and becomes 'soft'. When it is again used, this portion quickly wears away leaving the stone an uneven shape.

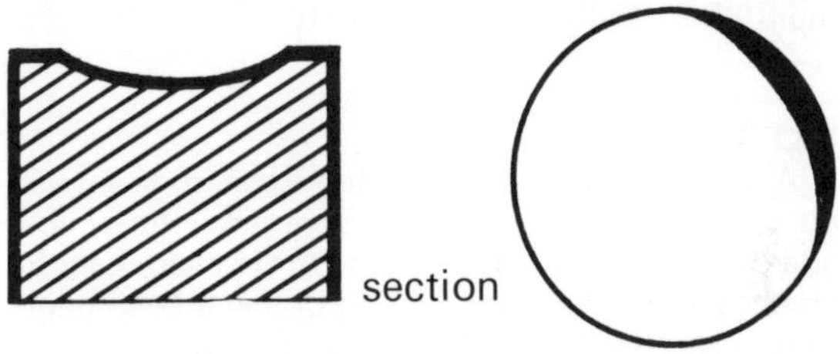

Although the tool blade can be moved from side to side the stone is likely to wear hollow. It can readily be re-trued by rotating it against the sharp edge of a cast-iron pipe.

Most grindstones have an adjustable frame or *tool holder* which ensures that the blades are ground to the correct angle.

GRINDING WHEELS

These small-diameter wheels can either be driven by an individual motor or can be attached to the motor of a lathe.

The wheel is usually made from a manufactured stone such as 'Alundum' (aluminium oxide) which grinds quickly but tends to 'burn' or 'draw the temper' of the blade as no lubricant is used. This means that the burned area of the blade is softened and will not keep a cutting edge.

To some extent this can be avoided if the blade is moved constantly from side to side and is frequently cooled in water.

The wheel rotates towards the tool edge and does not leave a *burr.*

When using a grinding wheel the transparent wheel guard should always be in place. If this is not provided then goggles must be worn.

HORIZONTAL WHEEL

Horizontal grinding stones, or wheels, are now in common use and have features superior to those of the traditional grindstone or wheel.

1. The artificial wheel is open-grained to allow the lubricant and waste steel to pass through.
2. Its structure, being artificial, is constant so there are no hard or soft patches.
3. The wheel rotates at only 110 r.p.m. grinding the blades quickly without the danger of 'burning'.
4. The master arm is adjustable between 15 and 30 degrees ensuring very accurate grinding.
5. The special oil is evenly distributed over the wheel, lubricating, cooling and cleansing to ensure maximum life.
6. The oil is filtered and pumped back for further use.
7. Attachments make the sharpening of carving gouges much easier and more accurate.
8. The machine is designed to operate to the maximum effect with complete safety.

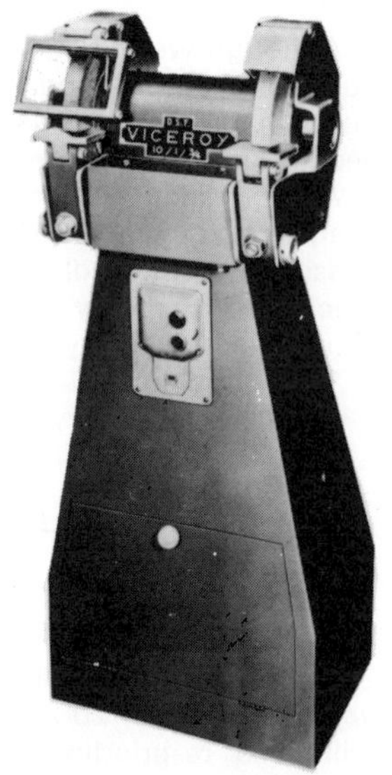

FILES

A small fine flat file is needed to sharpen a twist bit and a centre bit. The centre point, the scriber and the cutter are easily accessible, and can be finished with a fine stone file to obtain a keen edge.

A triangular file is necessary if saws are to be sharpened.

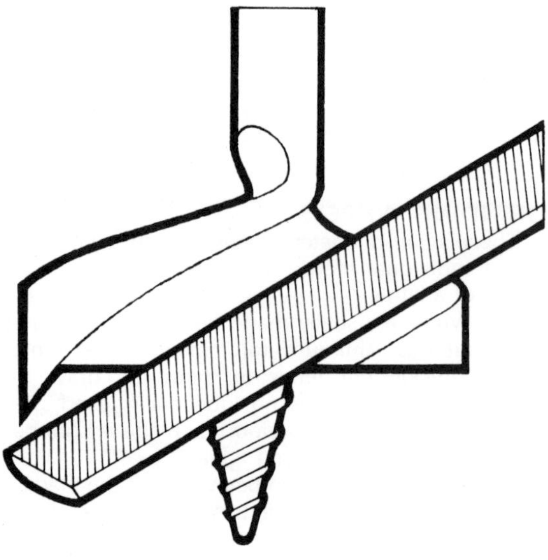

Motor driven grindstones

26 SHARPENING—OILSTONES

Natural oilstones imported from the USA, such as the Arkansas, cut very well but are expensive. Most people use an artificial stone, such as the India, which is made of Alundum.

Artificial stones are a *standard size* (200×50×25 mm) and are available in three accurately controlled *grades: fine, medium* and *coarse.*

A stone combining two of these grades is available, but as they are not expensive it is as well to buy all three. The stones are brittle and to protect them from accidental breakage, as well as from dirt and dust which clogs the pores, they should be kept in strong wooden boxes.

To allow the blade to be sharpened along the full length of the stone without slipping off, the stone is held firmly in place by hardwood wedges, finished with the end-grain flush with the surface.

Although this evens out the wear on the stone the constant honing of smaller blades eventually produces a hollow in both directions.

This prevents the blades of smoothing and try planes from being sharpened square, so *the stone must be re-trued* which can be done in at least three ways:

1. rubbing face downwards on a piece of flat *sandstone* lubricated with water.
2. rubbing in the same way on a flat surface, e.g., plate glass, covered with *abrasive powder* and lubricated with paraffin.
3. rubbing on a strong *abrasive cloth,* e.g., 'Metalite'.

As the stones are pre-saturated with oil at the factory only a small amount of *thin machine oil* is needed as a lubricant. The stone must not be used 'dry' and linseed oil would quickly clog the surface. The surface is occasionally cleaned by scrubbing with paraffin.

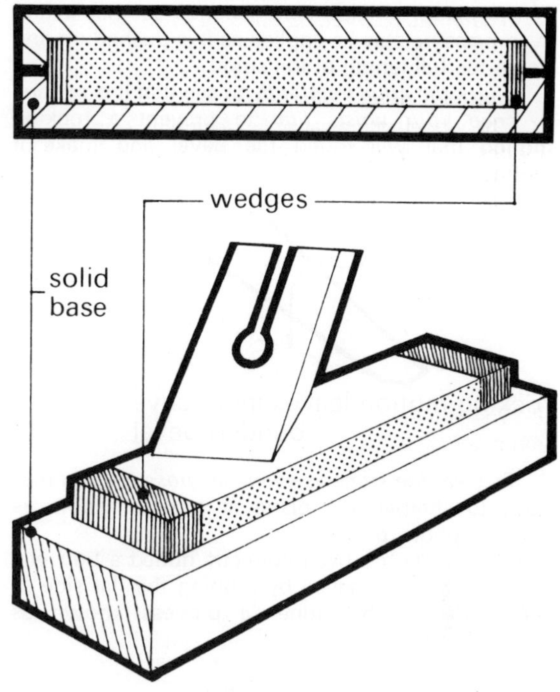

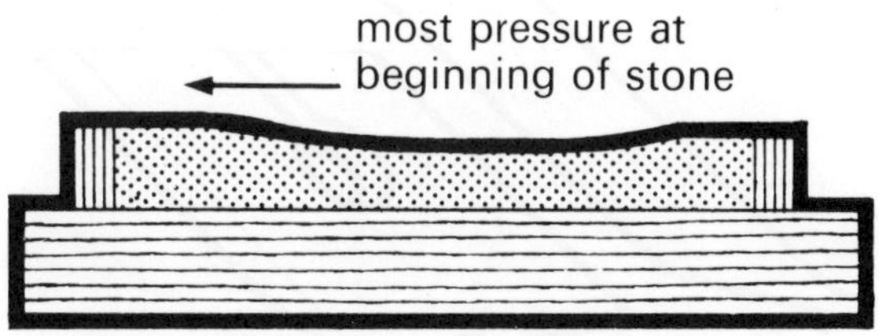

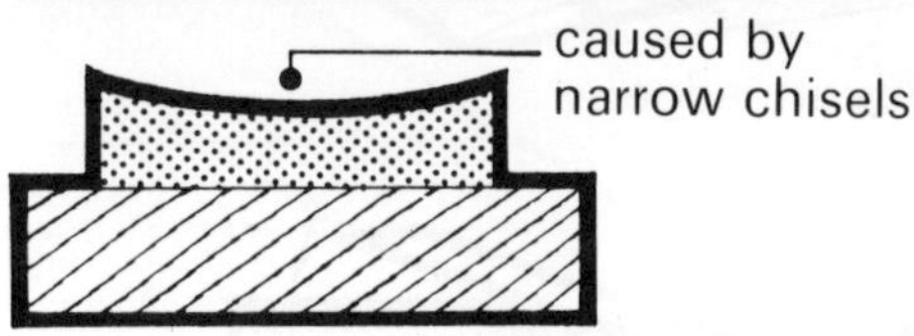

HONING GAUGE

The honing gauge is a simple but effective aid to the beginner in sharpening a plane blade at the correct angle.

The type shown has a screw which passes through the blade slot and is tightened in place by a knurled nut. The wheel allows a firm even pressure to be applied but the stone has to be reversed for wear to be even.

SHARPENING — THE SMOOTHING PLANE

Although some people prefer to have only one grinding/sharpening angle as is produced on a horizontal wheel, most prefer to grind an angle of approximately 25 deg. and hone a steeper cutting angle of between 30 and 35 deg. on the oilstone.

The blade is held in both hands so that a firm even pressure may be applied as it is pushed up and down the full length of the stone.

1. *Check the edge frequently* to see that it is square.
2. *Keep your wrists firm* to prevent a rocking motion that will round the bevel and make it ineffective.

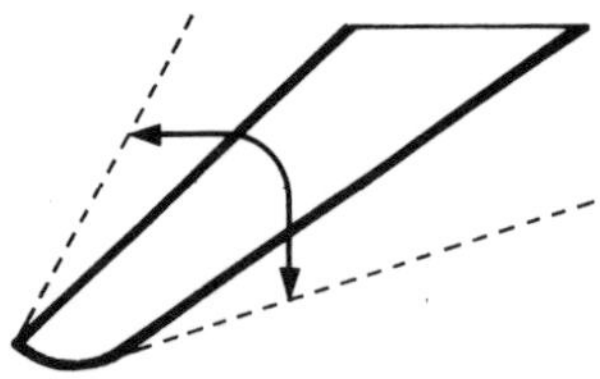

rocking motion leaves ineffective rounded bevel

3. To *wear the stone as evenly as possible* you may have to sharpen the plane at a slight angle as shown (photo p. 82)

If the blade has been correctly honed a burr will appear. This is removed by rubbing the flat side of the blade on the stone—a process known as *'backing-off'*.

'burr' or wire edge

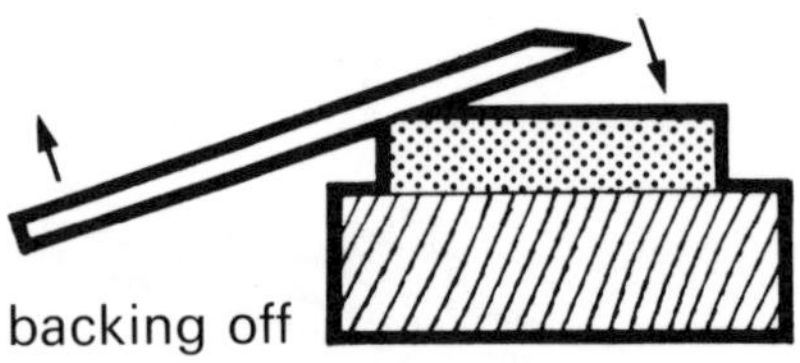

backing off

It is important to keep the blade flat as the slightest bevel on the wrong side will cause a gap between the blade and the back iron which will clog.

The corners of the blade are slightly rounded to prevent them 'digging-in'.

The back iron is carefully re-set, taking care not to touch and damage the new cutting edge. When the back iron is in position it is tightened with a large screwdriver, the blade resting on the edge of the sharpening bench and not in the hand—this would be dangerous.

27 SHARPENING—SPOKESHAVE

The spokeshave blade, although smaller, is sharpened in a similar way to that of the smoothing plane.

A simple *wooden holder* is made in which a saw slot or kerf is cut and the blade is slotted into it.

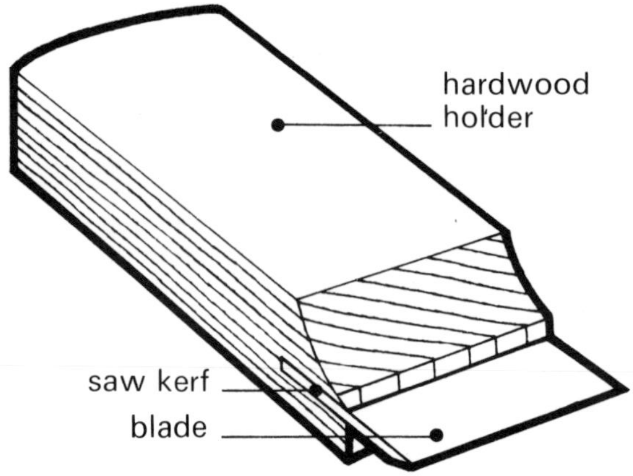

CABINET SCRAPER

In section seventeen you read how a well-set smoothing plane was used to finish off a surface prior to glass papering and polishing. Only in a few cases does the grain prove too difficult to manage, and then a cabinet scraper is used, which *produces a very fine shaving*.

It is manufactured from high quality tool steel and several different shapes and sizes may be bought. A cheaper alternative would be to make one from an old saw blade.

In use the tool is held with both hands, and as it is pushed away from the user it is slightly bowed and leaned forward to engage the *cutting hook*.

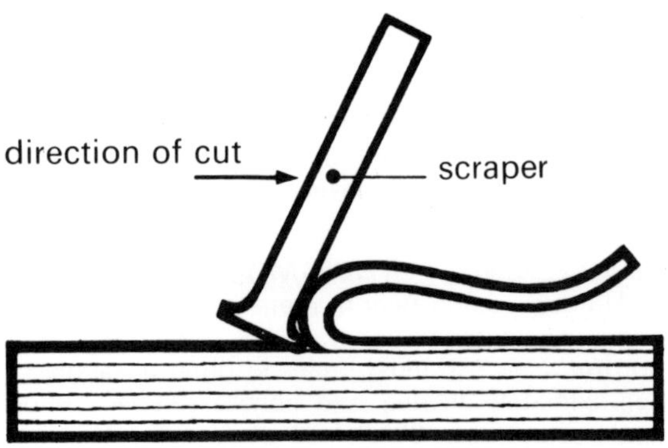

1. The edges are filed square and true and are smoothed on the side and top of an oilstone.

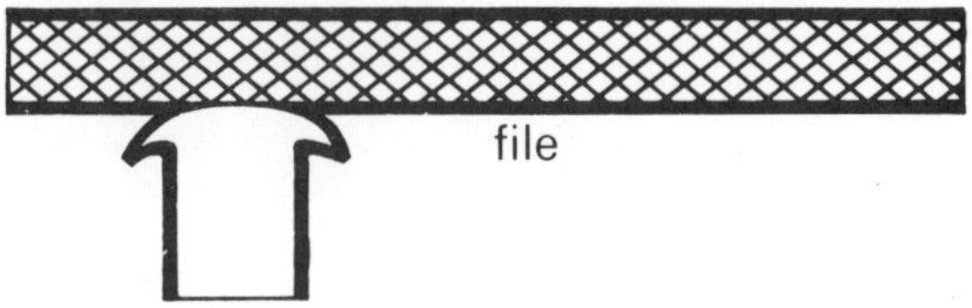

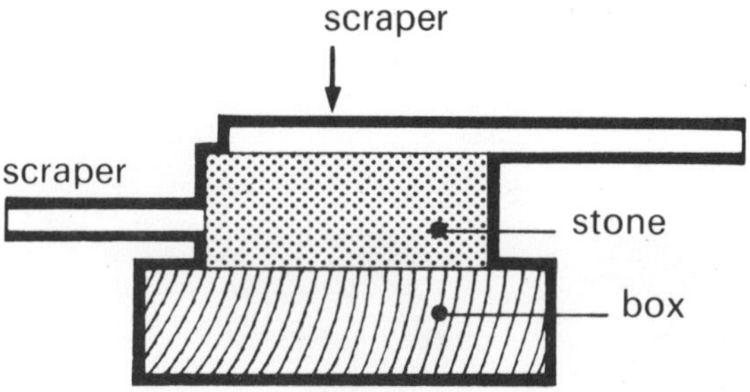

2. A hard steel *burnisher* is then drawn up the edges to pull them over slightly and produce the cutting 'hook'.

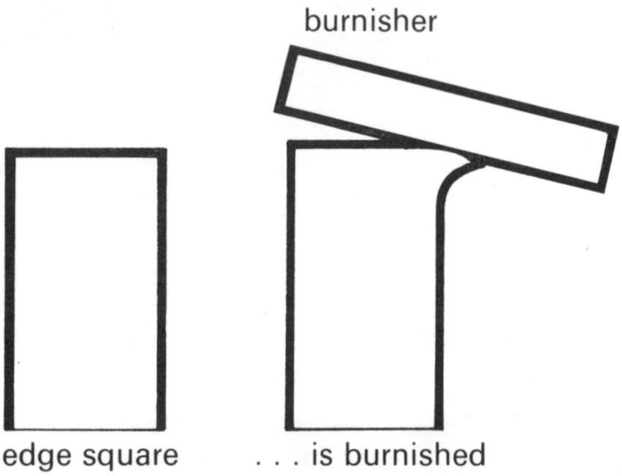

3. The scraper is easily misused. Its main disadvantage is that because of its cutting action *it tends to produce a slight hollow* on the surface of the work.

This may show after polishing.

Only use the scraper when absolutely necessary.

SPECIAL STONES

There are many dozens of *slips, shapes and files* in all three grades which are designed to sharpen every kind of cutting tool.

The round edge slip and the special gouge slip are the most popular for general use, and the machinist's stone is ideal for putting the final edge on centre and twist bits.

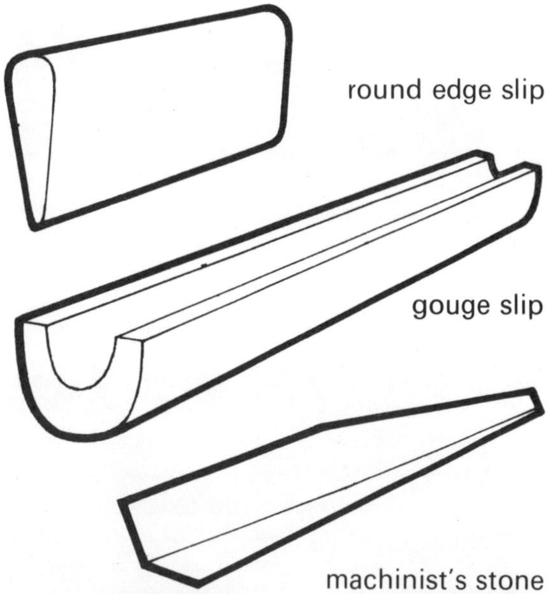

A slipstone is used to sharpen a carving gouge.

The files are designed for the metalworker but their simple shapes make them useful in the woodwork shop.

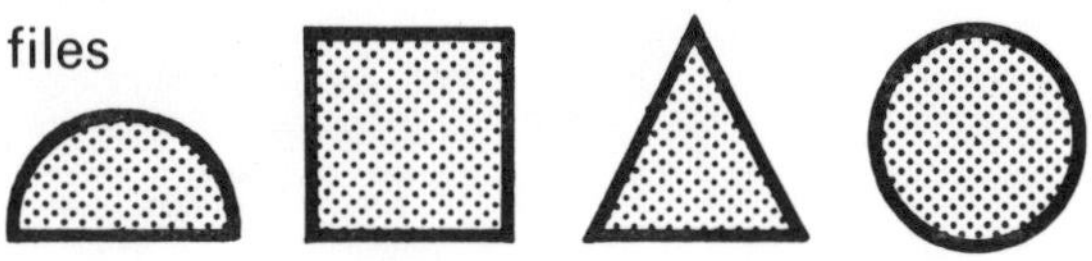

A horizontal grinding wheel ensures that tools are accurately ground to the correct angle

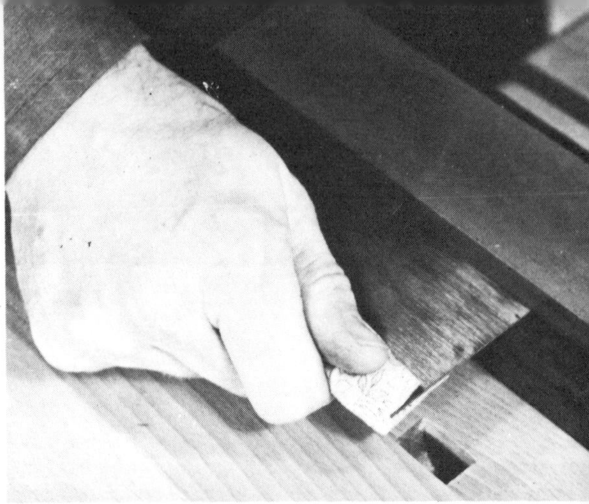

The edge of the scraper is trued on the side of an oilstone.

A plane blade is held at an angle when being honed to wear the oilstone evenly.

The cutting hook is produced by pulling over the edge with a burnisher or the back of a gouge.

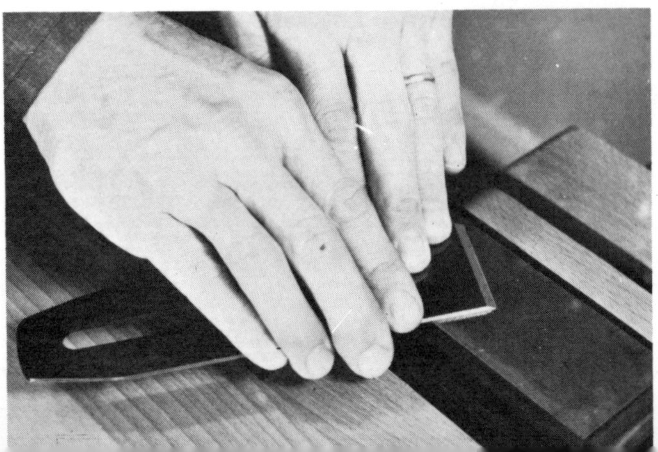

'Backing off' a plane blade to remove the burr or wire edge.

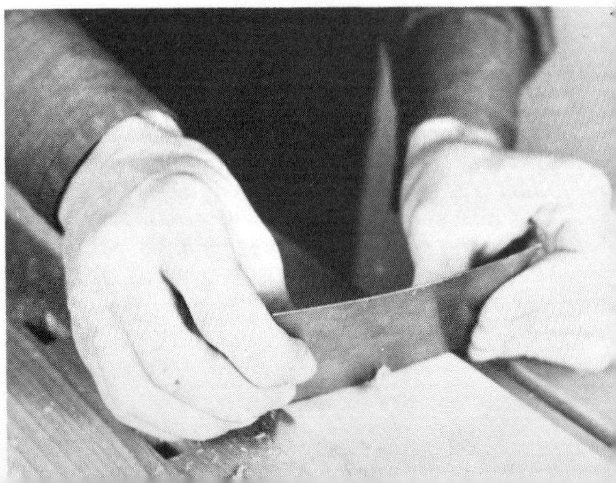

The scraper in use—producing a fine shaving to smooth awkward grain.

28 WORKSHOP EQUIPMENT— THE BENCH

A strong workbench is the basic piece of equipment needed to produce good work. The working surface must be at a convenient height or planing, sawing and chiselling become backbreaking occupations! The top itself should be a solid piece of hardwood, such as 50 mm thick beech or birch, firmly attached to the supporting table construction and supporting a strong vice (see section 23).

1. A *well* which will accommodate planes and chisels, etc., when temporarily not in use is an essential feature of a good bench. If a small lipping is screwed at the end of it, a plane can be rested without being damaged.
2. A hardwood *bench stop* which can easily be adjusted.
3. A good bench may have storage cupboards fitted and will be soundly made. The heavy-sectioned softwood timber used being mortise and tenoned together and the through joints being wedged.
4. Fitted cupboards for storing small work and the basic tool kit (commonly at the ends of the bench) help to keep the workshop tidy.

BASIC APPLIANCES

A *bench hook (sawing board)* is used for sawing small pieces of wood. It is often made of beech with the ledges, which can be made for left or right hand use, secured by dowels and adhesive.

For vertical chiselling the bench hook is often used but the surface quickly becomes uneven and an offcut of blockboard makes a very sound *chiselling board.*

The bench hook in use—supporting the rail for a tenon shoulder to be accurately sawn.

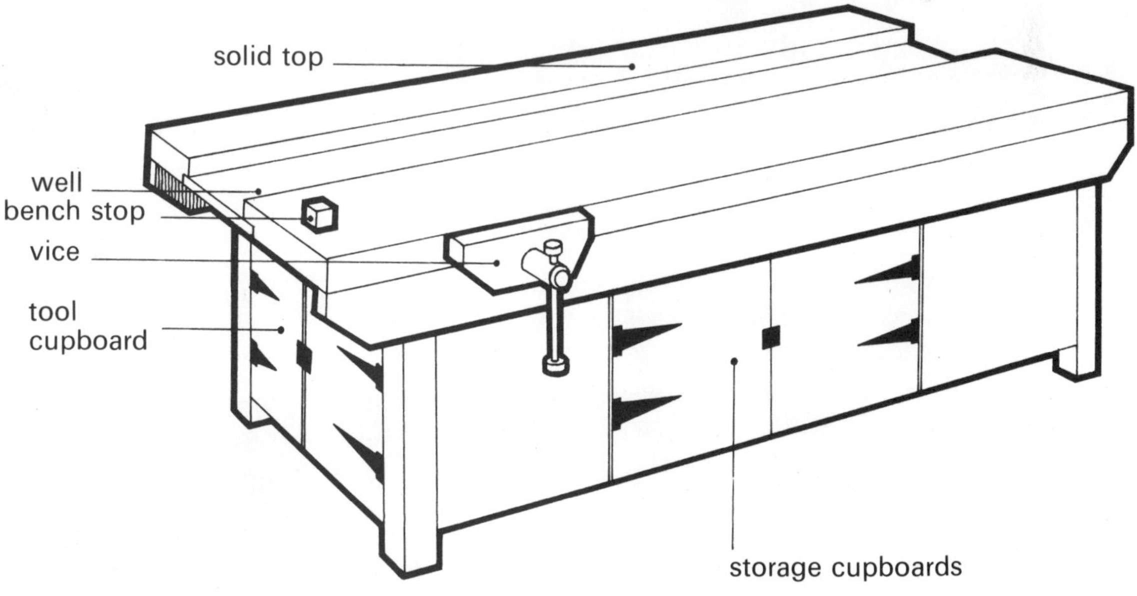

SAWING STOOLS

Although many of your workshops will have a power saw there are occasions when boards need 'ripping' by handsaw and more frequently have to be cross-cut to length.

A well made sawing stool should be stable when in use.

The Black and Decker 'Workmate' is a sophisticated stool—ideal for sawing but can be raised to a more convenient height for chiselling and planing.

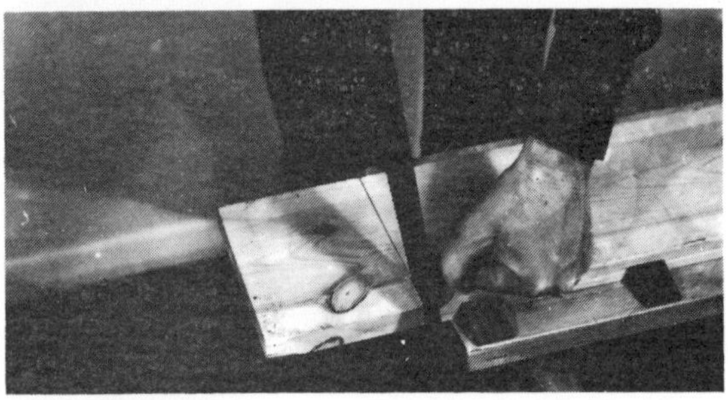

Above: Boards can be held in the vice-pegs to be cross cut to length.
Below: Thin sheets of hardboard or plywood are supported by the vice-bars on each side of the cut.

THE MITRE BLOCK AND BOX

Metal mitring tools have to some extent replaced wooden ones. But they are expensive to buy and, like most appliances, wooden ones are both cheap and easy to make from hardwood or laminated board.

Both the mitre block and the mitre box are used *for cutting timber at a set angle.* This is usually 45 degrees, for picture frames and the like, but it can be adapted for cutting any angle. The block can only be used for small timber, whereas the box will not only take thicker and wider timber but the *tenon saw* is accurately positioned by the two sides.

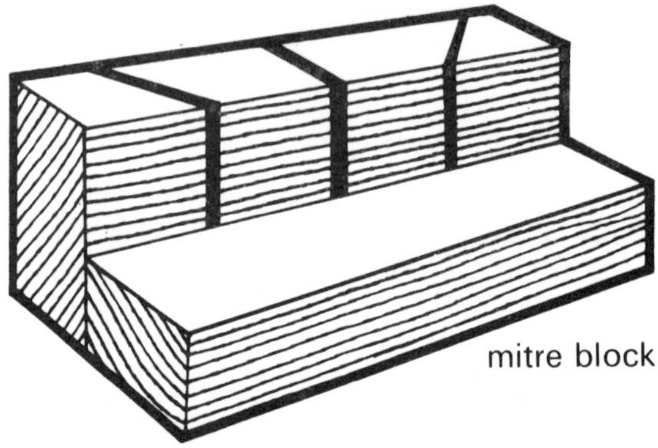

mitre block

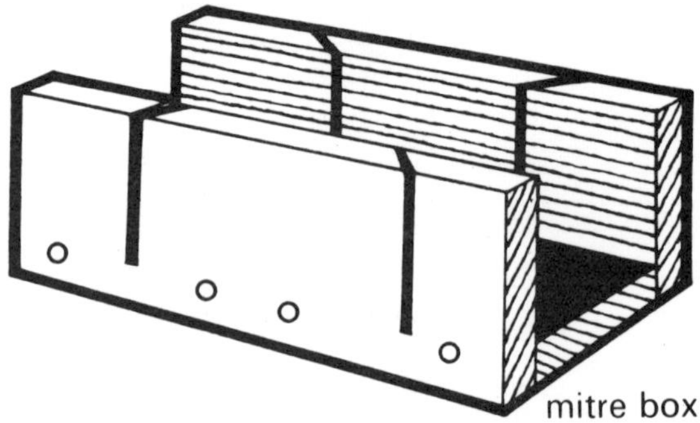

mitre box

Wear will be avoided and a more accurate cut will be made if *adjustable metal guides* are fitted to the top edge.

29 APPLIANCES— SHOOTING BOARDS

The sawn ends of many timbers will need trimming or squaring-off.

1. Picture-framing mitred on a wood block or in a box may need trimming to ensure an accurate fit.
2. The shoulders of dovetails and lap joints are often gauged from the end of a board which can be squared off on a shooting board.

Both the mitre and shooting boards are similarly constructed and are between 600 mm and one metre in length. *The differences are in the stops*—the mitre board having a block screwed to the centre of the top board (A) and the shooting board having a stop at one end, tapered to ensure a tight fit (B) (although a stout block, well screwed down, is both strong and more easily trued when necessary (C)).

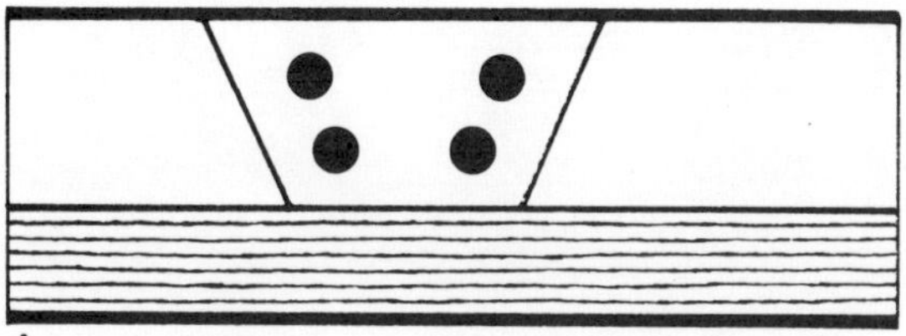
A

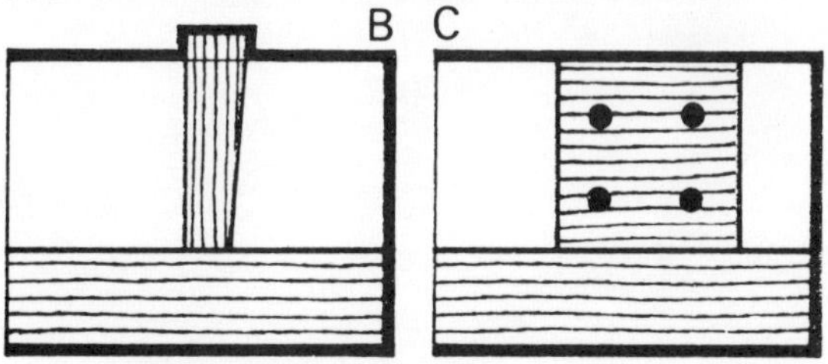
B C

The *base boards* must be of well-seasoned hardwood or 19mm blockboard which keeps its flatness and ensures an accurate 'rebate' for the plane to run in. Accurate cutting is necessary, and to avoid dirt and dust interfering with the plane, the top board is chamfered or grooved on its underside.

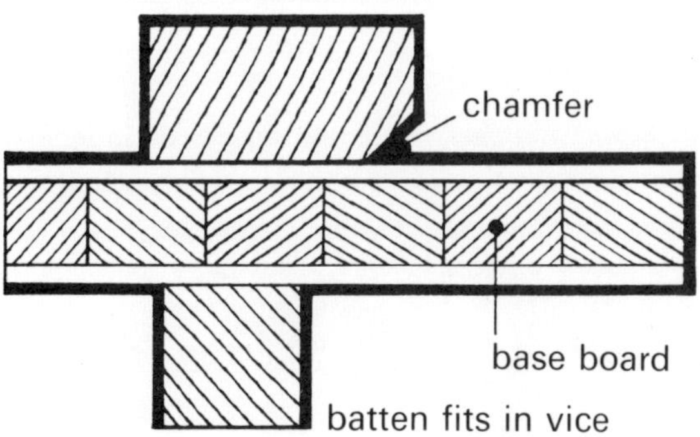

Accurately machined metal planes give a more reliable square cut than wood planes. The *technical metal jack planes* have a handle which can be screwed into either side of the *extra wide web* of the cast-iron body.

A technical metal jack-plane.

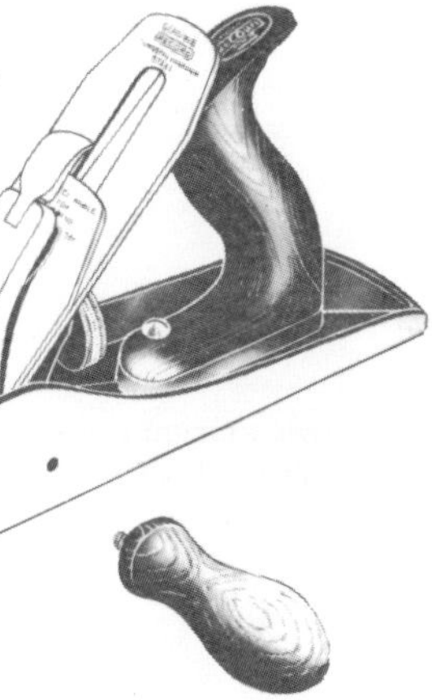

Small shooting boards are useful for trimming the ends of rails that are to be dowelled and the *block plane* does this job admirably (photo over).

THE CRADLE

The simple cradle enables such objects as stool legs to be *chamfered*, or to be partly *rounded* before being turned between centres on the lathe.

It can be made from any softwood but should have a hardwood stop.

An alternative stop would be a piece of slotted dowel which can easily be adjusted by tapping with a hammer.

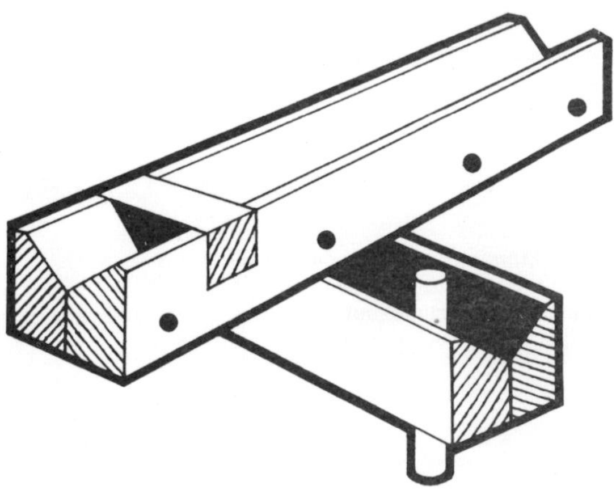

Small-sectioned timber can be accurately trimmed to length with a block plane.

A hardwood mitre block with adjustable metal guides in use.

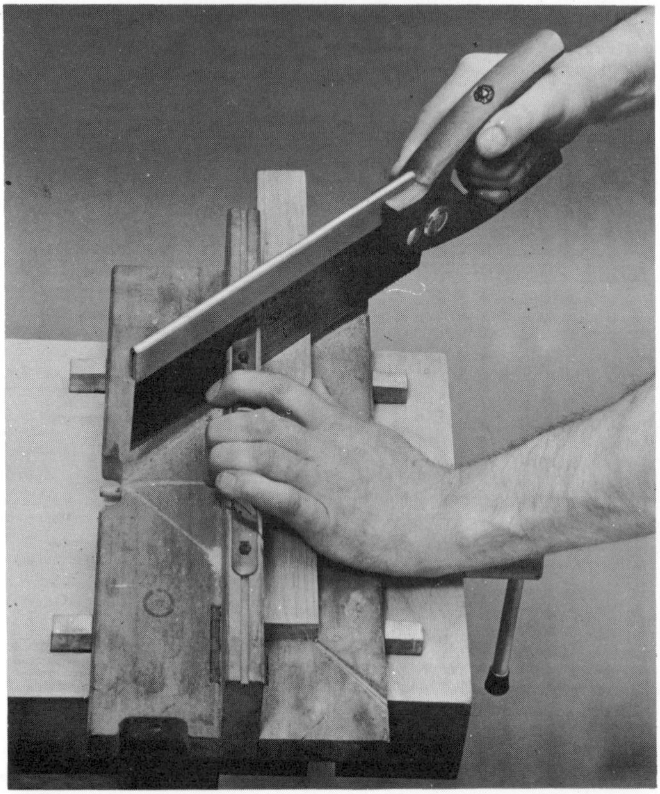

Metal Mitre blocks which can be set at any angle from 45° to 90° have two saw guides to ensure an accurate cut.

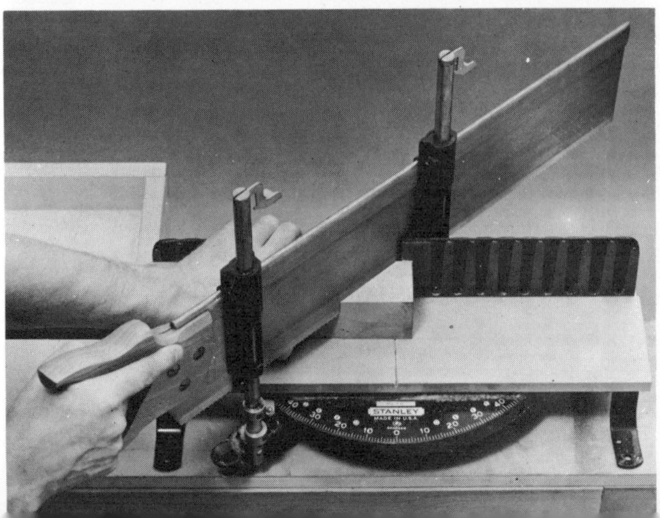

JIGS AND TEMPLATES

These are patterns which *help to speed up work and increase accuracy* by avoiding tedious repetitive marking out. Such as in Design 10 (see page 178) where each of the eight stool rails are prepared to receive dowelling.

The materials from which it is made will depend on the size of the job to be marked out and the number of times it will be used.

1. The *dovetail template* is in constant use and should be *made from metal.* Two of many possible designs are shown.

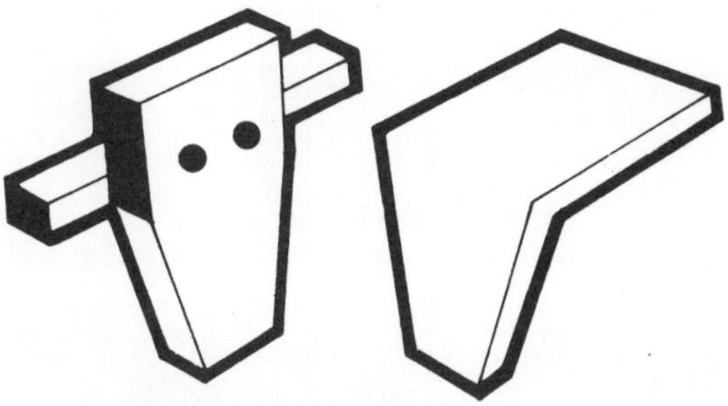

dovetail templates

2. Large templates which need to be accurate are made from *cardboard.* If a template is to be stored and frequently used a *hardboard* template would be ideal.
3. When a number of holes have to be bored an *aluminium template* is useful for accurate positioning of the centres
4. *Paper or card templates* should be used for shapes to be drawn only once. It is often convenient for these to be cut out of a full-size working drawing and to be pasted on to the work while the shape is cut
5. *Jigs* are usually made when a considerable number of identical shapes or holes need cutting, e.g., cutting squares for a chess board or drilling for dowelled joints.

A cardboard template would be ideal for this table.

Above: An aluminium template used for marking out holes in a pencil holder.

Below: A paper template is glued onto the surface (left) and is cut through on a bandsaw (below).

DOWELLING JIGS

The use of wood dowelling to make joints has become common, but the strength of the joints depends partly upon the accuracy of the drilled holes into which the dowel rod fits.

The Record dowelling jig requires a minimum of marking out and can be used to drill three hole sizes (6·3 mm, 8 mm and 9·5 mm) in a wide range of timber thicknesses (16 to 75 mm).

This makes it ideal for drilling corner and leg joints on frame and stool constructions. The long slide rods enable corner and side joints to be made in box and carcase constructions up to 460 mm wide.

To be used successfully the timber must be well prepared with marked faces and the jig must be secure before drilling.

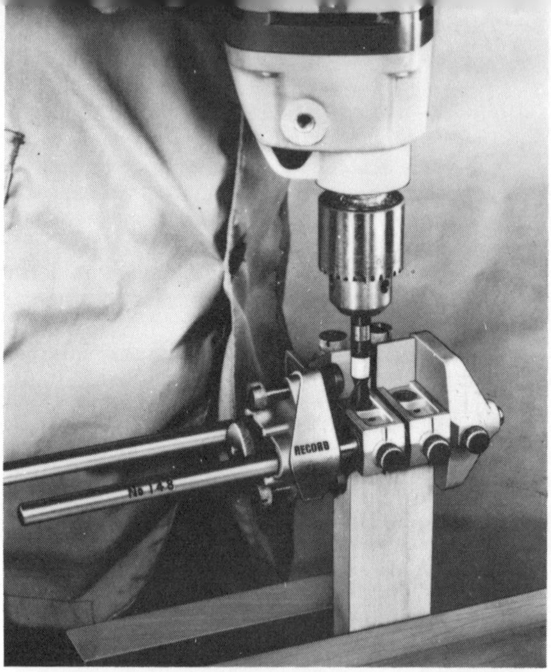

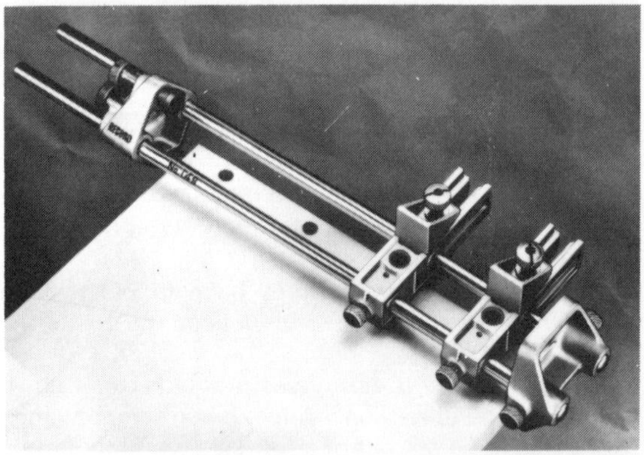

The Shapercraft Dowelmate is a simple jig for preparing corner joints for box or carcase constructions in manufactured boards. The three dowel sizes (6 mm, 8 mm and 10 mm) are suitable for boards ranging from 12 to 23 mm in thickness.

The board ends are cut square but the matching holes do not require any marking out. After drilling, the vertical board shown is turned through 180° before the dowel is inserted.

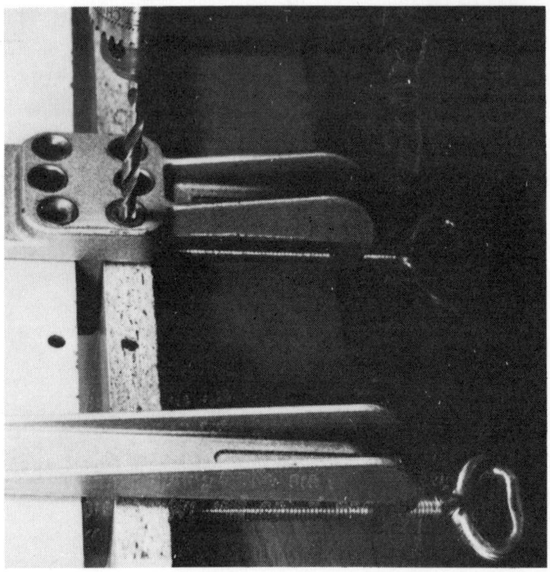

30 ADHESIVES—GLUE

Adhesives are used in two ways:

1. To apply large surface areas of material, as when laying veneers.
2. To stick together relatively small surface areas such as woodworking joints.

"An efficient adhesive is one that *maintains an adequate bond* between the wooden elements under the *conditions of service* that the joint has to withstand."

This means simply that for an adhesive to be efficient it must be carefully selected for a particular job. Obviously the demands on an adhesive for a fireside chair are totally different from those on an adhesive for a sheet of plywood which forms the outside wall of a prefabricated house or the cabin of a sea-going yacht.

DURABILITY OF ADHESIVES

For durability, adhesives are classified in the following groups:

1. *WBP*—weather and boilproof.

These are of two kinds, *phenol-formaldehyde* (PF) and *resorcinol-formaldehyde* (RF) which are red in colour and are *synthetic resins.* PF resins are used to bond WBP plywood (see section 11) and RF resins, such as Aerodux, are used for laminating and boat-building.

2. *BR*—boil resistant.

One of this type, *melamine-formaldehyde* (MF) is often used to improve other resins. It sets very hard and in one form is used as a protective coating for laminated plastic veneer, e.g., Formica and Warerite.

3. *MR*—moisture resistant and moderately weather resistant.

These are *urea-formaldehyde* (UF) resins which, being relatively cheap and easy to apply are most used in the school workshop, e.g., Aerolite.

4. *INT*—resist cold water only and are for internal use.

Animal (Scotch), *casein, PVA,* and *contact* adhesives are in this category and are mostly used in furniture making.

COMMON WORKSHOP ADHESIVES—ANIMAL GLUE

Animal glue is derived from the hide and bones of cattle and is sometimes referred to as 'Scotch' or 'French' glue.

Its *basis is gelatine*—the sticky jelly that remains after boiling the initial ingredients in water. The process has changed little over the past 3000 years and the glue, in refined form, is still used in modern furniture factories.

Animal glue is available in several solid forms such as slabs, cakes, pearls and powder, and in a jelly form as in Croid Aero.

PREPARATION AND APPLICATION

The solids are immersed in a covering of cold water and gently heated in a glue pot until they will run from the applicator (usually a brush) in an even flow. If a jelly is used it merely requires warming.

The glue should not be boiled as its strength and colour will both deteriorate.

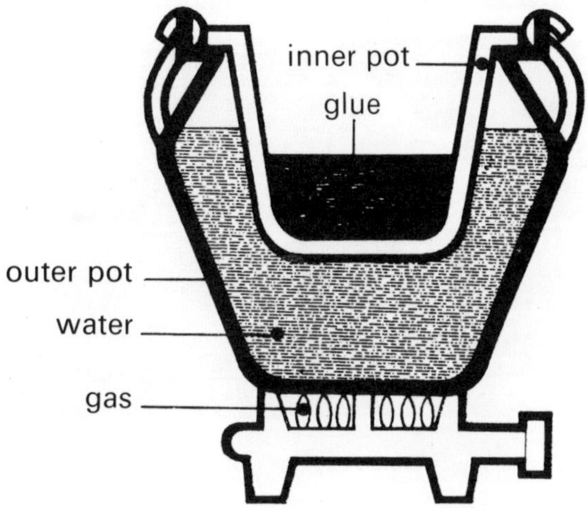

ADVANTAGES AND DISADVANTAGES

1. The glue forms a good natural bond with the wood.
2. The glue is sticky and quickly begins to set, so that small items, such as corner blocks, are easily fixed without much pressure.
3. The glue is easily cleaned off when it has 'jellied' and when it is properly hardened it does not blunt plane or chisel blades.
4. It is *non-staining and cheap* to use.
5. Early preparation and planning is necessary.
6. The glue has *very little resistance to water.*
7. Modern additives to control the setting time and to lighten the natural colour of the glue often need to be used.

Main uses are for most indoor woodwork, general furniture making and laying veneers.

PVA glue brushed onto an edge joint.

CASEIN ADHESIVE

This 'natural' glue is made from the curds of milk mixed with hydrated lime and caustic soda.

It was developed in the early days of the aircraft industry but is now regarded mainly as an indoor adhesive, e.g., Casco Casein.

PREPARATION AND APPLICATION

It is obtained in a powder form and the addition of cold water, generally in the proportion of one to one, is all that is required. The liquid quickly stiffens after mixing and should be applied to both surfaces with a wood or plastic spatula.

ADVANTAGES AND DISADVANTAGES

1. It is *easily stored, mixed and applied* and gives a strong joint in most normal woodworking conditions.
2. The *cramping time is short*—cramps are soon available for use on other jobs.
3. It has a *good resistance to cold water.*
4. It has a *tendency to stain* some timbers, leaving a visible joint line.

Main uses are general woodwork, laminated work, small boat building and when working with oily woods, such as Teak.

31 ADHESIVES—POLYVINYL ACETATE EMULSION (PVA)

This white, water-based adhesive has been developed in the last twenty years. The liquid has a cream-like consistency and is bought ready to use. Common brands are Evostick Resin 'W', Polybond, Timbabond 606, Dunlop Woodworker Adhesive.

PVA glue squeezed through a nozzle into a mortise.

PREPARATION AND APPLICATION

No preparation of any kind is required. The adhesive is applied with a brush or a spatula to both surfaces to be joined to avoid glue starvation. Wash brushes immediately in warm soapy water and rinse thoroughly to keep them in good condition.

Alternatively the adhesive may be applied from a conveniently nozzled dispenser.

ADVANTAGES AND DISADVANTAGES

1. Its shelf life (i.e. the length of time that it can be stored) is limited to about one year.
2. The adhesive *requires no preparation.*
3. There is *little waste;* it is economical to use.
4. It is *easily applied* and spreads smoothly and easily.
5. It sets within a few hours at normal room temperature and like most adhesives the cramping time is reduced by an increase in temperature.
6. It is not brittle when set and is therefore easy to clean up.

Main uses. It has a good resistance to damp but is generally used for indoor woodwork of all kinds.

SYNTHETIC RESINS

There are three main types of UF resin adhesive belonging to the MR group.

1. In powder form with the resin and hardener combined—Cascamite One-shot.
2. A powdered resin and a separate liquid hardener —Aerolite 306.
3. The resin and the hardener both in liquid form—Aerolite 300.

When the adhesives have set all three types have very similar properties. They are extremely brittle and surplus adhesive should be removed immediately after cramping-up.

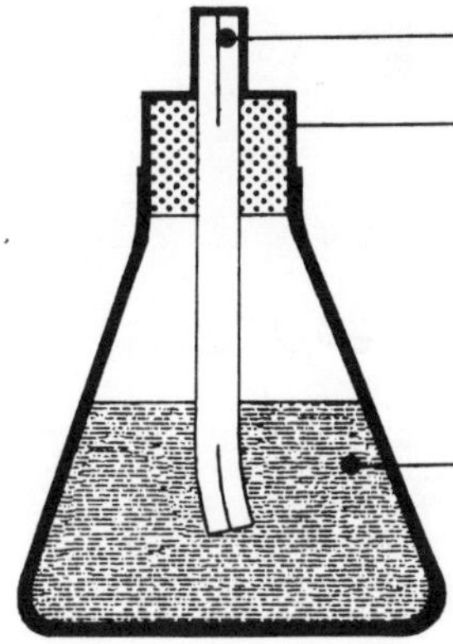

PREPARATION AND APPLICATION

Type One. The mixture is three parts of powder to one part of water by volume to produce a thick substance. Do not add excessive water.

This mixture is best applied to both parts of the joint with a spatula within about fifteen minutes of mixing as it quickly begins to set.

Once mixed, it is not possible to store the adhesive, and to avoid waste, *only sufficient for immediate use should be prepared.*

Type Two. Two parts of the resin powder are mixed with one part of water by volume.

The resin and hardener are applied separately to opposite sides of the joint, and when these come into contact setting rapidly begins.

To *prevent accidental contact between the liquids* they are carefully stored in distinguishable containers—both clearly labelled.

1. The sketches show the resin in a large bottle, wide-based to prevent spilling and the underside of the top waxed to prevent sticking. The wooden handled brush keeps soft in the resin.
2. The smaller bottle contains hardener and is corked to prevent evaporation. A piece of felt or similar material is a useful applicator.
3. Used in this manner there is no waste and the glue is economic.

Type Three. This has identical properties to type two, the difference being that the resin is already mixed when purchased.

Main uses are for canoe and boat building and for all external work since they have a high resistance to moisture.

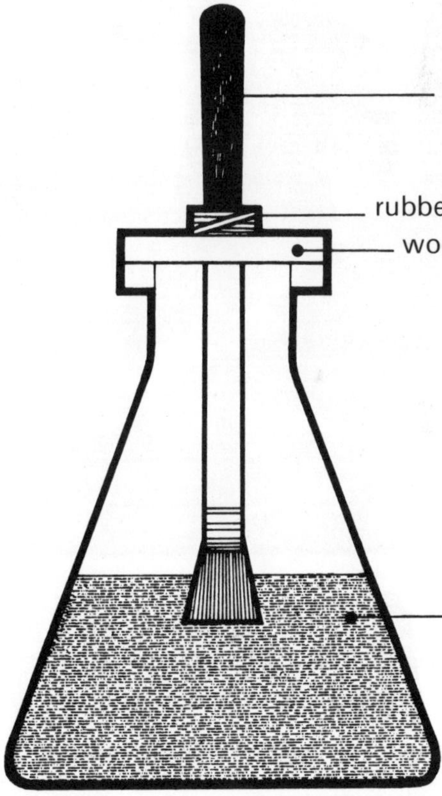

CONTACT (IMPACT) GLUES

These are mainly rubber-based viscous liquids in a solvent, e.g. Evostik 528, Dunlop Thixofix and Unistik.

PREPARATION AND APPLICATION

No preparation is needed.

The adhesive is spread evenly on to both surface areas with either a plywood or a metal comb.

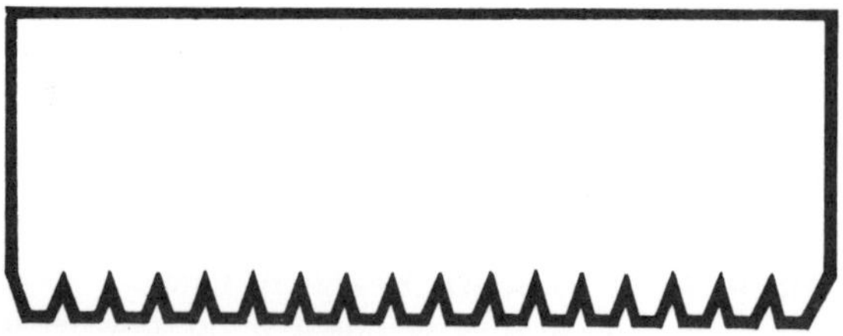

CIBA (A.R.L.) Ltd

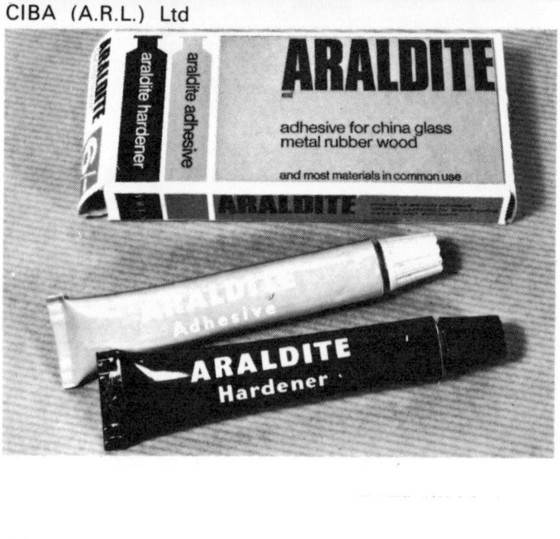

The joint is left 'open' for about fifteen minutes when firm hand pressure is usually sufficient to form a contact bond, although light cramp pressure may be used.

Main uses are for bonding plastic laminated sheets to plywood.

EPOXY RESIN

This adhesive has a separate resin and hardener and being particularly suitable for *gluing wood to metal* has a valuable place in the workshop.

The manufacturer's instructions for preparation and application must be carefully followed. Examples are Araldite and Britfix.

32 COMMON NAILS

Many different types of nail are available, the commonest being mainly used in carpentry and joinery.

Nails are a quick and effective means of joining wood together but as they mainly hold by the friction of the nail against the fibres of the wood, their strength is limited.

For the greatest efficiency carefully select the correct type and size of nail for the job.

CUT TYPE (BRAD)

Often referred to as a 'brad' this heavy nail is stamped from sheet metal—usually steel—and because of its square edges has considerable holding power.

The nail shown is 50 mm long and should be used for such jobs as fixing 16 mm floorboarding where its holding power will be employed to the greatest advantage.

Sizes from 25 to 125 mm.

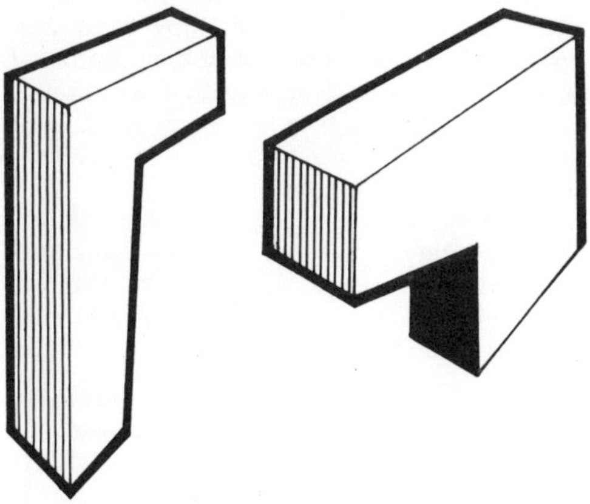

ROUND WIRE

These cheap nails, made from wire, have a large flat head designed for easy withdrawal. Used mainly in softwood work—a good example being *wood packing cases.*

Sizes from 25 to 150 mm.

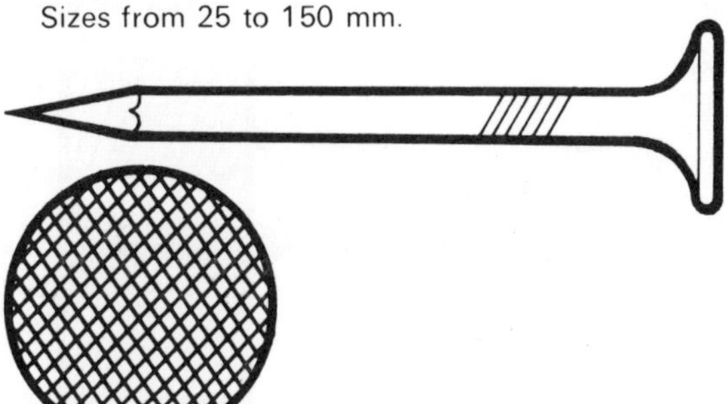

OVAL WIRE

Commonly used in *house joinery* as the oval wire and comparatively small head are quickly driven or punched below the surface of the wood. Sizes from 12 to 100 mm.

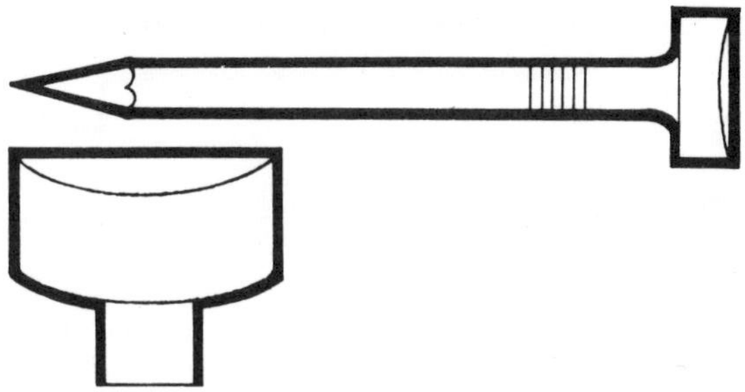

PANEL PINS

These fine round wire nails have small heads and numerous uses, particularly for fixing *plywood panels* and simple lapped joints. The diameter of wire nails, such as panel pins, varies and is based on the Standard Wire Gauge (see table 1 page 187).

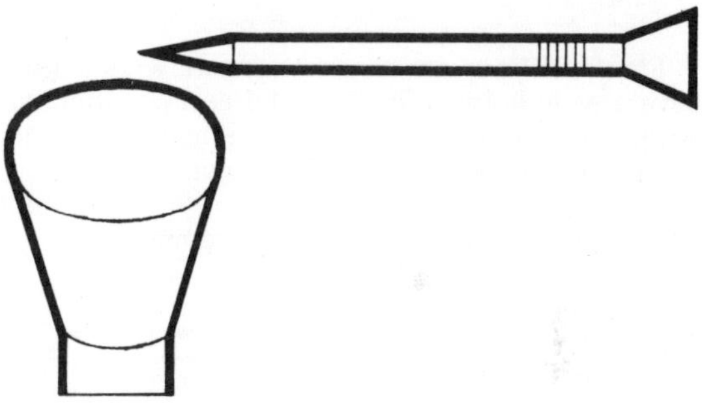

CLOUT NAILS

These short large-headed nails are mainly used for fixing *roofing felt* and are galvanised to prevent rust.

Common sizes from 12 to 50 mm.

When larger nails are being used a hole should be bradawled or pre-bored to prevent splitting.

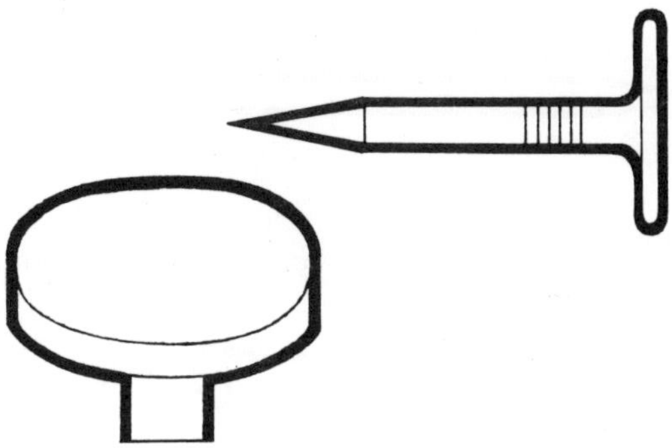

NAILS FOR UPHOLSTERY

Gimp pins. These small wire nails which are often made of brass are used in upholstery. Sizes from 9 to 19 mm.

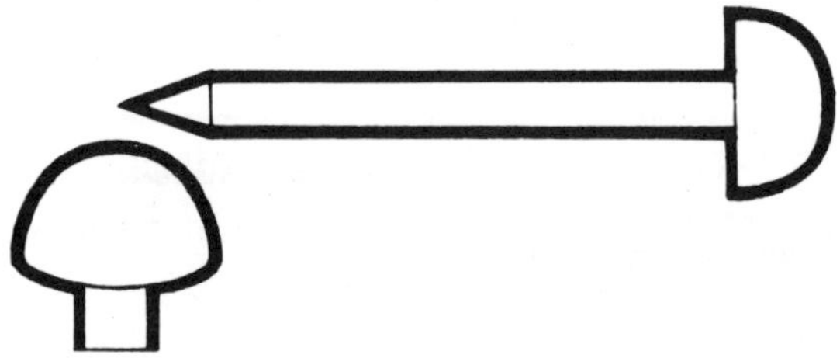

Cut tacks. These are short, sharp-pointed, flat-headed nails of black mild steel used for fixing upholstery material. Sizes are from 12 to 25 mm.

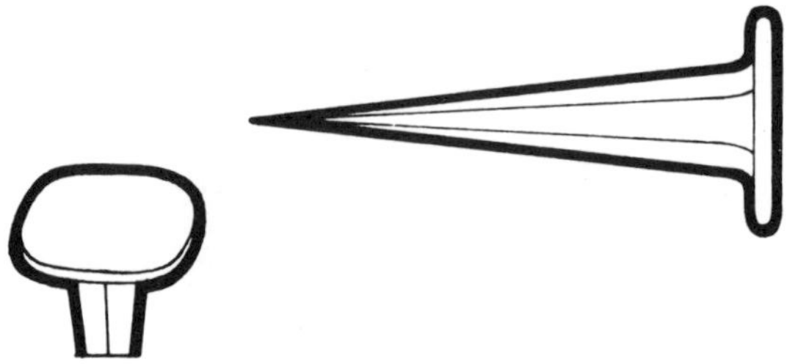

Staples. These are quick to insert with a gun, have a wide holding area, can be easily withdrawn without damaging material and are neat in appearance, particularly if made from copper.

Common widths vary from 5 mm for fixing light panels to 50 mm for large frame assemblies.

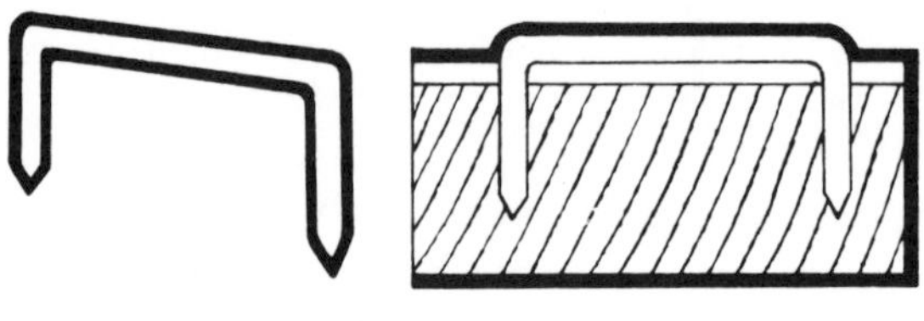

SPECIAL NAILS

Veneer Pins. Similar in appearance but of thinner gauge than a panel pin. Originally used for holding veneers until the glue had set.

Sprigs. These are small headless, tapered steel pins traditionally used for securing picture frame backs.

Escutcheon Pin. A short nail, commonly made of brass, designed to fix the protective plate of a keyhole.

Hardened Fixing Pins. A newly developed nail made of zinc-coated steel which *will penetrate brick* and plaster, etc., where plugging and screwing would previously have been necessary. They are expensive and sold by quantity. Sizes from 20 to 100 mm.

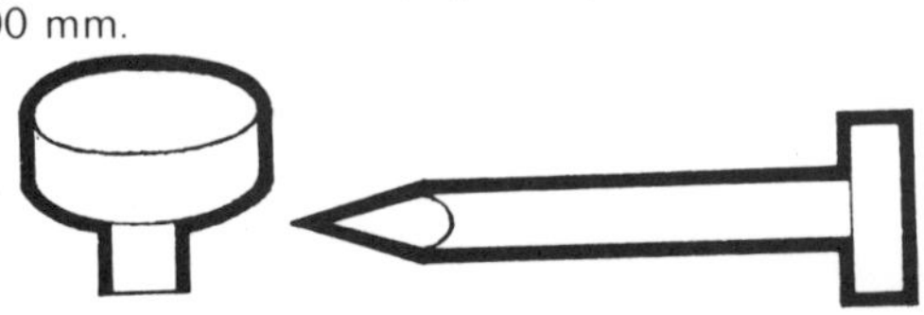

'Gripfast' Nails. Specially designed *for boat building.* These silicon-bronze alloy nails are as strong as steel yet will not rust or stain timber. The shank is barbed in such a way that withdrawal is most difficult. The grip is as much as a slightly shorter but much heavier screw and five times that of an equivalent round wire nail.

Available in sizes up to 150 mm long, pre-boring may be necessary to prevent splitting. They are not cheap, and like screws are sold by the gross. Countersunk and flat heads are made, both being suitable for a large variety of *permanent fixing jobs.*

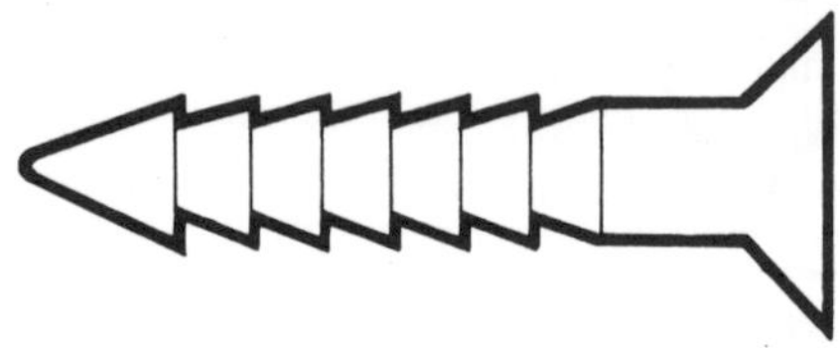

MAXIMUM STRENGTH

This is obtained by choosing a nail of the correct length, gauge and type of head. A reliable guide is: when possible use a nail the length of which is three times the thickness of the piece of wood being fixed.

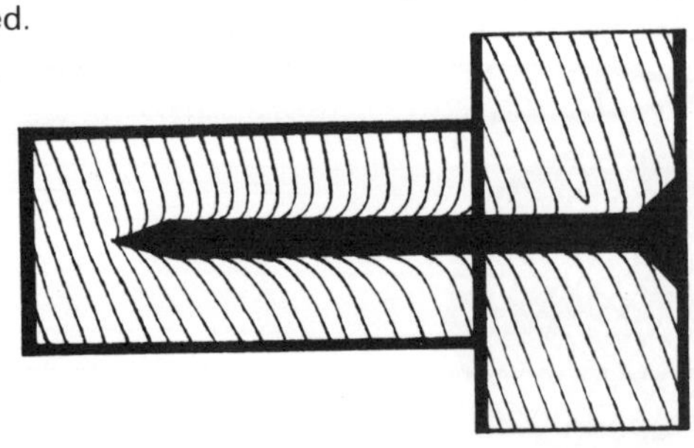

33 METHODS OF NAILING

DOVETAIL NAILING

Plain butt or lapped joints at the corner of simple boxes are strengthened if they are dovetail nailed. The nails are inserted on the 'skew' to obtain maximum holding power.

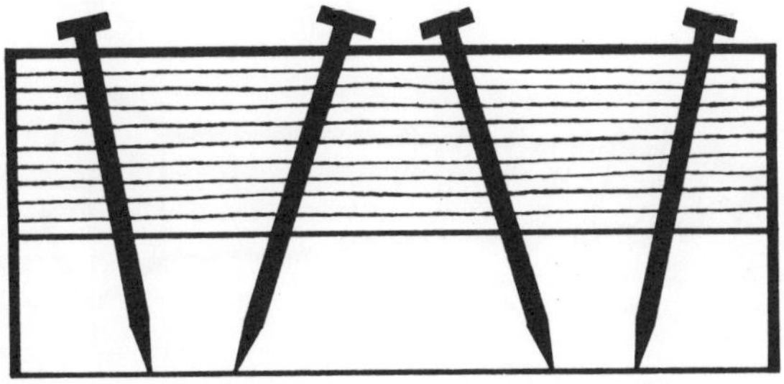

CLENCHING

Where thin boarding is being fixed, say on a garden gate, the nail is often driven right through for strength and clenched (bent over) when it emerges from the back.

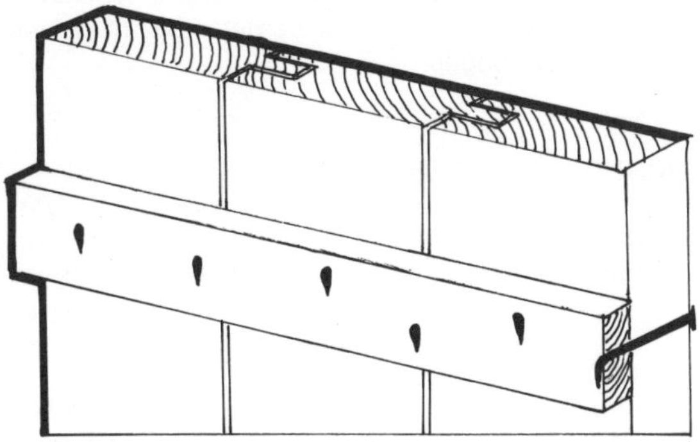

STAGGERING

When nailing near the end of a batten there is a danger of splitting. This can be prevented by staggering the nails across the width of the wood.

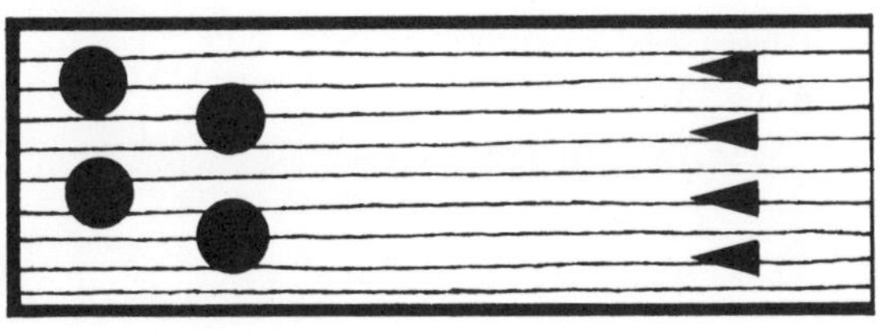

INSERTING NAILS

Hold nails between thumb and finger and tap into position at the required angle.

Hold the end of the shaft and swing the hammer from the elbow to drive the nail in. If you grip the hammer shaft near to the head the nail may bend.

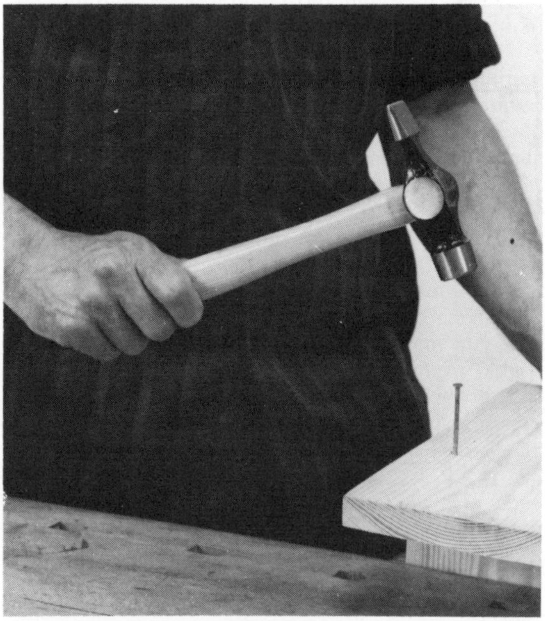

WITHDRAWING NAILS

Nails are usually withdrawn with pincers although a claw hammer may be used on heavy or rough carpentry work.

The surface must be protected from damage, as the nail is levered out, by a pad of waste wood.

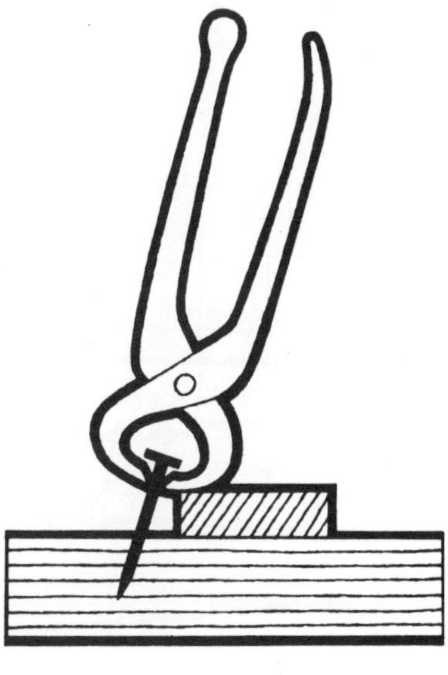

34 SCREWS—VARIOUS TYPES

SCREWS

Screws are an effective way of joining most solid materials together. Their main advantages over nails are additional strength and ease of withdrawal. They are therefore most suitable as a temporary fixing device (nails are much more permanent).

The most common materials used in wood screw manufacture are *steel and brass* although these are frequently coated with chromium, zinc, nickel or black japanning. Silicon bronze and other special alloys are occasionally used.

1. Steel screws are both the strongest and the cheapest.
2. Brass screws have a better appearance and will not rust but they are not very strong.

The most commonly-used screw, the steel countersunk head, is available in sizes from 6 to 150 mm and in gauges (i.e., the diameter of the shank) from 0 to 22 (see table 1).

The likely range of screws in your workshop, which will cover nearly all the necessary jobs, will be 9 to 63 mm in length and in gauges from 4 to 12.

Screws are made with three common types of head:

1. countersunk
2. raised countersunk
3. round

They are sold by number (usually in boxes holding one gross) and when ordering, the following information is necessary; the quantity, the screw length, thickness (gauge), material and type of head.

Examples:

1. 200, 38 mm, no. 8, steel, countersunk.
2. 100. 19 mm, no. 4, brass round head.

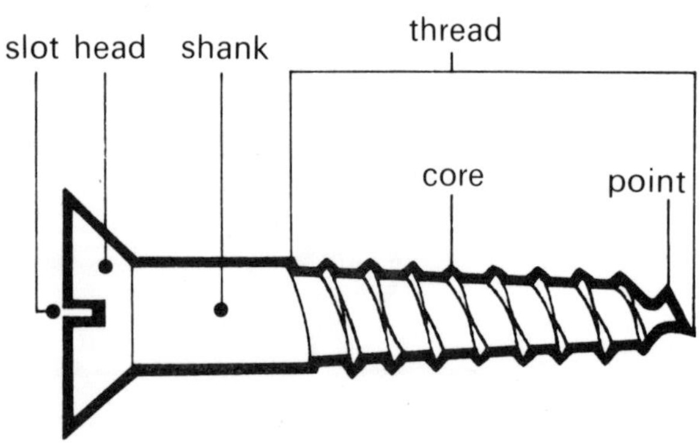

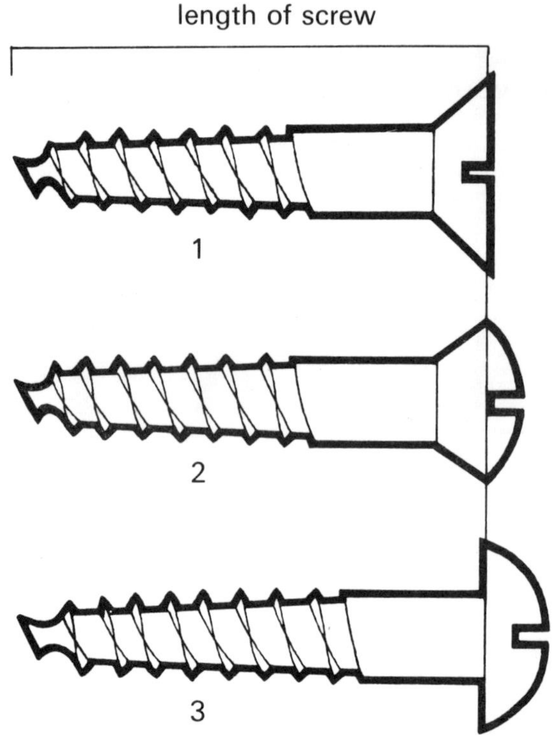

COUNTERSUNK HEAD

Used mainly *for joining wood to wood* where the head has to be flush or sunk below the surface and for securing hinges.

RAISED COUNTERSUNK HEAD

A less common screw used *for fixing door plates* and metal bathroom fittings, etc., it is often made of chromium-plated brass or other matching material.

ROUND HEAD

Frequently used *for securing external metal fittings* and in joinery work, e.g., fixing tee-hinges and shelf brackets to wood. Accordingly they are often black japanned over steel and are resistant to rust.

GKN TWINFAST SCREW

The Guest, Keen and Nettlefold (GKN) Company have developed a screw with two threads instead of the usual one. It has the following advantages:

1. A self-centreing point—the screw starts straight and drives in true.
2. Only half as many turns are required to insert the screw.
3. Greater holding power than an ordinary screw (the thread length is 4/5 total).
4. A smaller shank which lessens the risk of splitting.

These improvements make the screw particularly suitable for chipboard and blockboard furniture.

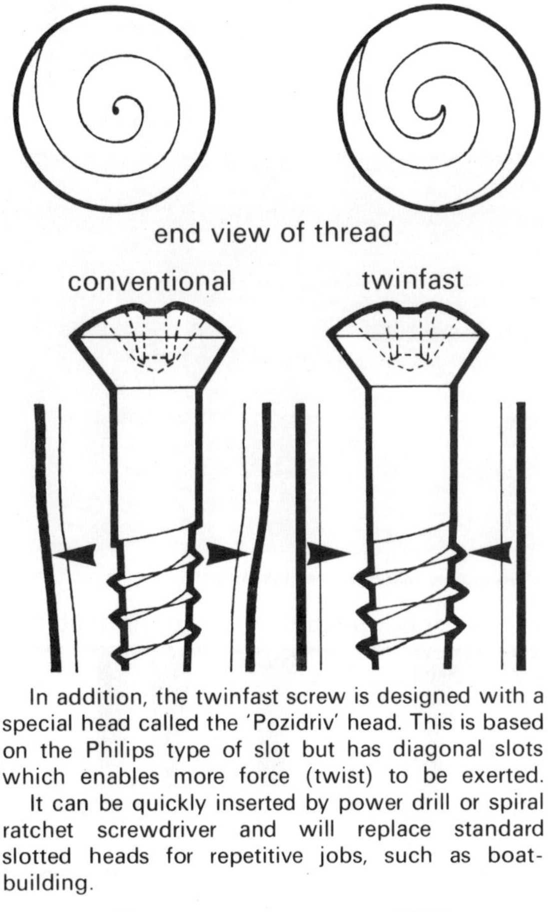

In addition, the twinfast screw is designed with a special head called the 'Pozidriv' head. This is based on the Philips type of slot but has diagonal slots which enables more force (twist) to be exerted.

It can be quickly inserted by power drill or spiral ratchet screwdriver and will replace standard slotted heads for repetitive jobs, such as boat-building.

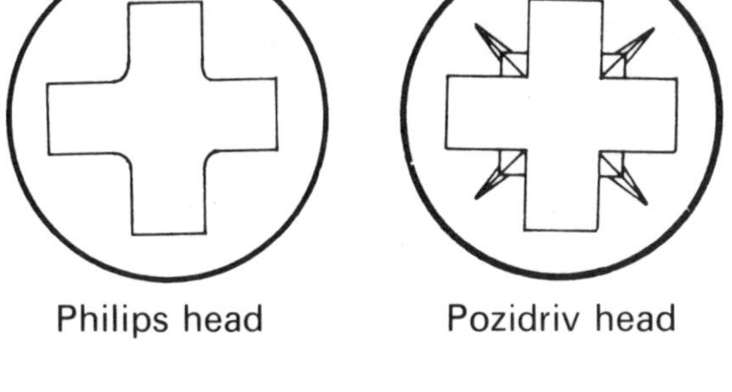

POZIDRIV HEADS

The use of Pozidriv recess in the head:

1. enables more twist to be put on the screw
2. prevents the driver from slipping out and damaging the surrounding work or the screw head
3. allows more vertical pressure which also
4. makes withdrawal of screws much easier.

One disadvantage is that a small deposit of paint or polish will cause the accurately machined driver to 'ride-out' of the slot.

Three sizes of screwdriver, called simply 1, 2, and 3, cover a screw gauge range from 4 to 12.

This new slot is used with all three common head shapes. Screwdriver bits for braces, hand drills and power tools are available.

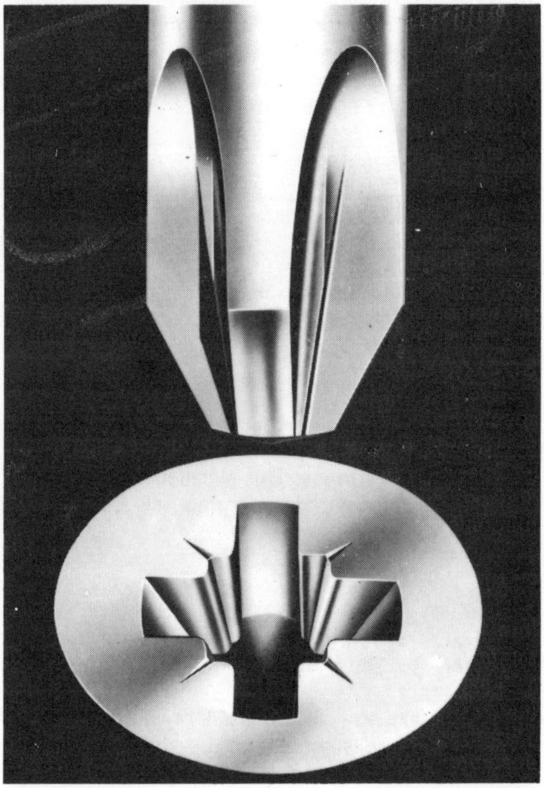

The photograph below shows a plastic cover cap which can be pushed into the Pozidriv recess of a countersunk head to give a neat appearance.

METHODS OF SCREWING

Wood to wood. Where possible the screw length should be three times the thickness of the top piece.

When making pilot holes for small gauge screws in softwoods a bradawl hole will be adequate.

For heavier screws or in hardwoods, holes must be drilled to prevent splitting and when brass screws are used in hardwoods a steel screw of the same size must first be inserted, to prevent the weaker brass screw from being over-twisted and broken.

1. A hole is drilled in the top piece giving clearance to the screw shank.
2. In the bottom piece a hole is bored about half the thickness of the shank.
3. If necessary the hole is countersunk. This can be done in one operation by a Stanley Screwsink of the correct size which fits any 8 mm chuck, e.g., the hand drill or electric drill. The wood surface is 'scored' and the fibres compressed when the screw is driven in.

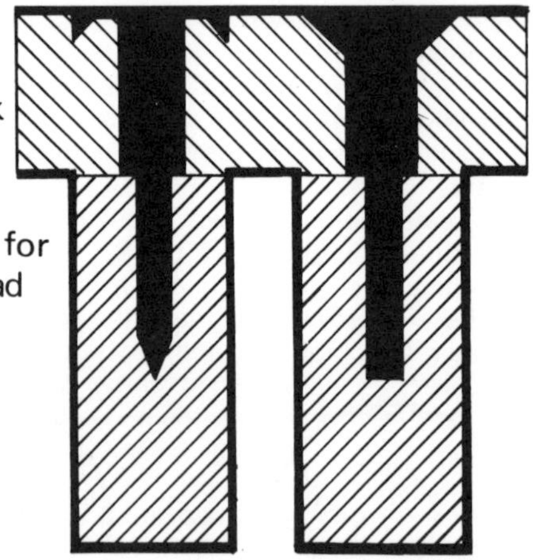

4. The screwsink is used in the electric drill to bore a hole (6–8 mm deep) so that the screw head is well below the surface. This is called *counterboring.*

A plug cut from matching materials is then glued into the hole.

Plug cutters match Screwsink sizes.

Metal to Wood. If ordinary screws are used two holes, one for the shank and one for the thread will be necessary.

1. If twinfast screws are used only one hole, the diameter of the shank, need be drilled to slightly less than the screw length.
2. In all cases insertion and subsequent withdrawal of screws is helped by waxing or lightly greasing the screw thread before driving it in.

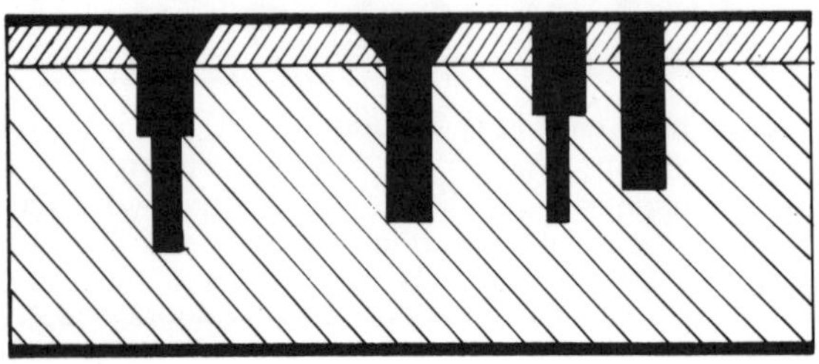

Sizes of Bits or Drills to Bore Holes for Wood Screws

Number of screw	4	5	6	7	8	9	10	12
Drill size for pilot hole (mm)	2·80	3·20	3·60	4·00	4·40	4·80	5·00	6·00
Suitable common drill size (mm)	3·00	3·50	3·50	4·00	4·50	5·00	5·00	6·00

ABRASIVES

From the times when the Egyptians used sandstone blocks, abrasives have developed relatively slowly but with the comparatively recent introduction of new materials it may not be long before the glasspaper we use today will be a thing of the past.

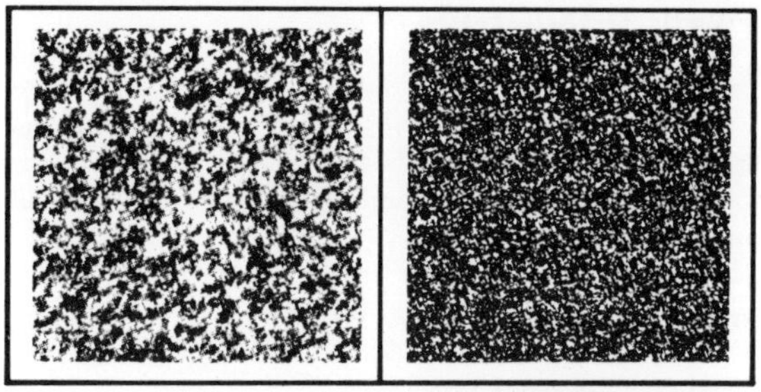

VARIOUS GRADES

The variety of abrasives now in use is considerable. The materials are stuck to paper or cloth backing sheets by animal or resin glues. Comparative grades are tabled on page 188 at the back of the book. The abrasives sheets are termed 'open coat' or 'close coat' depending on whether the grains are spaced out or close together on the sheet.

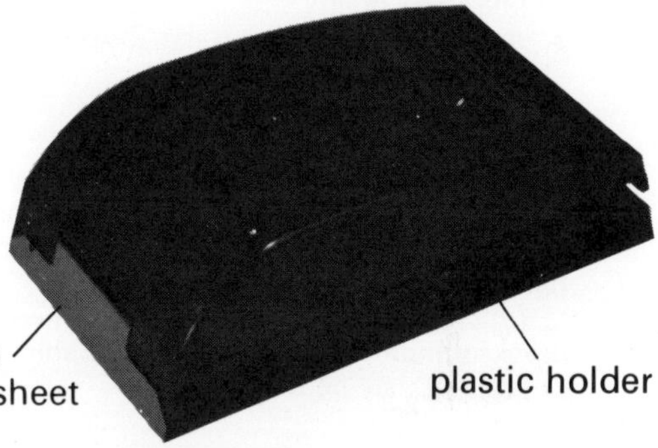

COMMON TYPES

1. Glasspaper—crushed bottle glass which quickly blunts and clogs.
2. Garnet—Red in appearance, is harder than glass but still tends to clog.
3. Aluminium Oxide—artificial abrasive used on machine sanders. It is especially good on hardwoods, keeping sharp and therefore not burning by friction.
4. Silicon Carbide—artificial abrasive which is hard and brittle. The backing paper is waterproof and the finer grades (220 upwards) are ideal for flatting cellulose, etc.
5. Tungsten Carbide—this is made by Cintride Ltd., and has an exceptionally long life. It cuts quickly and as the backing sheet is metal, can be cleaned with a wire brush. Best suited for joinery work and is effective on plastic laminate and grp.

Most of these abrasives are available in disc and sheet form for machine use. Sheet sizes are 280 × 230 mm and cut lengthwise once, and twice across, they fit a standard size block.

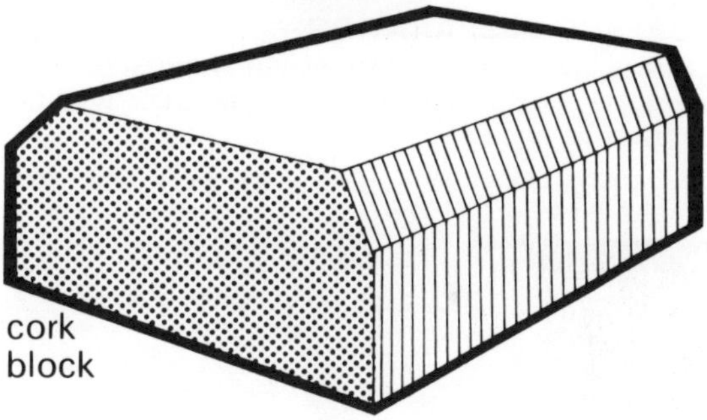

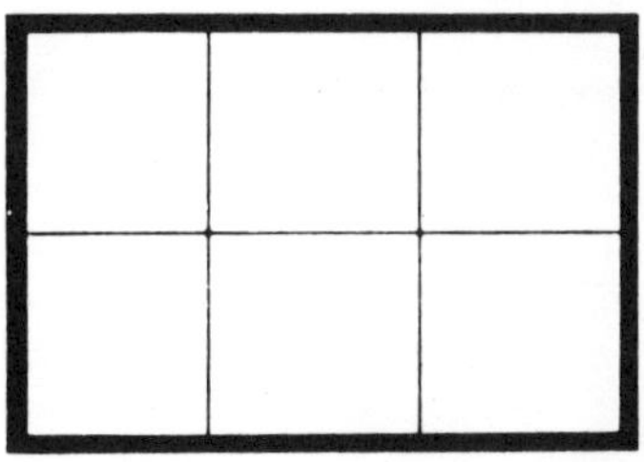

ABRASIVES IN USE

The cork block has the necessary 'give' to achieve a fine surface except on the most difficult grain. Abrasives must be used in the direction of the grain to prevent unsightly scratches. Mouldings must be done with specially shaped blocks. *Steel wool* in grades 3, 2, 1, 0, 00, 000 can also be used as a finishing abrasive and *flatting paste*, used between coats of synthetic finishes, consists of a fine abrasive powder in a solvent.

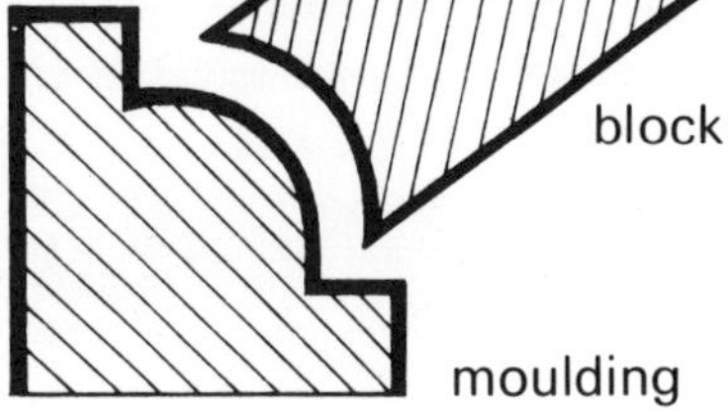

35 FINISHES

Finishes are applied to wood surfaces for the following reasons:
1. to give surface protection against dirt, grease and moisture
2. thus making surfaces easier to clean and more hygienic.
3. the grain is often sealed completely giving resistance to warp etc.
4. to improve appearance by changing colour or emphasising grain
5. to give a variable surface gloss, satin or matt.

CHOICE OF FINISH

There are hundreds of finishes available for timber and your choice may depend upon:

Type of Work—Table tops must resist heat and garden furniture, moisture.

Type of Wood—There may be a need to match other furniture for colour or surface shine and filling or staining may be necessary.

SURFACE PREPARATION

To obtain a good finish all wood surfaces need adequate preparation and this is true whether hardwoods or softwoods are used.

THE SURFACE MUST BE FLAT AND SMOOTH

This is best achieved with a smoothing plane and, if necessary, a cabinet scraper.
1. Surfaces to be painted, usually softwoods, should be glasspapered diagonally across the grain working with a medium grade (80).
2. Hardwood surfaces generally are given a clear finish and should be glasspapered with the grain working through the grades (80 to 180).

FILLING THE GRAIN

In most cases this is not necessary, but to obtain a high gloss on open-grained timbers such as oak, filler must be used.

Ready-made fillers, transparent or tinted to all shades of timber, can be purchased and these are superior to homemade types. If stain is to be applied to the timber it should be added to the filler before it is applied.

The paste can be rubbed in across the grain with a rag, and as drying time is from only a few minutes to one hour (depending on whether it is water or spirit based), any excess must be quickly rubbed off across the grain with linen and finished along the grain with a soft cloth.

Most finishes may be applied over them but in all cases the *manufacturers instructions must always be followed.*

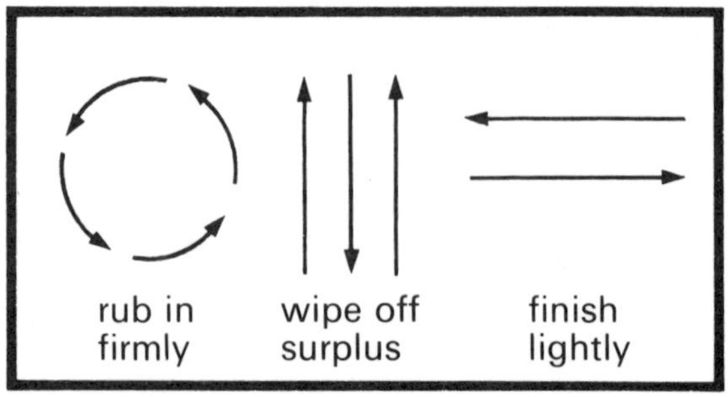

Most surfaces require glasspapering before a finish is applied—the abrasive paper is wrapped round a cork block.

Right: A spirit stain in cream form being applied with a foam pad.

Far right: A heatproof finish being applied with a brush. Note the adhesive tape protecting the gluing surfaces of joints.

FINISHES—STAINS OR DYES

Stains are usually applied:

1. To darken the surface colour of the wood—perhaps to match other furniture.
2. To imitate a more expensive or rare wood.
3. To emphasise the natural grain patterns in the wood, making it more attractive.

Apart from the colour which is in some polishes or finishes there are three main types of stain.

1. Water
2. Oil
3. Spirit

Water stains are easily mixed from powders and crystals and are easy to apply but they tend to fade and raise the grain (this can be avoided to some extent by previous wetting of the wood and rubbing down).

Oil stains are effective, but sometimes deaden the natural beauty of the grain and prevent some modern finishes from adhereing.

Spirit stains are quick drying and penetrate the wood fibres giving an efficient, fade-resistant dye. To prevent streakiness it must be applied quickly, although the recent introduction of a cream stain makes this hazard a thing of the past.

APPLICATION

The stain is usually applied with a brush or rag, but the cream stain is readily applied with a pad of foam (waste upholstery material can be used for this purpose).

Cautionary measures are:

1. Before staining the actual job, always test the colour on a waste piece of similar material. Stain is not easily removed!
2. Modern finishes are complex and it is advisable to use recommended stains:

e.g. With Ronseal 'Hardglaze' use Colron wood dye; with Furniglas 'Hardset' use Furniglas fadeless wood dye.

WORKSHOP FINISHES

The development and use of superior synthetic finishes has made the traditional use of french polishing materials inadequate, and they offer distinct advantages.

1. They are easily purchased
2. Relatively simple to apply
3. Extremely resistant to wear
4. Each is designed to do one type of job well.

Most jobs that are designed and made in the school workshop can be finished with:

Paint or enamel
Brush polish and wax
Oil
Cellulose
Acid-catalysed lacquer
Polyurethane lacquer

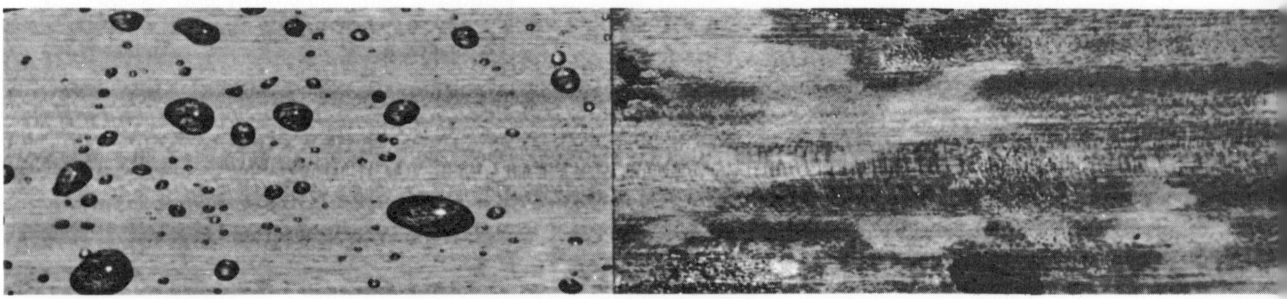

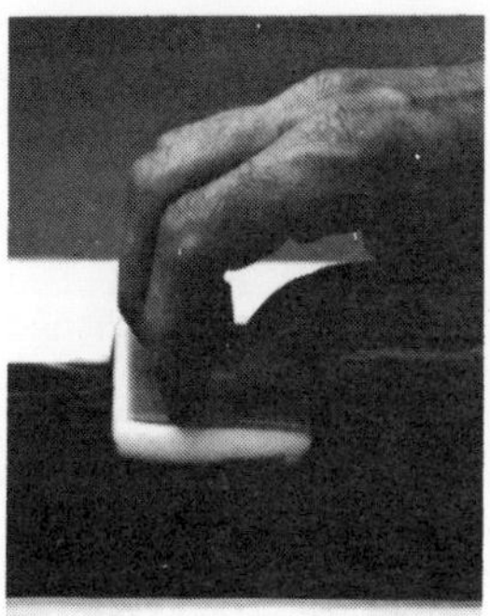

Above: Protection against liquids on table tops is necessary—in this instance a polyurethane finish (left) is effective.

36 FINISHES—MATERIALS

The materials required for giving a protective coating to wood surfaces, apart from the liquids themselves, are relatively few and are:

1. Abrasive—glasspaper or garnet paper and steel wool
2. A quantity of rags including coarse linen and soft cloth
3. Brushes of the best quality that can be afforded
4. A supply of jars with screw tops and labels
5. Appropriate thinners—white spirit and methylated spirits, cellulose thinners and those supplied for acid-cured lacquers

Let us now look at the different methods of finishing various objects you are likely to make in your school workshop.

PAINTING

Internal; softwood door to be painted.

1. The surface is prepared.
2. Resinous knots which may spoil the finished surface are sealed with knotting (shellac and meths).
3. A priming or sealing coat, probably with a lead base, is applied.
4. Any nail holes or cracks are then filled with stopping.
5. Surface is glasspapered (100) by hand to remove roughness caused by raised grain. Remove dust.
6. Apply thin layer of undercoat.
7. Lightly glass-paper when dry, care being taken on edges. Dust.
8. A protective coat is then applied with varying degrees of gloss.
9. All coats should be thinly and evenly applied to obtain the best finish. Additional coats of under- or top-coat may be used.

Hardboard-covered doors that require painting must be sealed with hardboard sealer prior to painting. Boards that are pre-sealed may be bought (see section 12).

External; garden gate to be painted. Procedure as for indoor work, but taking particular care to seal the porous end grain.

The polyurethane type, such as Kingston 'Diamond', dry quickly and form a thin high-gloss film which has a high resistance to weather, abrasion and chipping.

The undercoat is an eggshell paint which can be used internally as a finish.

Manufacturers' instructions must be carefully followed in regard to intervals between coats.

ACRYLIC PAINTS

Acrylic paints are fairly common nowadays and one of the features that make them easier to use than ordinary paints is the fact that brushes can be cleaned in running water.

Acrylic is a plastic which, when dry—in about four hours—is hard-wearing, water- and steam-resistant. The absence of oil means that the white is permanent (no yellowing) and all colours are fade-proof. It can, therefore, be used on wood surfaces that are subject to direct sunlight or heat.

The silky, gloss finish is for indoor use only, e.g. kitchens, bathrooms and particularly nurseries, since it is free from lead.

USE ON NEW MATERIALS

It is possible to apply acrylic paint direct but the following primers are recommended:

Pink Wood Primer or *Acrylic Undercoat* for **soft-woods.**

Aluminium Styptic Primer for **resinous soft-woods** and **hardwoods**.

Primer Sealer White for **hardboards** and **fibre-boards.**

HIGH SPEED ACRYLIC UNDERCOAT

This undercoat dries in an hour which means that two undercoats plus a topcoat can be applied in one day.

APPLICATION OF ACRYLIC PAINTS

Apply the paint generously and spread it evenly and quickly. It will soon touch-dry and brushmarks should disappear.

Clean all equipment with water immediately after use.

ADVANTAGES OF PAINT

Paint is readily available in a large variety of colours and surface finishes. It is easy to apply and gives a truly protective finish.

CARE OF BRUSHES

Brushes may be temporarily immersed in water to prevent hardening but should be cleaned as soon as possible in white spirit or other brush cleaner.

WAX FINISHING

Internal; walnut cigarette box to be wax polished.

1. Before gluing-up the joints are masked and the insides polished.
2. The outer surface is prepared. This close-grained hardwood does not require filling or staining.
3. A thin coat of brush polish (a mixture of shellac and meths) is applied.
4. After about 30 minutes this will be dry enough to

glass-paper lightly (180) and a second thin coat applied.
5. Drying time will be about an hour—warmth quickens drying—when the wax may be applied.

There are two ways of doing this;
1. Lightly glasspaper, dust, and apply wax evenly with a soft cloth. When dry, polish with a coarser linen-type material.
2. Apply wax directly on a pad of ·00 steel wool. This method allows the wax to penetrate the shellaced surface and leaves an attractive sheen rather than a high polish.

TYPES OF WAX

Excellent wax can be made by adding pure turpentine to beeswax.

Ready-made polishes of good repute have additives, such as silicones, which give greater protection against abrasion and water than just beeswax.

Wax finishes are not resistant to harsh treatment or heat and although they *can be easily renovated* are not suitable for table tops etc.

OIL FINISHING

External; garden seat in Burma Teak to be oiled.
1. The surface is prepared, down to 120 glass-paper only, as the oily grain clogs finer papers.
2. The seat may be assembled before the finish is applied.
3. The oil is applied with a rag and rubbed well into the grain.
4. When dry glasspaper lightly and apply second coat with a brush.
5. Treatment must be annual to preserve the rich colour of the wood. If neglected it will go a 'silver' colour but will not rot.
6. When used internally the surface may be finished with wax on steel wool.

TYPES OF OIL

Teak is a naturally greasy timber which may reject finishes other than oil. An oiled finish gives excellent protection and emphasises the attractive grain patterns.

Boiled or raw linseed oil, mixed with a small amount of turpentine to quicken drying and warmed to make application easier, is commonly used.

Special *teak oils* are made with additives of *synthetic resins* which *accelerate drying and* give high *resistance* to *heat and moisture.* e.g. Rustins Teak Oil (6 hours) Granyte Ultra-Rapid (2 hours).

CARE OF BRUSHES

Wax finishing—brushes may be stored in the brush polish or cleaned in methylated spirit.
Oil finishing—rags used to apply oil soon harden and should be thrown away—the brushes cleaned in white spirit.

CELLULOSE & ACID-CATALYSED LACQUERS

Internal; nursery stool in Parana pine, to be cellulosed.
1. The surface is prepared as for hardwoods.
2. No filling is necessary because of the high solids content of the cellulose.
3. Sanding sealer is applied and when dry is lightly glasspapered and dusted.
4. One or more coats of cellulose finish are quickly and evenly applied by brush. They soon become touch dry but must be left overnight.
5. Gloss finishes can be improved by rubbing down with fine steel wool between coats and burnishing the final coat with paste—finally polishing with a soft cloth.
6. A non-gloss finish may be achieved by rubbing down the final coat with wax on steel wool and lightly polishing.

TYPES OF CELLULOSE

Remarkable improvements have been made in the quality of cellulose. It can be bought with a variety of surface finishes and qualities and is easily applied.

A contrast to the natural wood finish is provided by a white enamel cellulose—ideal for use in nurseries, bathrooms etc.

Both finishes are resistant to abrasion and hygienic in use.

Because the material is highly inflammable the room must be well ventilated and free from dust.

ACID-CATALYSED LACQUER

Internal; a tea tray in sapele-faced plywood to be lacquered.
1. The surface is prepared. If filling is necessary, it should be one that is recommended by the lacquer manufacturer.
2. The acid hardener is added to the resin in the quantity stated on the bottle and mixed. A screw-top straight-sided graduated jar is ideal for this job.
3. Apply mix quickly and do not overbrush.
4. This coat will soon be touch dry and after one hour may be rubbed down with grade 400 wet and dry paper.
5. The second coat (and third if necessary) are applied in same way.
6. The final coat must be left overnight and finished to a gloss by burnishing or to a satin/matt finish with steel wool and wax.

Note—Avoid any *metal fittings* on the tray. Keep the air-tight jar in a cool place.

TYPES OF LACQUER

Mainly of the 'two-pot' type they offer high resistance to water, heat, alcohol, fats, acids and abrasion.

The introduction of a small quantity of melamine increases their performance—raising the solids content and eliminating the need to fill the grain. Ideal for surfaces in kitchens, bars, dressing tables and bathrooms, but not for exterior use.

CARE OF BRUSHES

Brushes may be stored or cleaned in cellulose thinners and when used in acid-cured lacquer must be washed in supplied thinners and a detergent immediately after use.

VARNISHING

External; WBP grade plywood canoes need absolute *protection against abrasion and water.*

1. Surface is prepared and all the nail-holes are filled.
2. First coat of varnish, thinned with 10 per cent white spirit, is applied with a rag and rubbed well into the grain.
3. The next day a second coat may be applied with a brush.
4. This should be glasspapered down before the third and subsequent coats are added. The resistant qualities of the finish will be directly related to the number of coats that are applied.
5. The edges of the plywood should be sealed with special care.

POLYURETHANE TYPE

Although oil varnishes are still extensively used for marine and outdoor work, polyurethane-based finishes are now in common use. The most reliable types are similar to acid-cured lacquers in that they require the addition of a hardener, i.e. they are two-pack types.

The one-pack type is easier to use—the addition of oils prevent the curing or drying from taking place in the can. It also allows a small amount of white spirit to be used as a thinner and brush cleaner.

Internal; It is useful for coffee table tops and in its matt form for the currently popular wall panelling.

Coloured polyurethanes include Oak, Walnut, Teak, Blue, Red, Yellow, Orange, Green and Purple. These are effective on light-coloured woods such as Birch faced plywood and blockboard.

Internal; It is useful for coffee tables tops and in its matt form for wall panelling.

PRESERVATIVE

There are many branded types of wood preservatives on the market—many of which are oil-based to repel water (see photo p. 101). As Western Red Cedar cladding on building is popular, many are designed to maintain the attraction of that particular timber and contain a suitable stain.

CREOSOTE

This is a dark liquid derived from coal tar and is used to preserve exterior woodwork, such as fences and garden sheds etc.

For home use it is applied with a brush. Paraffin will act as a thinner and will also clean brushes.

Surfaces mellow to a deep brown colour, require annual treatment and are not suitable for painting at a later date.

BRUSHES

Ideally, brushes, which are a most expensive item in the finishing kit, need cleaning after use.

Some may be temporarily stored, paint brushes in water and cellulose brushes in thinners.

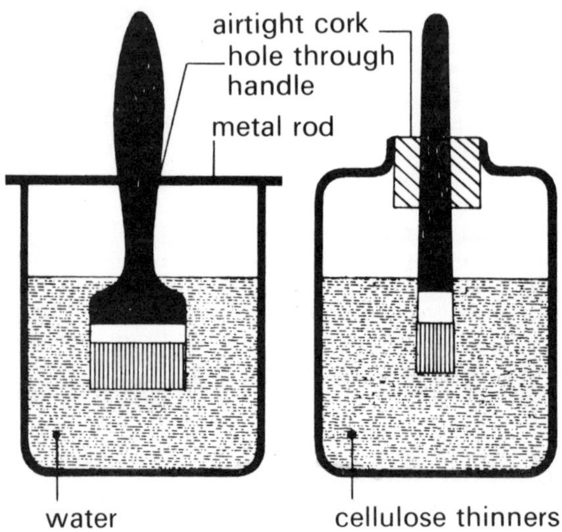

EXAMINATION QUESTIONS

25-26 GRIND & OILSTONES

1. What lubricant is used *(a)* when grinding on a sandstone; *(b)* when finishing an edge on a sharpening stone? (SE)
2. Describe the faults that may develop in grindstones and oilstones and state what results these faults may have when tools are being ground and sharpened.

How would you true a worn *(a)* oilstone *(b)* grindstone?

3. Name the object shown below and state what it is used for.

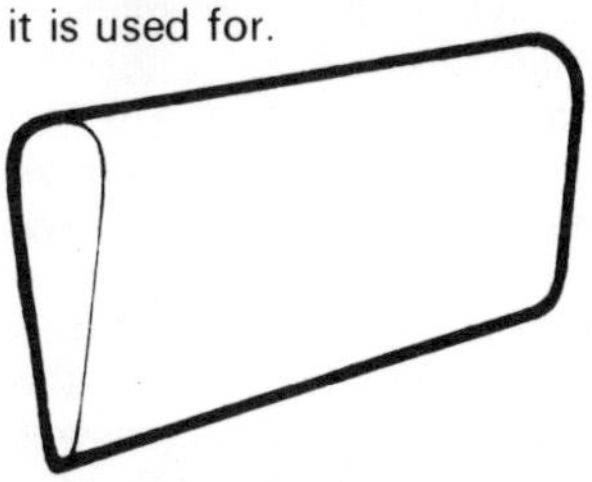

4. How should a worn oilstone be restored to good cutting condition?
5. Why is it essential to use a flat stone and not one that has worn hollow? Why is a lubricant used when sharpening? (WM)
6. What advantages have artificial grindstones and oilstones over natural materials?
7. The blade of a wooden jack plane needs sharpening (not grinding). Describe in detail, how to remove the blade from the body, to sharpen the blade and then to replace the blade so that the plane is ready for use.

27 SHARPENING

1. Three of the finishing processes are planing, scraping and glasspapering. Imagine that you are instructing a beginner how to carry out these processes in cleaning up an oak table top.

(a) What advice would you give him about using the smoothing plane?
(b) Explain (using sketches with notes) how to put a cabinet scraper in working order, and also how it is used.
(c) What advice will you give about glasspapering? State suitable grades for this job. (SE)

2. Sketch the section through the edge of a cabinet scraper when sharpened and ready for use. (MET)
3. Make a sketch of a scraper and explain how it is sharpened.

28 WORKSHOP EQUIPMENT

1. If you were to design a small workbench for use at home what good qualities would you expect it to have?

Make a concise list of any fittings you would include.

2. You are to design and make a sawing stool.

Make a neat pictorial sketch of the finished job and a large size detail of the joints used.

When necessary make written notes to explain your design.

3. Sketch a bench hook (sawing board) showing how you would fix the parts together.

Name a suitable material with which to make it. (WM)

29 APPLIANCES

1. You are required to make a set of dominoes. The overall dimension of a single domino is 50× 30×8 mm. The 28 piece set is from 0/0 to 6/6 with the spot marking as illustrated below:

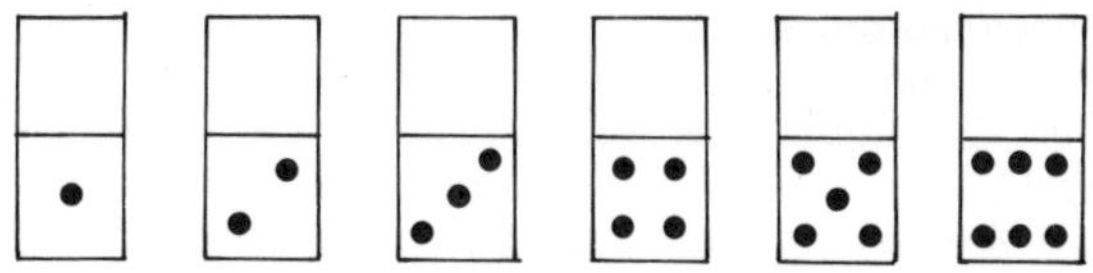

The dominoes are to be produced from a piece of planed hardwood 1450 mm long, 30 mm wide and 8 mm thick.

Design and make a freehand drawing of a jig to assist in *(a)* the cutting of the material into 28 equal lengths. *(b)* the marking of the centre line. *(c)* the marking of the spots. (The spots may be produced by drilling a shallow hole with a 4 mm drill.)

N.B. You may, if you consider it to be an advantage, design a SINGLE jig that will assist in the performance of all THREE FUNCTIONS. (MET)

2. Make a sketch of a template or pattern you have used in the workshop. State the material from which it is made and why that material was chosen.
3. You are to make a chess board from 50 mm squares of solid wood 6 mm in thickness.

By means of notes and sketches, show an appliance you might make to ensure that the squares are accurately made.

30-31 ADHESIVES

1. Name a glue that it is necessary to heat before use. Name a glue that it is not necessary to heat before use. (MET)
2. Which glue would you consider to be most suitable for the following purposes:

(a) making a rubbed joint between two long boards to form a table top
(b) applying a sheet of Formica to a fitted kitchen working surface, so situated that no pressure may be applied to assist in the adhesion
(c) gluing a brass tube into a hole bored in a wooden table lamp base
(d) gluing together several veneers between

curved formers to make laminated ribs for a canoe
(e) gluing the frame of a stool (S)
(f) hammer veneering
(g) securing the mortise and tenon joints of garage doors? (SE)
3. What glue is used for making a rubbed joint between two long boards? Write about the glue you have chosen under the headings: *(i)* composition of the glue *(ii)* method of preparation *(iii)* advantages and disadvantages in use with respect to other common glues used in woodwork.
4. Many types of glue are now on the market. Name one and make a short list of its advantages over animal glue. (WM)
5. Giving reasons for your choice state the type of glue or adhesive you would use in each of the following processes;
(a) laying a veneer with a hammer
(b) securing dowels in the end of a plate rack which will be in contact with hot water.
6. Most gluing jobs in the home consist of gluing wood to wood, both indoor and out of doors, and occasionally metal to wood, pot to pot and similar jobs.

You are to purchase three types of adhesive to do these jobs. State the types you would choose, giving your reasons for doing so. (Remember that the adhesive may have to be stored for a considerable time).

32–33 NAILS AND NAILING

1. Make enlarged sketches of a panel pin and an oval wire nail. Name each nail. (S)
2. Which kind of nail would you use to fasten *(i)* boards to a garden fence *(ii)* a canvas top to a folding stool? (S)
3. Name and sketch five common types of nail and describe their uses.
4. By means of notes and sketches show how nails are effective in holding pieces of wood together. Show how the design of the nail can increase its holding power.
5. Explain by drawing in the nails with dotted lines on a copy of the drawing below how you would nail together the two boards shown.

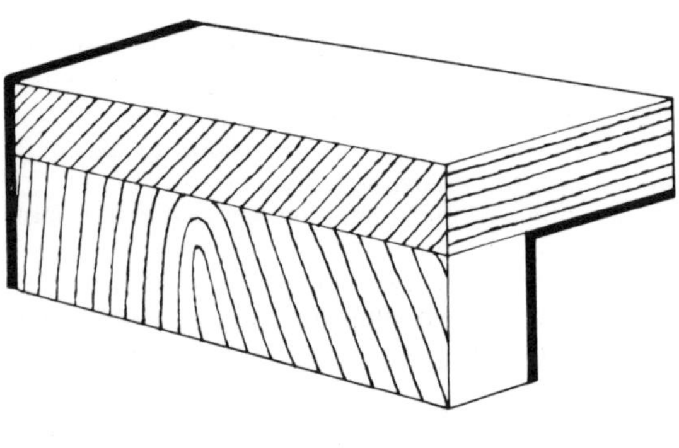

6. Make a sketch to show what is meant by 'dovetailed' nailing. Why is this done? (WM)
7. Give four examples with sketches of the use of nails in woodworking and two different examples where screws are best used.

34 SCREWS AND SCREWING

1. An order for wood screws reads as follows: 100 of 45 mm No. 8 Csk. Hd. steel screws. Explain what this means.
2. Write notes to explain why screws are made in such a wide variety of materials.
3. A box made of 15 mm softwood has a 6 mm plywood base fixed by means of 12 wood screws. Write down a specimen order for the screws required.
4. Chipboard is a difficult material to screw into.

How can screws gain an effective hold in this board? Use sketches to illustrate your answer.
5. In a wood screw, what is the purpose of— *(a)* the slot; *(b)* the head; *(c)* the shank; *(d)* the thread; *(e)* the tapered point on the end of the screw? (WM)
6. The backrest of an oak garden seat consists of 50 mm by 15 mm slats screwed to a 32 mm frame.
(a) specify the type of screw that you would order for this purpose and give reasons for your choice.
(b) describe the steps that you would take to insert one of these screws without causing damage to either the screw or the timber.

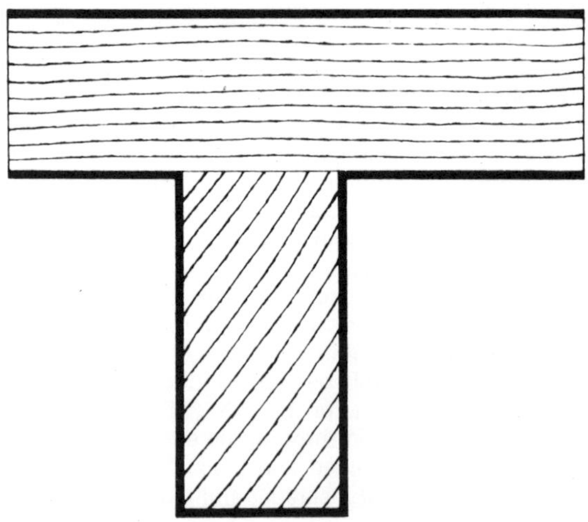

7. The sketch shows the actual thickness of two pieces of wood to be screwed together. Make a copy of the sketch and draw lines to represent the holes bored to receive a countersunk screw. (W)

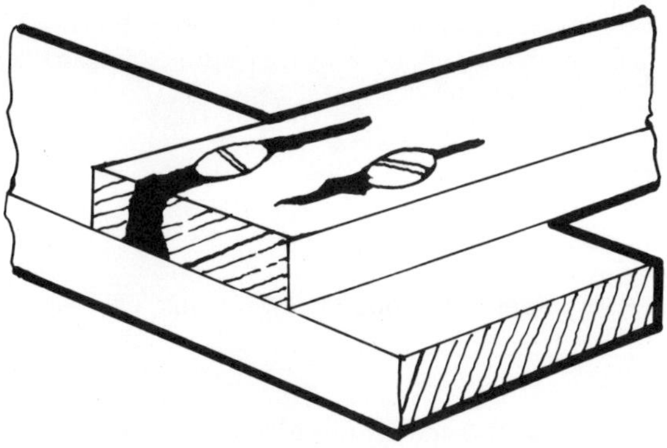

8. The drawing shows an example of bad screwing method. How could the problem have been avoided?

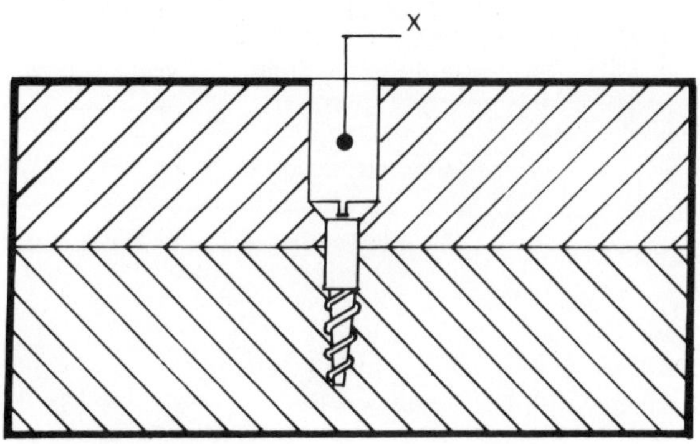

9. The section shows two pieces of wood screwed together. *(a)* What is the name of the hole labelled 'x'? *(b)* How might it be filled?

ABRASIVES

1. Various types of abrasive papers are used in woodwork. Write an account of such papers, covering the following points:
(a) the purpose of abrasive papers;
(b) the types available and how they are graded;
(c) when and how abrasive papers should be used. (JMB)
2. Why is a glasspaper block usually made of or faced with cork? (WM)

35-36 FINISHES

1. Name a suitable finish for:
(a) a hardwood stool frame;
(b) a model yacht;
(c) a guitar or other instrument.
For each of these describe in detail how you would carry out the finishing process. State: *(i)* the wood to be used; *(ii)* why the finish has been chosen; *(iii)* how the surface is prepared; *(iv)* how the finish is applied; *(v)* any special precautions necessary to ensure a good finish.
2. A bathroom cabinet made from softwood is to be finished in white enamel. Describe the stages necessary to obtain a good finish. What should be done with the brushes between stages and on completion of the work?
3. Describe in detail the process of painting a newly-made softwood gate.
How would you deal with *(a)* knots; and *(b)* make notes on the qualities required in the paints used and reasons why such qualities are desirable.
4. Wood very often has a finish applied to it. Why is this necessary? What finishes would be suitable for:
(i) a whitewood bathroom cabinet; *(ii)* part of a gatepost which is sunk into the ground; *(iii)* an elm bookcase; *(iv)* a finely figured table top?
Give reasons for your choice in each case.
5. As above for the following:
(i) a teak or elm garden seat (S)
(ii) a garden frame and light (S)
(iii) a wood book trough (S)
(iv) elm fruit bowl (S)
(v) columbian pine door
6. Assume that you have just finished turning a bowl from teak and that it is intended for use as a salad bowl.
Give an account of the steps you would take to finish the bowl ready for use.
7. Complete in your own rough book the following sentences:
(a) French polish is made from ....
(b) paint brushes are cleaned in ....
(c) wood floors are protected by ....
(d) the basis of paint primer is ....
8. How would you think three of the following materials?
(a) French polish
(b) Emulsion paint
(c) Oil bound paint
(d) Cellulose lacquer? (SE)
9. Give brief 'step-by-step' outline information to provide protective finishes for the following newly constructed jobs. In each case let No.1 be glass-papering.
(a) a greenhouse (European Redwood)
(b) a solid oak table requiring a natural finish
(c) a mahogany table requiring a high gloss finish. (SE)
10. Why is it important *(a)* to stir priming paint thoroughly before use? *(b)* to secure the lid of a paint tin after use? *(c)* to clean a paint brush after use?

STANLEY TOOLS LTD

SPECIAL TOOLS 4

You will be able to refer to this small section on 'special tools' when you use them for practical work. In addition, your teacher may also use it to supplement the work done in the theory schedule.

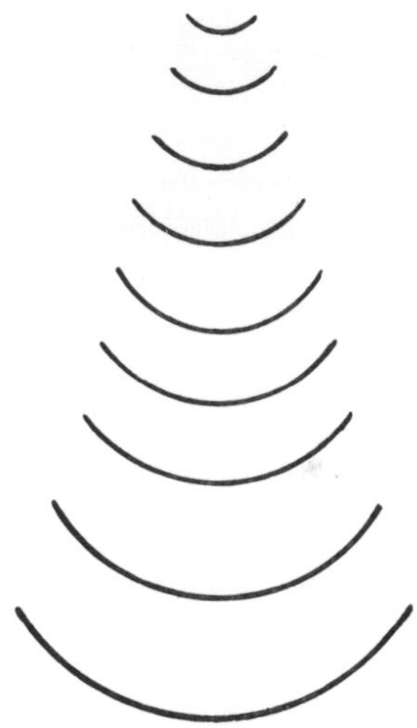

'E' sweep sizes

CUTTING TOOLS—GOUGES

Carving gouges vary considerably in both the shape of the blade and the curve of the cutting edge. These are more fully described in *Woodwork* 2.

In the days when much handwork was done with gouges the degree of curve of the edge was described by letters beginning at 'A'. This was almost flat like a chisel and 'F' was almost a semicircle.

The old 'E' sweep (this is found to be adequate for most work) in sizes from 6 to 38 mm, is generally available.

FIRMER GOUGE

Irrespective of its width the blade has the same curved section with the cutting bevel sharpened on the outside (the burr on the inside being removed by the appropriate oilstone slip). Its *main use is for hollowing out* such things as hand carved bowls and other sculptural work.

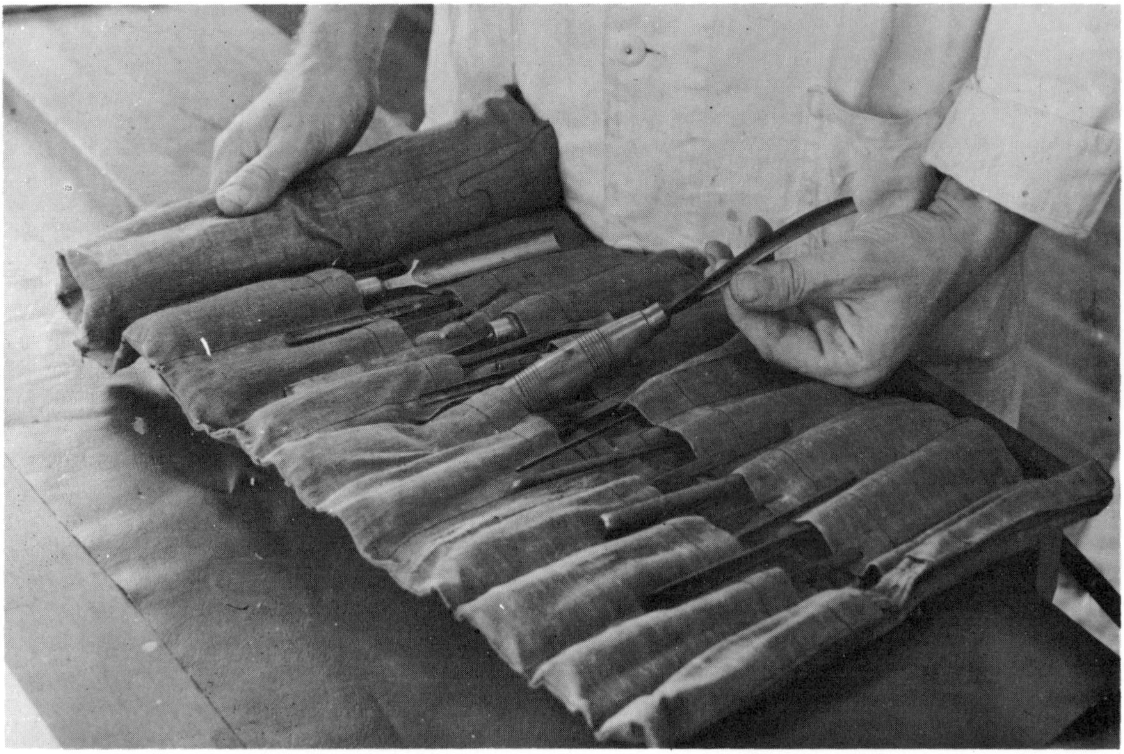

A set of carving gouges is stored in a protective canvas roll.

SCRIBING GOUGE (PARING)

A long version of the scribing gouge is called a paring gouge but both are used in a similar way *for cutting external curves.* The grinding bevel of 25 degrees is cut on a conical shaped wheel, the sharpening bevel with an oilstone slip and the burr removed on an oilstone. In effect, the sharpening process of the firmer gouge is reversed. Handles are either of the round ash or carving boxwood type (section 16).

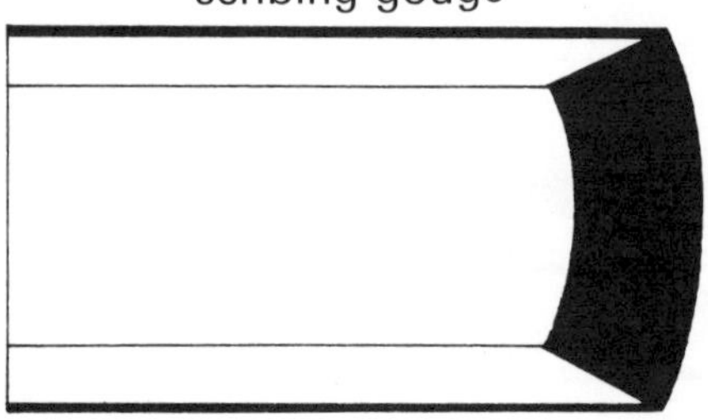

SPECIAL PLANES

To produce a fine shaving, all 'special planes' must have a sharp and finely set blade and a small mouth (this is not always adjustable). These planes are 'special' in that they are designed to do jobs other than produce a flat surface and the main difference from the bench planes (section 17) is the absence of a back-iron.

A lever cap is usually used to prevent 'chattering' in use.

BLOCK PLANE

This plane has the sharpening bevel uppermost and the blade is held by a lever cap at the low angle of 20 degrees.

The simplest kind is only adjustable for depth of cut but more expensive versions allow for lateral movement, as on the bench planes, and have a fully adjustable mouth.

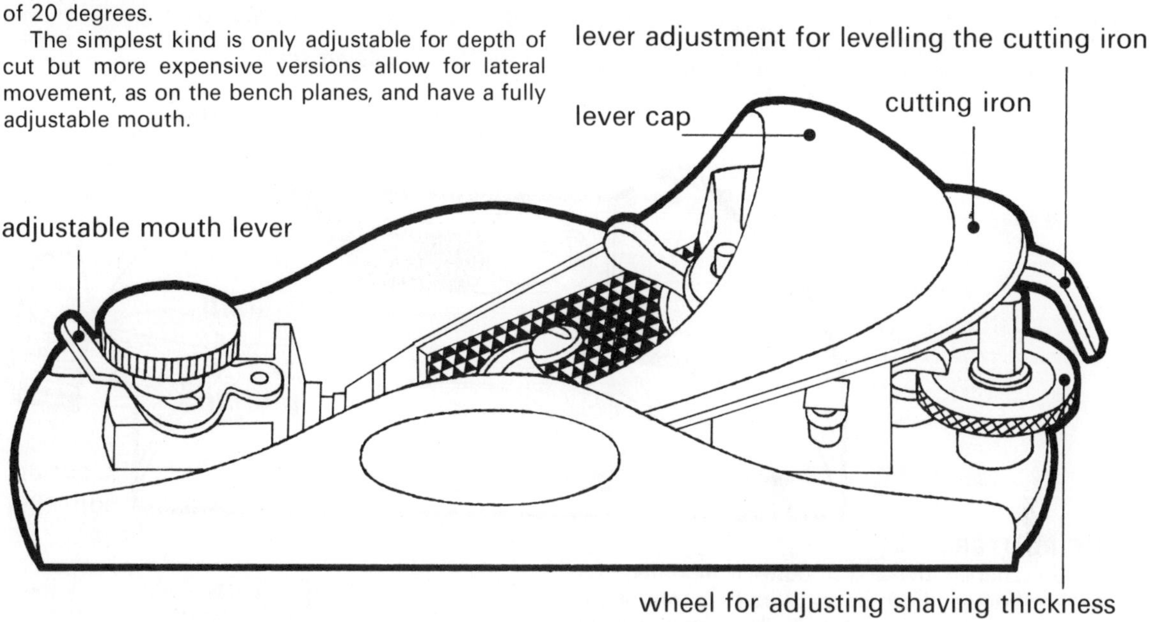

This extensive range of adjustment and the compactness of the plane make it *ideal for one-handed use, trimming mouldings, chamfering and cutting end grain.* It can also be effectively used on small shooting boards.

One model, the Stanley 60½, can be successfully used on laminated plastic veneers because the blade is set at only 12 degrees.

SHOULDER PLANE

This accurately-machined metal plane has a low-angled blade, bevel uppermost, and varies from 15 to 38 mm in width (the narrower versions being of most use) and from 100 to 215 mm in length. Generally they are *used for trimming shoulders* of large tenons *and for truing rebates* etc.

The blade must be sharpened perfectly square and lined up with the edge of the plane or it will dig-in or leave a step. It is held in position by an intricately shaped lever cap and the best types have a screw depth-of-cut adjustment.

A shoulder plane clearly showing the low-angled blade.

BULL-NOSE PLANE

This works on the same principle as the shoulder plane, and at 115 mm long can be considered a smaller version of it.

It can work close to the ends of stopped rebates and in some models the front can be unscrewed. In this state it acts like a mounted chisel.

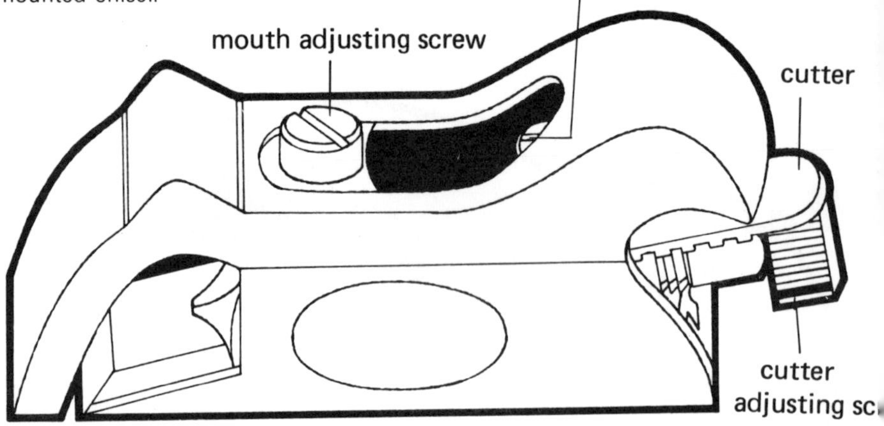

THE ROUTER

The L-shaped low-angled cutter is mounted in a cast iron body and can be adjusted for depth of cut by a nut on a vertical thread. The cutter is held firmly in place by an iron collar fixed by a wing nut.

Some planes are fitted with an adjustable depth stop and fence.

Its *main use is to clean out and level grooves and housing to a set depth*—the bulk of the wood usually having been removed by other means, such as a chisel.

There are two sizes of router, the larger having two hardwood knobs which can be firmly gripped with both hands. It has 6 and 12 mm cutters, and a V-shaped cutter for working into corners and because of its shape will also remove bulk waste.

The smaller, cheaper version has only a 6-mm cutter and as it can only be pushed with the thumbs is used for light work.

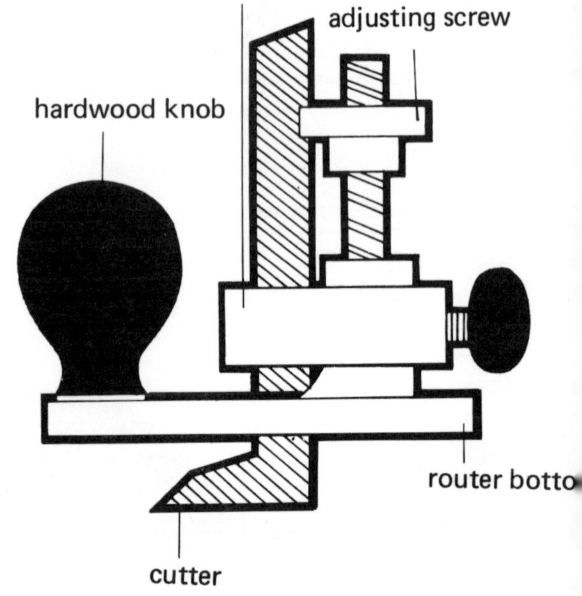

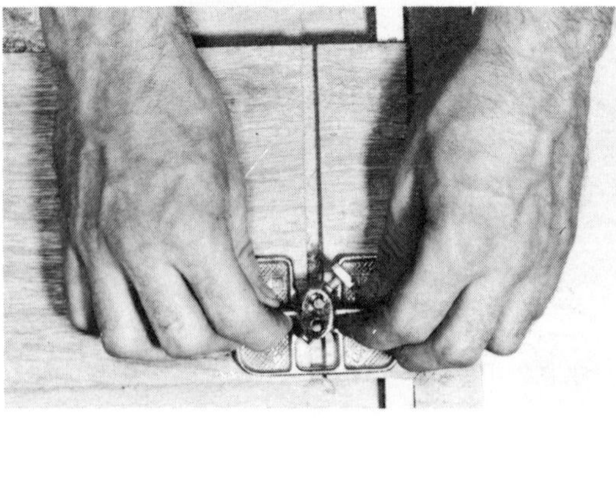

A bull-nose plane being used to trim shoulder

A hand router shown with alternative cutters.

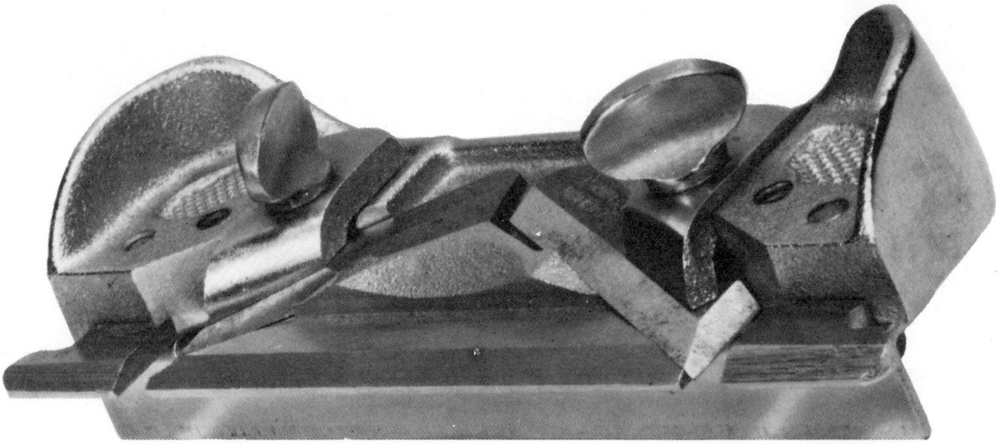

SIDE REBATE PLANE

The sides of housings and grooves are sometimes *in need of cleaning up or enlarging.* This can be done with one of these small planes which are

The front may be unscrewed for working up to the end of a stopped housing and a depth gauge can also be fitted to avoid digging-in.

The side of a housing being trimmed with the Stanley side rebate plane.

REBATE PLANE

Used for cutting rebates, the most useful type is called a Fillister rebate plane and has two cutter positions—one for bull-nose work (in this position the depth-of-cut adjusting screw is not in operation) and one for normal use.

It has a blade that will cut rebate widths up to 38 mm wide and an adjustable fence to regulate lesser widths.

A depth stop operated by a wing nut is fitted close to the spur, which can be brought into action to sever the wood fibres in front of the blade when cutting across the grain of a piece of wood.

Depth-of-cut adjustments are usually made by a knurled nut slotted into the end of the blade but some types are operated by a lever. A firm lever cap eliminates vibration when in use.

Remember three things:

1. begin cuts at the far end of the wood and work back.
2. keep the fence close to the wood by applying side pressure with the left hand.
3. keep the plane upright to ensure that grooves and rebates are square.

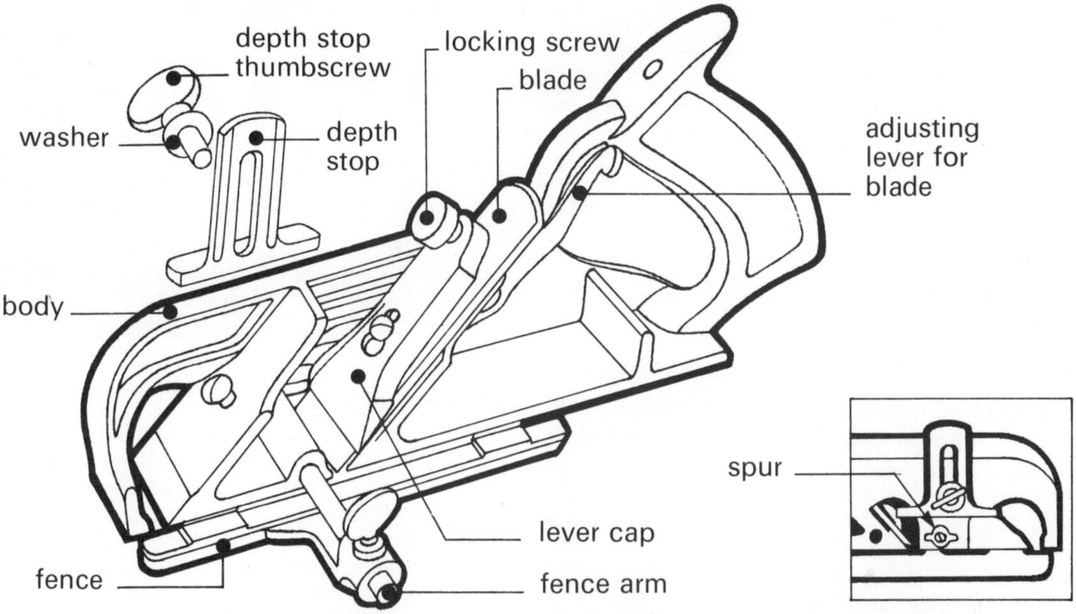

rebate plane in use—
ote that the rebate is worked
ack from the end of
e wood furthest away from the user.

PLOUGH PLANE

The main use of the plough plane is *for making grooves* to accept plywood and hardboard panels, glazing, sliding doors etc. In addition it can cut *rebates and housings.*

The eight standard cutters (3 to 14 mm wide) can be finely and accurately set with screw adjustments and special cutters for plywood panels (4, 6, 9 and 12 mm widths) can be obtained.

The standard plane has;

1. a double arm adjustable fence which can be used on either side of the cast-iron plane body.
2. a depth stop, adjustable to a depth of 15 mm.
3. extra long arms (bars) to allow for working up to 125 mm from the edge of a board.

The simplest plough plane is lighter and smaller than the traditional type. It will plough grooves from 3 mm to 12 mm wide, to a depth of 16 mm and up to 100 mm from the edge.

It lacks the fine screw-adjustment on the blade but the fence and depth stop are adjusted in the same way.

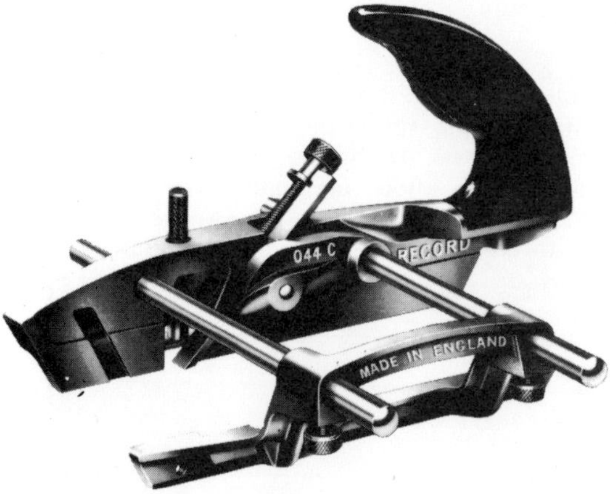

The latest plough plane design is styled for more comfortable handling with an open plastic handle replacing the closed saw-type handle.

PLANE SETTINGS

Although it might appear so, the setting-up of these special planes to do a job is not complicated. *Always check:*

1. the thickness of the cut
2. the depth (from the cutting edge of the blade)
3. the fence (which must be parallel to the side of the plane).

When setting the plane for use the measurements can be accurately made using any steel rule.

checking the depth

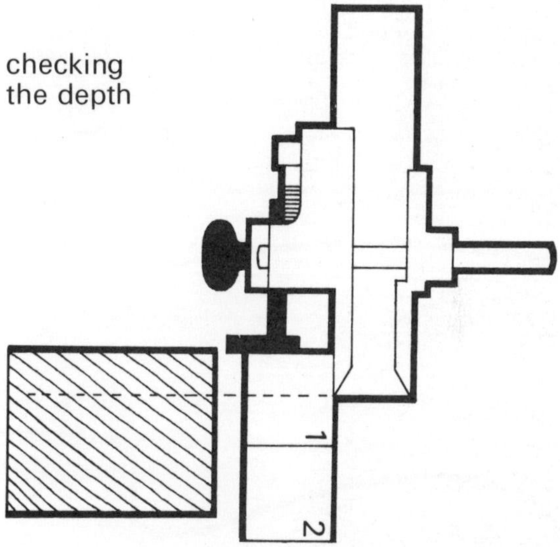

corner jointing

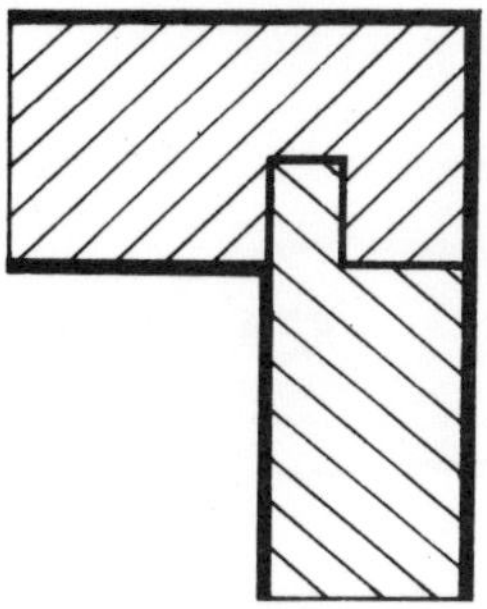

for edge jointing

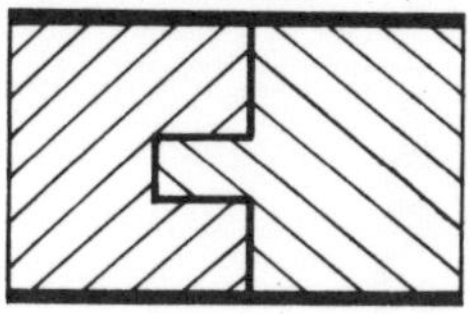

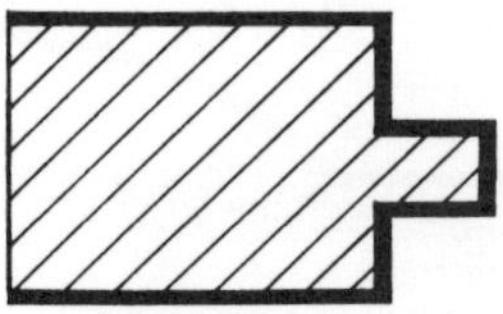

tongues

grooves 0 to 15 mm

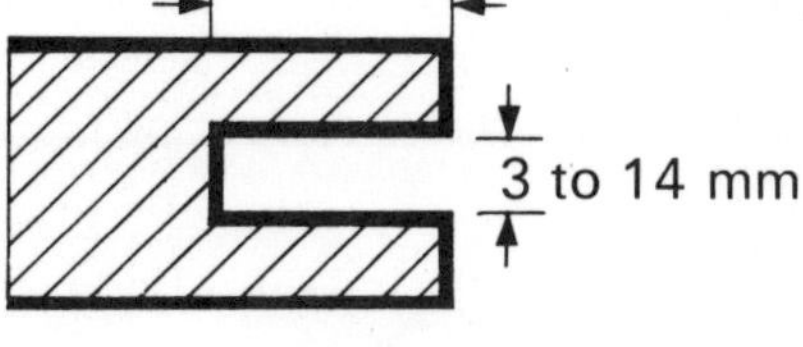

rebates 0 to 14 mm

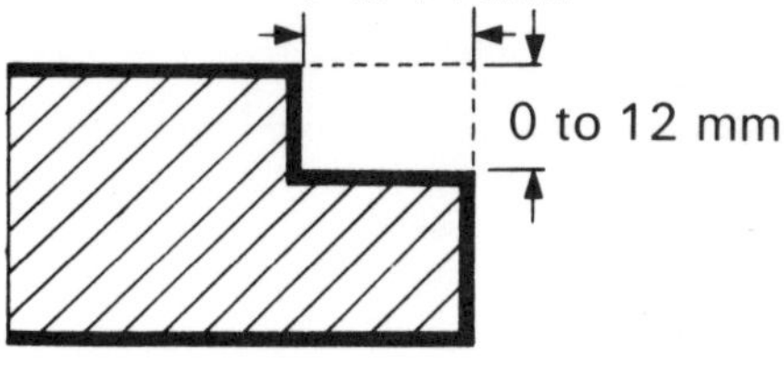

checking the fence

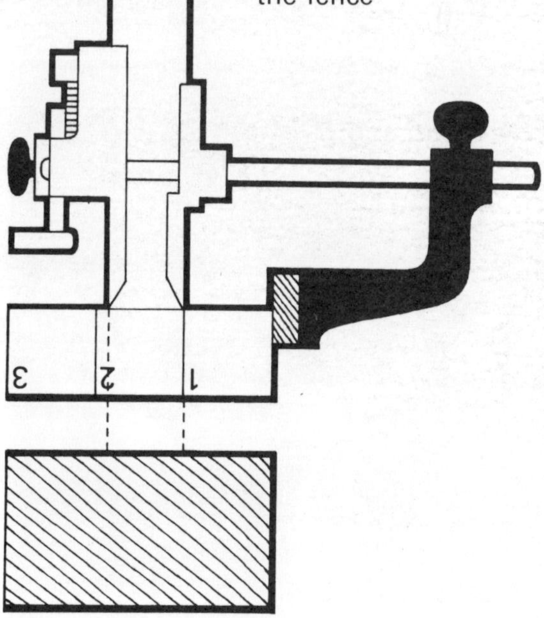

WOOD AND METAL SPOKESHAVES

Roundfaced wood spokeshaves made from close-grained boxwood are most pleasant tools to use, but their mouths wear out quickly and ill-fitting blades are a nuisance.

Although they are being replaced with two kinds of metal spokeshave (of malleable or cast iron) with identical blades (sharpening described in section 27) small wood spokeshaves are still of value. This is because they can hollow out tight curves which metal spokeshaves would not reach. Metal spokeshaves are similar in shape to the wood versions, but one has a *round face (for internal or concave curves)* and the other a *flat face (for external or convex curves.)*

Hollows for the thumbs are provided so that the 'wristy' pushing action needed is possible.

The thickness of shaving and lateral movement of the blade is effectively adjusted by two knurled nuts. The blade is firmly held by a lever cap which helps to break the shavings, but the mouth cannot be altered.

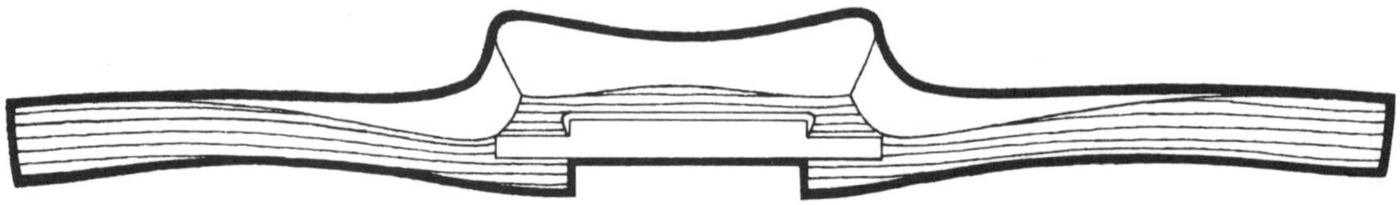

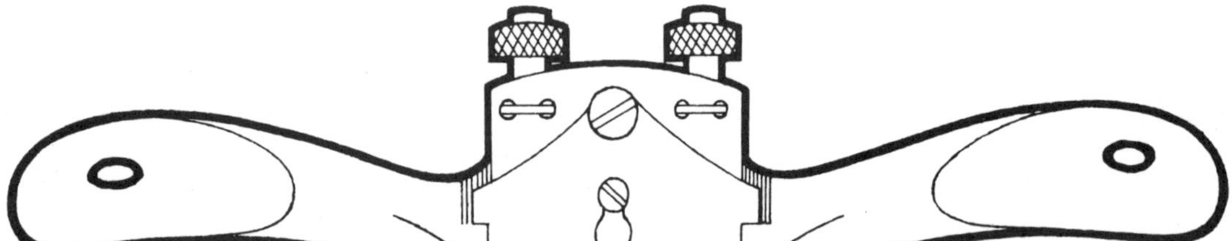

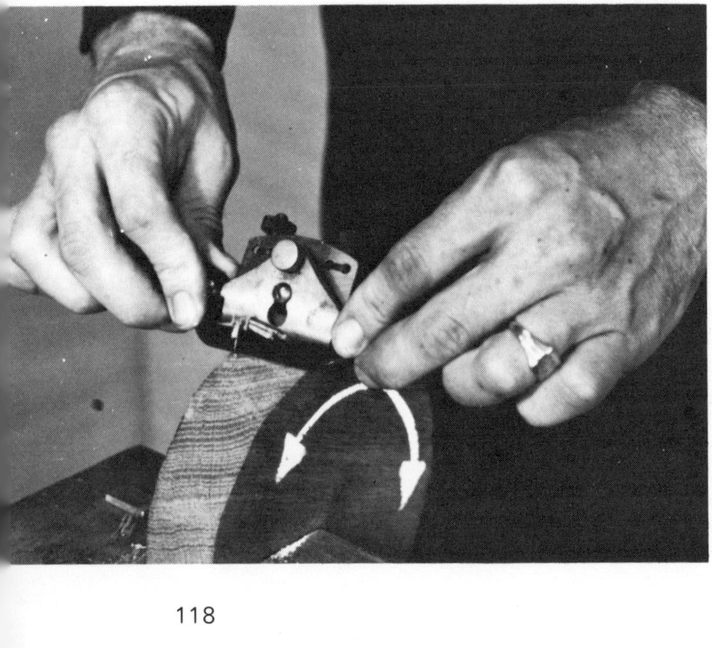

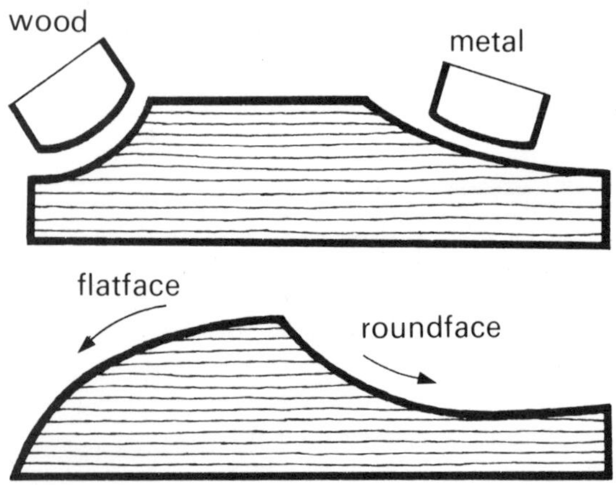

All curved work must be done 'down' the grain and considerable practice is needed to become proficient in their use. The skill, once acquired, enables bold stopped chamfers to be cut and wood carvers find them useful for finishing work.

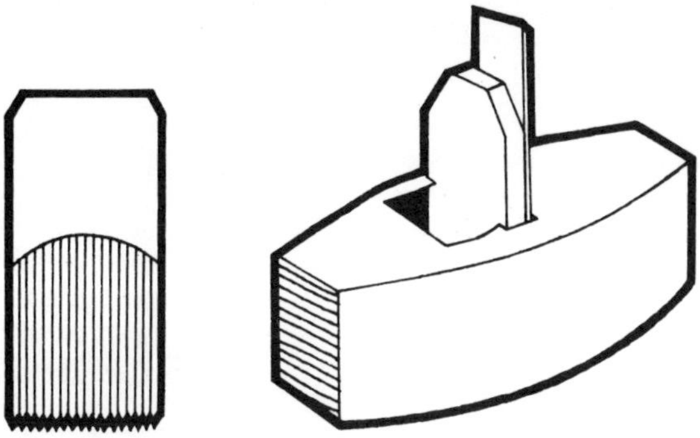

TOOTHING PLANE

The plane is *used when veneering by hand.* Similar in both shape and size to the old wood smoothing plane, it has a steeply angled blade without the support of a back iron and this, combined with closely cut V-shaped grooves on the face of the blade, produce more of a scraping than a cutting action.

It is *used for providing a key for glue* and *for making sure that the surface* to be veneered *is perfectly true.* Now that hand veneering is not common it is most often used when preparing thin strips of timber prior to laminating shapes.

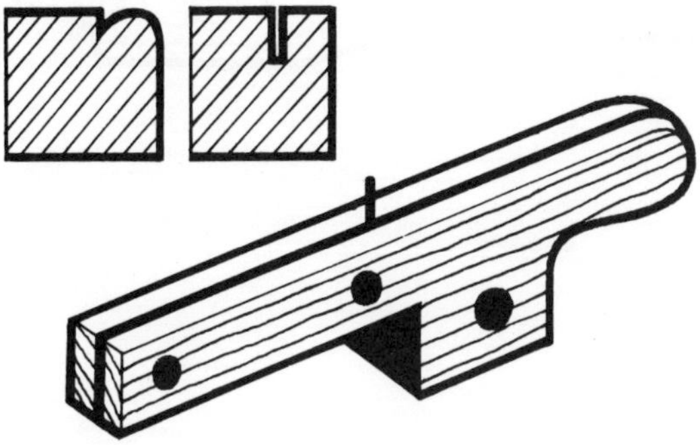

SCRATCH STOCK

A home-made tool with many uses including *cutting small mouldings* on panelling and *narrow grooves* for inlay.

Two pieces of hardwood are cut out to form a right-angle in which a blade is held by screwing the two pieces together.

Blades made from pieces of old hacksaw or similar material can be ground to any shape and grooves for inlay may be made with a bradawl blade.

SCREWDRIVER BIT

The joiner's brace (section 18) has strong jaws and with the wide sweep of the cranked handle is capable of exerting considerable force. This makes it ideal for inserting and withdrawing large screws and for this purpose a screwdriver bit is made.

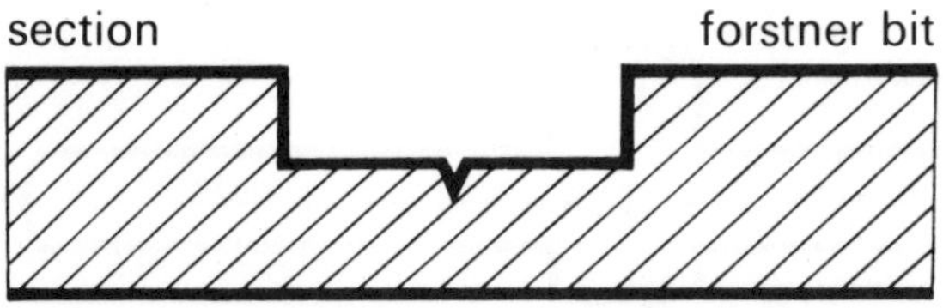

FORSTNER BIT

This has a shallow centre and a scribing ring inside which are two cutters. It bores a clean shallow hole which is unaffected by knots or awkward grain. It is not easily sharpened and should be stored carefully in a box. There are 24 sizes from 9 to 50 mm.

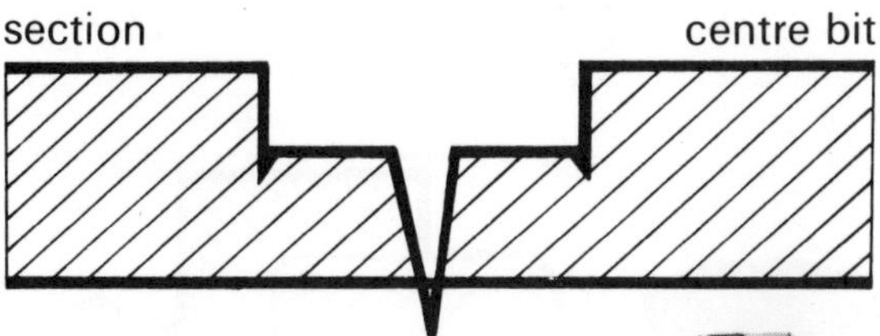

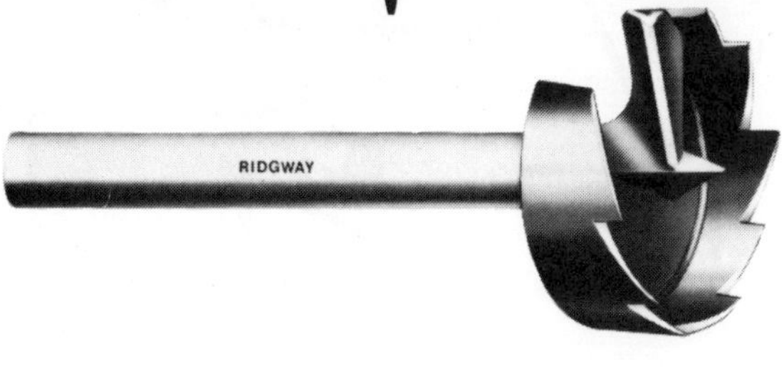

SAW TOOTH CENTRE BIT

Although it is designed for use in a power drill it is worth looking at because it will bore shallow holes (like the Forstner bit) up to a diameter of 89 mm. It is less expensive than the Forstner Bit and is much easier to sharpen. It bores clean, smooth holes with and across the grain, and can be used to remove waste in sculpture and carving.

EXPANSIVE BIT

The bit has a threaded centre, one scriber and two cutters, one of which can be adjusted *to cut holes up to 150 mm in diameter.*

The sketch shows the best type available, with a non-slip serrated cutter which is adjusted by a spring-loaded fixing plate.

The scale is helpful when setting the scriber but to be accurate, the diameter of the hole should first be checked by testing in a piece of scrap wood.

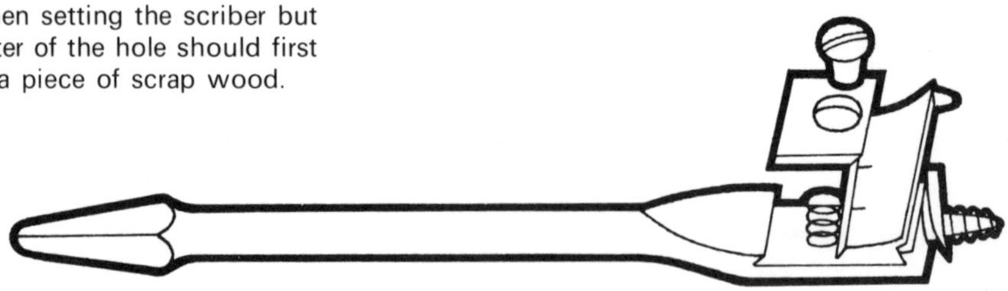

COMPASS CUTTER

If *holes larger than 150 mm in diameter* need to be cut (such as for speakers) they can be done with the compass cutter.

This uses a special high-speed bit with a side cutting action which can be fitted to any electric drill.

Holes up to 450 mm diameter may be cut in timber (50 mm) sheet metal (4 mm steel), aluminium (6 mm), plastic laminate hardboard, chipboard and plywood.

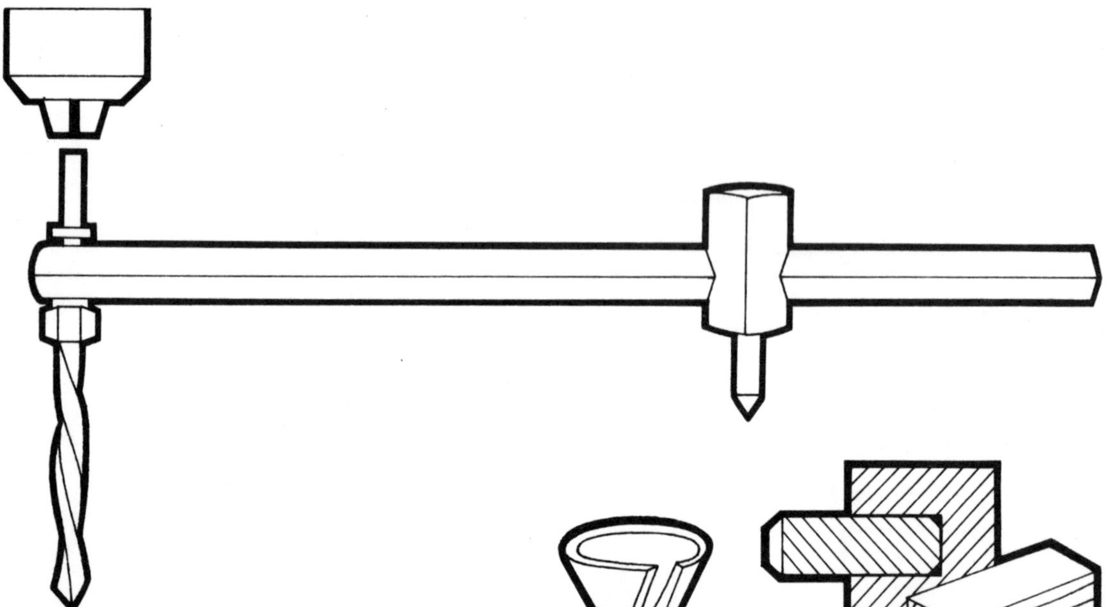

DOWEL BIT

This is a funnel shaped cutter 19 mm in diameter *used for chamfering the ends of dowels.*

It allows easy entry of dowels into holes and is useful where a number of dowelled joints are being used.

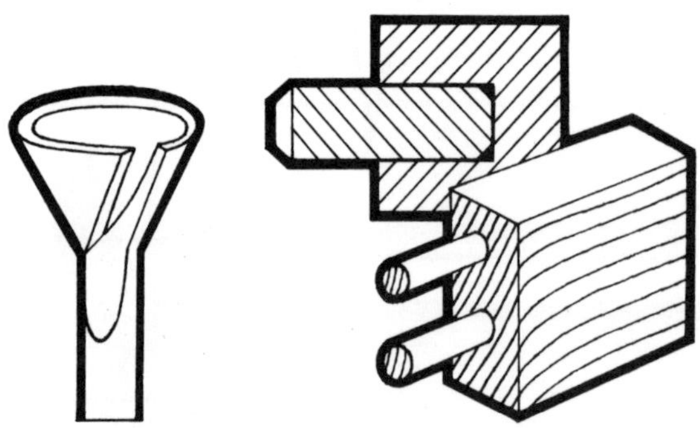

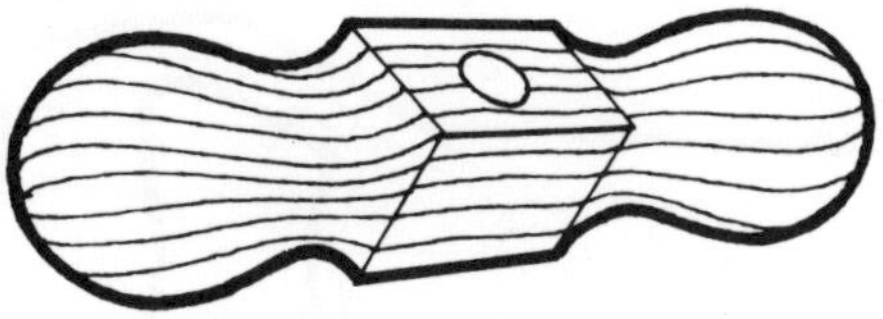

SHELL AUGER

This long bit is from 300 to 900 mm in length and from 6 to 12 mm in diameter. Using a rest or a special attachment it is fed into work on the lathe, e.g. *for boring deep holes* such as in lamp bases.

COUNTERSINKS

Snailhorn bits (for use in softwoods) and roseheads bits (for hardwoods and mild steel) are used for *countersinking for screws*.

Snailhorn

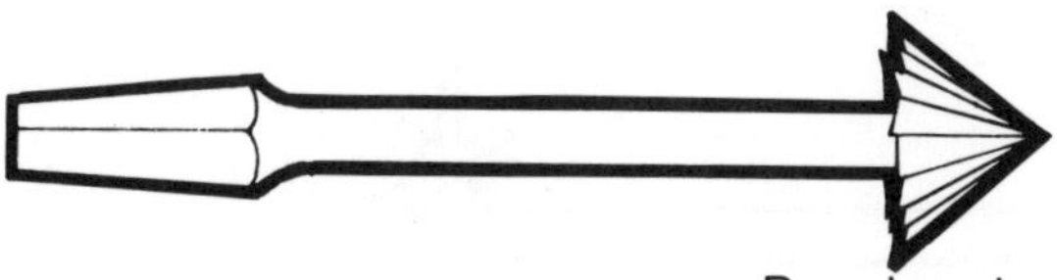

Rosehead

SAWS—PAD SAW (KEYHOLE)

The saw consists of a hardwood handle which is slotted throughout its length to receive the tapered blade. In this way only the amount of blade required need protrude.

It is fixed by two screws threaded into the brass ferrule. Blades 200 to 300 mm long.

Stanley produce an effective 150 mm blade *for cutting keyholes and similar cuts started from a hole*, and which fits into the handle of a trimming knife.

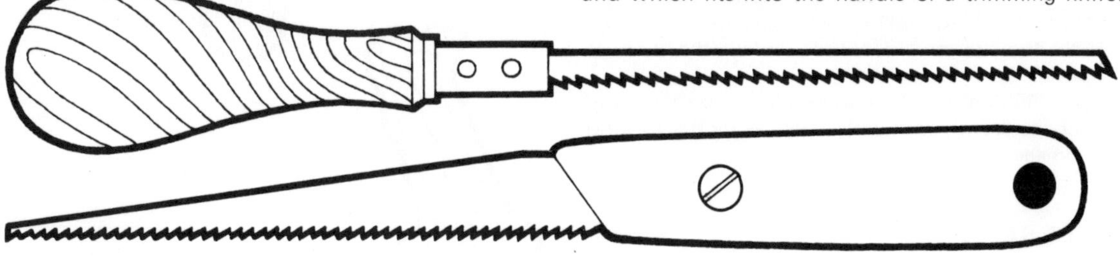

COMPASS SAW

Used in a similar way to the pad saw the longer and stronger blade is fixed into a more orthodox saw handle which allows *heavier work* to be carried out.

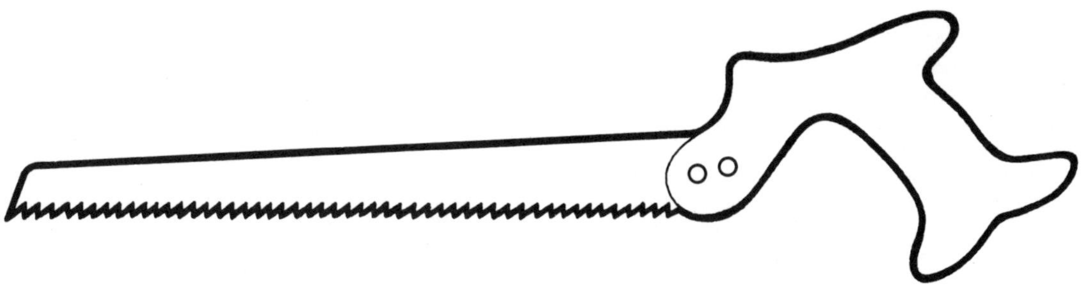

GENERAL PURPOSE SAW

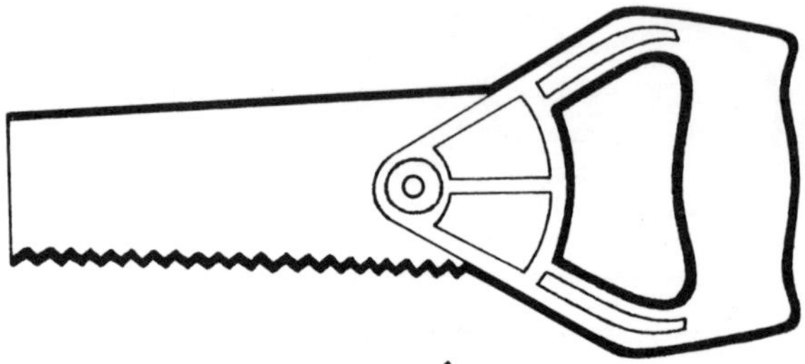

The Eclipse company fits a high-speed blade (for use on both metal and wood) into a symmetrical alloy handle.

The blade can easily be adjusted to nine different working angles and is fixed by a wing nut.

It is ideal *for sawing in awkward places.*

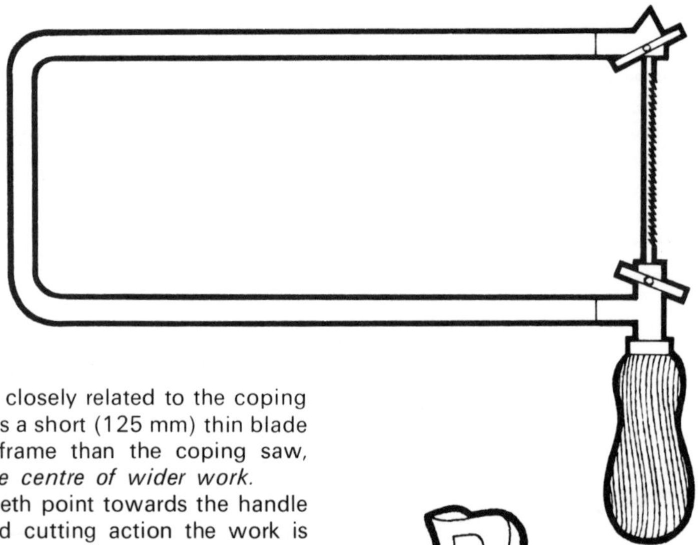

FRET-SAW

This is a frame saw closely related to the coping saw (section 20). It has a short (125 mm) thin blade and a much deeper frame than the coping saw, *allowing access to the centre of wider work.*

In use, the blade teeth point towards the handle and for the downward cutting action the work is supported on a V-board.

It is intended *only for cutting curves in thin wood* and consequently is mostly used in model making and similar crafts.

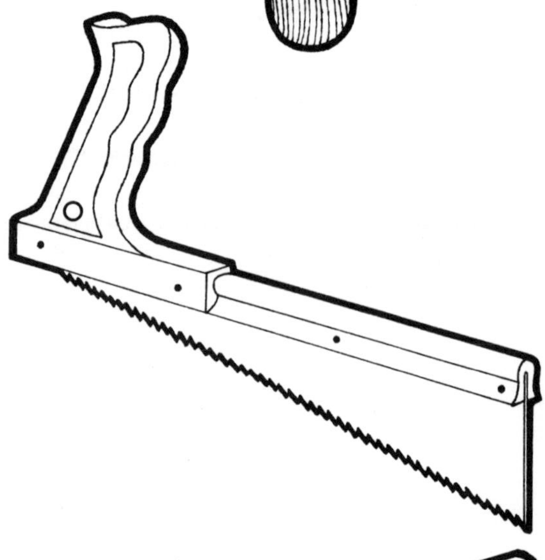

SHEET SAWS

High speed steel blades, similar to those used in hacksaws (which are not sharpened but replaced when blunt) are made to be screwed into a firm alloy back.

They enable the woodworker to make effective cuts in wide boards of both wood and laminated plastic without splitting or cracking the surface. They are also useful where hidden nails may be suspected since they will cut mild steel.

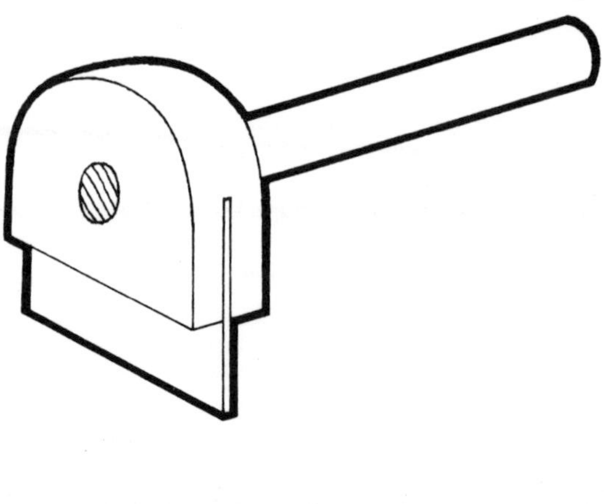

VENEER HAMMER

In an age when most veneers are laid by machine or are self-adhesive this tool is less often used. It is not a hammer in the normal sense of the word (it is not used for striking) but is used for 'driving' out surplus glue from beneath the surface of a veneer.

The sketch shows clearly its simple construction —the brass or alloy 'blade' being rounded and polished to prevent damage to the thin surface of the veneer.

SPIRAL RATCHET SCREWDRIVER

This is of most use where large numbers of medium sized screws have to be inserted—such as in some types of boat building.

1. It drives in or withdraws the screw when pressure is exerted.
2. It can be used as a fixed screwdriver.
3. It is of most value in awkward corners where its length from 340 to 700 mm is used to advantage.
4. It is fitted with interchangeable bits which vary widely in size.
5. For easy use, careful lubrication with light oil is necessary.

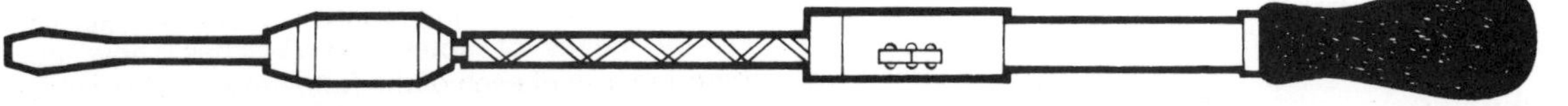

POZIDRIV SCREWDRIVERS

These are specially designed for use with the Pozidriv screws described in Section 34.

They are designed to exert great pressure on the screw head which, besides making for stronger joints means that stubborn screws can be more easily withdrawn.

The Stanley Pozidriv drivers are available in three sizes (1 to 3) to match the screw heads.

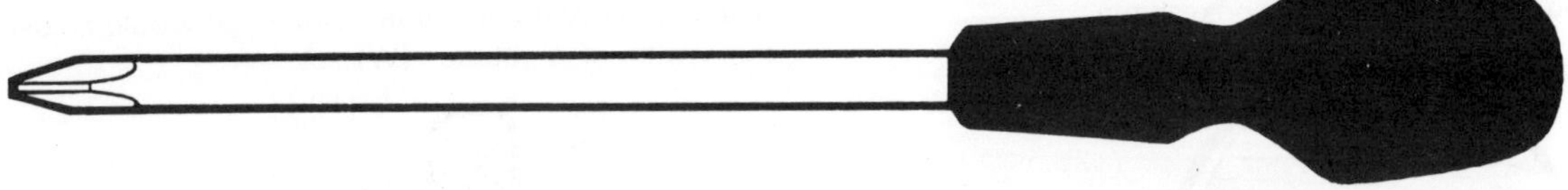

HOLDING DEVICES—HANDSCREW

This tool is of ancient origin and although G-cramps and holdfasts are now more common the handscrew still has many uses.

It is made of beechwood chops with boxwood or metal screws, and works on the lever principle, the forward screw acting as the fulcrum.

1. It has a large jaw capacity.
2. Is capable of cramping awkward angles.
3. Spreads pressure over a wide area.
4. Thus no cramping blocks are necessary.

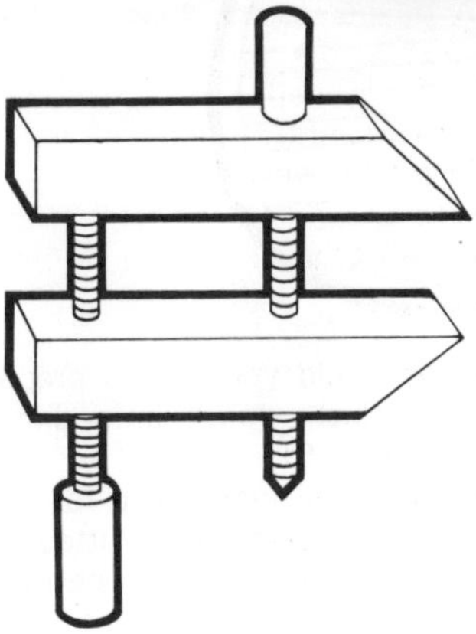

THE MITRE CRAMP

For securing mitred joints a cramp is made to take frames (up to 100 mm wide) enabling gluing and pinning to be carried out.

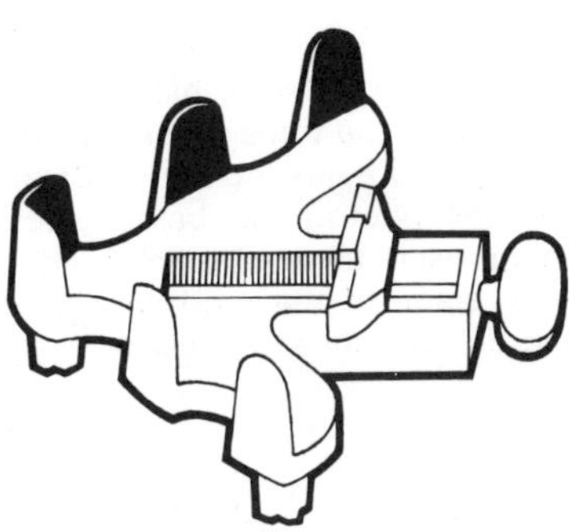

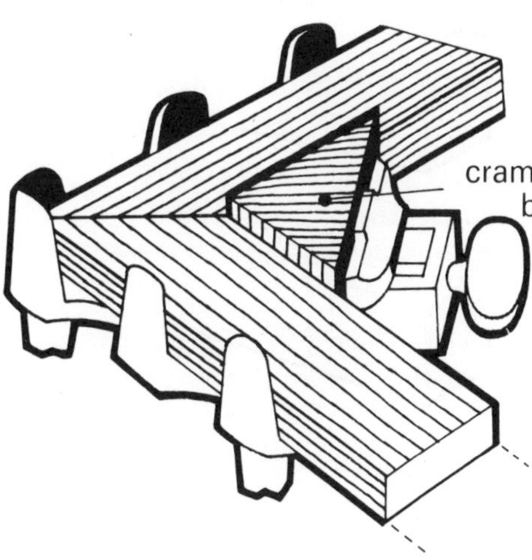

EXAMINATION QUESTIONS

GOUGES

1. Some gouges are sharpened inside, others outside. Name both kinds.
2. Describe briefly how you would sharpen—*(a)* a scribing gouge; *(b)* a firmer gouge.
   Make a sketch of any special stone which you may have to use.

PLANES

1. Name one type of plane that does not have a back iron.
2. Name a plane that may be used to cut a groove. (MET)
3. Name the tool used to clean up a very long housing joint.
4. The drawing below shows a circular coffee table. On your copy of the drawing insert arrows to show the direction of the cutting action when truing the edge to shape with a spokeshave.

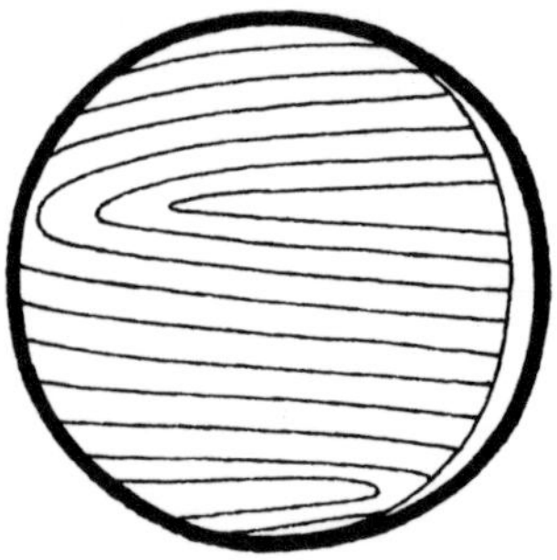

5. Which plane would you use to prepare a wide surface (e.g. a flush door) immediately before gluing on a veneer? (SE)
6. Name the tools you would use for—(i) cutting a slot to enable a 'ply' panel to be fitted. (ii) cutting a recess to enable a glass panel to be fitted.

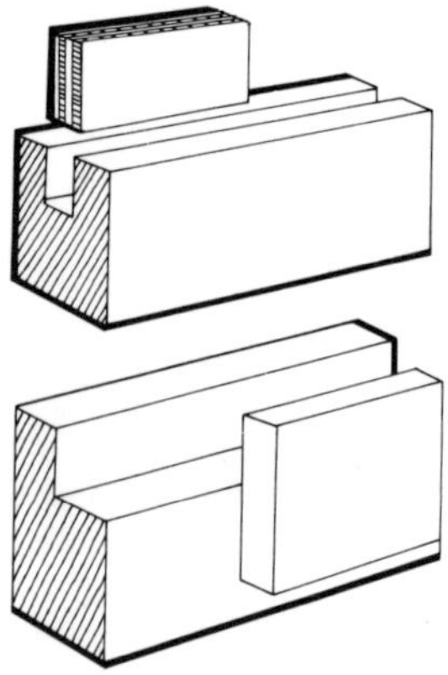

7. What is the approximate angle of a pitch for the cutting iron for these tools:
(a) smoothing plane.
(b) shoulder plane? (SE)
8. Which tool would you use to smooth an outside curve that you have sawn on a piece of wood? (S)
9. Name the plane you would use to make level and true the base of a trench for a housing joint, running across the grain. (S)
10. Sketch a block plane and indicate its use. (S)
11. By means of notes and sketches show one important use of each of the following—*(a)* shoulder plane *(b)* plough plane *(c)* router plane.
   It is not necessary to draw the planes.
   Make a full size pictorial sketch of the blade of each plane.
12. When would you use a spokeshave with a round sole? (S)
13. The drawing below shows the end of a rebate plane. Make a copy of the drawing and on your copy indicate with a letter D the part you would adjust to set the plane to the required depth and with a letter W the part with which you would adjust the width of a rebate. (W)

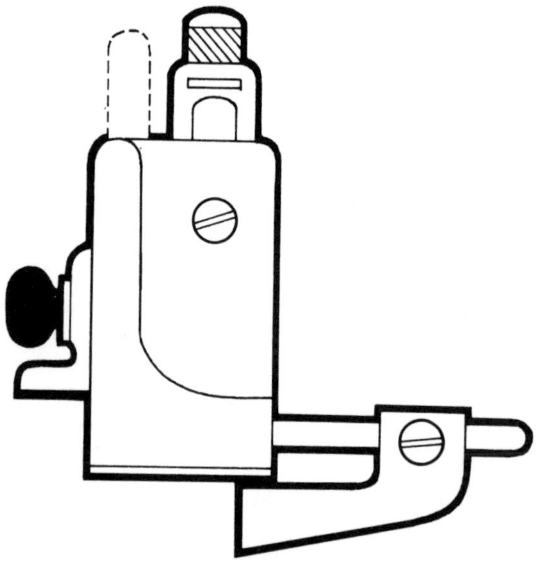

14. In woodwork various planes are used. *(a)* name **three** different planes *(b)* give a typical use of **each** of the three planes *(c)* explain in detail the cutting and adjusting action of **one** of the planes.
15. The photograph below shows a hand router being used to level a stopped housing. State at what stage of the work you would use the plane and use sketches to show how you would adjust it.

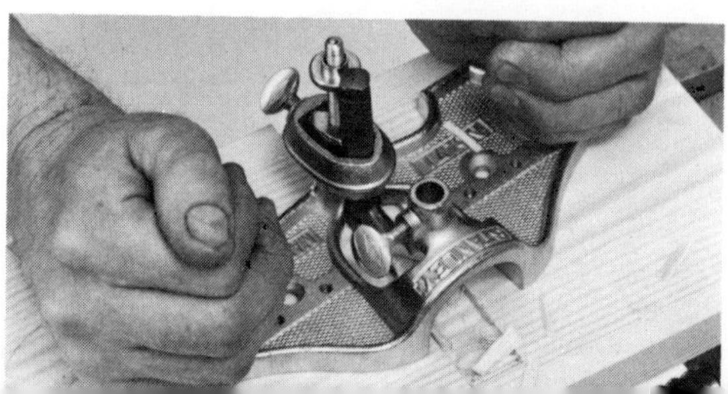

BORING TOOLS

1. What is the advantage of a Forstner bit for certain jobs? (SE)
2. Name these four types of bit, which are commonly used in a woodworker's brace.

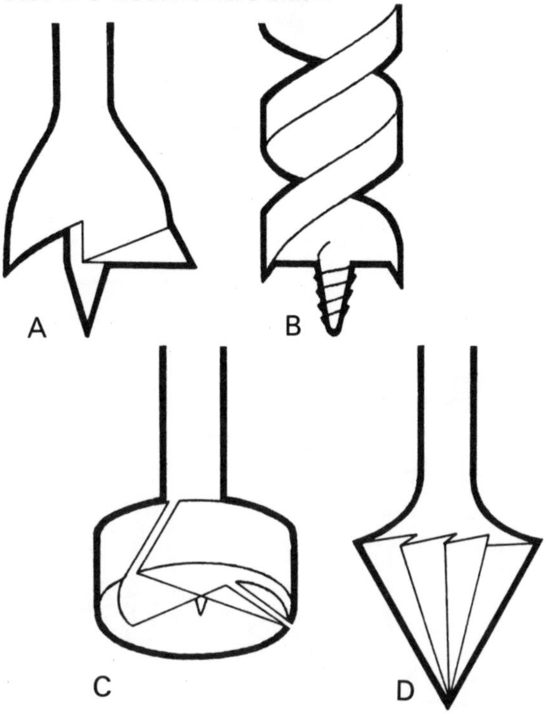

3. The section below shows the hole in a desk-top into which an ink well will fit. Describe how you would cut the hole and name the tools you would use.

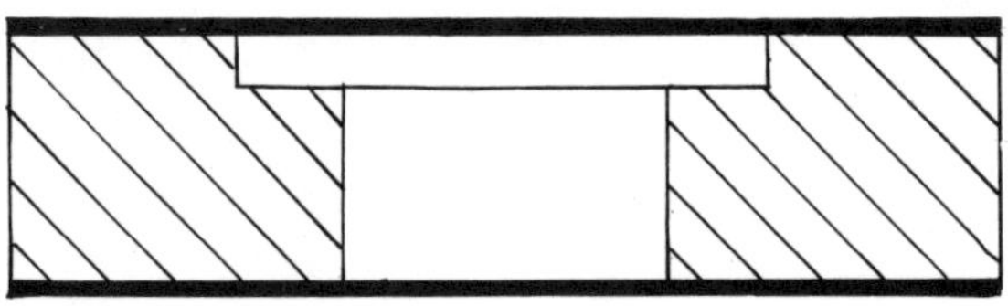

SAWS

1. Back saws and hand saws form two groups of saws, the third group are special saws. Name four in this group. (SE)
2. Name the saw you would use to cut a 100 mm diameter circular hole in a piece of plywood 200 mm square. (MET)
3. Name the saw you would use to cut a 100 mm diameter circular hole in the middle of a large sheet of plywood. (MET)
4. Fret saws and coping saws are similar in appearance but each have certain advantages for particular jobs.
   State what these advantages are and if necessary use sketches to illustrate your answer.

DRIVING TOOLS

1. What is a spiral ratchet screw-driver?
   Make a list of its advantages and disadvantages over a fixed screw-driver.
2. The normal screw-driver and screw head can have several faults. Name and sketch these faults and say if and how the use of 'Pozidriv' drivers and screw heads avoid them.
3. Old steel screws corrode and are difficult to remove. Explain at least two methods of 'releasing' such screws and state how you would treat replacement screws to prevent the fault recurring.
4. What is a veneer hammer? Illustrate your answer with a clearly labelled pictorial drawing.

HOLDING DEVICES

1. Describe with the aid of sketches two instances where handscrews are preferable to G-cramps. Give reasons for this.
2. Two holdings tools are illustrated below. Name them and give an example of where they may be used.

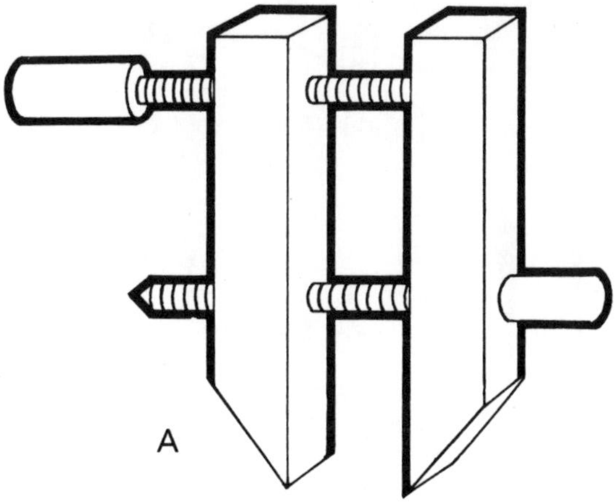

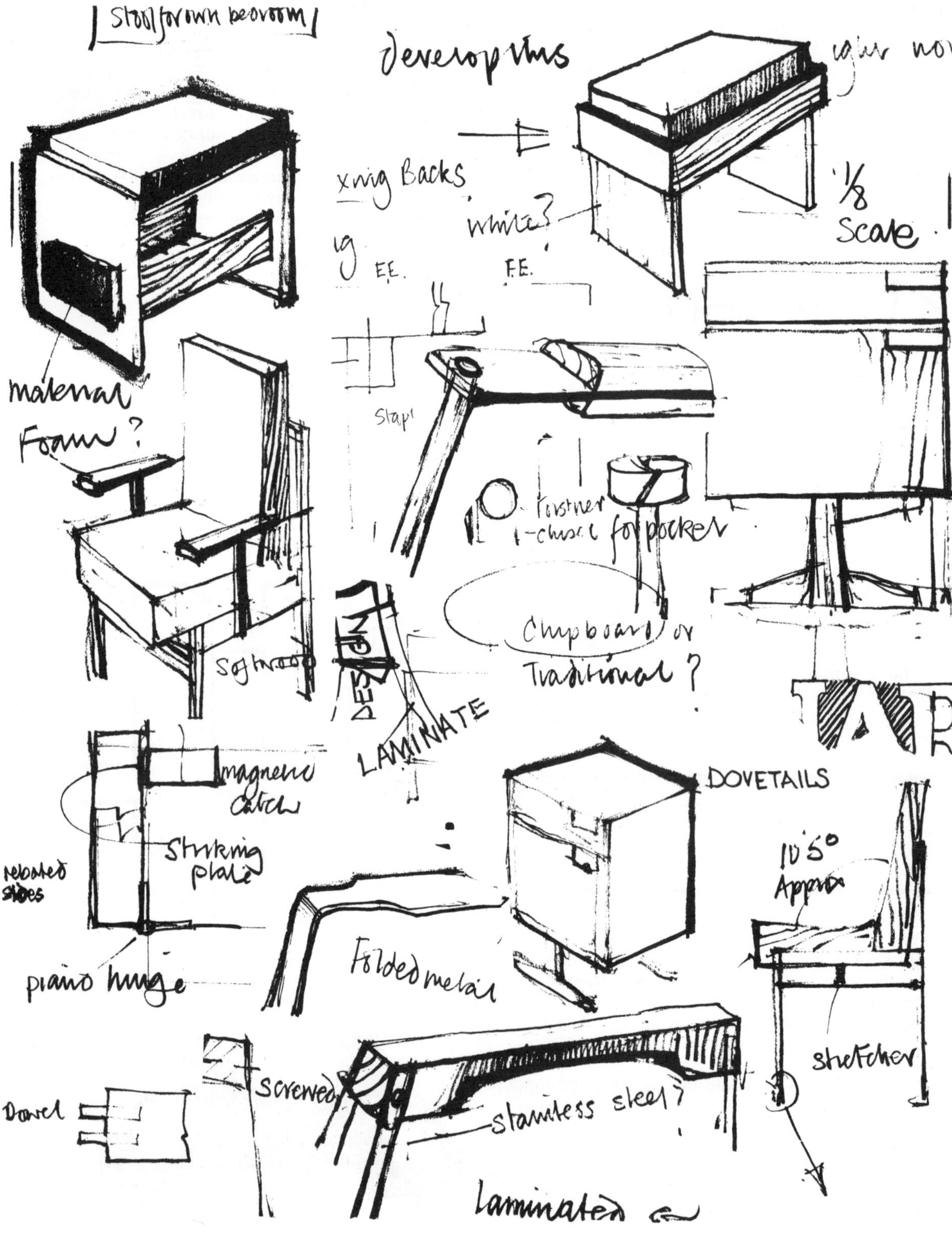
Stool for own bedroom
Develop this
colour now
Fixing Backs
white?
1/8 Scale
F.E.
F.E.
material
Foam?
Forstner chisel for pocket
Softwood
Chipboard or Traditional?
LAMINATE
magnetic Catch
Striking plate
rebated sides
piano hinge
DOVETAILS
10 5° Approx
Folded metal
stretcher
Dowel
screwed
stainless steel?
laminated

DRAWING 5

To the Student

Technical Drawing is a subject on its own and many of you will be taking examinations in it. If so then you will already be familiar with what you read.

Although this chapter includes some basic formal work it is mainly concerned with showing you how to produce working drawings for Woodwork.

Much of the work is freehand sketching, which can be done at home, thus saving valuable workshop time.

And the Teacher

Although a glance at the timetable may give the impression that the fourth year have a generous time allowed in the workshops this is generally an illusion.

Many boys will not have machine tools to assist them with their handwork, and performing the basic craft skills takes time. In addition some hours are necessarily involved with workshop 'theory'.

It is hoped that the ground covered here and in the chapter on design will show students some ways of approaching their individual design problems and recording them (perhaps in their own time) in such a manner that you are readily able to give advice.

For this purpose you will find that a sketchbook/pad for each student makes reference to earlier work and preliminary preparation for a new job that much easier.

SKETCHING—LINES

Freehand Sketching

One of the greatest assets a woodworker can have is to be able to sketch, i.e., to record quickly and fairly accurately his ideas and designs as they occur to him and to develop these ideas until a working drawing can be produced.

To describe some shapes or processes is extremely difficult and a sketch can convey more to another person than any number of words.

You may have a teacher who has developed this facility of sketching and who rarely has a pencil out of his hand. You may notice that his outline sketches of joints are the quickest means of giving you the required information and a visual image recorded is the best way of remembering things.

This is one reason why firms and organisations spend so much money on visual advertising.

Do you know the meaning of the symbols shown below?

The chances are that your teacher is not an artist—he will not have been born with the 'gift' of being able to draw. Rather he will have set himself the task of how to do it and proficiency has come as the result of considerable practice.

Sketching is one of those subjects in which undoubtedly 'practice makes perfect'.

The quality of line produced will make or mar a drawing and to produce lines of good quality you must use a sharp HB or B pencil.

Work from the top left-hand corner of the sheet and sketch a series of horizontal lines about 100 mm in length.

Drawing lines, just for the sake of it, may seem monotonous, but look critically at your sheet and notice how the lines vary. You have produced a variety of lines—now you must become aware of the kind of line you are drawing, so that you can control it.

Close your eyes, and holding the pencil lightly draw more lines, occasionally gripping the pencil harder. Notice then how the line varies according to the amount of 'grip'.

Note: The heaviness of a line has little to do with how hard you 'press-on'.

Practise drawing lines of a given length, say 100 mm.

Mark the beginning and end of the line, place the pencil on the left mark and transferring your eye to the right mark . . . draw the line.

Note: The line must have a good beginning and a clear end: if it fades in the middle it is not particularly important.

Draw squares and rectangles with lines of good quality.

Increase the number of squares drawn and vary their size without losing the quality of line, the correct shape or the accurate angles. Use lightly drawn lines to build up your 'constructions'.

Drawing will be easier if the paper is tilted towards you on a firm board and if you stand to work.

QUALITY OF LINE

Right handed people should work in the direction of the arrows.

Do not hold the pencil too near to the point nor too tightly.

All types of line must have a positive direction and must be drawn without hesitating, which will produce a faltering line of poor quality.

Horizontal Lines should be straight and parallel with each other and it helps if you draw with the arm rather than the wrist, which will inevitably produce some form of a curve.

Vertical Lines are also drawn without wrist movement. In fact if you transfer the weight of your body from the toes back onto the heels and keep your arm 'fixed' a straight line will result!

Drawing squares involves deciding where two lines meet or cross and that the angle is accurate.

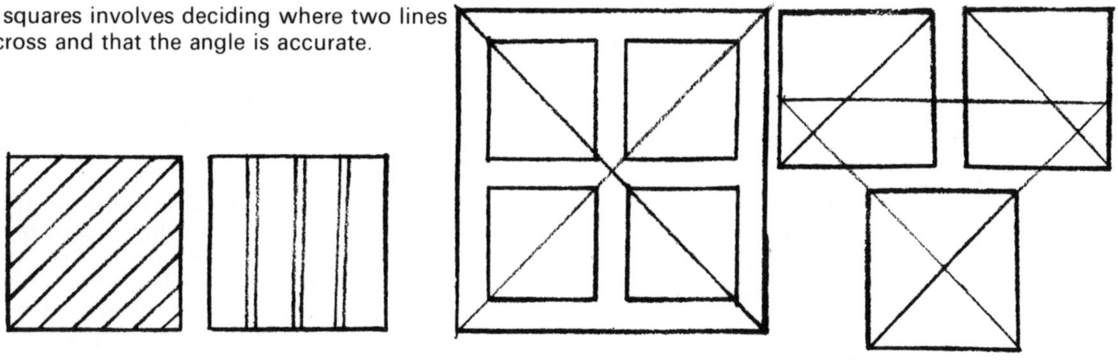

New schools usually look utilitarian and are designed to be functional. Such buildings are made up of varying areas of rectangles and views of three dimensional shapes which provide good drawing practice.

SKETCHING—SIZE AND PROPORTIO

Your sketches must never be so small that detail cannot be put in nor so large as to be unmanageable.

Draw a series of parallel construction lines and space out equal rectangles within them.

Regard these rectangles as front views of much larger objects such as bedside cabinets and wardrobes, etc., and on this scale you can quickly determine whether or not a proportion is 'correct' or needs adjusting.

You are now dividing quite short lines into accurate proportions. Next see if you can do this on a larger scale. Afterwards check your results with a ruler.

To divide a line into an even number of spaces judge half the length by eye and then halve each of the halves.
To divide a line into an uneven number of parts, draw a line of any length and mark off the equal distances.

Note: In most cases the actual size of the drawing is not so important as correct proportion. Unless objects are to be directly compared to each other, say the comparative heights of a table and chair, then scale need not be a major consideration.

Practise at home by drawing the front views of items of furniture, large and small. Ignoring scale, draw them between parallel construction lines and make the proportions accurate (see below right).

You will soon notice that two rectangles of exactly the same size can be made to represent vastly different objects by breaking the area up into varying shapes.

You may be aware that much of the furniture in your home is symmetrical in design, that is, it is the same on the left side as on the right. Sideboards are often a good example of this.
In these instances you may save yourself time by only completing half the sketch up to a centre line.

SCALE

When you are sketching or designing an object you will eventually want to produce drawings to scale. There are no strict rules to obey but it is best to draw as large as possible, within reason;

Example: If you were asked to draw a matchbox holder in an examination you should do it as near to full size as possible, whereas a sideboard would be about $\frac{1}{5}$ scale, i.e., a length of 500 mm on the job is drawn as 100 mm on your paper.

SIZES AND PROPORTIONS

These sketches of cabinets are in proportion to each other and are simply rectangles broken up in a variety of different ways.

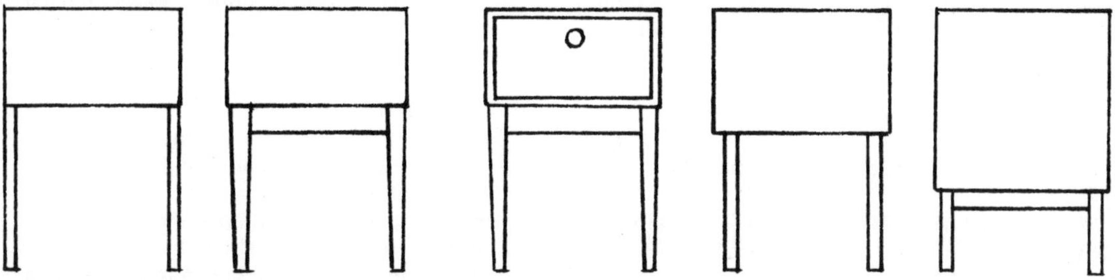

When you have trained your eye to divide a line up into equal spaces, the layout of dovetails on a given width of wood is not difficult. It is easy to see if the tails are too large or too small.

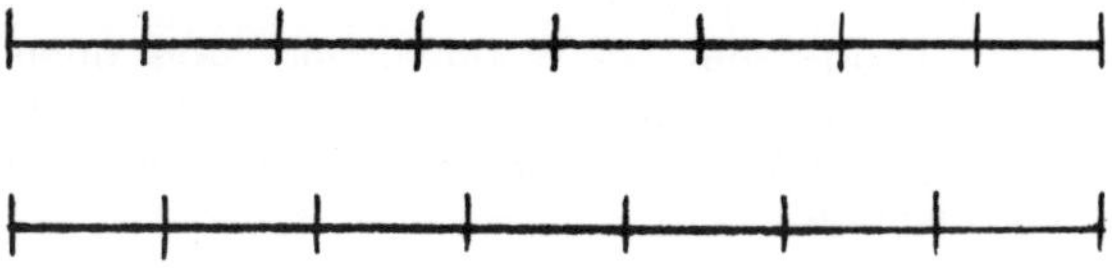

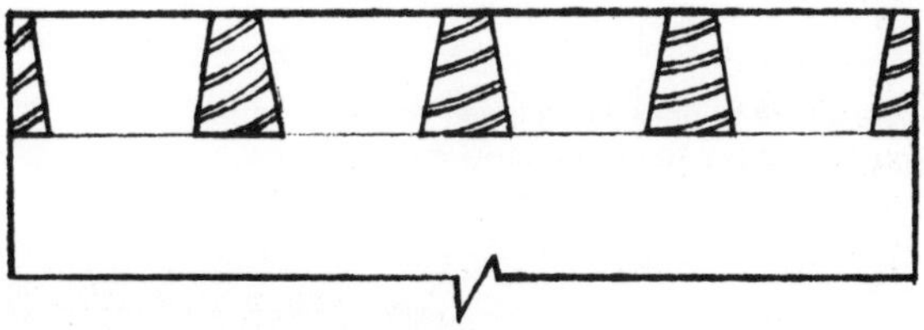

BREAK LINE

This symbol is used to show that there is a break in the wood. Shorter lines need only be uneven.

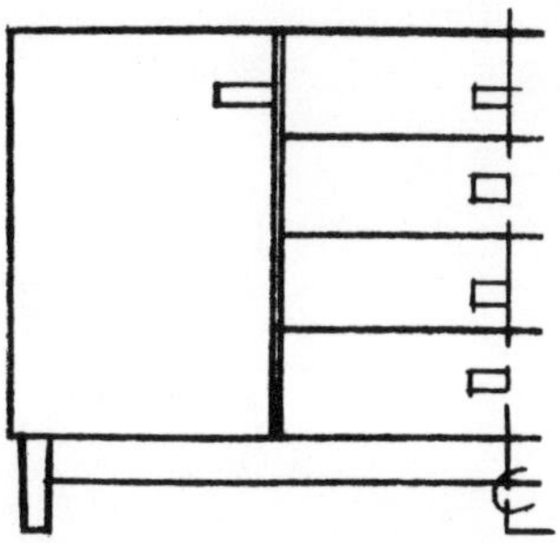

CENTRE LINE

This is shown as a lightly drawn long-and-short chain and may be labelled, although its position is usually obvious.

milk holder   wardrobe   stool   television   bookcase

SKETCHING—CURVES

CURVES

Fairly long shallow curves can be accurately drawn using the elbow as a pivot and without using any wrist.

Curves with a small diameter are almost entirely done with a wrist action.

Practise drawing both concave and convex curves with a variety of curvature.

CIRCLES, SEMI-CIRCLES AND ROUNDED CORNERS

Provided that you have mastered the 'square' and the curve, drawing a circle will present few difficulties as it can be built up of four squares with curves drawn in.

Draw a series of circles of different diameter, perhaps using the edge of a piece of paper to mark the radius on the diagonal construction lines.

You will soon be confident enough to draw small-diameter circles freehand, without the aid of construction lines.

Also note that semi-circles are simply half full ones and are based on two adjacent squares.

The corners of many jobs are rounded and they should be carefully drawn, particularly if the detail is full size.

OUTLINE DRAWINGS

You should now be able to draw:

Horizontal and vertical straight lines
diagonal lines at any angle
make-up areas of squares and rectangles
free curves and formal circles
judge proportion in relation to overall size.

You will be able to practise drawing the outline shape of almost any object from a cigarette lighter to a cooling tower and be able to gradually eliminate some of the guide lines as you become more confident and proficient.

The large variety of woodworking tools offers plenty of opportunity for practice, bearing in mind that proportion and not size is the most important consideration.

The ability to draw firm curved shapes enabled one group of boys to create these wall carvings.

CURVES AND CIRCLES

Like straight lines, these must always be of good quality, having a definite beginning and end.

For large-diameter curves you may have to turn the board round so that the elbow may be used as a pivot.

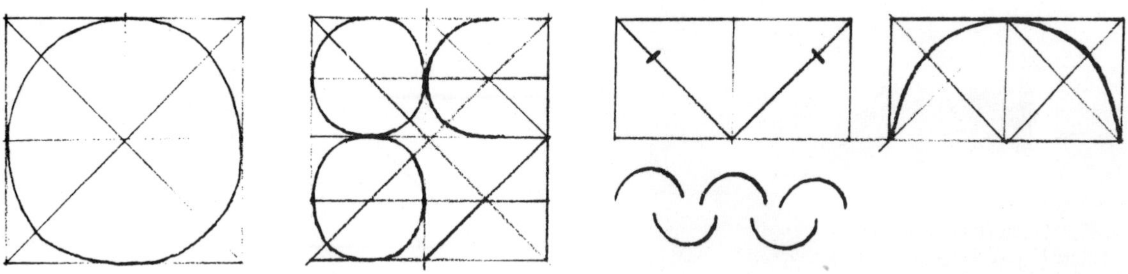

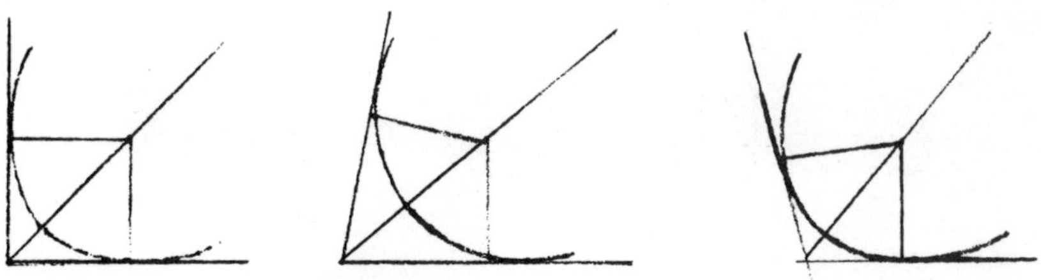

Note that rounded corners, whatever their angle, are constructed by using a bisector. Perpendiculars are drawn from the edge of the work to determine the radius of the curve.

OUTLINES

Quick outline sketches of tools are as useful for answering examination questions as the ability to produce small well-proportioned elevations is invaluable in the preliminary planning of a piece of work.

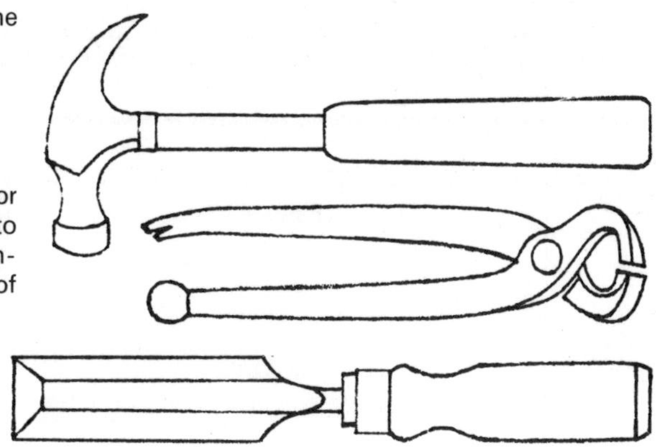

SECTIONING

This is a technique which will often show much more than a complicated pictorial exploded drawing, when it is necessary to explain such things as the fitting of tool blades to their handles.

Imagine a section or 'cut-through' of some simple objects and draw them. Where possible they should be full-size as they would be on a working drawing.

The detailed fitting of many woodworking joints can be revealed by sectioning, such as a mortise and tenon used on a basic stool construction.

The diagonal lining is referred to as 'hatching' which is usually done at an angle of 45 degrees, except where confusion may arise, when it may be at another angle.

Adjacent pieces of wood should be hatched in opposite directions and be evenly spaced.

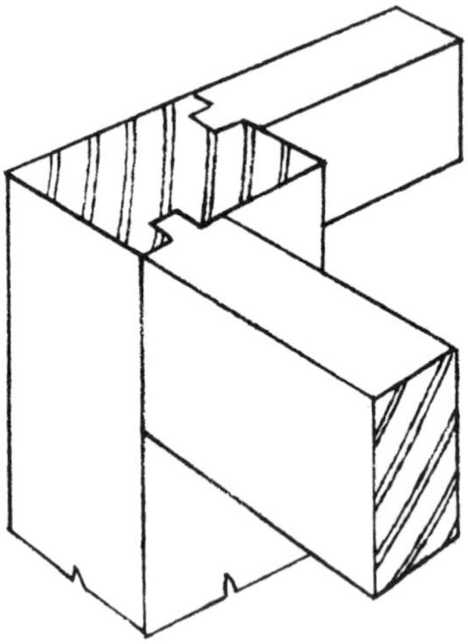

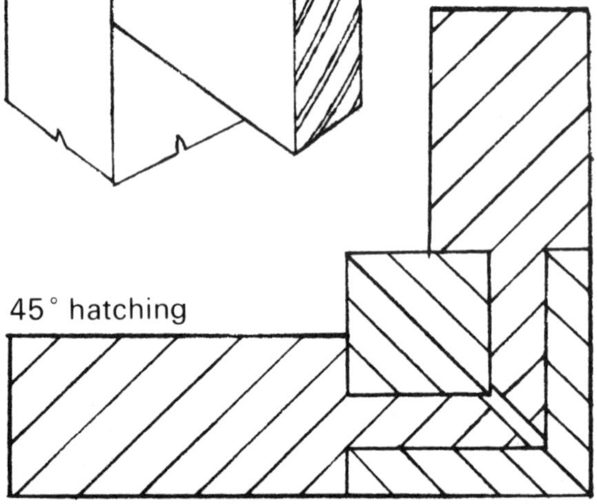

The section below shows the sizes and position of the two grooves in the table side rail into which the glass top and plywood base fit.

A section through any of the sugar bowls would not indicate their shape. A side view with a half-section is more effective.

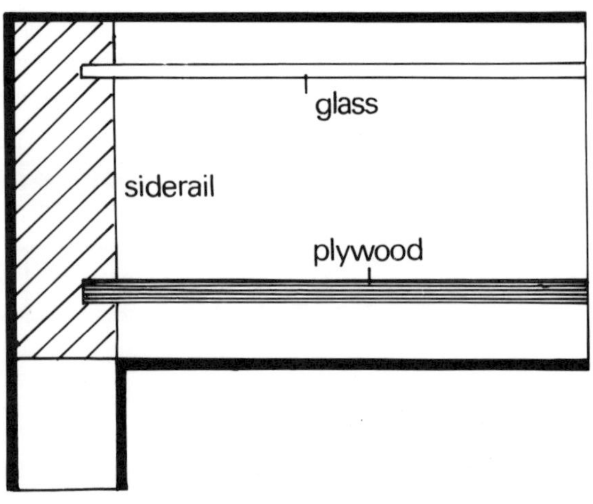

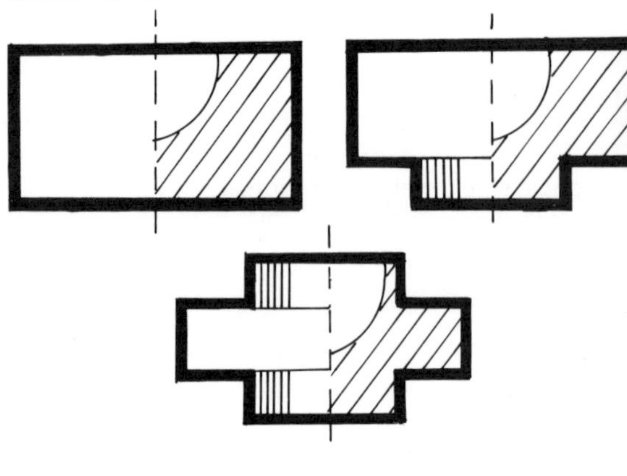

DIMENSIONING

'Full-Size' freehand sketches are not absolutely accurate and must be given dimensions. Such dimensioning is even more essential when sketches are either scaled up or down.

Figures detract from the actual drawing and should be kept to a minimum and not repeated. Practise by dimensioning some of your outline drawings.

Projection and dimension lines should be full light lines with neat sharp arrows about 3 mm long.

Measurements on vertical lines should be inserted from the right-hand side of the sketch.

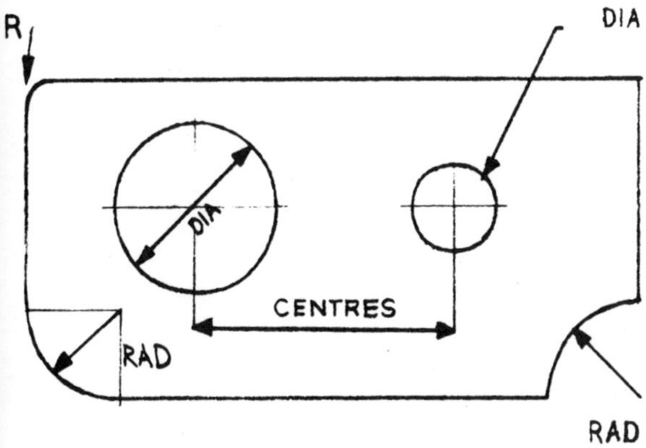

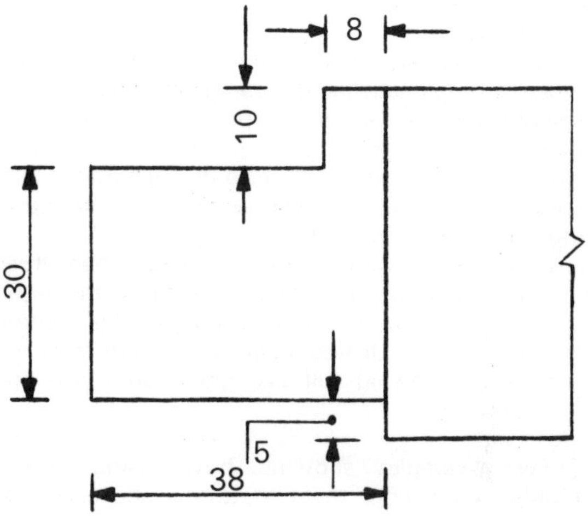

LETTERING

Clear labelling in an examination counts for much but it must be done quickly. Therefore, it will pay you to develop your lettering so that it can be speedily written and be clearly legible.

Practise an alphabet that is free from fancy 'curls'. It can be either upright or slope forward.

Keep the amount of written work to a minimum—using a short note form, and letter between faintly drawn guide lines which will not need erasing.

Letters should not be more than 4 mm high, except for major headings—6 mm high.

Lower case letters may be used where it is desirable.

ABCDEFGHIJKLMNOPQR
STUVWXYZ 123456789

ABCDEFGHIJKLMNOPQR
STUVWXYZ 123456789

abcdefghijklmnopqrstuvwxyz
abcdefghijklmnopqrstuvwxyz

LABELLING

Good outline drawings can be further improved by the method of labelling used.

The use of leaders is most effective but remember that they must touch or cross a line on the drawing at a steep angle, and should not be drawn parallel to the lines on the drawing or confusion may arise.

Leaders must end in a dot on the drawing or an arrow at a line.

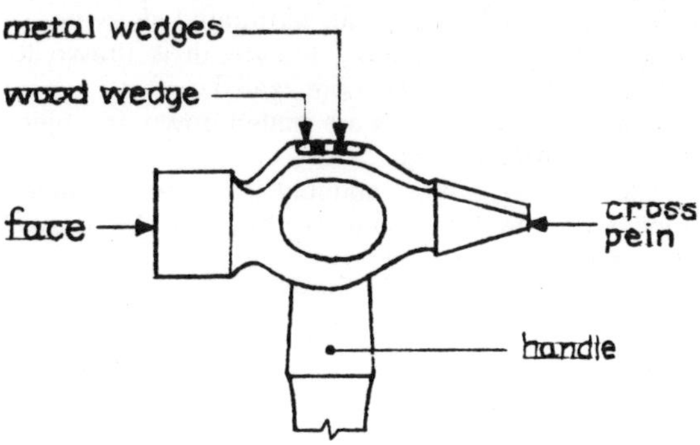

ORTHOGRAPHIC VIEWS

A pictorial view conveys the best impression of the actual appearance of an object and there are three main ways of doing this:

- Oblique drawing
- Isometric drawing
- Perspective drawing

An outline sketch or sectioned drawing is ideal where a simple labelled diagram is required as in an examination, or where proportions have to be determined. But when you are designing a job to make, you will have to visualise its appearance, and record it for future reference (when a working drawing can be made from it).

> If outline views only are used, then three drawings will be needed to show the front, end and top of an object. We call this method of drawing 'Orthographic' and it is of most use when drawing full-size detail on a working drawing.

Two examples showing how, using Orthographic projection, three views are necessary to show three faces of an object.

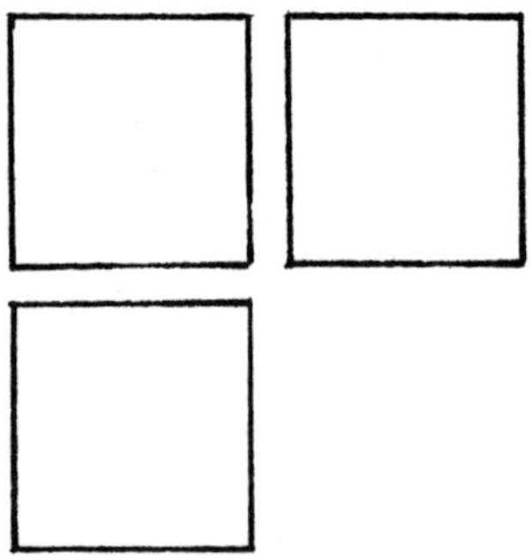

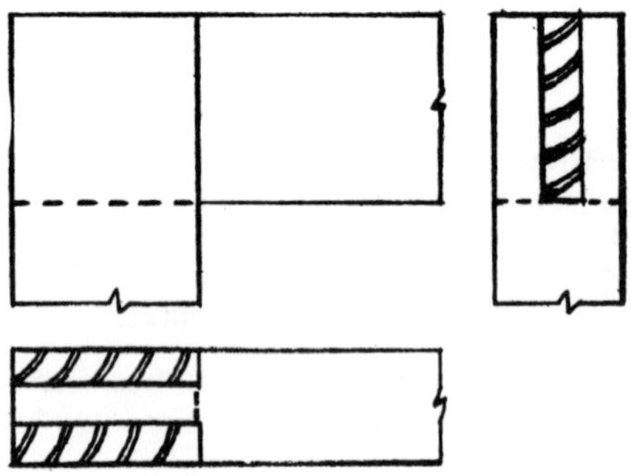

PICTORIAL VIEWS

OBLIQUE

The front of the object is drawn accurately and the depth drawn in at an angle of 45 degrees. This gives the appearance of an elongated drawing.

Note: If the line indicating the depth is drawn to half scale it will appear more realistic.

Unless the depth lines are scaled down an object appears to be too long.

The method is most suitable if curves or circles appear on the front face as they can be drawn accurately.

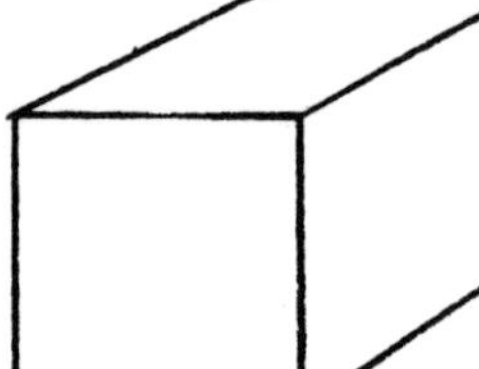

ISOMETRIC

The Oblique method gives one true surface (the front) but does not represent the way in which we would normally see an object.

An Isometric view is much nearer to this, using parallel lines drawn at an angle of 30 degrees to the horizontal.

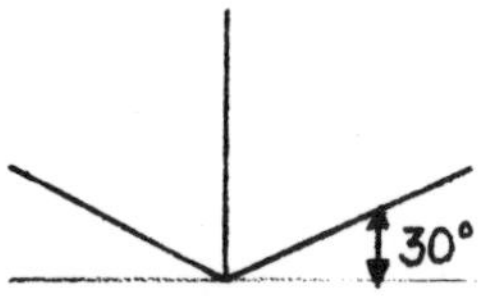

Until you are able to judge angles of 30 and 45 degrees you may find it useful to practise your sketches on specially ruled paper. If this is not available, check the angles occasionally with a set square.

Isometric drawings are ideal for drawing small things such as metal fixing plates and corner joints but the appearance of larger objects is often unrealistic as the viewpoint appears to be several metres above the object.

The only satisfactory method of obtaining a realistic sketch is to draw in perspective.

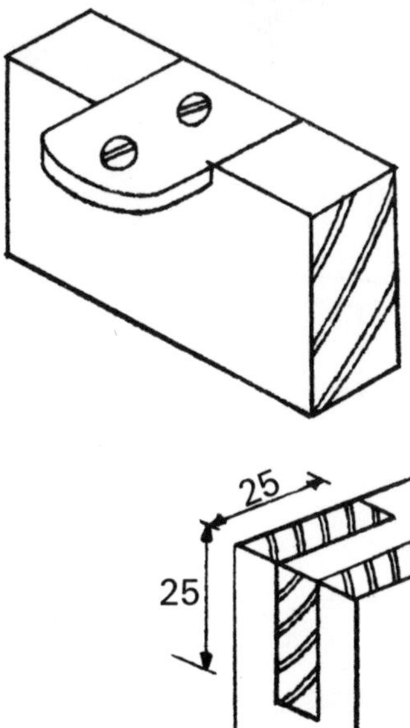

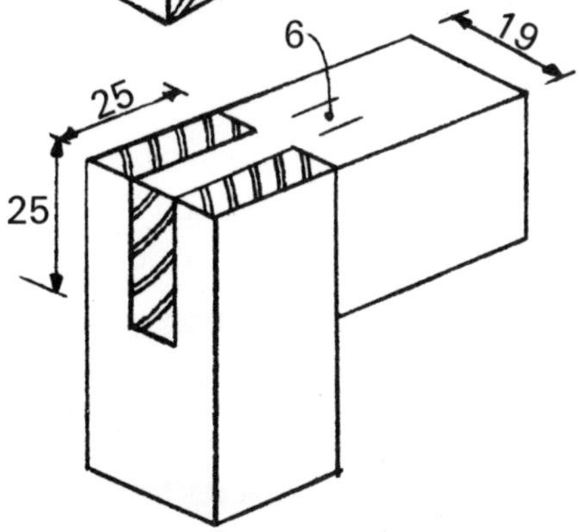

Full size details of joints drawn in Isometric projection are easily dimensioned; but the rule of drawing in measurements from the right hand side of the paper has to be modified slightly to make them readable.

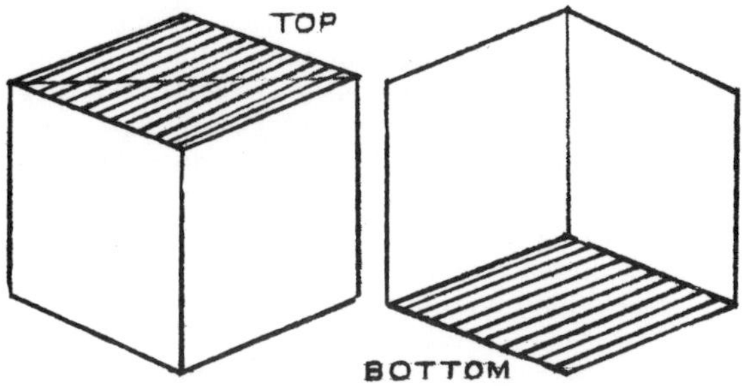

The Isometric drawing of tall objects is not satisfactory—not many people would see the top of a wardrobe in this way.

wardrobe

The far corner of long objects such as sideboards appears to stick up into the air in an unrealistic way.

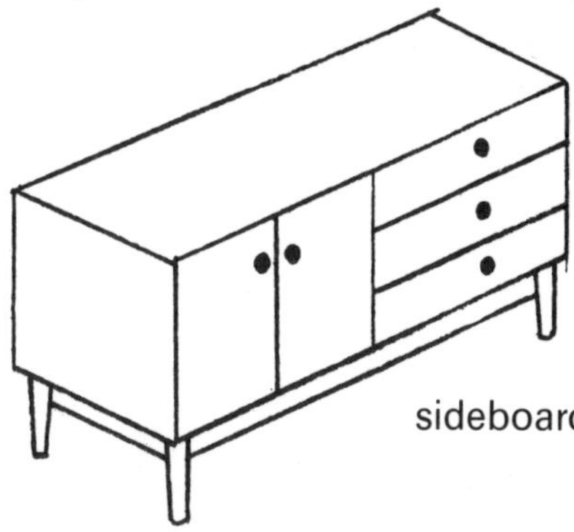

sideboard

Compare these sketches with the ones in Perspective on page 138.

PERSPECTIVE

In many ways using 'perspective' is only drawing what we actually see.

You must first fix a point where the *centre of vision* (marked by a vertical line) crosses the *eye level* (represented by a horizontal line). *Vanishing points* are fixed on that line at an equal distance from the centre of vision.

An object is constructed in a similar way as in the Isometric sketches but with the base lines converging on the VP and not the set angle.

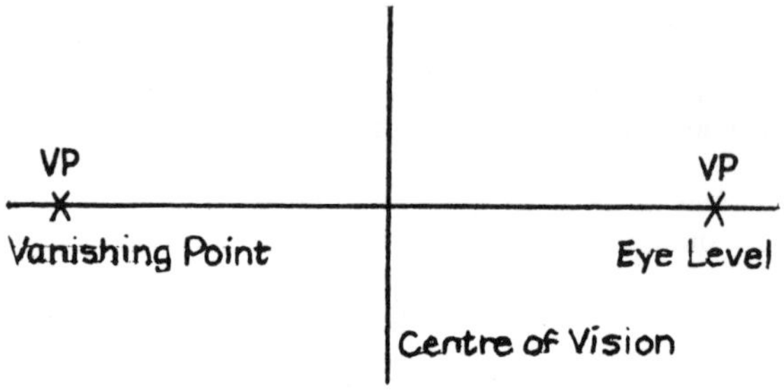

Using Perspective compare the realistic shapes of the sideboard and wardrobe compared with the Isometric sketches.

Note: The closeness of the vanishing points to the centre of vision affects the appearance of the drawing.

Large objects need the vanishing points quite close whilst smaller objects can have wide VP's producing lines that are almost parallel.

Note: If the VP's are too close together they may give an unhelpful view of an object where little can be seen.

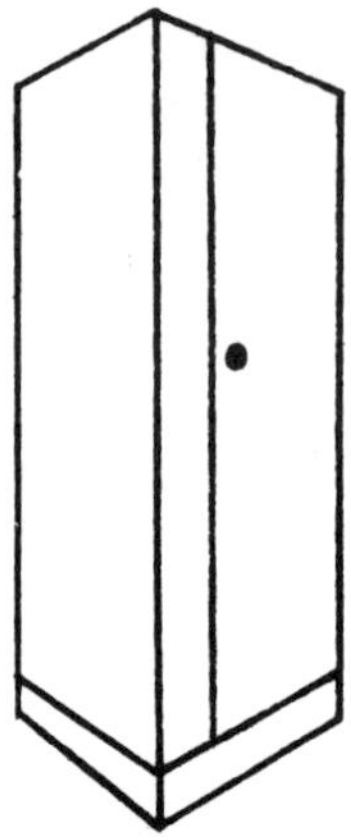

wardrobe

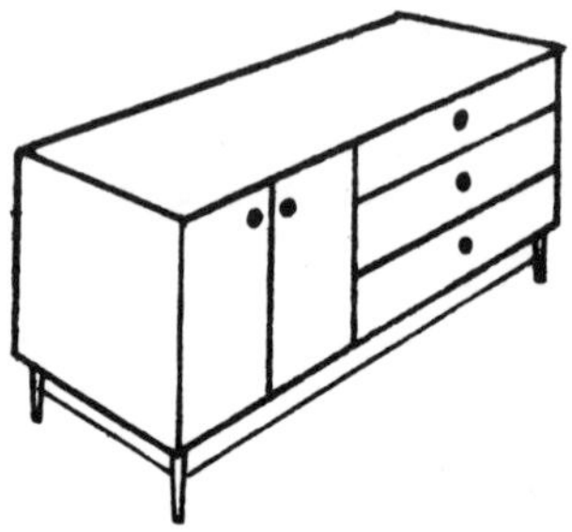

sideboard

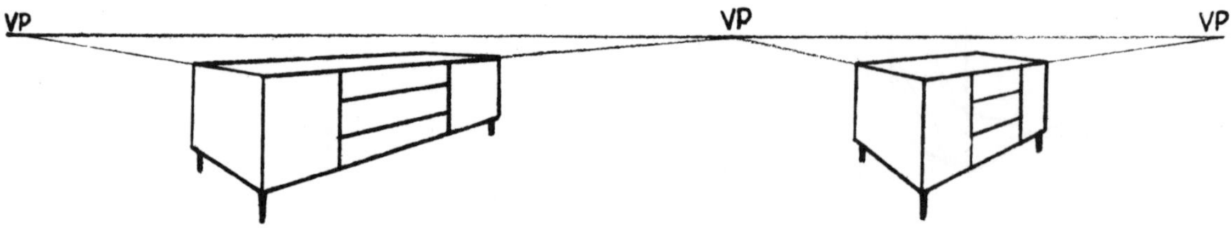

Note that you are able to see the top of a cube below eye-level and the base of one above eye-level.

Surfaces which are at eye-level are seen as straight lines.

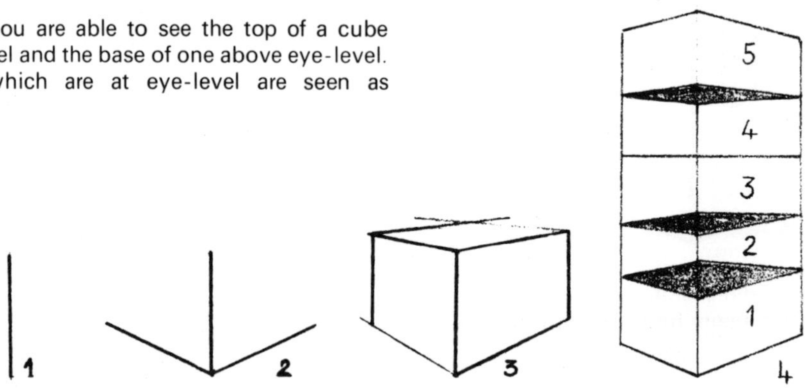

There is virtually no limit to the practise you can do with 'boxes' that may be cut out and added to become 'furniture' or sculptural forms.

You might find it worthwhile to prepare a softwood cube and cut from it two or three 'slices'. Rearrange these pieces and glue them together to produce blocks which will be fascinating to draw from any angle.

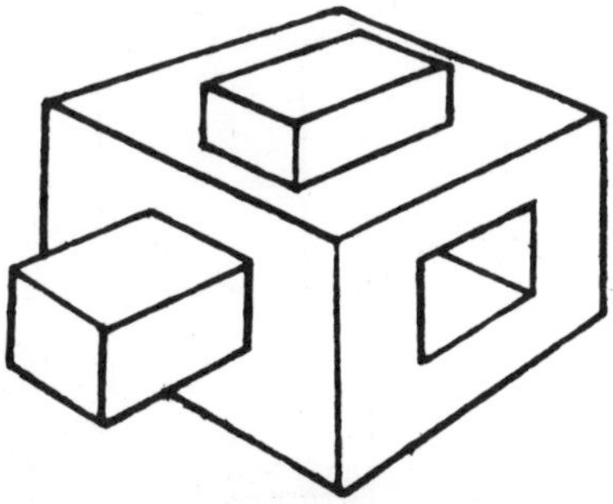

CIRCLES AND ELLIPSES

Except in Oblique sketching when we may see a circle on the front face of the surface, all circles are shown as ellipses. This means that one circle axis is longer than the other, called the 'Major' and the 'Minor'.

Ellipses are constructed in a similar way to circles and are not so difficult to sketch freehand.

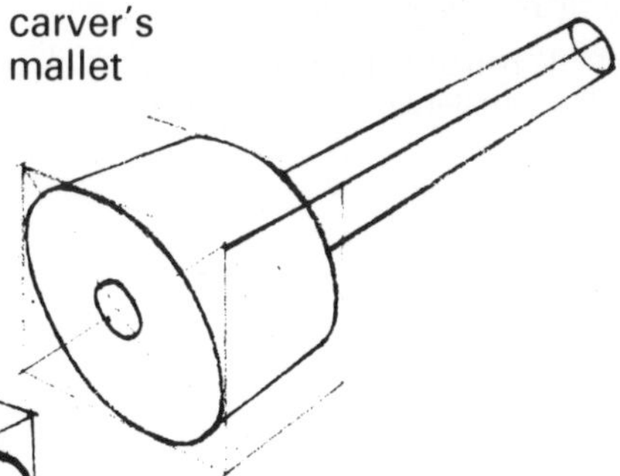

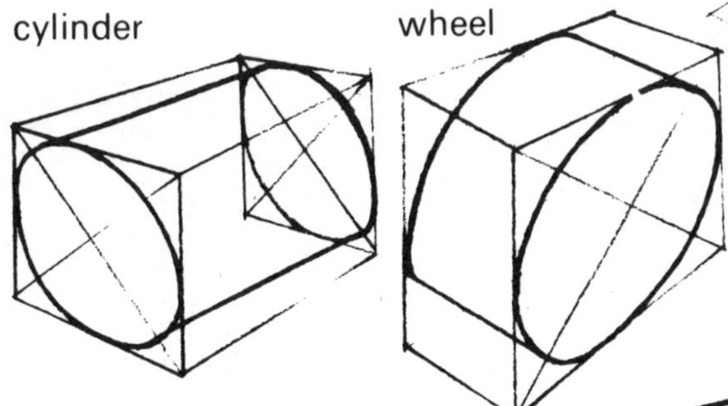

Long objects such as a mallet handle or a screwdriver need a centre line to avoid being 'crooked'.

DIVISION OF LINES AND AREAS

With practise you will be able to divide lines into 'equal' lengths with little difficulty but may find the use of some guide useful in the early stages.

Two ways are shown of using diagonal lines to divide up the front of a sideboard into doors and drawers.

Most other shapes can be based on a 'guide box'.

You will soon forget that VP's are 'needed' and you will be able to design in perspective.

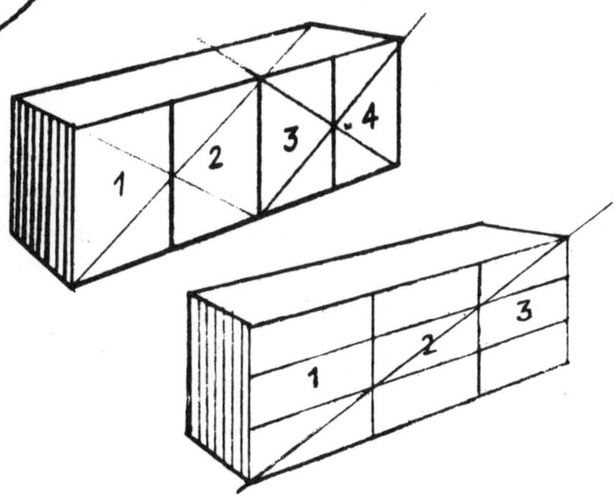

SKETCHING

EMPHASIS

We can emphasise the shape of objects by 'weighting' lines or by introducing 'toning', but for the emphasis to be effective it must be carefully done.

(1) In a cube the edges nearest to the eye can be weighted and if a hole is bored through the cube then the inside shape can be treated in a similar way.

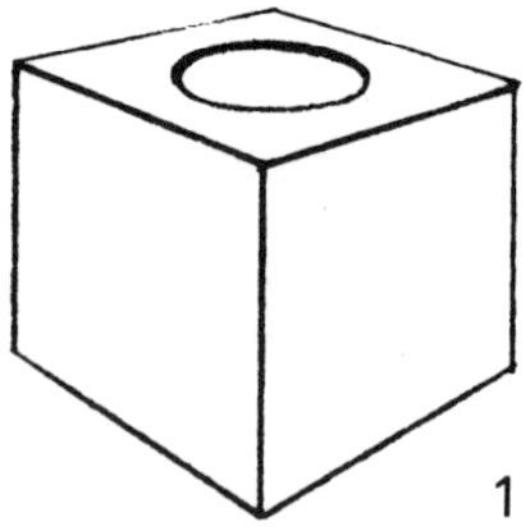

1

(2) The use of heavy lines is most effective when combined with 'toning' or other surface treatment.

A 'B' pencil is best used to draw in the closely spaced parallel lines—the surfaces are not shaded.

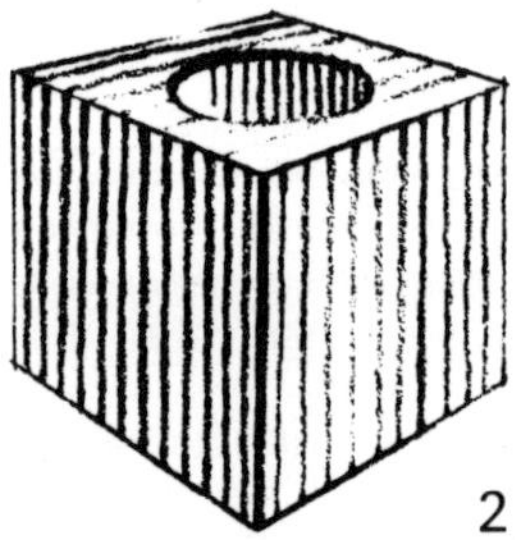

2

(3) A grain effect to emphasise the material should not be overdone or else it detracts from the shape of the design. It is unsuitable for narrow surfaces such as chair legs.

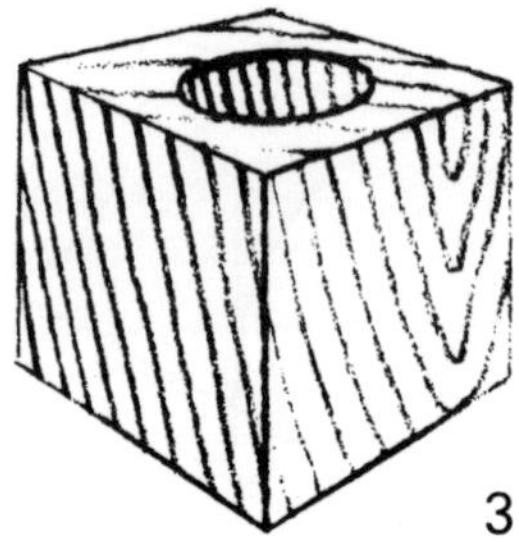

3

(4) An even softer pencil may be used to tone the background, throwing the shape into sharp contrast with the background.

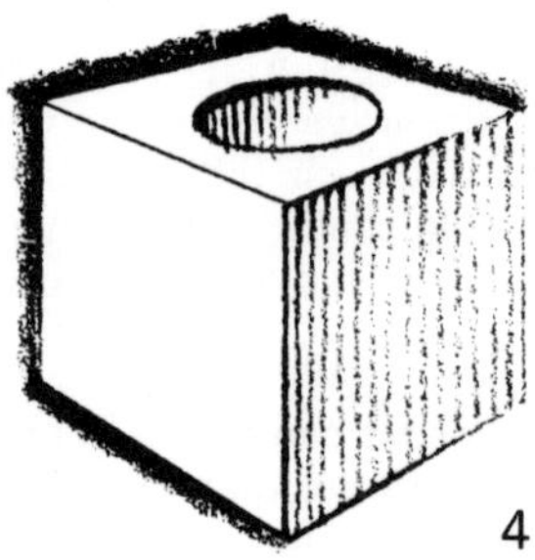

4

TONING, GRAINING

Straight lines are often used for 'toning' metal fittings or curved surfaces that have been turned on the lathe.

Note: The heaviest toning is not on the 'edge' of the cylinder.

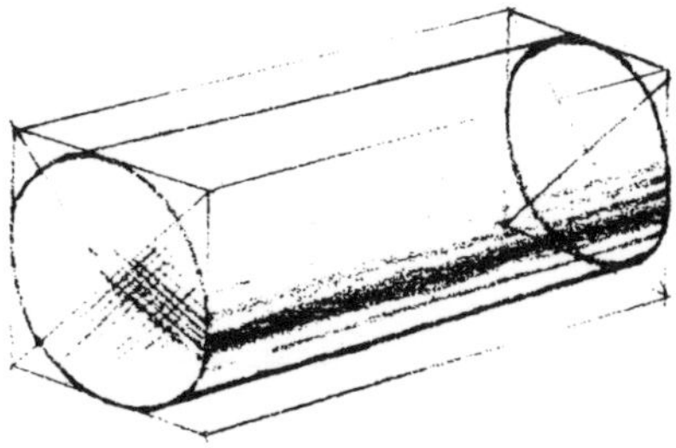

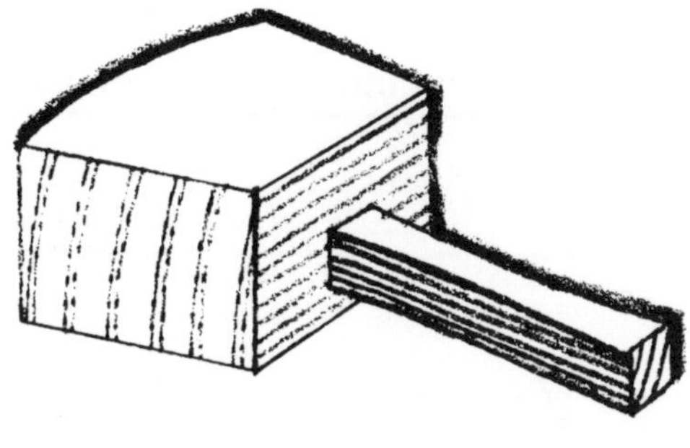

You should now be able to illustrate any examination question with a good-sized, well-proportioned sketch clearly labelled and showing all the detail required.

More important still, you should be able to record your design ideas on paper so that your teacher will be able to help you to work up to a so-called 'working drawing'.

COLOUR

Pictorial drawings of such room settings can be highlighted with the careful use of colour wash. Black and white illustrations can not do justice to such work and your teacher will help you to use colour effectively.

> Do not use toning, graining or colour unless the drawing will be improved in some way—line drawings are often very effective and all that is necessary.

Using the techniques of pictorial sketching and toning you will now be able to draw tools in a more realistic way. Even more important, these skills can be put to use in your preliminary design work before a job is made.

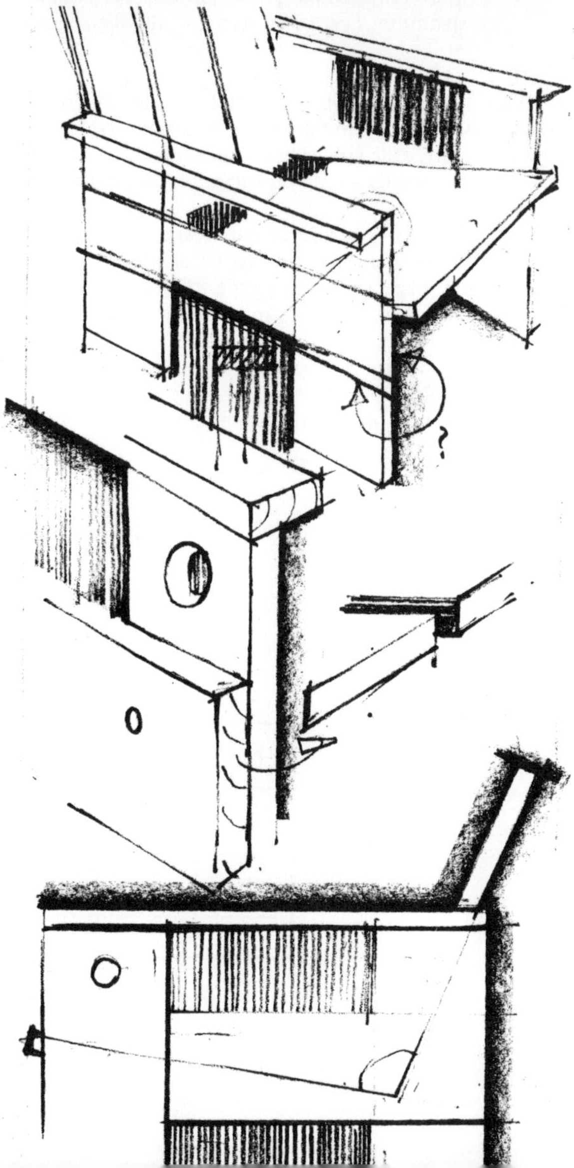

THE WORKING DRAWING

The outlines and pictorial sketches you draw may be adequate preparation for most of the jobs you do in the workshop. However you will sometimes need to have accurate or larger drawings from which to work.

A working drawing is the name we give to the recorded facts that will enable you or any other person to make the job you have designed.

Opposite is a tenth-scale drawing which would either be drawn directly onto the full page or drawn separately and glued onto a suitable portion of the larger drawing sheet. See Design 1 page 154.

SMALL-SCALE DRAWINGS

When all the details have been considered a small scale drawing is made, usually showing three views and giving the overall dimensions.

Large objects such as tables are often drawn to one-tenth scale while others, bookracks, for example, can be drawn to one-fifth scale.

THE PAGE

You should always make full use of the paper provided in an examination or available in school, drawing jobs full size where possible.

Joint details in any projection must be full-size.

Irrespective of the size of your paper your teacher will most likely indicate a layout, standardised for your use. If this is not so, then the following information or data, as it is called, must be given in a well-lettered panel.

Title of drawing, scale, date, your name and form. Rub-on lettering, such as 'Letraset' may be used to give a professional finish to working drawings.

TYPES OF LINE

The types of line shown are those recommended in the British Standard Specification 308 : 1964.
Note: The outline and section lines are not thick lines but are 'heavier' in weight. They may be drawn with a very sharp HB pencil so that they are clear.

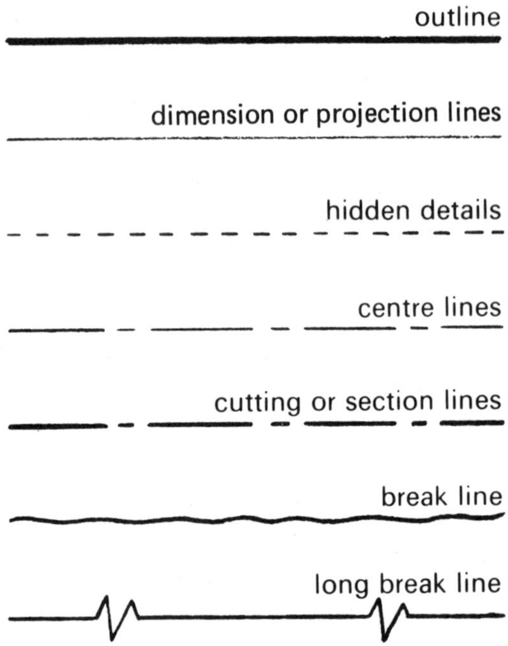

CUTTING LISTS

A concise summary of the timber and other materials required for the job is usually inserted. This is called a cutting list.

A formal layout with sub-headings should be drawn up for complicated jobs, but is not necessary if only one piece of wood is needed, as for instance, when making a table lamp.

Where boards are specified planed both sides (PBS) or scantlings planed all round (PAR) very little planing is necessary.
Note: State whether sizes given are 'nett' or include waste to allow for planing and sawing to the required length.

No	Description	Timber	Condition	L	W	Th
4	legs	Elm	P.A.R.	420	50	32
2	top rails	Elm	P.A.R.	1050	70	25

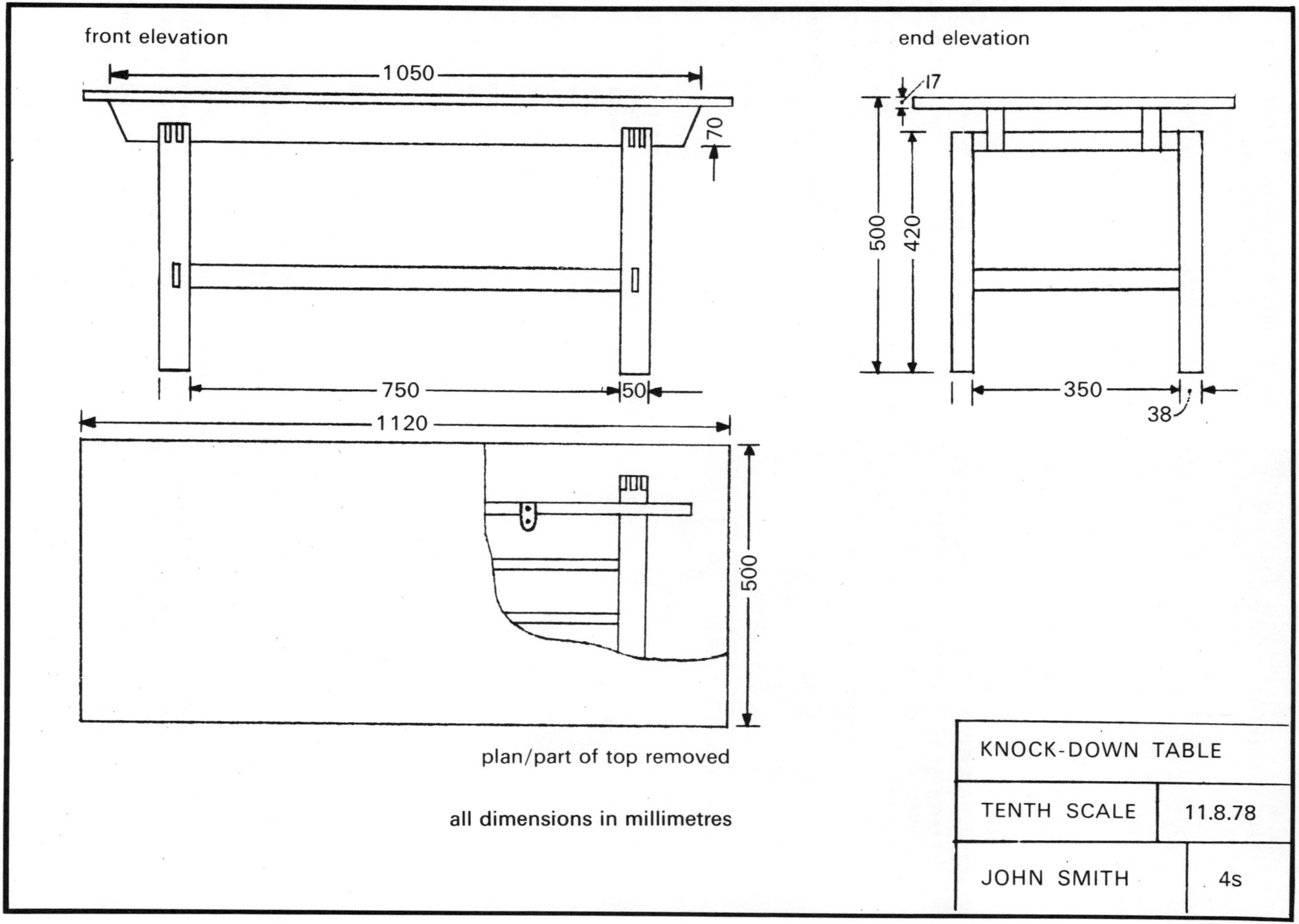
front elevation
1050
70
750
50
1120
end elevation
17
500
420
350
38
500
plan/part of top removed
all dimensions in millimetres
KNOCK-DOWN TABLE
TENTH SCALE
11.8.78
JOHN SMITH
4s

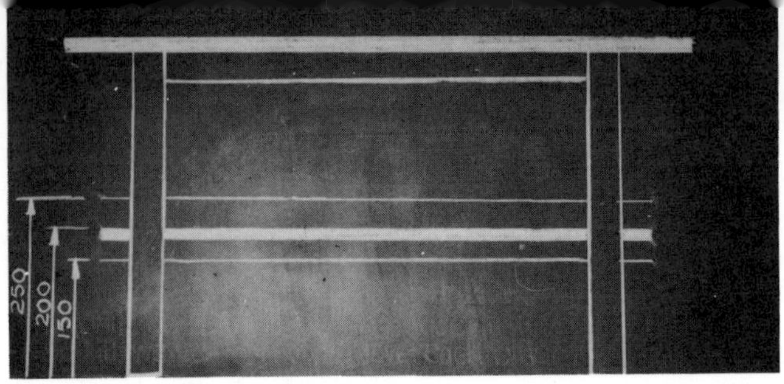

A full-scale blackboard drawing helps to decide the best height for an occasional table shelf.

THE WORKING DRAWING—FIRST AND THIRD ANGLE PROJECTIONS

First and Third Angle Projections can be used to illustrate working detail in most drawings.

It is possible to use more than the three views or elevations shown but this is rarely necessary.

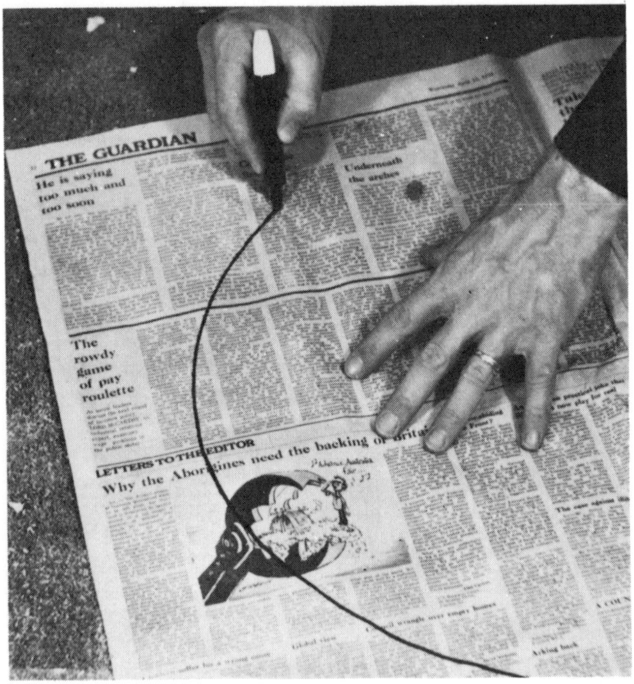

Full-size drawings can be made on newsprint—large shapes can later be cut out and used as templates.

FULL-SIZE ELEVATIONS

When you are making a large object such as a table or a pair of step-ladders, and wish to gain an accurate impression of their size, full size drawings may be produced on a blackboard (see photograph top). Adjustments can be made with coloured chalks.

A less messy and more permanent method is to draw on newspaper or lining paper with a fibre tipped pen. A further advantage of this method is that the drawing can easily be stored for future reference.

SECTIONS

It is usual to draw sections in Orthographic Projection and, where, for example, a metal fitting is used to fix a sheet of plate glass to wood, it will be clearer if colour is used.

The following colours are recommended:

Steel	Purple
Brass	Light Yellow
Copper	Crimson Lake
Aluminium	Light Green
Wood	Burnt Sienna
Glass	Pale Blue

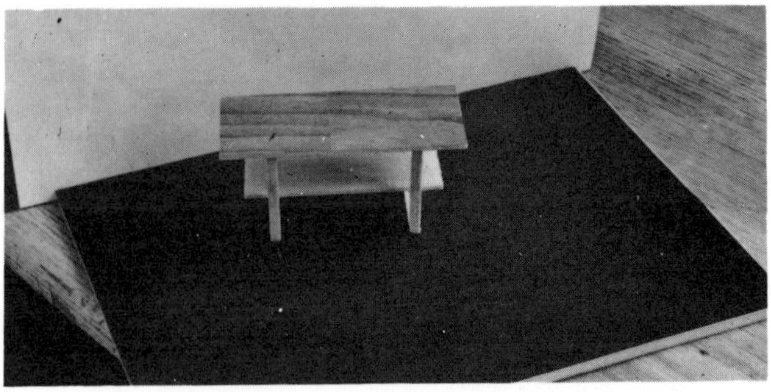

A scale model in balsa wood or cardboard is an extension of the drawing and makes the design more realistic.

SCALE MODELS

A good number of well-proportioned pictorial sketches combined with full-size drawings will give you an excellent impression of the final appearance of your job. (Photograph left). Even more realistic would be a carefully scaled model of your design. For this, one evening with a small quantity of balsa wood should be adequate time in which to make a scale model in three dimensions.

Note: If balsa wood is not available, cardboard and small pieces of softwood may be substituted.

ELEVATIONS

In the first angle orthographic projection, each view is placed so that it represents the side of the object furthest away from it. This is in contrast to the third angle projection where the view is placed nearest to the side it represents.

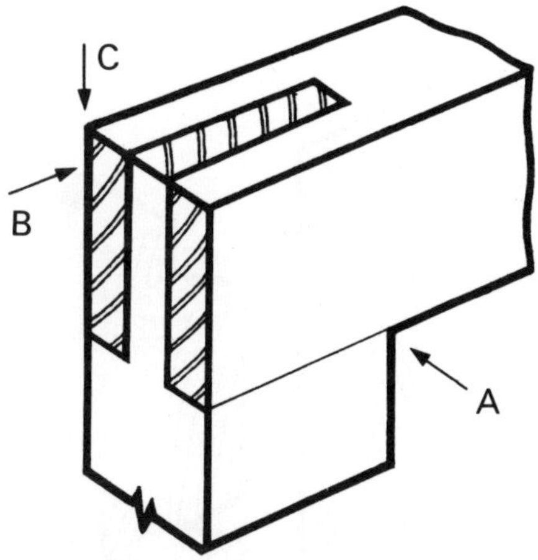

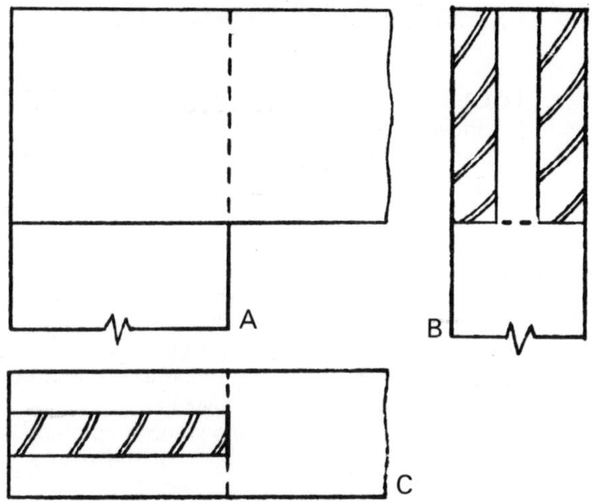

"CUT-AWAYS"

You may wish to show the inside of a joint in an Isometric view if a sectioned elevation is inconvenient.

This can be done by 'cutting away' part of the joint to show the detailed fitting.

A simple example is the through, wedged mortise and tenon joint illustrated.

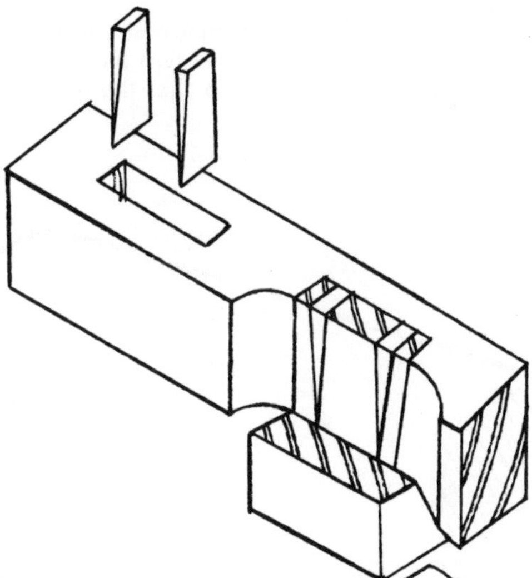

EXPLODED VIEWS

Exploded views are most frequently drawn with the Isometric method of projection to show pictorial detail of a joint. Choosing the best view is most important.

Example: The corner bridle joint can be easily illustrated in a true 'exploded' or 'pulled apart' view, whereas a forked mortise and tenon joint as used on a wide rail must have the leg turned round to show the mortise clearly.

Bridle Joint

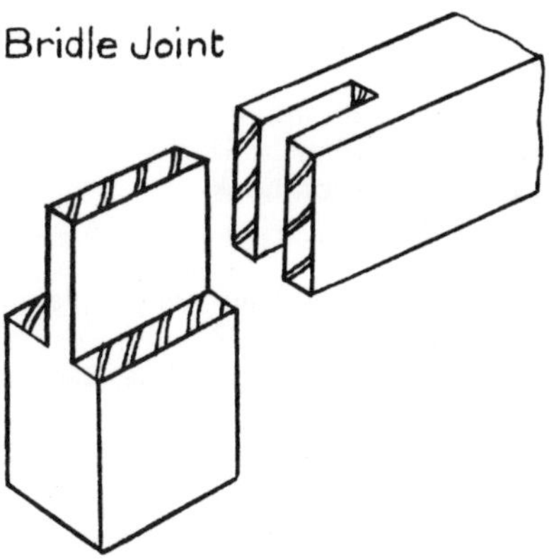

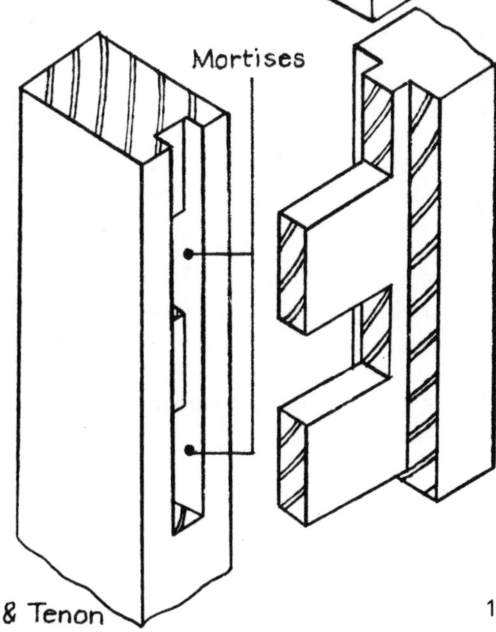

Forked Mortise & Tenon

EXAMINATION QUESTIONS

TOOLS

1. Show by a *diagram* why a smoothing plane used to plane the edge of a long board could make the edge hollow. (WM)
2. Make a large *sketch* of the cutting iron and the cap-iron of a metal smoothing plane showing the cap-iron in the correct position. (S)
3. Make an *exploded sketch* of the firmer chisel. Explain how you would make this chisel fit for use, if it had been badly damaged by a nail. (S)
4. *Draw* four tools used in marking out and cutting a mortise and tenon joint. (MET)
5. *Draw* the cutting end of a smoothing plane blade (iron) and indicate the angles of the bevels on it.

JOINTS

1. The incomplete drawing below shows the corner of a panelled door. *Sketch* the two pieces (the stile and the rail) *pulled apart*, so that the joint can be seen. (S)

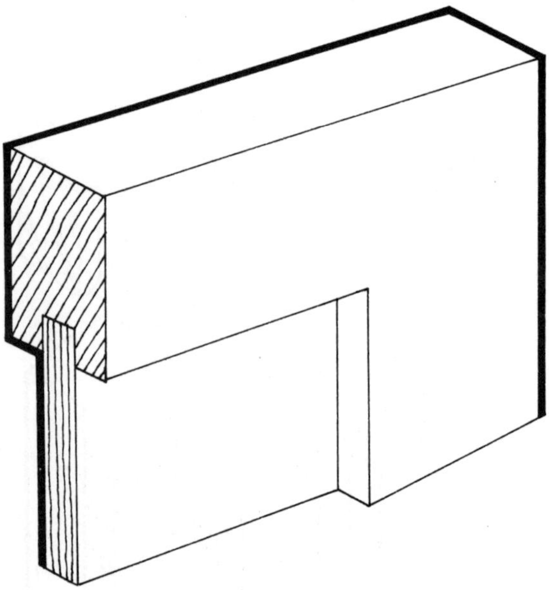

2. Make a *clear sketch* of a stopped housing *pulled apart.* (S)

3. The sketch shows the materials used at one corner of the front of a drawer with the two tails cut on the drawer side. Give in detail, using *sketches* where possible, the procedure for completing the joint. (WM)

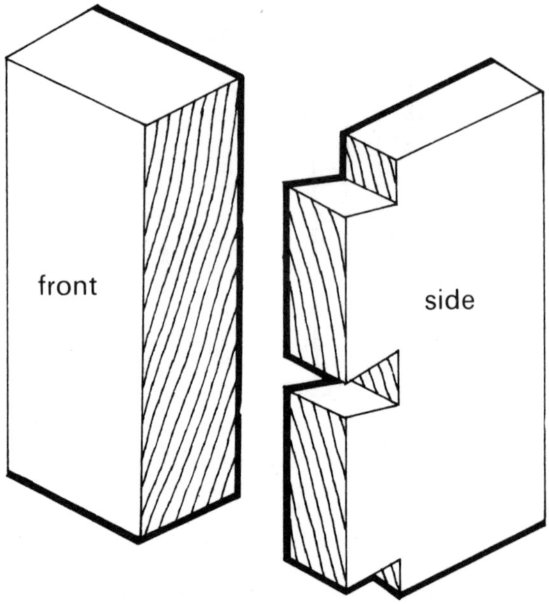

4. A table-top has to be made up from three hard-wood boards.
 (i) Name and *sketch* two methods of joining the boards edge to edge.
 (ii) *Illustrate* how you would arrange the boards to minimise warping. (NW)
5. *Sketch* and describe how you would secure the solid wooden top of a small table to the rails.
 State why you adopt the method you describe. (S)

EQUIPMENT

1. *Sketch* and describe with approximate sizes and state the use of the following:
 (i) A sawing board or bench hook.
 (ii) A shooting board.
 (iii) A mitre box.
2. Why are precautions necessary when planing the end grain of a piece of wood?
 Describe with sketches four methods used to prevent mishaps.
3. By means of a *labelled diagram* show how the bench holdfast applies pressure.

DESIGNS AND CUTTING LISTS

1. A piece of even-grained and easily worked hard-wood 350 by 225 by 32 millimetres is to be made into a shallow dish.
 (i) *Draw freehand* a suitable shape for the dish.
 (ii) *Draw a cross-section* through the centre of the dish. (MET)

2. Design on underframe for a circular coffee table 375 mm high with an 450 mm diameter top.

Show clearly the kind of joints you would use and *add a cutting list* of the material you would require for the underframe and the top. (S)

3. Make a *pictorial sketch* of a tool box indicating overall sizes. Then make out a cutting and materials list (excluding interior fittings).

4. From the sketch below.

(a) Make a *complete cutting list* of the carcase of the cabinet—excluding the plywood back and the door.

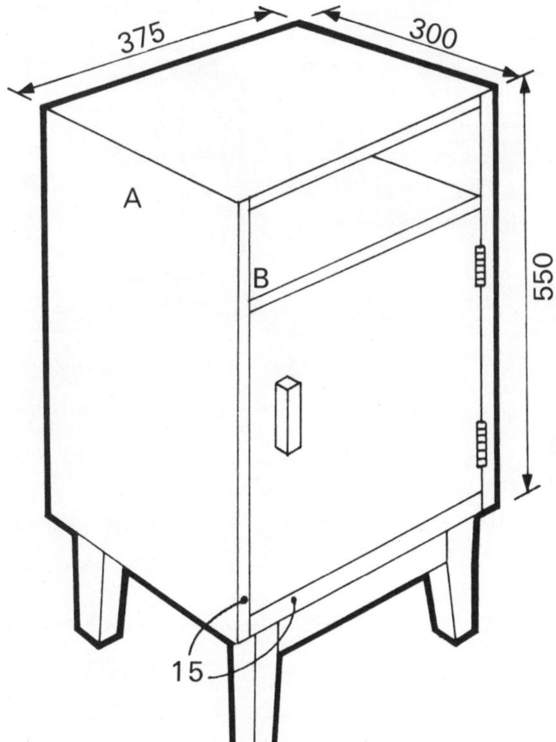

(b) By *notes and sketches* show the joint you would cut at A.

(c) Describe by notes and sketches how you would mark out and cut the joint at B.

(d) Show the construction of an alternative door to be made of solid timber with a panel.

(e) Show by notes and sketches how you would hinge the door, using suitable butt hinges.

5. Make out a *cutting list* for a joiner's mallet; then use a diagram to show how the head is fixed to the handle.

6. From the bookrack shown below;

(1) Make a *dimensioned sketch* to show the size and shape of the end P.

(2) Name the joint used between the ends and the shelf, and in a further *sketch* show the exact arrangement of this joint.

(3) Describe in detail how you would make the joint between the end P and the back rail.

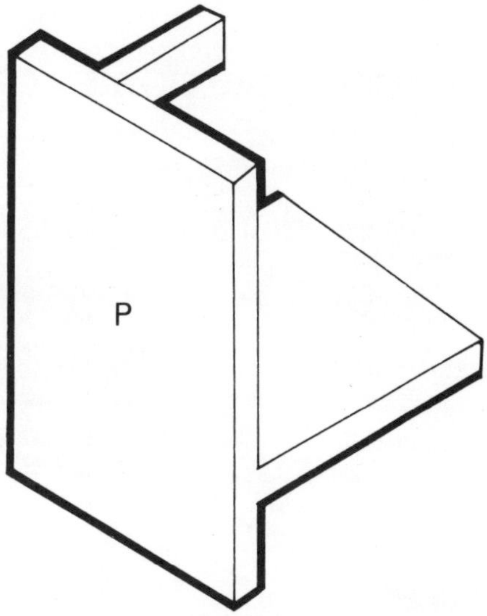

7. The photograph shows a crudely made gardeners' seed tray made into a kitchen spice rack. It does its job, that is—it is functional, but it does not look very nice.

Design a rack to hold between eight and twelve jars of your own choice. Sketch the joints that you would use and state the material(s) from which it could be made.

Photo: Courtesy GORDON RUSSELL LIMITED.

DESIGN 6

A dictionary will tell you that the word design can mean many things from a 'mental plan' to a 'pattern'.

People often talk about a car or a chair as being 'well designed'. It is only when the car fails to start or the chair leg breaks that we realise that they are talking about appearance and are not concerned whether these objects do their job efficiently i.e., that they are functional.

They are also expressing an individual opinion which really amounts to 'taste', and as many people like only what is popular at the time they are only trying to be fashionable.

Whilst fashions in clothes change almost overnight and cars every year, for most people an item of furniture is made or bought to last for a much longer period. Some people do change furniture quite frequently, but, in spite of the newly developed 'throw-away' paper chairs, these people are in a very small minority.

Our furniture must therefore be made to last and should also be of satisfying appearance to last visually.

The joiners of Shakespeare's time made furniture that is still strong and usable. With today's materials we could make furniture of equal durability but with more emphasis on design and fashion we accept the limited life-span of such work.

So your task, when you design and make a table, stool or cabinet is a difficult one. Somehow you must find a balance between function and appearance.

In some of the designs shown you will see how the emphasis switches from one to the other. For example, the table lamp must look well in its living room setting, whereas the milk bottle holder must work, and its appearance is a secondary consideration.

Your teacher and your examiner do not expect you to conceive a new idea—although it would be a pleasant surprise if you did!—but to work out problems drawing upon all the knowledge of construction that you have experienced or gained from textbooks, magazines and workshop practice.

Less common is the opportunity to refer to items of work that are well designed. Your teacher may have a catalogue of photographs of good work but you could collect designs from magazines, etc., to use as a source of reference.

Professional designers have many ideas that may be borrowed.

Designs, then, are solutions to problems and it is usual to use both words and drawings to solve them.

Some of the designs in this section are suggested methods of approach to specific problems set by examination boards—others are open to a looser interpretation.

You will find the solutions to these problems helpful in the work which you are preparing and making.

The solutions to the problems are functional. To the author they are also of good appearance. You may not agree and to alter appearances will usually mean using different constructions—as in the coffee table designs 3 and 4.

Use the constructions most suited to the job and always use your skill to the best advantage. On the other hand do not be afraid to use simple effective joints, modern materials and fittings where the job demands it.

The jobs shown are varied and you may be able to use some of the ideas for your practical work. Because of this, overall sizes are sometimes suggested but details are left to your own discretion.

Drawings are not to scale.

DESIGN: AN INTRODUCTION

DESIGN 1 STOOL

Known Facts: The maximum and minimum dimensions.
Wood, metal and other materials may be used.

Examination requirements: Using the basic idea shown in the sketch:
Design and construct a stool.
The stool must have some form of lower rail construction.
The seat should be upholstered for greater comfort.
The completed stool should be given a suitable finish.

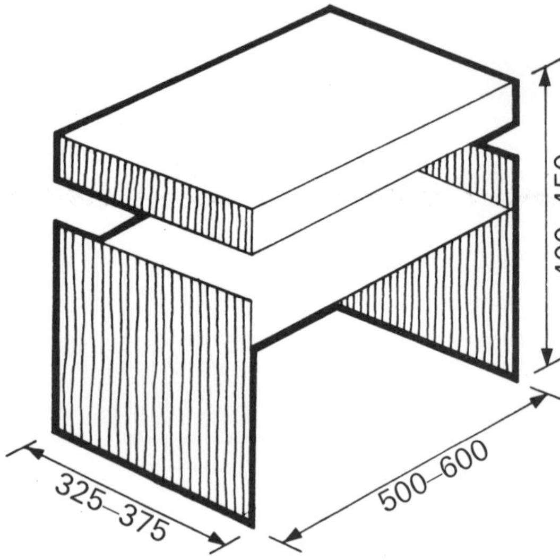

PROBLEMS TO ANSWER

What use is the stool to be put to? For example, a music stool is not the same size as a bedroom stool.

Is the design to be 'traditional' and make use of jointed legs and rails or are the large flat surfaces of manufactured board to be utilised?

Let us presume that the stool is for use in a study/bedroom and that simple flat surfaces of manufactured board are to be used.

APPEARANCE

Make sketches of the probable appearance, with a series of freehand sketches using your imagination and pencil freely. The drawings need not be all to the same scale but should be correctly proportioned and not too small.

Use the techniques of toning and line emphasis, to show clearly the form of the stool.

Freehand sketches and brief notes are an essential part of your design work.

PROPORTION

Carefully select the most promising idea (which is very often your last sketch) and set out a front and end elevation to $\frac{1}{5}$ scale.

Bearing in mind the use of the stool you must now decide upon the height, width and length within the considerable choice of shape offered by the dimensions given.

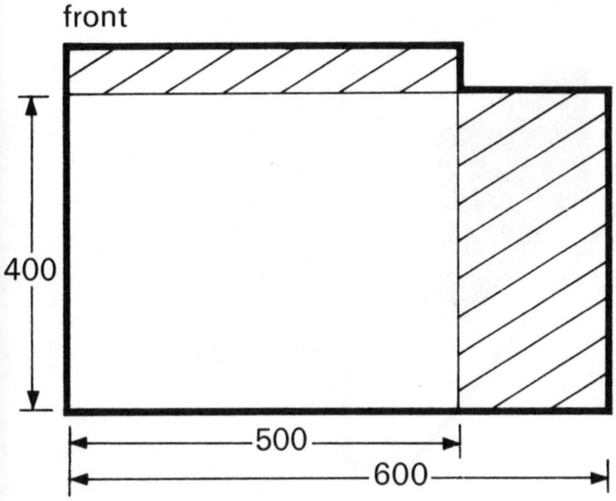

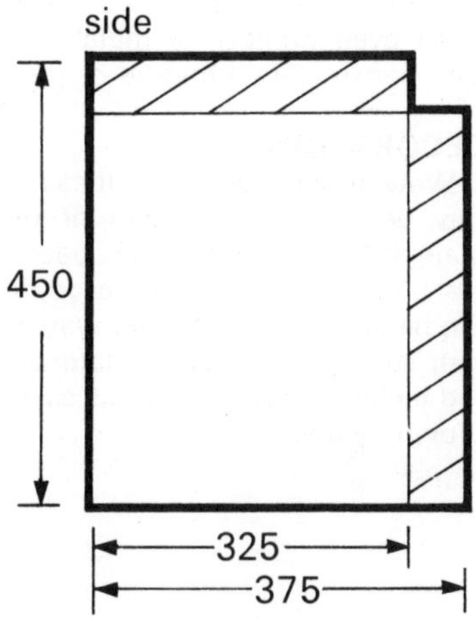

DESIGN FEATURES

Consider features that will make the design of real interest and base ideas on your $\frac{1}{5}$ scale elevations, perhaps using tracings to speed up the work. For example, the features could be the lower rail construction which will give the stool its main strength. Rails could be wide or closely set, near to the ground or to the seat.

Use sections where these will make your ideas clearer.

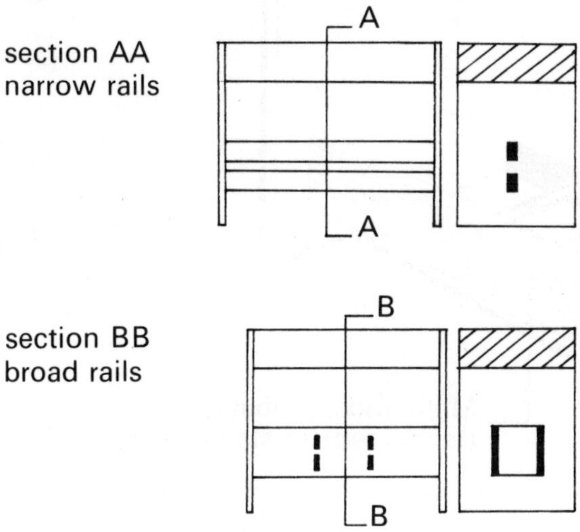

THE SEAT

Consider the need for a comfortable seat.

For example, plastic foam could be mounted on Pirelli webbing. Sketch this and add explanatory notes.

Alternatives: The webbing could be fixed to a frame made with corner joints or the middle cut from a sheet of plywood, which would eliminate unnecessary jointing and be in keeping with the design.

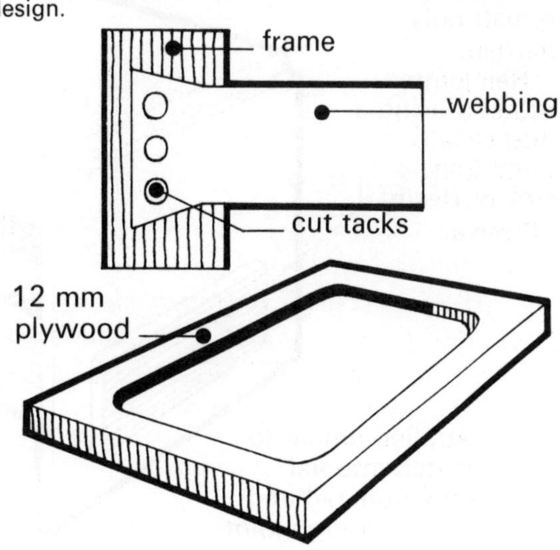

USE OF NEW IDEAS

Consider any new ideas that develop as you work.

For example, the cut-out waste from the seat might be trued-up and fixed on the stool ends and perhaps covered with seat upholstery.

Note: This would enable the rail joint, probably a form of mortise and tenon, to be brought through, wedged and covered.

The deep rails also suggest that a storage space for magazines, etc. could be made.

An even number of metal rods could be fixed with epoxy resin adhesive or inserted and left dry.

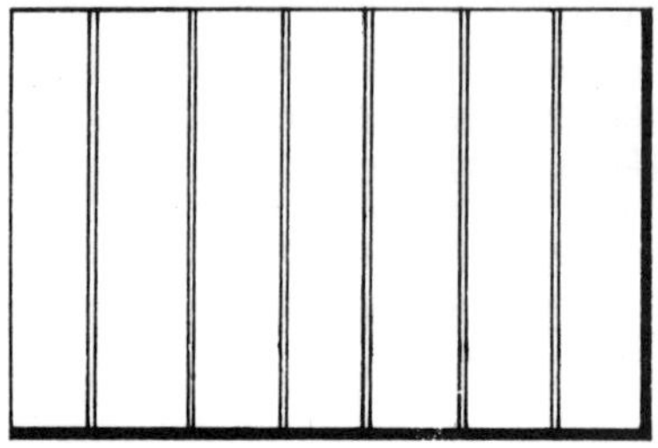

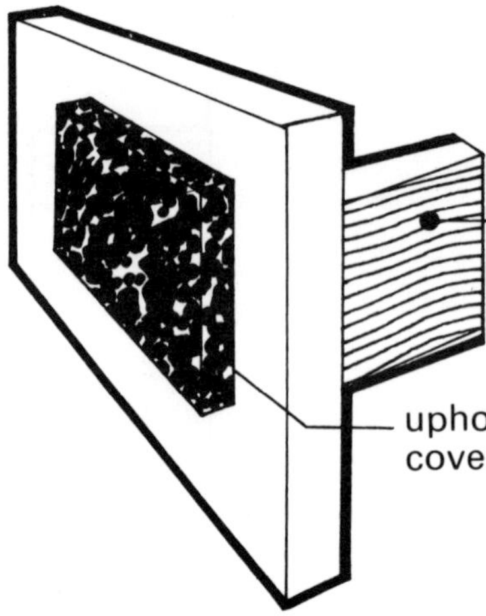

DECORATION

Write down your own ideas on how the stool may be given some form of decoration. In this example the decoration has been 'built-in' as work has progressed, by using large flat surfaces which can be treated in a different way. Contrast gloss and matt surfaces with other materials, make decisions and include these on a good-sized formal sketch as shown below.

FORMAL SKETCH

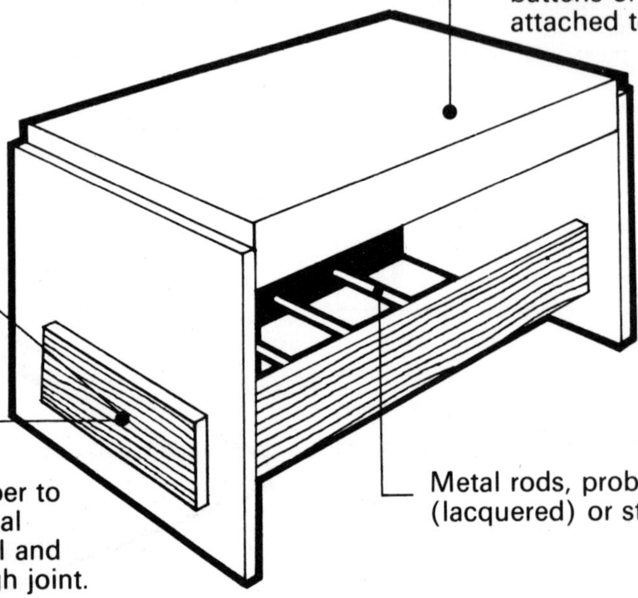

CONSTRUCTION

Although appearance has been a prime consideration, the use of wide rails as a design feature has been a sound basis from which to work as it ensures considerable stability.

The seat screwed neatly to a strip of aluminium angle guarantees more than adequate strength.

The examining board allows 20 hours to make the stool you have designed, and although this would be possible from the information already recorded in both note and sketch form, you will find a full working drawing invaluable.

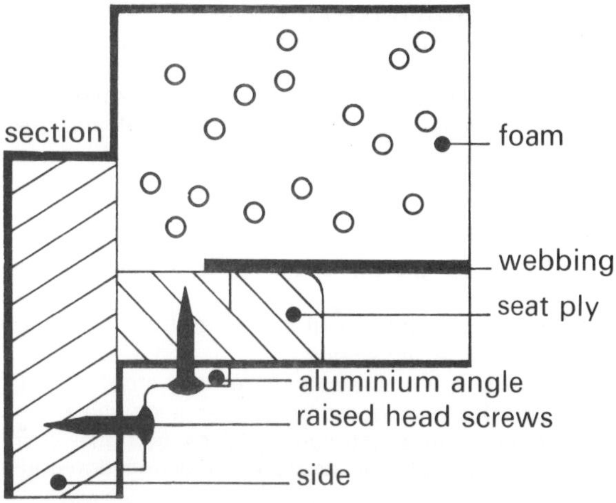

The finished bedroom stool uses wide rails to give strength and provide useful storage space beneath the seat.

FINAL ADJUSTMENTS

The sketch opposite includes some adjustments to the original ideas.

There will always be alternative shapes and joints whatever you are designing and if you are aware of these they should be considered before you make a working drawing.

The Seat: Webbing not to be used. The foam to be upholstered on to a solid plywood base and will therefore be one-third thicker than the loose cushion.

The deeper seat shown at the front is in keeping with the wide lower rail.

Draw a full-size elevation of the stool at the bottom of a blackboard and stand it on the floor. Consider carefully the suggested proportions, alter if necessary and then produce a working drawing.

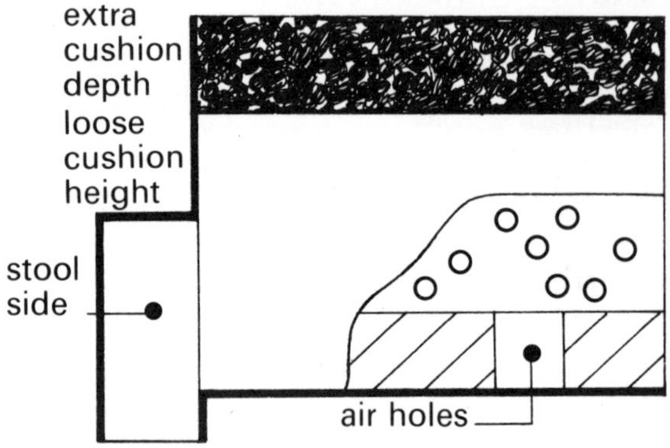

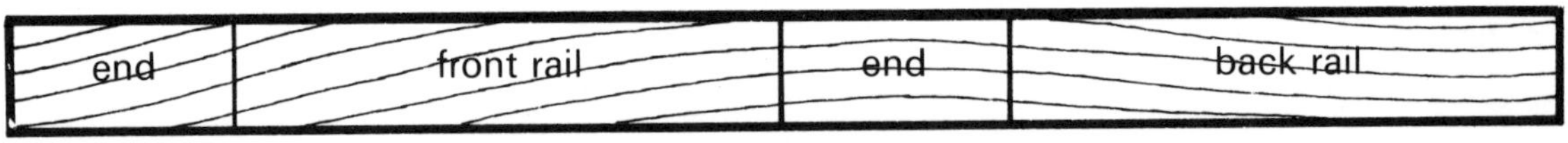

Marking out rail to achieve continuous grain effect.

THE WORKING DRAWING

The drawing should include any information, written or drawn, that is necessary for the stool to be accurately made. Thus, although you may include elevations and a plan to show overall sizes most of the work should be done full size. When the stool is being made, the position of joints, etc., can then be taken directly from the drawing.

Consider if complete elevations are necessary—in this, as many other cases, they are not—and superimpose them where there is insufficient space.

Space on the paper, that is the way the drawing is laid out, can be planned by making a fairly quick scaled sketch as shown.

Use written notes on the drawing to clarify details and have a panel to include the usual data, notes on finishes and list of materials.

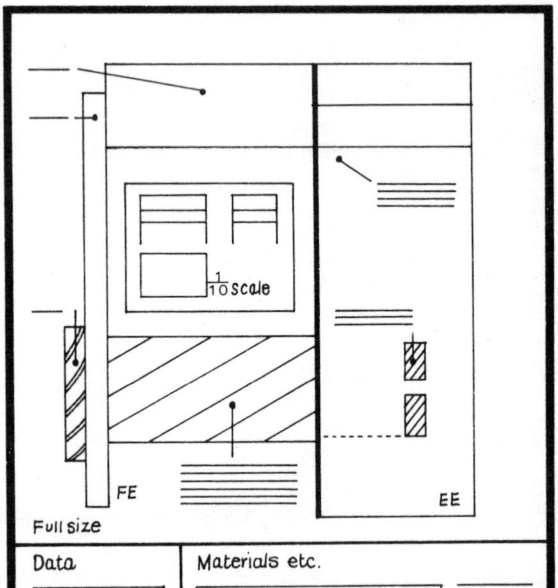

DESIGN 2 OCCASIONAL TABLE

Items of bedroom furniture are rarely seen or made in isolation, and if you have decided to make a stool for yourself, similar to the one described in Design I, then a matching table may be considered. It will help to make your room more personal and could be made to any convenient size.

DESIGN REQUIREMENTS

The table should be of similar appearance to the stool.

It may be of any size, but a surface 600 mm square and height of 400 mm is recommended where sizes are not limited.

APPEARANCE

In order to achieve uniformity of appearance the same materials should be used as in the construction of the stool.

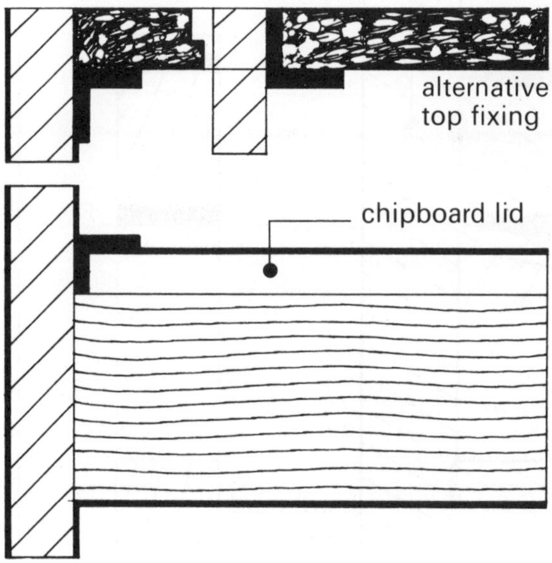

PROPORTION

If the size of the table is to be different from that suggested then the proportions should be carefully considered—from small scale sketches move to the blackboard and draw full-size elevations.

Top sizes must be determined by the use of folding newspaper.

Lay it out on your bedroom floor, and you will see how much space the table is going to take up.

DESIGN FEATURES

The top: This is of plywood and should be covered with a material of the same colour and texture as the stool seat and glued with PVA.

The aluminium angle support may be inverted to show a contrasting metal edge on the top surface.

The lid: This could be of plywood or veneered chipboard and is used to cover the large storage space between the deep rails.

The aluminium angle used here is an attractive feature as well as being of practical use.

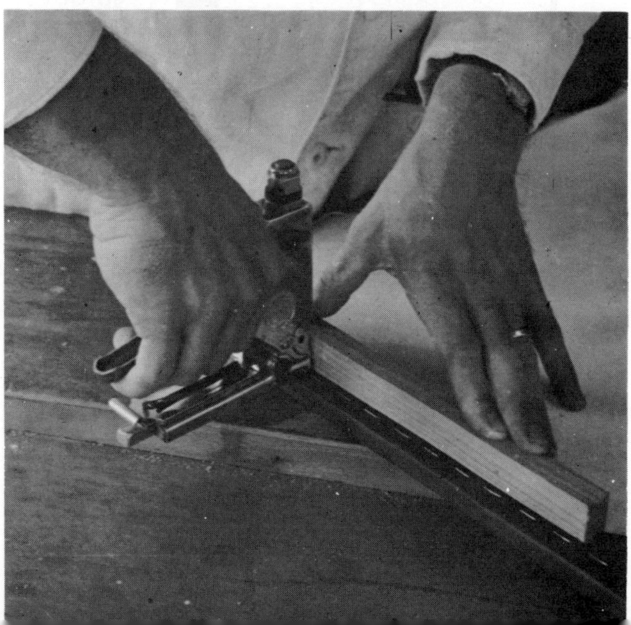

Right: The plywood top is covered with a PVC material which is glued with a PVA adhesive and stapled underneath. A straight-edge helps to make the staples look neat.

DECORATION

This is again provided by carefully contrasted surfaces. Strongly grained softwood rails, fixed to smooth white ends, both support a lid that could be veneered with a dark hardwood such as teak or mahogany. Satin smooth aluminium angle and colourful textured fabric on the top complete the 'decoration'.

CONSTRUCTION

The drawing shows a sectioned front view of the rail joint that may be used for both stool and table—the distance between the outside edges of the rails could be 455 mm to enable a standard width of chipboard to be used for the lid.

As the front elevations of the table and stool are similar, the rail may be made the same width.

A good storage space is created by using a hardboard base supported in the grooved rails and on bearers screwed and glued to the ends. Similar bearers support the lid (see photograph below) which is held in place by the aluminium angle.

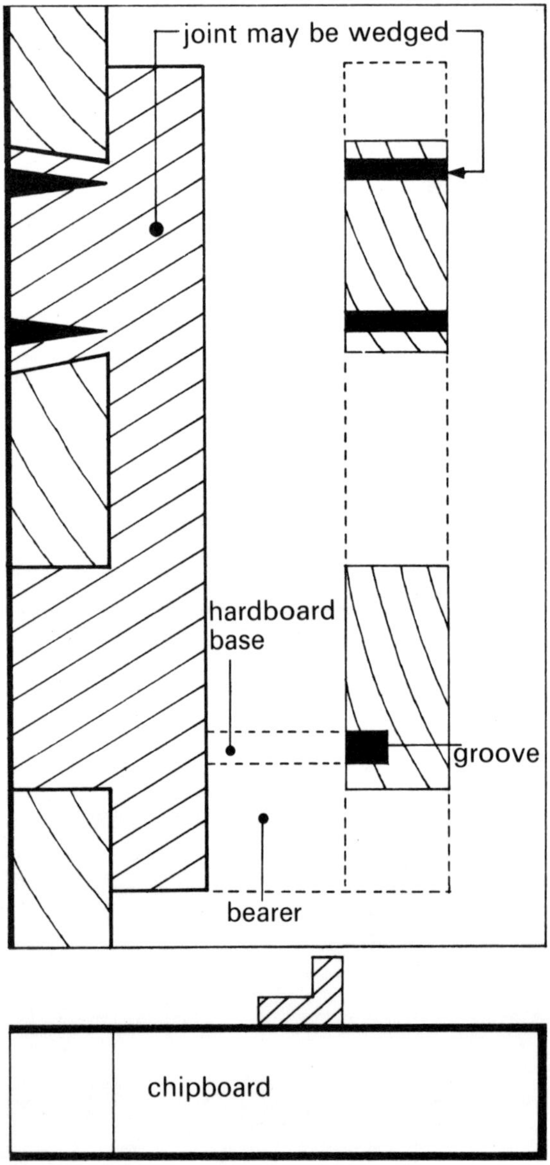

The wide rail is tenoned into the plywood sides. Bearers applied to the sides support a hardboard shelf and a sliding lid.

FITTINGS

The lid will need a small handle or finger grip at each side. This can be a piece of aluminium angle fixed with epoxy resin adhesive.

Consider other alternatives.

FINAL ADJUSTMENTS

Decide on the finishes to be used—these will be related to the materials used and should be the same as those on the stool.

Work through the same procedure as the stool making a good-sized sketch of the table and giving appropriate written information.

THE WORKING DRAWING

By superimposing one over the other, the side and end elevations of the table can be drawn full-size on an A1 sized sheet of paper. There is no need for a plan. Dimensions will not be necessary providing that overall sizes are stated, as measurements can be taken directly from the drawing.

DESIGN 3 COFFEE TABLE

Known Facts: Overall Dimensions are given.
The top is 1 m × 500 mm and height is 375 millimetres.

Examination Requirements: You are required to complete the front elevation, end elevation and plan of a small coffee table, $\frac{1}{5}$ full-size, indicating:

A suitable underframe to which the top can be attached.

One method of fixing the top to the underframe.

A pleasant and functional shape for the table top.

Any shaping and decoration you think necessary on the underframe.

The type of material you would use and the finish.

Further notes and sketches may be added to your drawing to give any other relevant information.

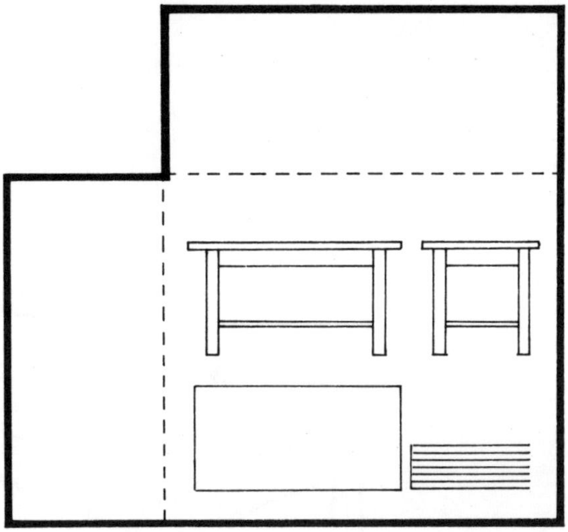

PROBLEMS TO ANSWER

What type of underframe is going to be used?

This will affect all other solutions so it must be established first. Make a series of quick clear sketches to develop your ideas.

Some basic constructions are shown below in simple line form. The variations in size, shape and form on these themes are numerous.

PRESENTATION

Quickly note the overall areas that will be taken up by the $\frac{1}{5}$ scale drawing.

In this instance it will fit either way on the paper, but the long vertical edge 'seems' to give more space for the important notes and sketches.

Indicate the space by drawing a faint line.

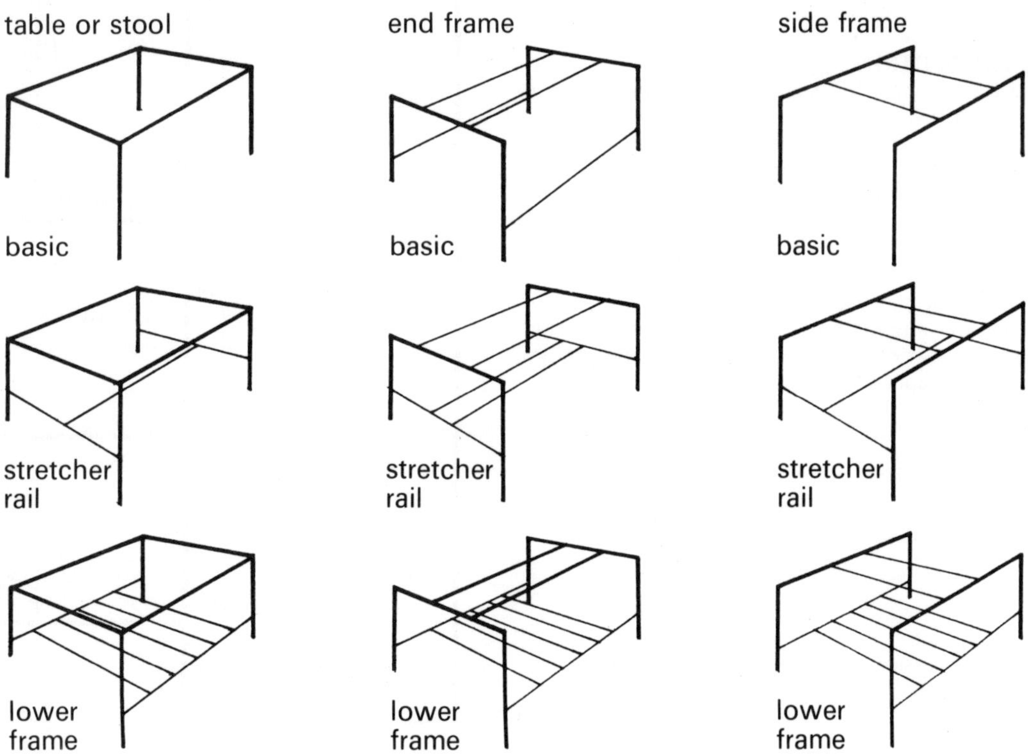

APPEARANCE

As an example let us consider the basic stool/table construction.

Shown below is a sketch that you might have drawn. On it you should insert leaders and record decisions on decoration, shaping finish, etc.

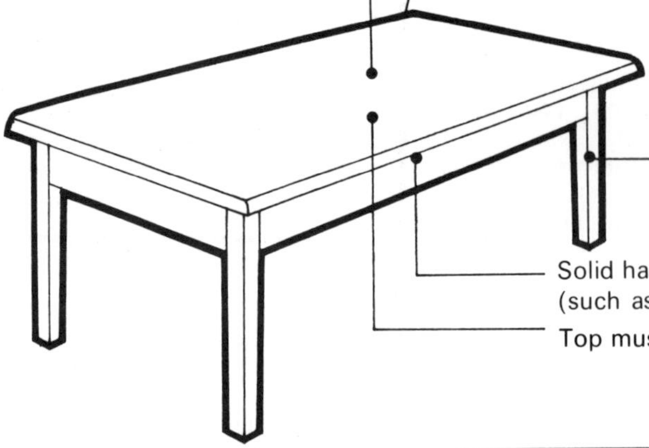

DESIGN FEATURES

You may think that in spite of the chamfer the table is too simple in line. A secondary rail would provide an additional feature and also give greater strength to the underframe.

CONSTRUCTION

Make a simple full-size sketch of the corner to determine the width of the rails and leg.

Time may not permit the sketch of an exploded isometric view of the joint—so its shape and proportion should be shown here.

DECORATION

Note how the use of a second rail as a design feature and strengthener also allows a much more effective use of chamfers cut with the natural sweep of a spokeshave.

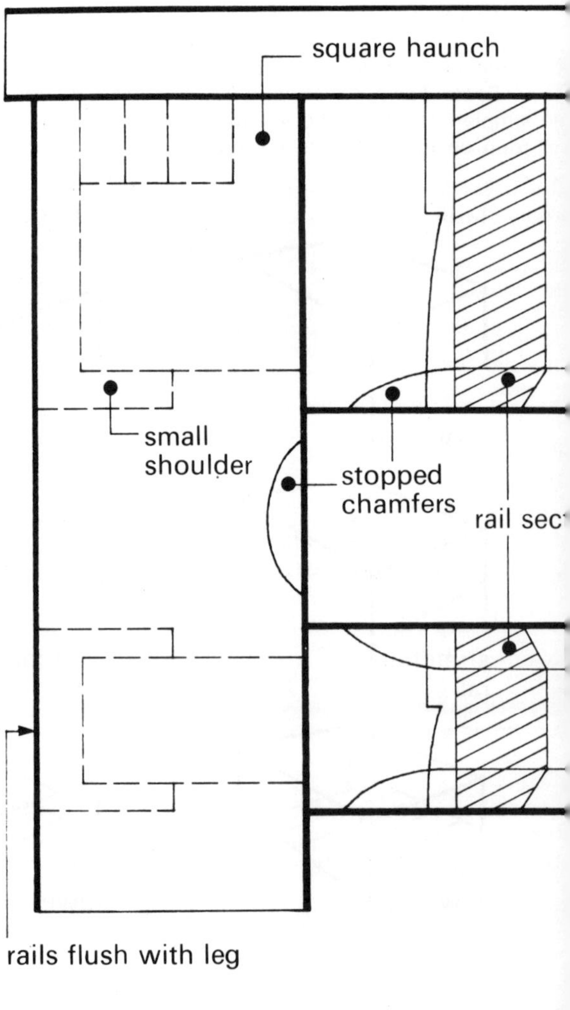

FIXING THE TOP

The plywood top can be fixed with metal plates.

Make a full-size pictorial sketch, indicating features by clear labelling.

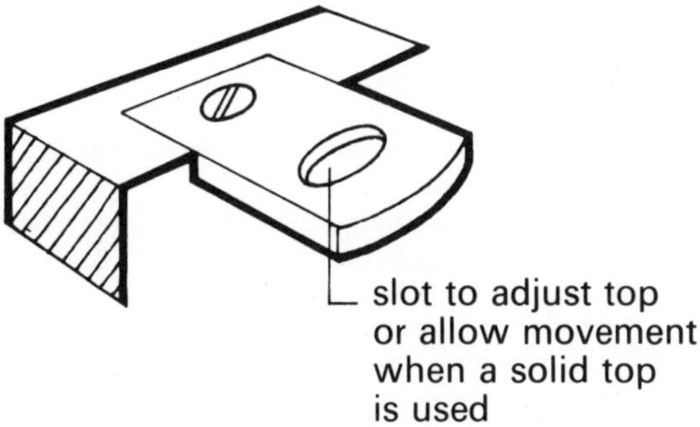

MATERIALS

You must indicate the materials used; you could use *almost any hardwood*—a close grained mahogany or teak would be ideal. Contrasting woods could be used for the top and underframe—attractive examples being:

oak and mansonia
mahogany and rosewood

STAINING

Probably the table will have to match existing furniture,—Whatever hardwood is used it is likely to require staining, and this should be carefully done in good light.

It is important that test stains be done on similar waste wood before doing the 'real thing'.

FINISH

For the top to be effective in use an A/C lacquer or polyurethane finish would be ideal since both are *heat and moisture resistant.* The table is likely to get considerable wear and a satin/matt finish may be more serviceable than a high gloss.

The underframe could be treated in the same way although a cheaper wax or cellulose treatment would be adequate.

THE DRAWING

From the information that you have recorded in note and sketch form, the $\frac{1}{5}$ scale drawing can now be easily made.

MAKING A COFFEE TABLE

In this examination question the sizes of the table were stipulated and although they would result in a well-proportioned table, any design for a table for use in your own home would need to be of a size and shape to suit your own needs.

The overall height should be between 375 and 450 mm depending on the type of easy chairs you have, but whereas a 1 metre table may be dwarfed in a very large sitting room it could be a nuisance in a small flat.

Determine the size and shape of the top:

When at home lay out a sheet of newspaper on the floor and fold it until you determine suitable dimensions.

Rectangular and square tables are common because they are strong and easy to make, but they can act as a barrier to walking about, particularly in a small room. Consider a round top which is pleasant to sit around.

Round tables are discussed in *Woodwork 2* (pages 53, 78, and 93).

A set of nesting tables is ideal when entertaining people. Three alternative arrangements are shown.

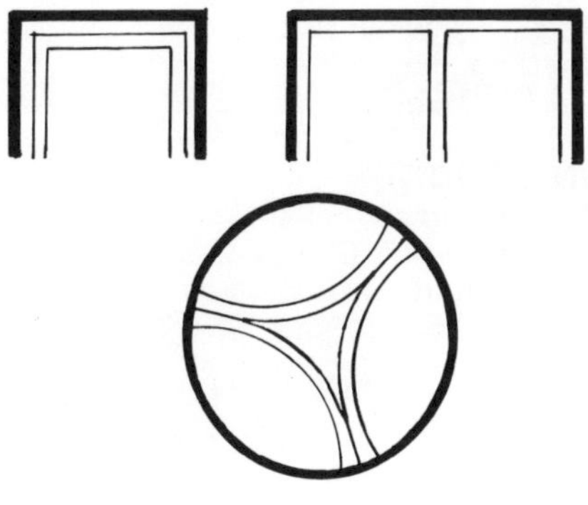

The plans show average sizes of tables at present being manufactured—they may be a useful guide in starting your design.

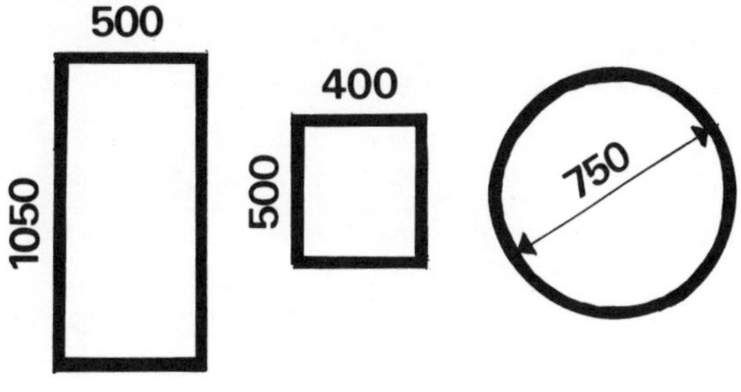

DESIGN KNOCKDOWN FURNITURE

AN INTRODUCTION

Large pieces of mass-produced furniture, such as wardrobes, are often packed flat by the manufacturers and fitted together with screws and catches when they reach the home. As you can imagine this saves time and money in transporting, storage and delivery, particularly up narrow staircases.

Furniture made in this way is called 'Knock-down' furniture. Other advantages are:

Work can be taken home more easily on crowded buses!

Damaged/scratched surfaces can be readily removed and renovated.

Furniture temporarily not required can be stored in little space.

Of course, with special fittings available, the possibilities of construction are numerous, but well-constructed items can be made without having to use specialised fixing devices.

Each of the KD items illustrated opposite consist of parts secured only by standard wood screws.

Right: The upholstered seat and detachable side frames of the music stool fit inside the music storage box for easy transportation.

Below right: The games table has two identical X-frames connected by a four part supporting column.

Above: This softwood occasional table, with a vinyl top, has detachable legs notched into the side rails and screwed from the inside.

Right: The armchair based on a design by Gerrit Rietveld consists of four separate frames screwed together.

DESIGN 4 KNOCK-DOWN TABLE

Example:

A coffee table based on the proportions set in design 3 and using the end frame with stretcher rail construction.

THE END FRAMES

These could be made from 50×25 mm planed hardwood.

The lower rail may be placed flat or on edge, but in either case the best joint would be through tenons which could be wedged.

The tenon shape can be repeated at the corners where finger joints may be used in place of the more obvious dovetails. The latter tend to look cumbersome in such a thick material.

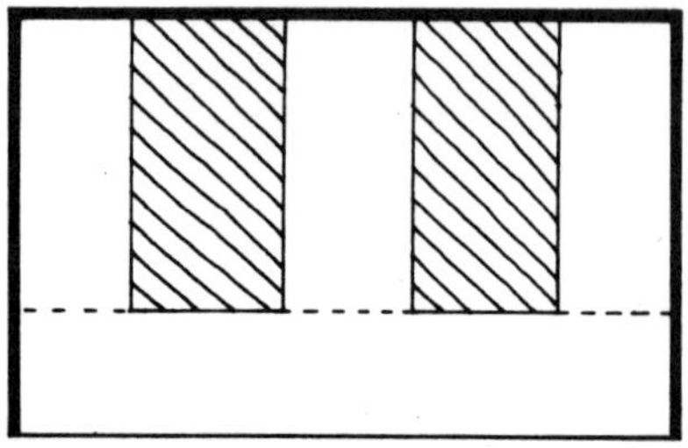

finger joint

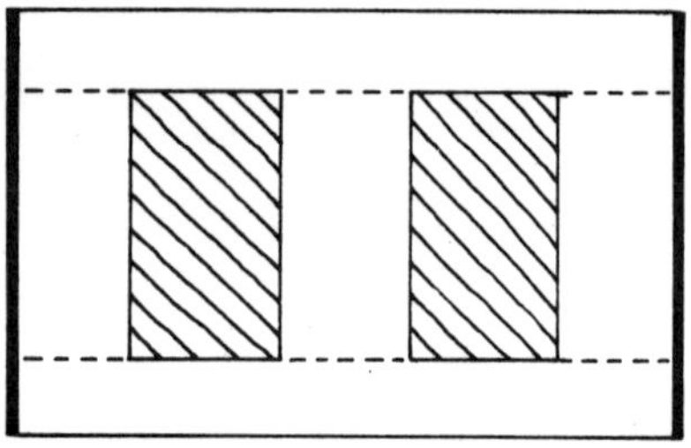

flat-rail

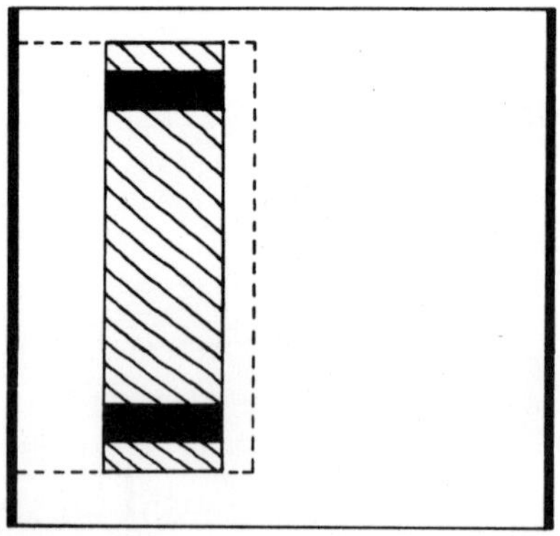

edge rail

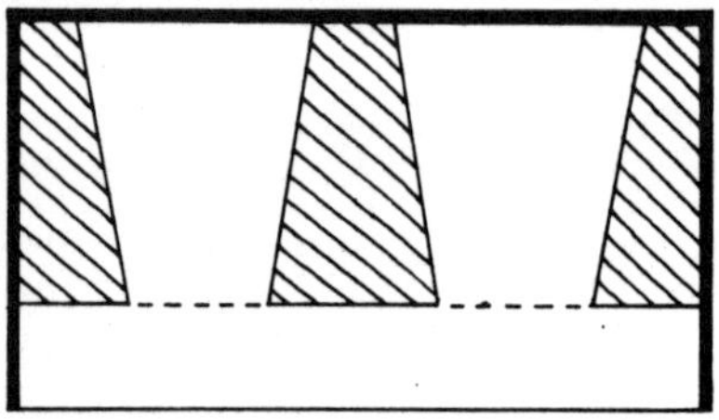

dovetail joint

TOP RAILS

The job of the top rails is to hold the end frames together and they are positioned to give adequate support to the table top. By being placed on end they elevate the top above the frames giving an appearance of lightness.

The rail endings should be simply treated—a slope like the one shown above is adequate. They may be housed to fit over the frames and are fixed from above by steel countersunk screws.

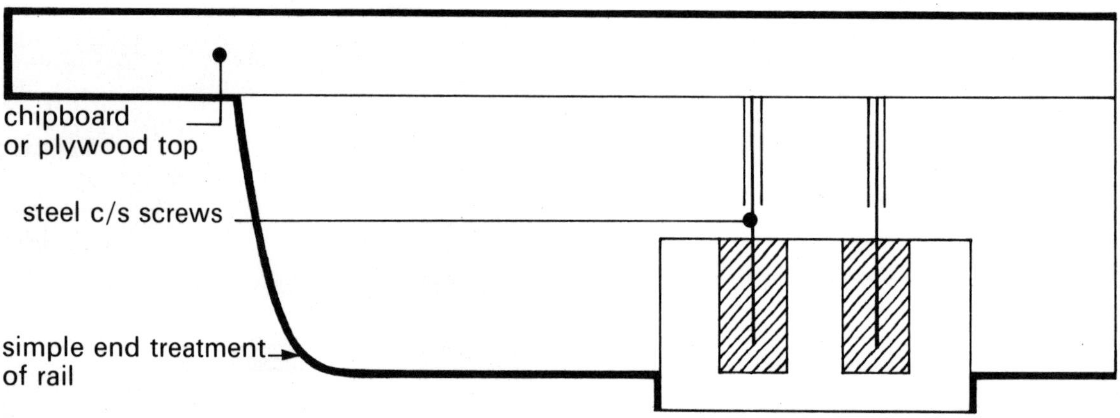

Above: A knock down table which combines traditional joints with special fixing devices.

Below: The table packs flat and is easily re-assembled with a screwdriver.

STRETCHER RAILS

Flat Rail. Like the top rails they may be housed and screwed but from below—using brass screws in surface cups.

Edge Rail. By being stepped and screwed from beneath with a steel round-head screw, a neat rail ending is achieved.

Note: When making the table, mark out the inside shoulders of top and stretcher rails at the same time.

sections

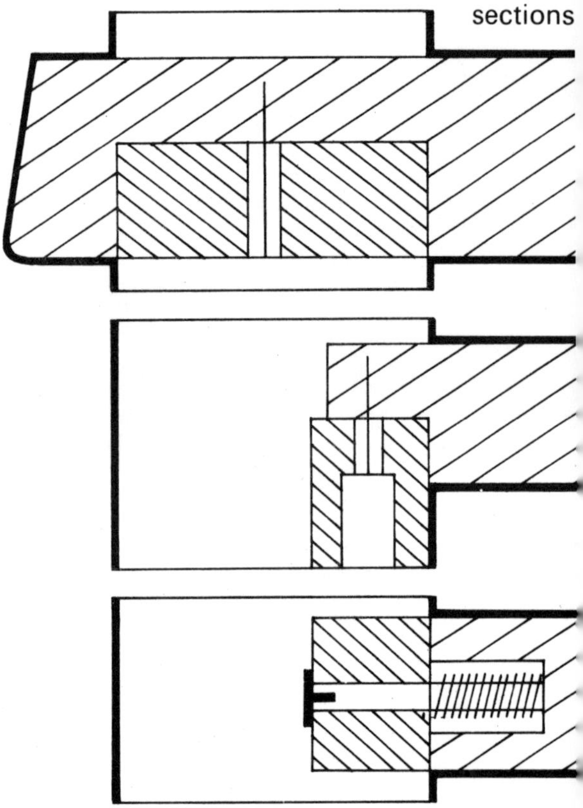

Alternative: Although requiring a special KD fitting this method is both neat and strong. A nylon bush is inserted in the end grain of the stretcher rail and a countersunk screw inserted. The screw-head is then covered with a threaded cheese-head cap made of brass.

The lower rails can be fixed with a KD screw fitting which is covered by a brass cap.

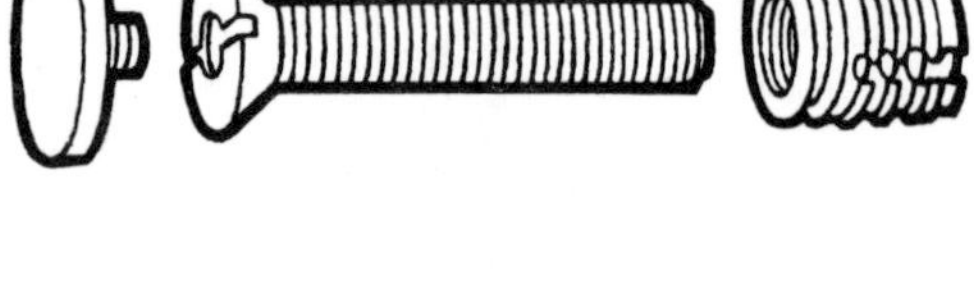

THE TOP

The rectangular shape of the end frames suggests a similarly shaped top.

Veneered chipboard (section 12) is a material which is available in standard widths and a strip of matching veneer is soon applied to the ends with a contact adhesive—the edges are already veneered.

The top may be attached to the rails with a metal plate (as in design 3) but using Twinfast screws.

Alternative: Plastic KD fittings are an efficient fixing device and are easily obtained from do-it-yourself shops. Special chipboard screws are supplied. (*Woodwork 2,* pp. 62 and 69)

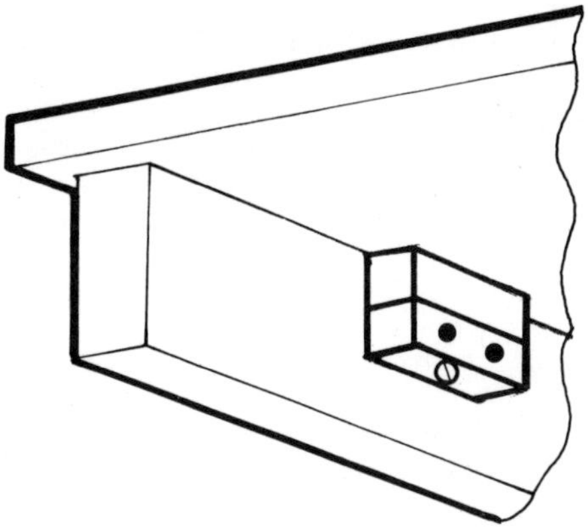

LOWER SHELF OR TRAY

If a lower shelf is fitted it should be of the same material and shape as the top and could be fixed in the same way.

Alternative: Have a moveable tray. For this to be effective the stretcher rails must be set well apart.

A tray needs sides and ends to prevent crockery, etc., from sliding off but the corners are most hygienic if left 'open' as cleaning is easier. The half end elevation below shows one of many ways of constructing such a tray.

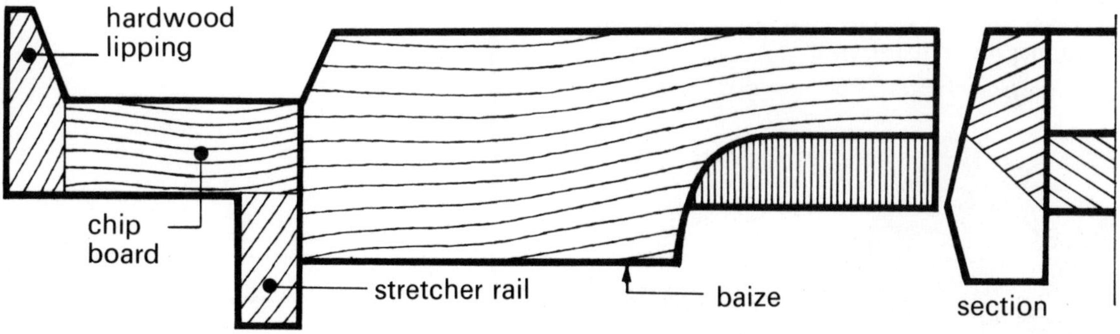

The side lippings can be shaped, glued and cramped on.

The ends of the tray can:

(i) act as handles.

(ii) act as feet when the tray is placed on a surface —could be covered with self-adhesive 'baize', e.g., sueded 'Contact'.

(iii) be used to position the tray between the stretcher rails.

Note that the shaping is simple and that the proportions of the tray, as well as its actual size, are important.

FINISH

This can be finished as in design 3, or if of teak, it should be coated with teak oil.

DESIGN 5 SHOE CLEANING BOX

Examination Requirements: Design a box to hold shoe cleaning materials.
It should have a lid and a footrest which can also be used as a carrying handle.
State the material and finish you would use. (S)

The answer is to be given as part of a written paper and suggests that a series of sketches and brief explanatory notes are required.

The size of the box—left to your own judgment as no information about contents is given.

The shape of the box—whatever its size, must make the contents easily accessible.

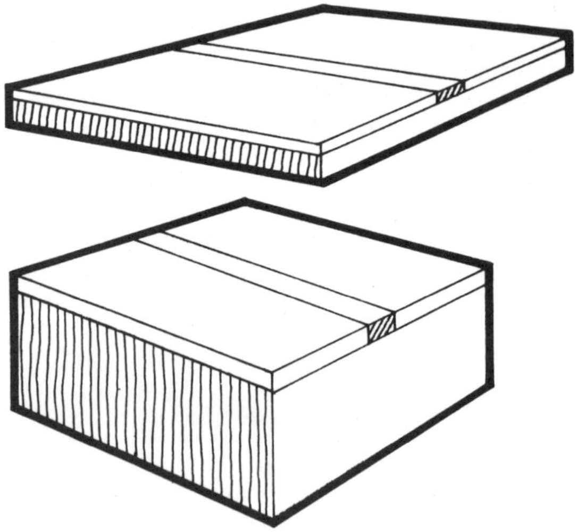

PROBLEMS TO ANSWER

A wide flat box would give good access to contents but would take up valuable shelf space, so a smaller but deeper box is preferable.

CONSTRUCTION

The sketch shows two *plywood lids* fixed to a central strip of wood by means of *butt hinges*.

They project at the ends to form a finger grip so that they are easily opened.

A *hardboard partition* can be slotted into a narrow through housing.

The glued and pinned/screwed hardboard/*plywood base* gives the box stability and enables corner joints to be simple.

Dovetails would, of course, be strongest and a suggested layout of the tails is shown in the sketch. (This is not drawn full size).

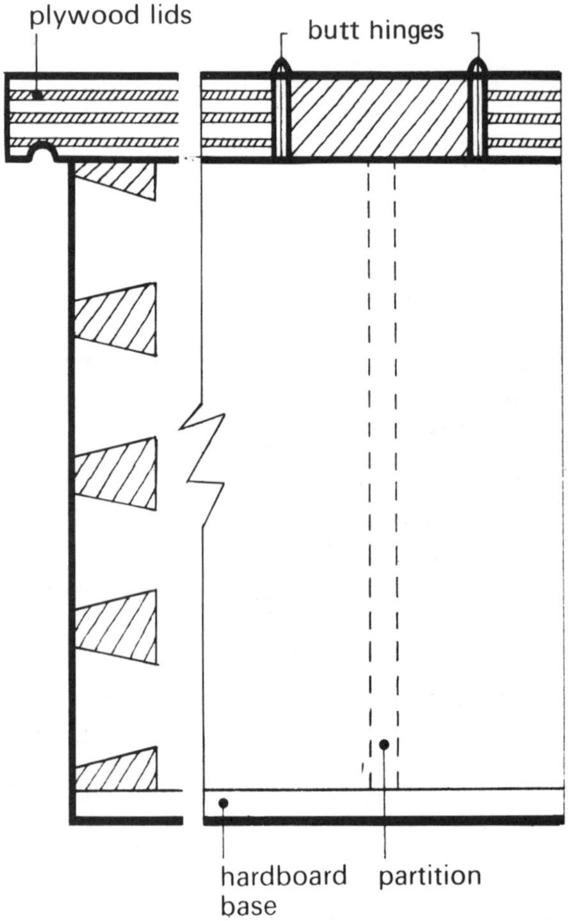

A strong shoe-cleaning box of Parana pine made without a shoe rest.

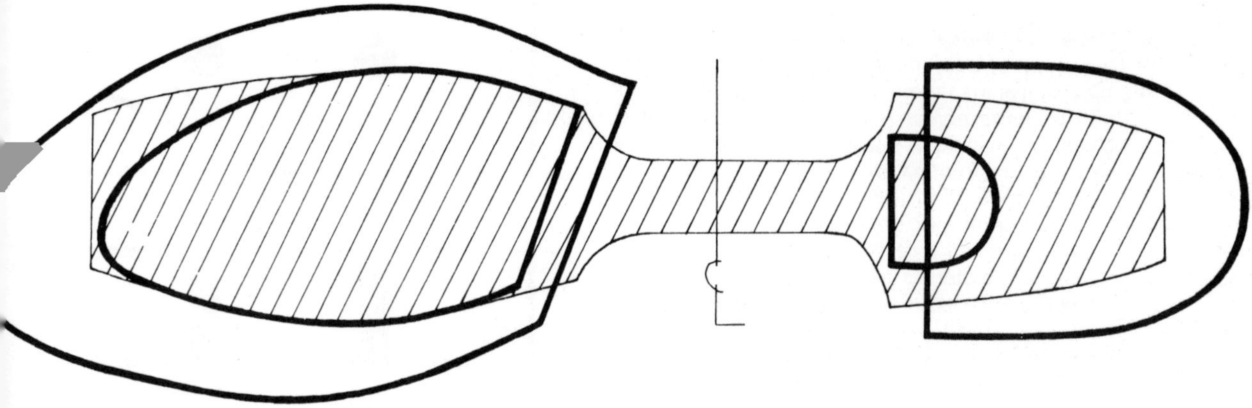

HANDLE/FOOTREST

The shape of shoes and hands bear little similarity and designing a handle-cum-footrest is the most demanding part of the problem.

A practical way of doing this would be to take off a shoe and draw round it, producing an outline of contact with a surface.

The sketch shows the shape of a large man's shoe and a smaller ladies size (not full size).

Note: The space between the soles and the heels suggests the position of the handle. For the box to be properly balanced this must be placed in the middle.

APPEARANCE

Because such a variety of shoe shapes and sizes will be placed on the rest it would be best to simplify the shape.

The example shown could be readily shaped from wood and perhaps screwed to a metal band to form a handle.

Alternative: An all wood construction using finger joints at the corners and with the vertical members screwed to the side.

MATERIALS

This is primarily a functional object and a softwood is ideal for the main box. Plywood for the lids would eliminate a tendency for them to warp and handles of flat sectioned mild steel are suitable. The footrest could be a contrasting hardwood.

FINISH

A hard wearing cellulose finish would be ideal and the plywood lids could be painted in distinguishing colours. The metal handle should be painted with a suitable lacquer.

MAKING A BOX

Determine the size required by measuring all your shoecleaning materials and considering any shelf space on to which it may have to fit. Consider the use of a small metal handle if a shoe rest is not required.

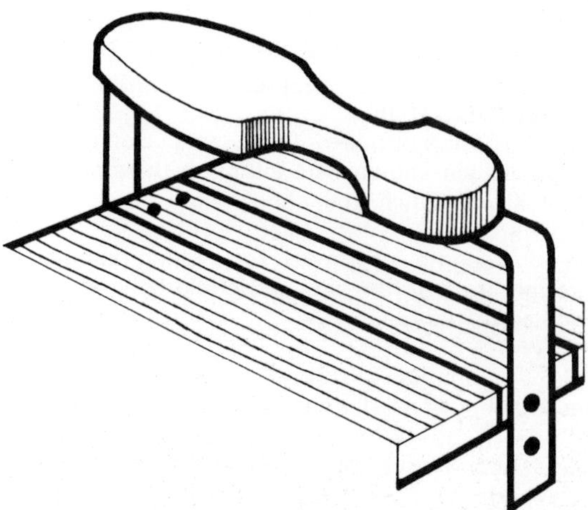

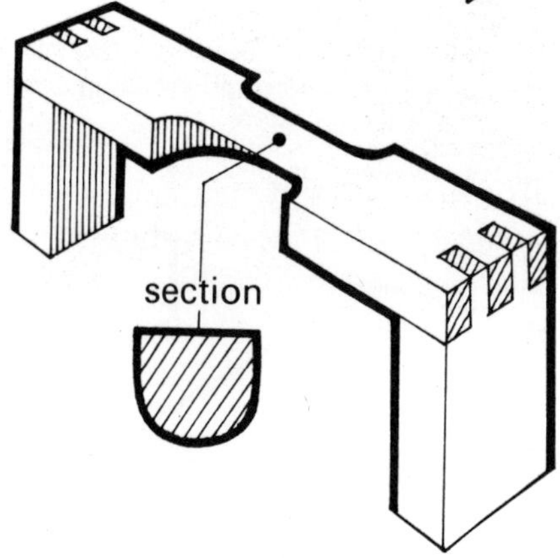

DESIGN 6 MILK BOTTLE HOLDER

Designing a milk bottle holder for home use requires similar treatment to the shoe cleaning box in that *its prime object is to be functional.* If it is to be useful it must do its job properly and *appearance is of secondary importance.*

Examination Requirements: Design a holder for three pint milk bottles.
It should have a carrying handle.
State the materials from which it is made, the type of adhesive used and a suitable weather resistant finish.

Firstly, three pint milk bottles must be measured and the minimum size of the holder determined.
Note: A space is needed between each bottle for a divider which will prevent breakage.

The handle will be placed above the bottles and if some form of foot is included the holder will be clear of wet ground.

A simple outline sketch states the basic needs of the design.

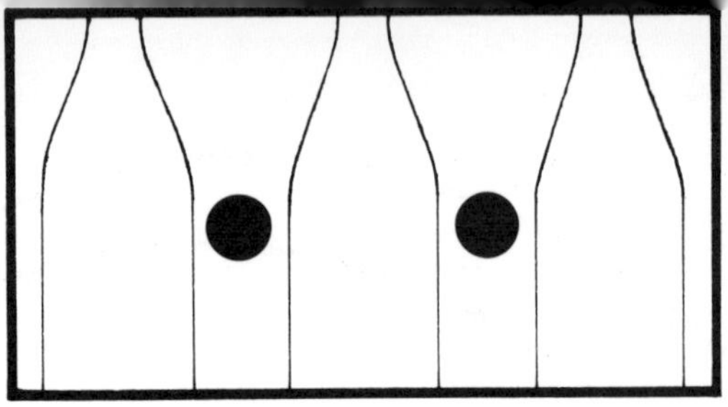

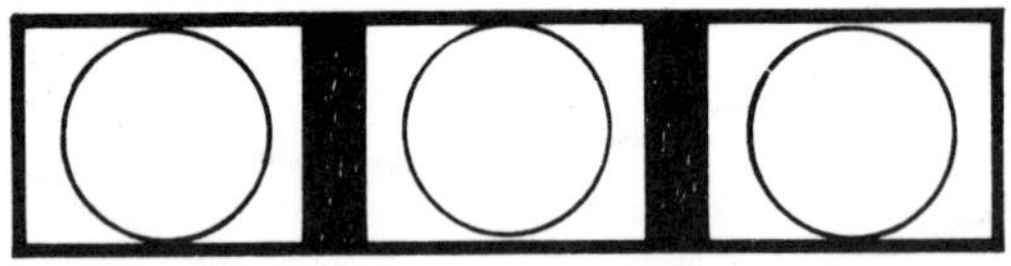

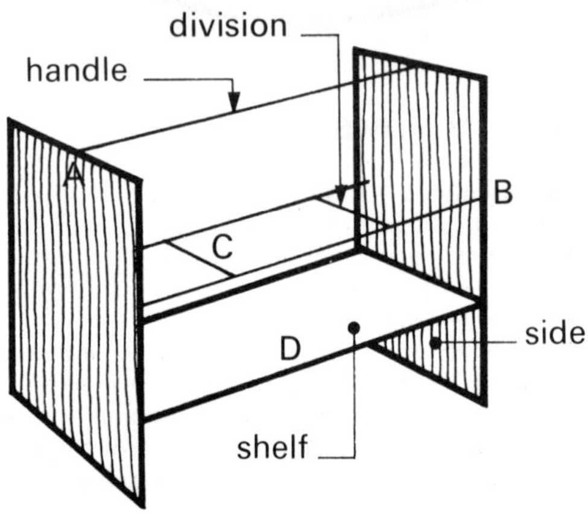

CONSTRUCTION

This design requires four joints. Some simple examples are shown here although there are many alternatives which you should consider.

(A) A length of dowel rod which should be brought through the side and could be wedged for increased strength.

(B) A common or through dovetail with a bare-faced tenon as an alternative. The latter is strongest.

(C) Short lengths of dowel rod may be used as an alternative to a rail fixed into a through housing.

(D) The shelf can be fixed by any number of variations on the through housing joint.

A

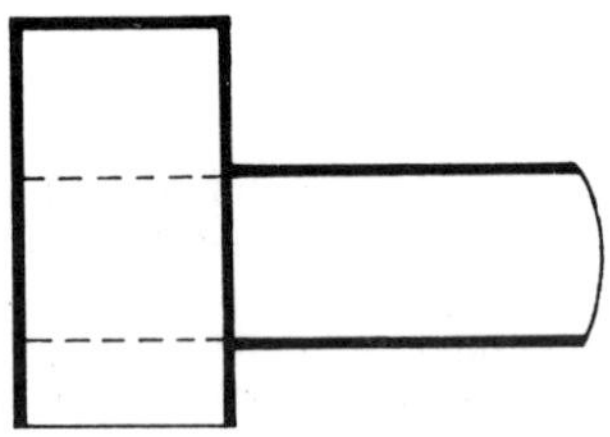

B

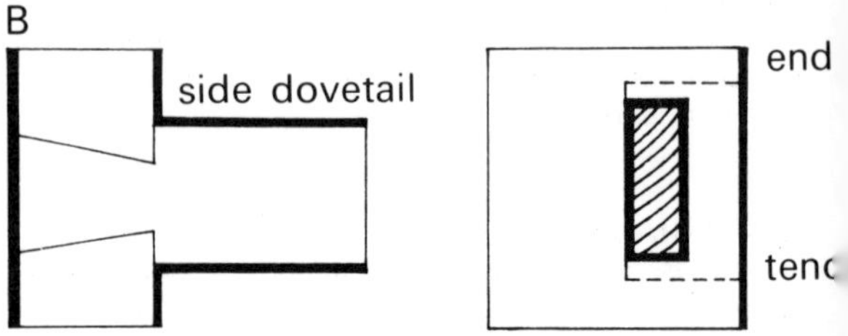

D

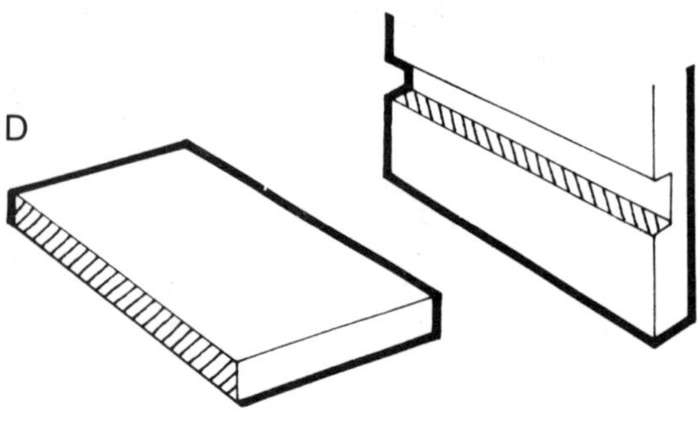

C

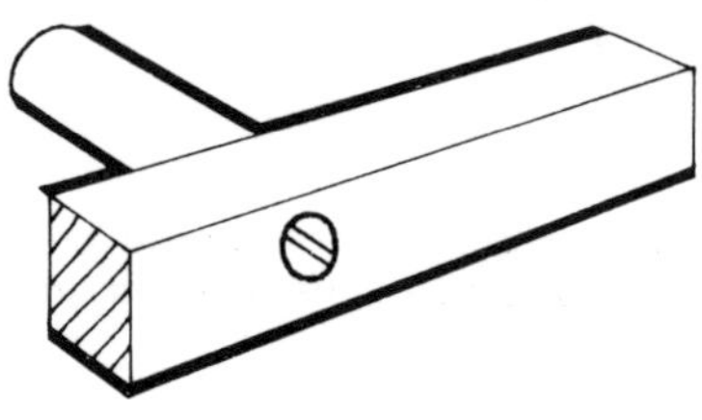

Position of Handle: A centrally placed handle could cause an obstruction.

There are two solutions to this:

Increase the height of the holder, but this might make it heavy and cumbersome.

Keep the same height and put the carrying handle off-centre to make access easier (see photo).

Take care when positioning the lower rail—it need not be very high to support the bottles and a high rail will prevent access. A full-size section will help to establish its best position.

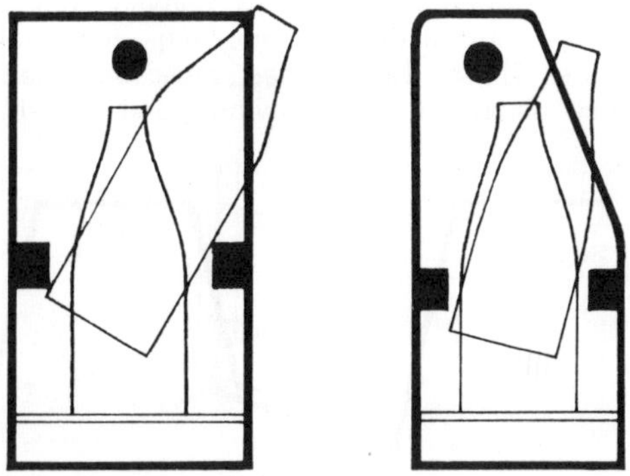

A softwood milk bottle holder with the dowel handle set off-centre.

MATERIAL FINISH ADHESIVE

1. Almost any timber would do the job well—a softwood is cheaper.
2. The finish is used outdoors and must be fully protective, e.g., a polyurethane varnish.
3. The adhesive must be waterproof; use any synthetic resin adhesive.

APPEARANCE

Acceptable shapes have been determined by functional considerations and can be improved by careful attention to detail, such as widths and thicknesses of material and edge treatment, e.g., use of small chamfers.

ALTERNATIVE DESIGN

Alternative Design: A box construction could be used with dovetailed corner joints used throughout.

Sloping sides provide access from both sides. Rubber stoppers may be used for feet. Handle shape needs careful consideration and a mock-up in scrapwood would be valuable.

MAKING A HOLDER

You may think that these simple solutions to the problem are rather heavy in both appearance and weight.

Using wood formers or the 'Flexiformer' (see *Woodwork* 2) the job may be laminated making a strong but light construction. Thin metal rods instead of timber will also refine the design.

The more adventurous you are as a designer and craftsman the more exciting will be your results.

The sketch shows the bottles fitted into holes drilled with an expansive bit and resting on metal rods which form the handle supports.

Details of construction and handle design need careful thought—that is your problem!

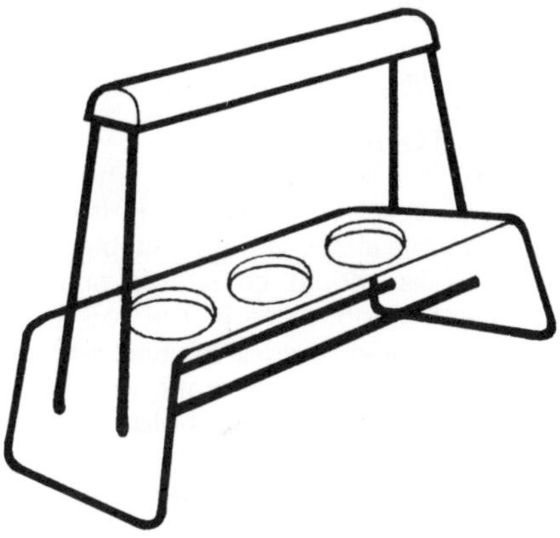

DESIGN 7 TABLE LAMPS

Table lamps are usually used as a secondary source of light in a living room or lounge and beside diffusing or spreading a pleasant light, they should look attractive.

DESIGN REQUIREMENTS

The base must be stable without appearing cumbersome—this is a safety factor.

The position of the bulb (the light source) must be determined.

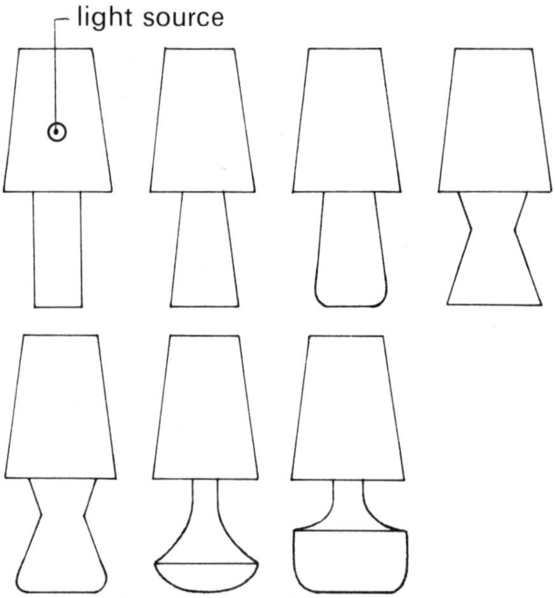

The shade must be effective, avoiding a glare but providing adequate light.

The relative size of the shade and base are most important.

DECISIONS TO BE MADE

You should first select a shade—when you have carefully made a beautiful base it is frustrating to find that a suitable shade is not available.

Ideally, shapes should be simple and of plain material—being unobtrusive in the room. A good selection of textured shades is available in most big stores or it is possible to make your own.

The shade frame and light holder will fix the position of the top of the base.

Make a series of scaled sketches of bases below your shade—which can be drawn with tracing paper, to save time and achieve great accuracy.

APPEARANCE

Lamp bases can be square in section but are more often round, having been turned between centres on the lathe. This means that with carefully chosen timbers—teak for example—a simple shape will bring out the grain markings. The cone, cylinder and bottle shapes all have firm bases and are stable. Only a few shapes are shown and many subtle variations of size and proportion could be developed from each one.

Grain which may be less attractive but is of regular colouring can be used between adjacent blocks of contrasting timber, e.g. mahogany/sycamore. These 'sandwiches' must be carefully prepared using full-size drawings, and the shape should have contrasting angles to obtain the maximum effect.

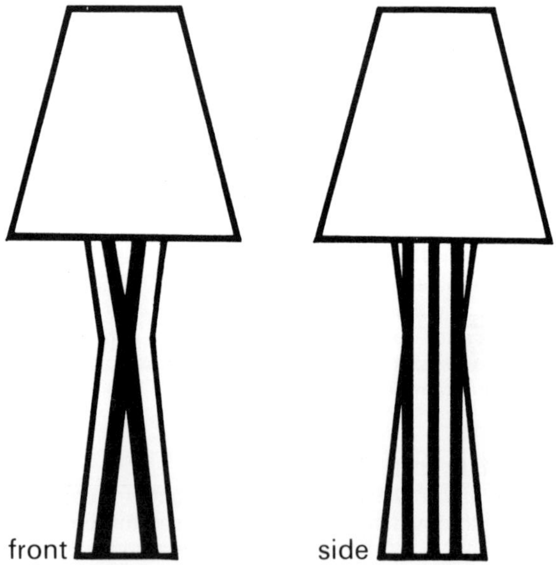

Wide flat bases are often turned on the face-plate of the lathe and laminations of plywood offcuts of good quality give an attractive effect in either direction, but a non-brittle glue (PVA) should be used, that will not 'fly' or blunt the turning tool edge.

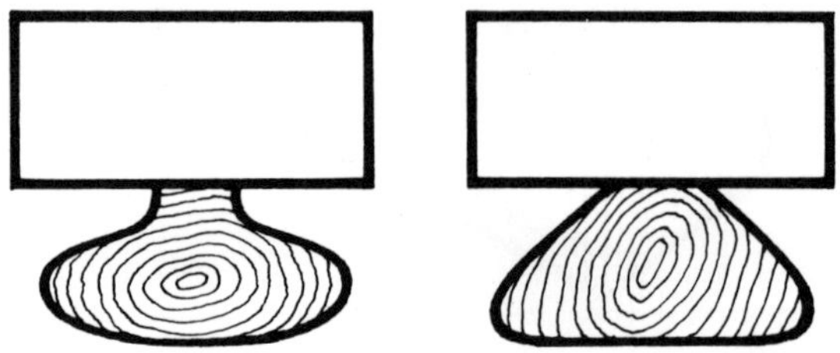

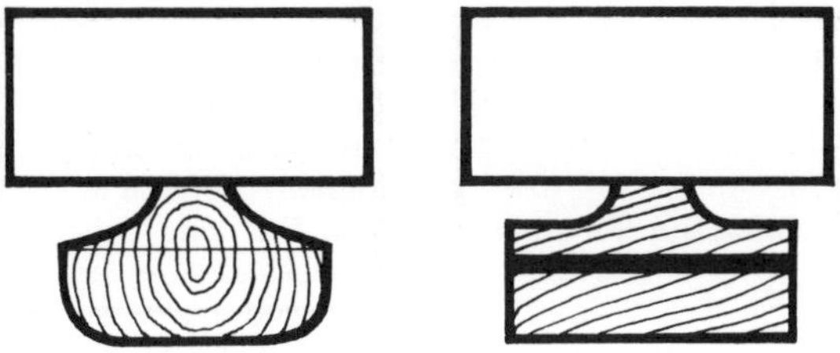

DESIGN FEATURES

The most simple of shapes, the cylinder, can be highlighted with bands of metal—teak and stainless steel being a good combination.

The high gloss finish on some lamps can be contrasted with a band of self-coloured linen or similar fabric (perhaps to match the shade) and secured with clear 'Bostick'.

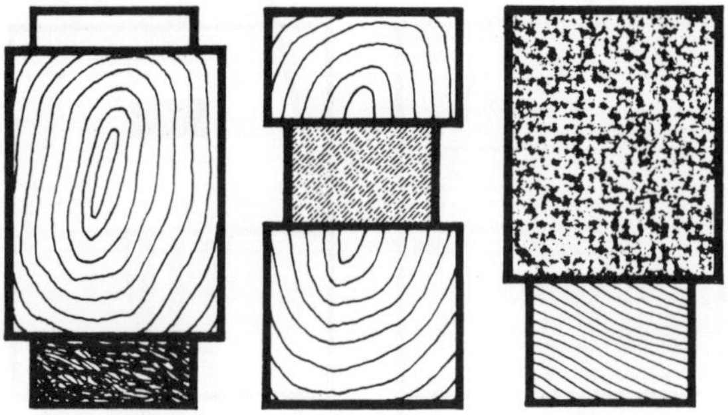

THE BASE

In the past protection has usually been given to table surfaces by covering the base with baize. This can now be done easily by applying a piece of self-adhesive sueded vinyl sheeting such as 'Contact' by Storeys Ltd.

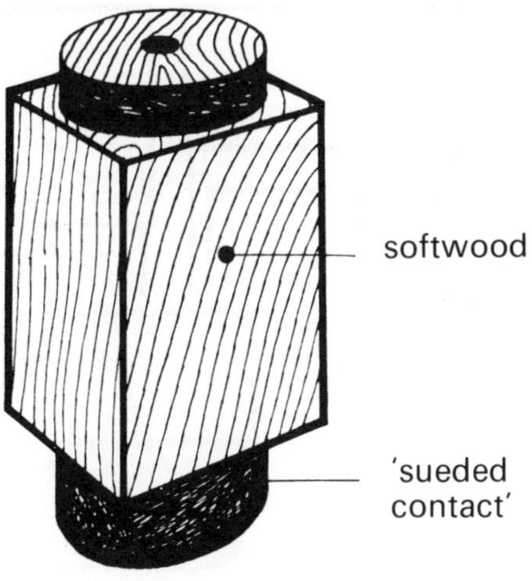

THE FINISH

As the lamps are for interior use only almost any finish is adequate.

If the work is turned it can be polished on the lathe for which a quick-drying cellulose is recommended.

LAMP FITTINGS

(a) The cheapest type of fitting on the market is usually made of brown plastic.
(b) The imitation candle wax in some holders may be 'in keeping' with the decorations of older houses.
(c) The white plastic holder has a clean modern shape which will look good on most bases.

Take good care in selecting a bulb with the most appropriate shape and remember that clear bulbs give a sharper light than pearl ones.

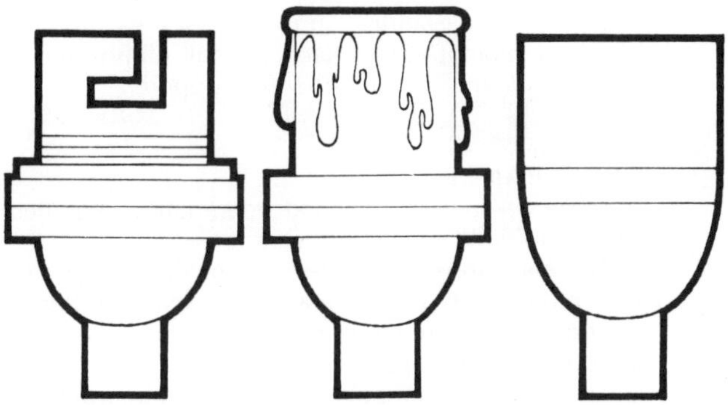

Contrasting forms of teak table lamps, one turned and the other carved.

DESIGN 8 BEDSIDE CABINET

Known Fact: The cabinet is to be 550 mm in height.

Examination Requirements: You are to show by a series of drawings, notes and sketches the design of a bedside cabinet.

It should have:

some enclosed storage space,

a plinth or stool to raise it from the floor.

Show clearly the joints to be used and the shape of the handles.

State the materials from which it is made and a suitable finish for the surfaces.

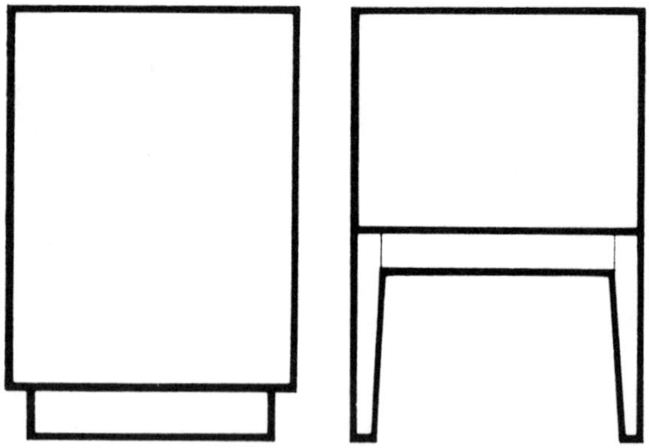

What amount or shape of *storage space* is required?

When this is decided it will be possible to determine the overall dimensions of the cabinet, which in turn, will enable us to design the underframe.

From the elevations shown it is clear that a 450 mm cabinet would need a small plinth, and a 250 mm cabinet a taller stool for support.

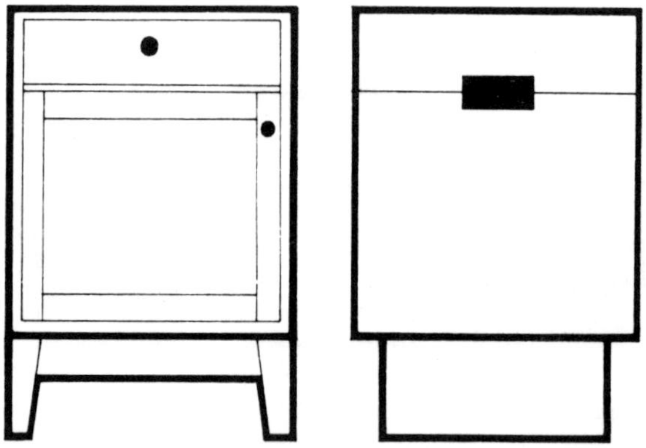

APPEARANCE

Make a series of freehand imaginative sketches of the probable cabinet appearance.

The elevations show how any basic outline can take on a variety of appearances by using different methods of construction, types of material, surface textures and handles.

The examples compare a traditional construction, using a drawer, framed door, applied handles and carcase on a stool with a construction using flat plywood surfaces, recessed finger grips and a plinth support.

PROPORTION

Where the amount of storage space is not critical make a series of freehand $\frac{1}{10}$ scale sketches to decide on the shape required.

If you were making the cabinet you would then prepare a full-size blackboard drawing to be seen at floor level.

A plan size of 375×300 mm is well proportioned and will hold large magazines.

Set out a $\frac{1}{5}$ scale front and end elevation of your design.

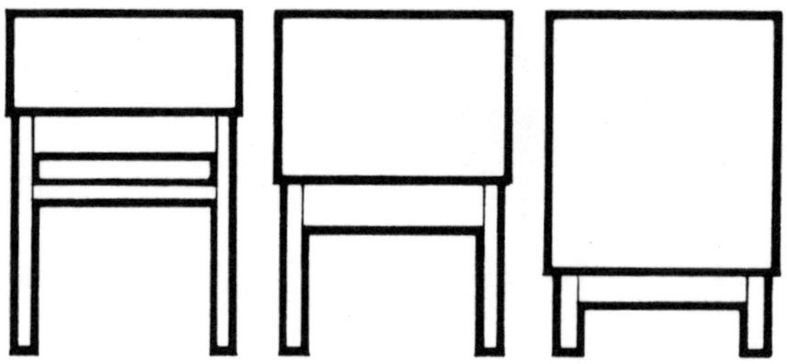

DESIGN FEATURES

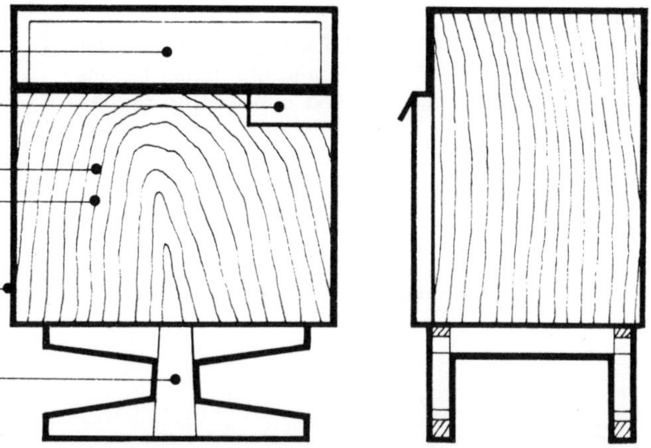

DECORATION

In the example shown above, 'decoration' is the contrasting of the stainless steel handles with strong and attractively grained veneers.

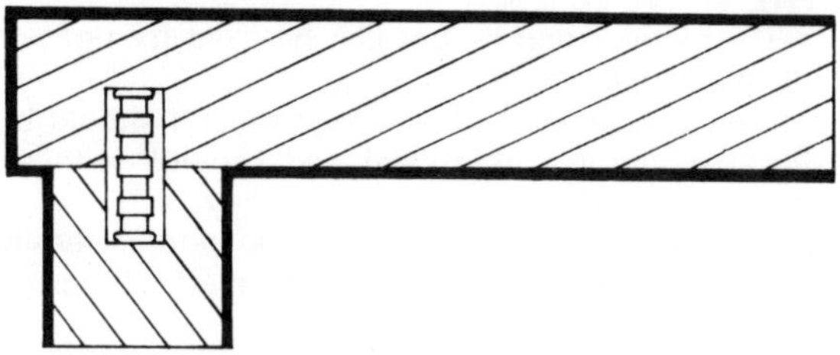

CONSTRUCTION

This can usually be made clear with labelled, sectioned elevations.

The Cabinet: The top can be glued and dowelled to the sides but the use of snap-in nylon dowels would enable the top to be removed and replaced if badly damaged.

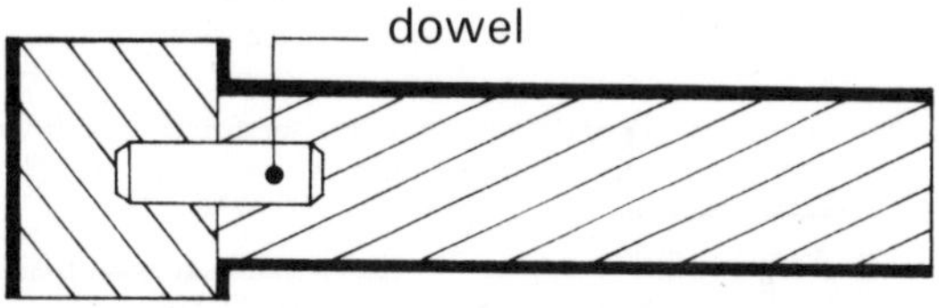

The fixed Shelf is secured with 6 mm dowel and glued with PVA adhesive. The use of a housing would weaken the 'grainless' chipboard.

The cabinet may have *a half shelf* on hardwood bearers or an adjustable one supported by nylon shelf supports.

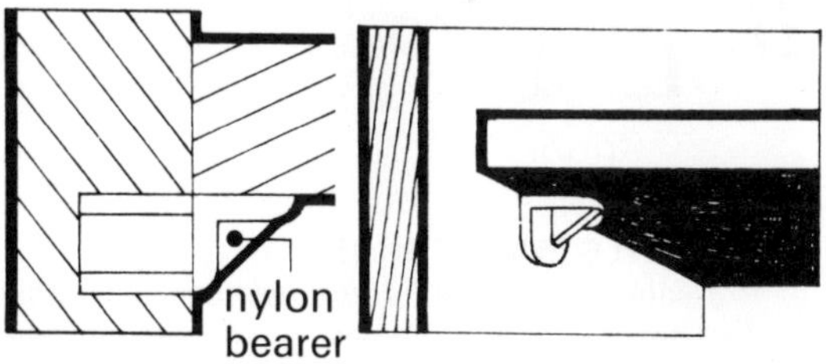

The bottom of the cabinet is fixed in the same way as the fixed shelf.

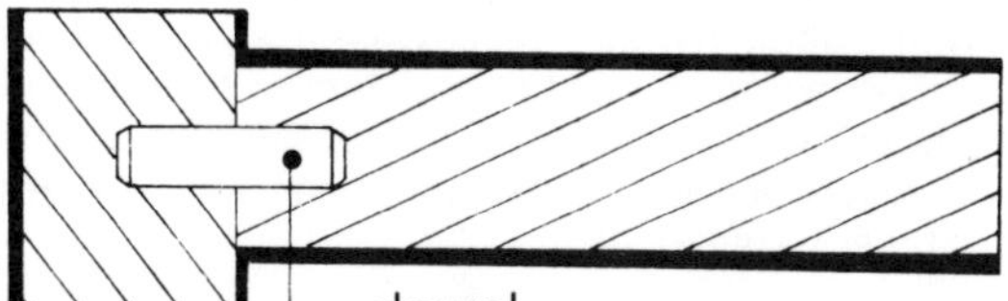

The fixed shelf and bottom are finished flush with the inside of the rebated sides. *A plywood back* is pinned in to the rebate and on to a fillet (glued and screwed to the top) to make the cabinet rigid.

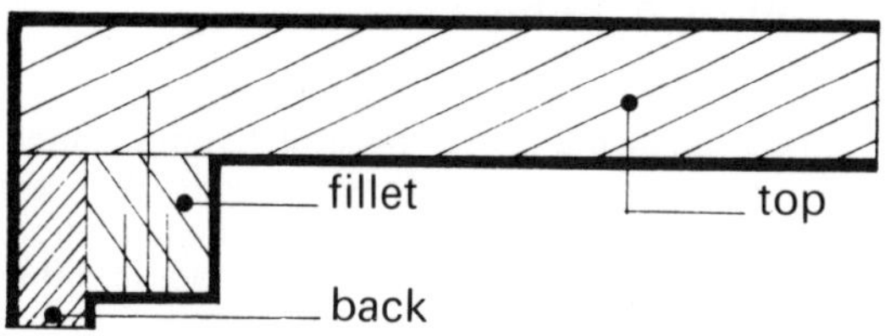

The door is cut from a 380 mm wide board—with an attractive grain pattern. The ends are covered with matching lipping or a piece of strip veneer.

SUPPORTING STOOL

The identical front and back frames can be constructed with T-bridle joints and are joined by one substantial cross rail dowelled into the top bridles.

The timbers are carefully shaped, but chamfers are not used as they would look out of place in the design.

The stool should not be less than 150 mm high to facilitate cleaning. A height of 175 mm will produce a square cabinet and will allow the chipboard sides to be cut from standard lengths.

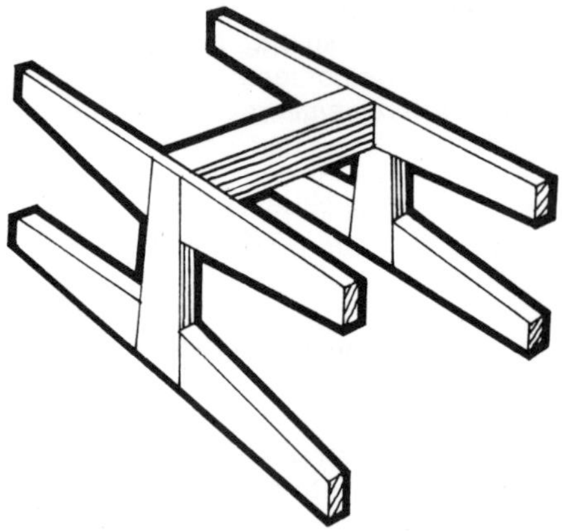

THE HANDLE

The handle (and hinge) can be fixed for right or left hand use.

Preferably made from stainless steel it should be recessed into the chipboard and secured with an epoxy resin adhesive.

It is set to one side so that the door is easily opened. It also provides an asymmetrical design feature.

The door is hung with a piano hinge and a magnetic catch holds it firmly in position.

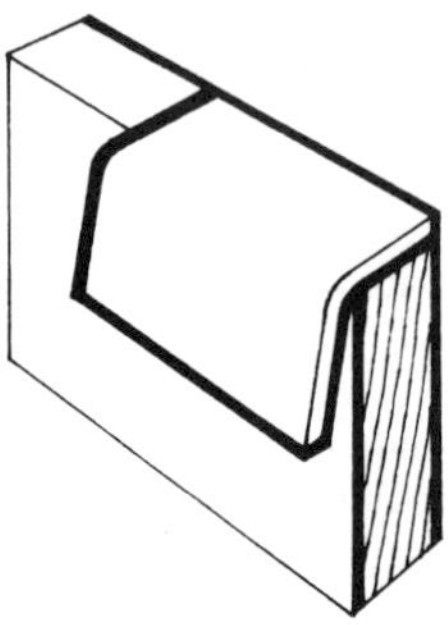

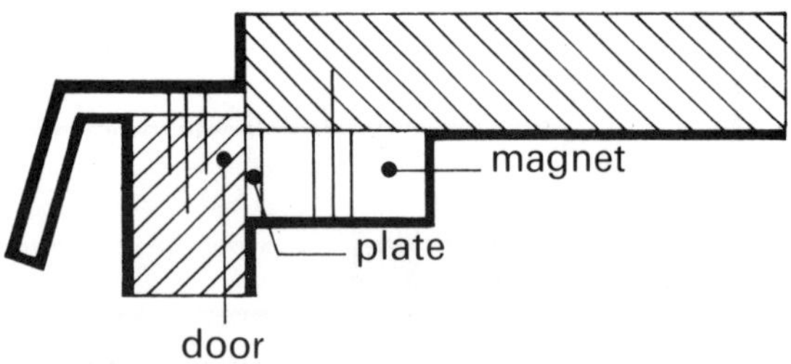

MATERIALS AND FINISH

Pre-sanded *veneered chipboard* can be obtained under several trade names such as vip-board, handi-board, and conti-board, and are surfaced with mahogany, oak, teak, walnut and rosewood.

The top finish must be resistant to heat, moisture and abrasion.

Inside surfaces must be 'finished' before the cabinet is glued up.

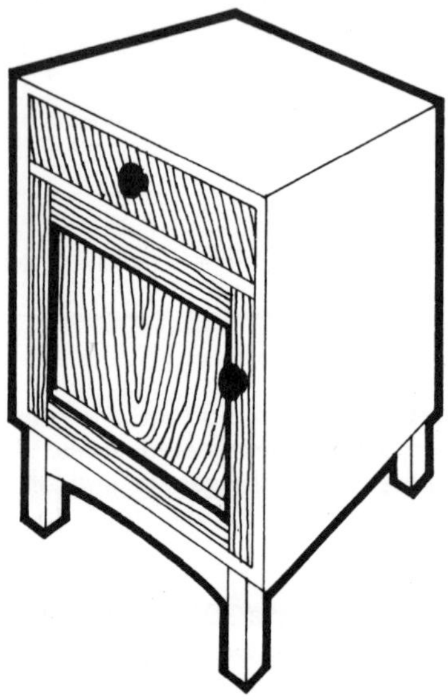

MAKING A CABINET

The decision on cabinet size will be an individual one based on personal requirements.

You may use a useful piece of furniture, such as this, as a means of showing off your skill, using solid timber and traditional forms of construction, or combine traditional and modern methods in different ways.

DESIGN 9 JARDINIÈRE (Plant Pot Stand)

Known Facts: The contents of the stand.

Examination Requirements: By means of notes and sketches show the design of a *jardinière* (plant pot stand).
It is to be used in the porch of a house.
It must hold four plant pots, each of which are 160 mm high and 175 mm in diameter at the top.
State the materials used and the finish applied to them.

PROBLEMS TO ANSWER

Are the plant pots to be placed on a tray so that they are seen, or placed inside a box construction so that only the plant is plainly seen?

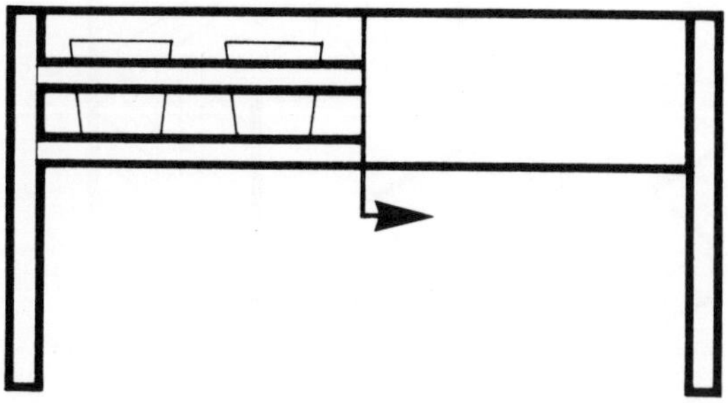

Sketch a series of front elevations to scale (approximate length is known) to determine the height of the stand.

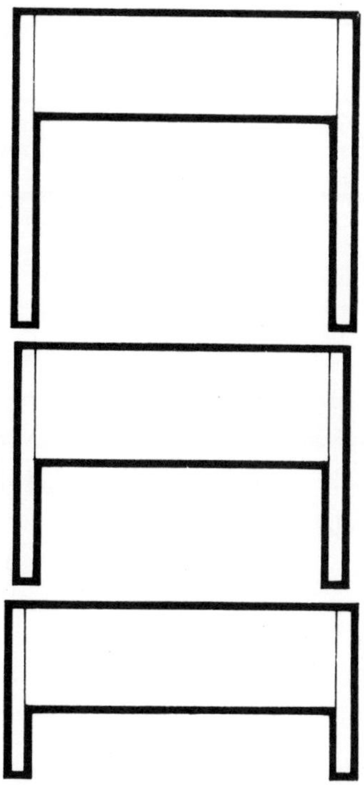

Then draw an end elevation to determine the width of the stand. If a box construction is being used it will need to be about 225 mm wide. A base dimension of that size would not be stable and this suggests that some form of sloping legs will be necessary.

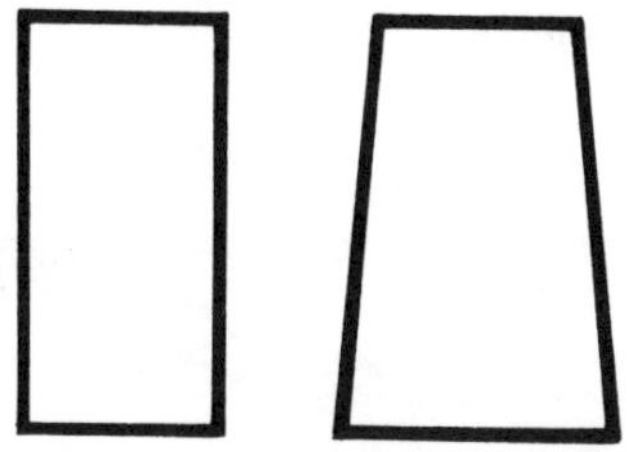

APPEARANCE

For the plants to be shown to their best advantage *the lines should be simple.*

Sloping legs are not easy to construct. One alternative would be slab sides, but they are too simple in appearance and lack interest.

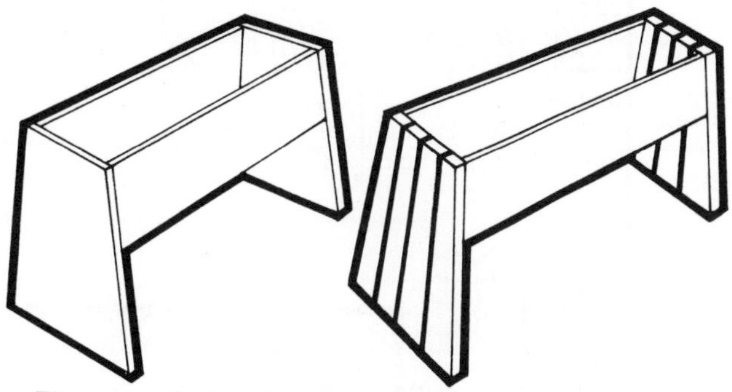

The use of slatted ends provides that interest without being complicated.

Make a series of pictorial sketches until you are satisfied, before working out constructional details. If you were making the stand you would now make use of full-size blackboard drawings to check the proportions.

CONSTRUCTION

The slats are attached to a simple frame which supports the box construction. They may be screwed from the inside with countersunk screws or from the outside using brass screws in external screw cups—giving a decorative effect.

The frame rails are through-tenoned into the end rails, the joint shown being housed between the mortises.

Note: There are many variations on this joint—wedging the tenons at right-angles to the grain is one.

Note: The inside edges of the slats are parallel—only the outside edges being sloped. This makes the plant pot holder, which is a straight-sided box construction appear to have slightly sloping sides.

Any suitable *corner joint* may be used.

If a softwood is used and is to be painted a glued and pinned lap joint is adequate.

If a hardwood is used and is to be given a clear finish then dovetails would show to good advantage.

The internal tray may be of metal or plastic and will rest on bearers glued and screwed to the inside of the box.

The box may be held in position by plates.

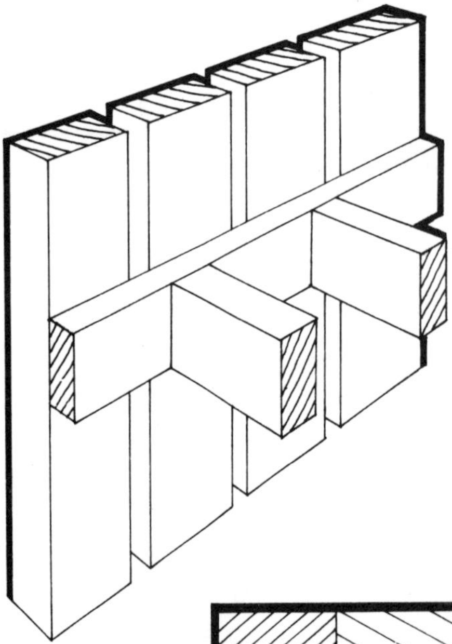

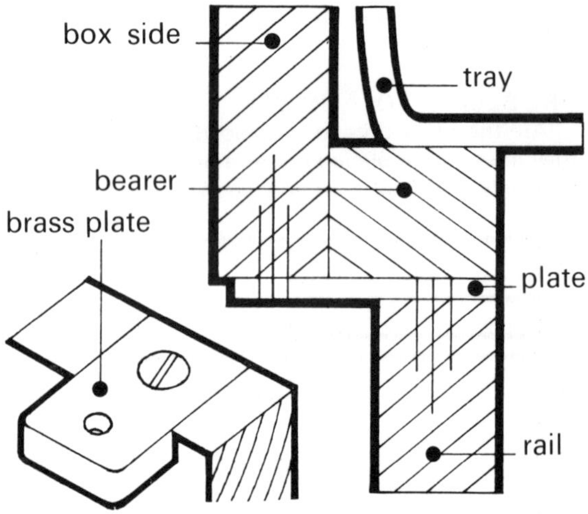

section

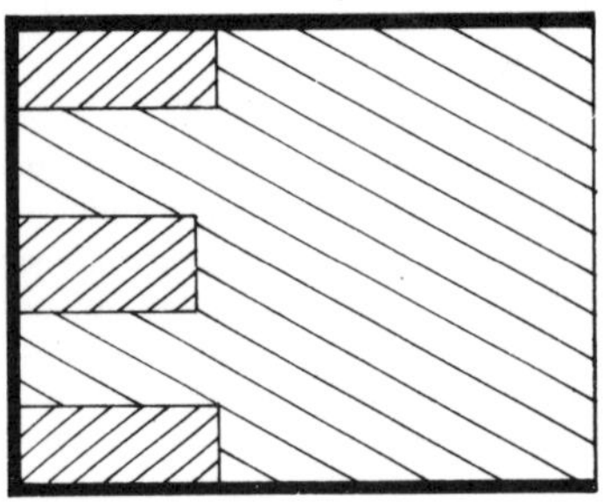

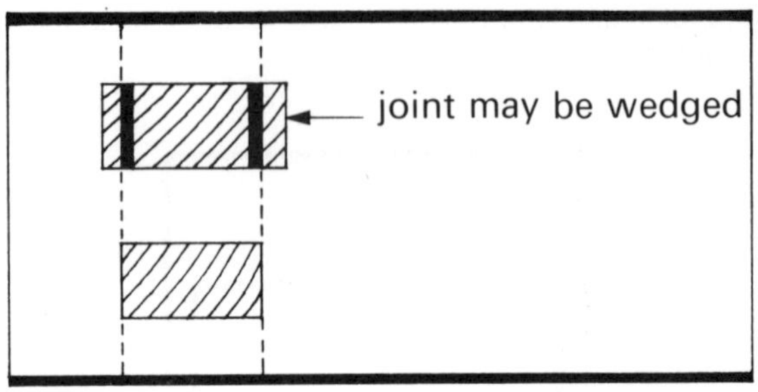

MATERIALS AND FINISH

Softwood slats and frame should be finished in white gloss paint and the hardwood box given a polyurethane finish to emphasise the grain.

Slats and rails made from western red cedar should be finished with polyurethane and the WBP plywood box painted white to contrast both texture and colour.

When making a jardinière consider the contents and its position in or around the home and use a metal or plastic tray in the box. This must be made or bought before making your full-size drawings.

Consider other constructions based on the stools in Design 3.

A simple but effective design suitable for both inside and outside use.

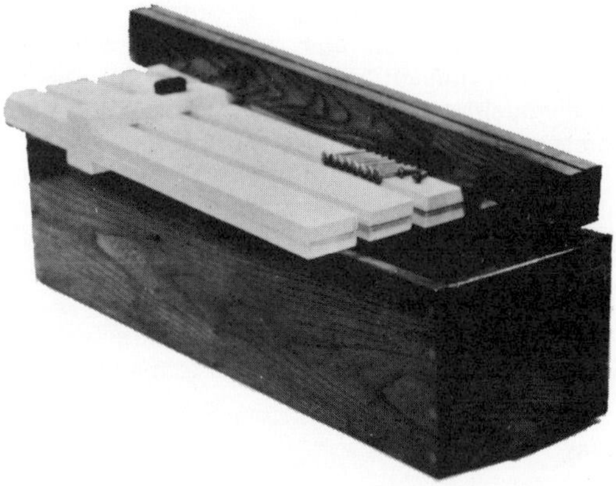

The use of knock-down fittings (see page 163) for the frame rails enable the unit to be stored away in the winter months.

Plastic KD fittings—an alternative to using metal plates to hold the box in position.

DESIGN 10 GARDEN FURNITURE

Group work is particularly useful when large items of work are being planned or when several identical items need to be made. In both instances simplified assembly line methods may be introduced. Group work is not uncommon before school activities such as Christmas plays when scenery and 'props' require combined efforts. Boatbuilding is another task in which both trouble and time are saved by group working.

Garden Furniture design is often neglected in school. Perhaps during a long cold winter we find it hard to imagine eating our tea outside on a warm summer evening. Storage during the wintertime may seem to present an insurmountable problem or an individual boy may think the task beyond him in a foreseeable length of time.

Imagination and good fortune are needed to overcome the first drawback. The second demands careful planning to see how the work can fold away or be 'knock-down' and the last is solved by working as a group.

This is an account of one such scheme—a design problem solved in practical terms by a group of fourth year boys.

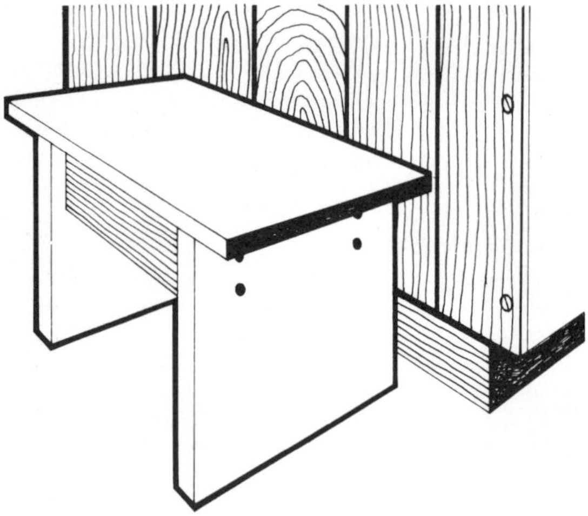

DESIGN REQUIREMENTS

A sturdy table for outdoor use which is large enough for four people to eat a full meal from.

When not in use, the stools to be protected from inclement weather under a surface which has a truly protective finish.

To be neat and attractive in appearance.

To be easily dismantled and reassembled—taking up a minimum amount of space for winter storage.

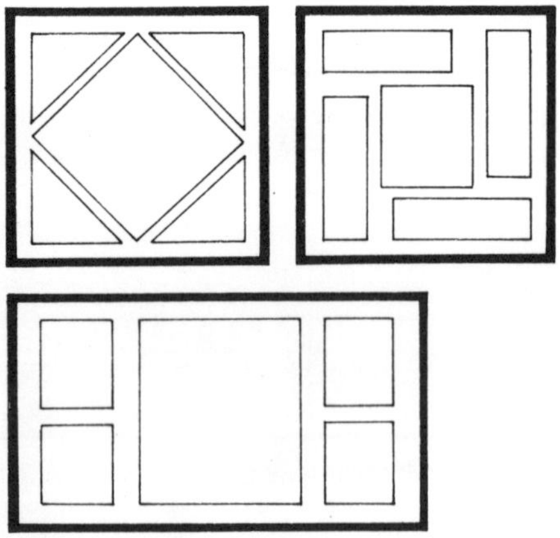

APPEARANCE

The eventual design began to emerge only after many dozens of sketches had been made.

Approximate known sizes were the height (750 millimetres) and the top (not less than 1 metre square) to accommodate four adults for a meal.

Spaces and forms were, at first, seen as simple rectangular forms and the design lost all its impact when, at a later stage 'legs' were drawn in.

This resulted in a return to the rectangular slab-sided stools and a box (made from four frames) to support the table top.

This column had to be of good size to be sufficiently stable, and scale drawings were used which soon showed that a rectangular table top would be most successful.

DESIGN FEATURES

We realised that the seats could be protected throughout an unpredictable Summer season by being suspended from the top. The idea was developed and *the suspended stools became the strongest design feature.*

The top was visualized as a smooth shiny surface supported by a contrasting textured base. This was achieved by using a plywood top and a base made up into panels from pine matching-board and raised from the ground on a 'plinth'.

The mahogany side rails which supported the stools provided a strong horizontal line in contrast to the vertical boarding. (See photo p. 183).

The stools kept the simple slab sides but added both colour and texture to the design with their

PVC covered tops.

The whole job was designed to be dismantled and reassembled with a screwdriver.

There was a considerable number of screws and a Stanley spiral ratchet driver (see 'Special Tools' section) saved many a weary wrist and blistered palm!

DECORATION

Decoration was, as with so many other successful designs, never thought of as a separate item. The size and shape of the pieces were decided and the materials specified only after preparing coloured pictorial sketches based on the most promising ideas.

Hard gloss paint, matt knotty pine boarding, dark mahogany rails, textured seats and fairly large metal fittings were adequate decoration. *Decoration which is 'applied' is less often successful.*

CONSTRUCTION

The top. This was conveniently sawn from a sheet of plywood, as were the stool tops and sides.

One standard sheet of board left material enough to be used for other jobs.

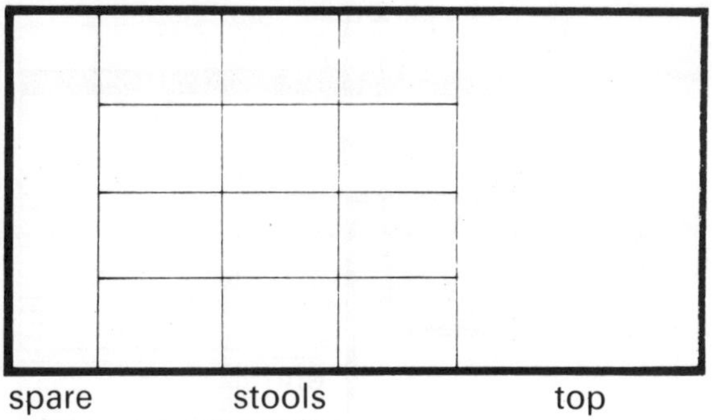

The supporting base or column consisted of two sides attached to two end panels by means of 45 mm no. 10 brass screws, to form a 'box'.

The corner joint was extremely strong being held by steel screws and a resin adhesive.

The matching board was glued and screwed (brass) or nailed (copper nails are also suitable) and the end tongue and groove planed off.

A constant gap between the boards was maintained by using a spacing strip of hardboard when securing the boards.

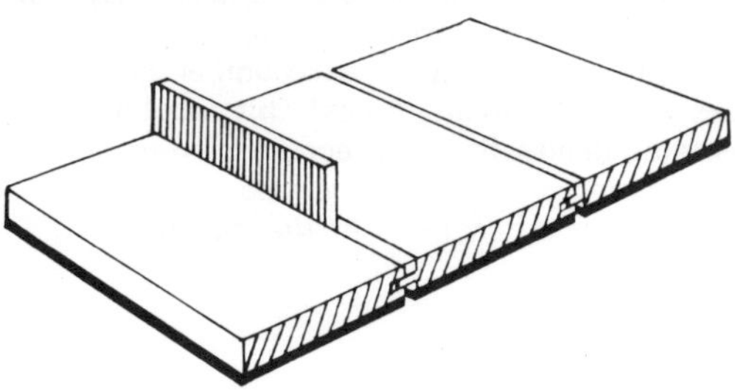

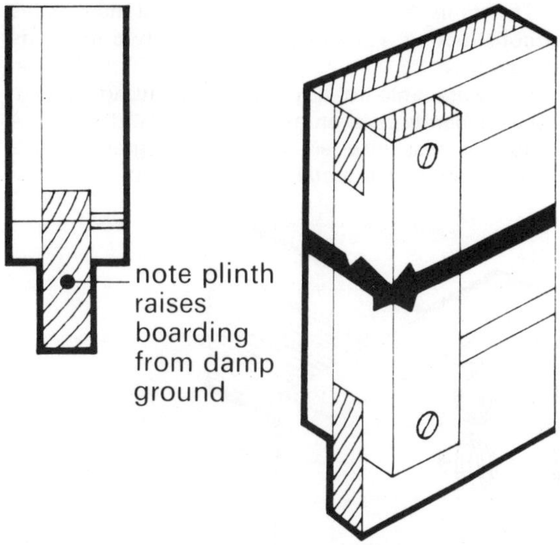

For the side frames a lighter construction was possible and the bottom rail (75 mm by 25 mm) was stepped to fit into the end frame.

A cam-locking device was used to secure the top but plastic KD fittings are suitable and more easily obtained.

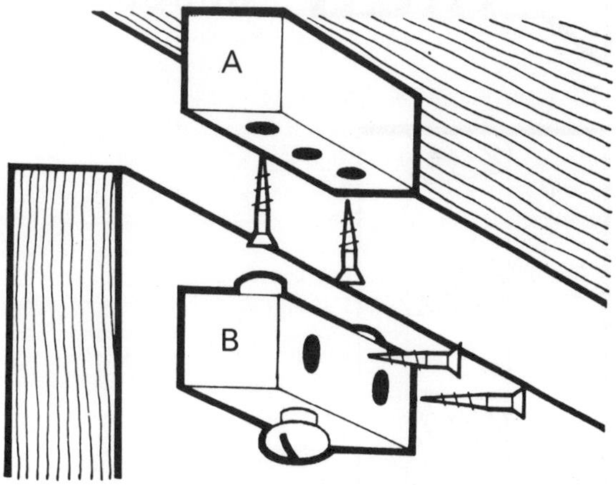

The stools. You will be able to think of many ways of constructing a stool other than the two methods shown here.

We were able to buy some KD fittings which gave tremendous strength to the rail/end joints. A metal coil was inserted into the end grain with a special tool and a metal screw inserted.

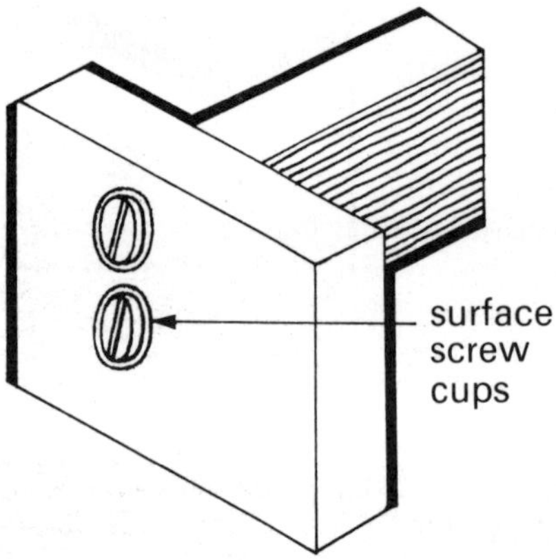

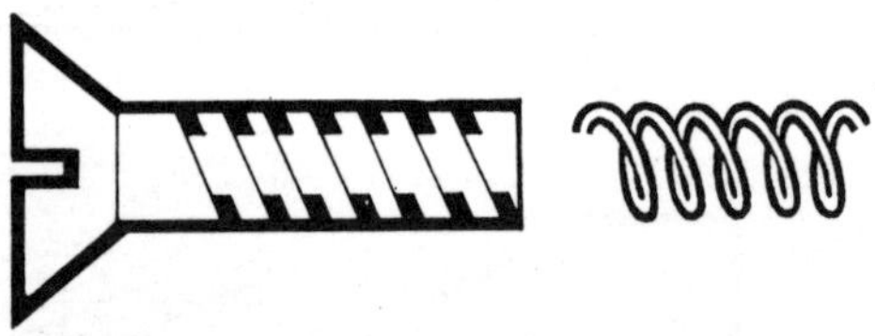

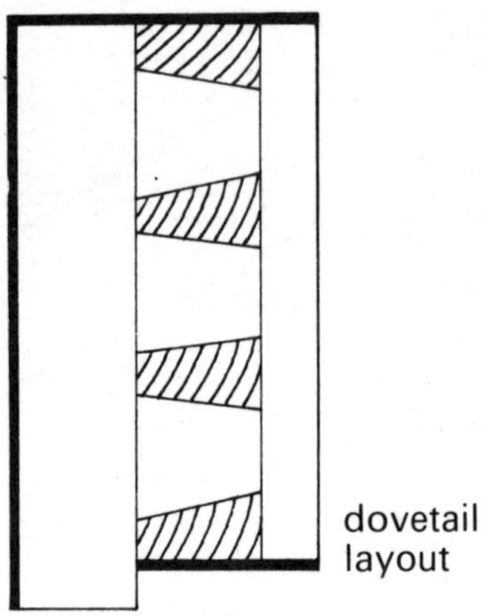

Alternative. You could construct a shallow box using a dovetail or comb joint, but this would not pack so well for storage.

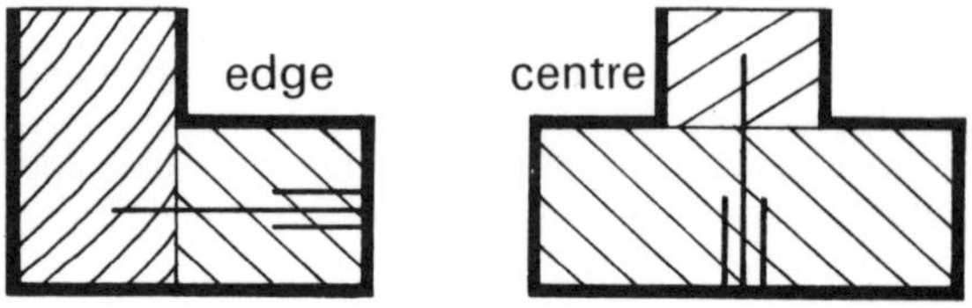

The bearers. These were glued and screwed through the top for maximum strength, the countersunk holes being filled with stopping or wood plugs.

THE WORKING DRAWING

Models of Balsa and full-size blackboard elevations convinced us that a height of 740 mm was preferable to 760 mm and still left good leg room.

Working drawings were restricted to full-size details of corner joints and clearances such as shown and $\frac{1}{5}$ scale elevations giving overall dimensions.

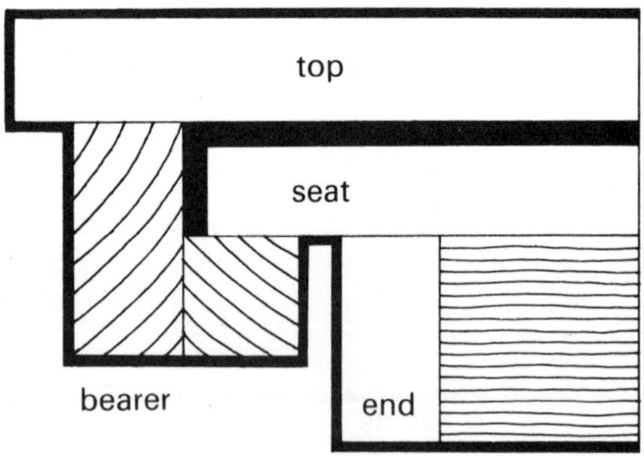

PLANNING THE WORK

For many reasons we were not able to plan a work schedule for the group down to minute detail, but contented ourselves with an 'open' list of jobs that we could envisage would need doing. In fact when work commenced this list was rarely referred to, as the jobs took on a natural progression and one foreman controlled his 'artisans'!

There are two ways of working as a group. One is for each member to complete a task—say a stool—and contribute it to the group; the other is for each boy to select a limited number of repetitive tasks—such as drilling holes! This repetition, using jigs, etc., makes for more accurate work produced in less time.

The finished design is shown opposite.

The completed set of Garden Furniture in use.

A dowelling jig ensures accurately bored holes in the end grain of the stool rails.

These holes are then countersunk with an attachment screwed to the drill.

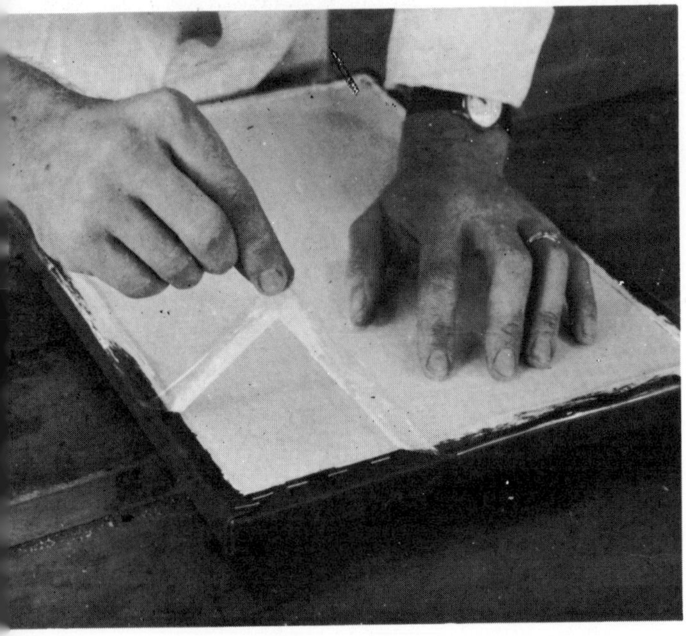

The seat bottoms are painted—on KD furniture all surfaces will be seen. Here masking tape, which gives a neat edge, is being removed.

The seat is neatly secured with a plastic KD fitting.

Right: The top is reversed to show clearly the positioning of the stool bearers.

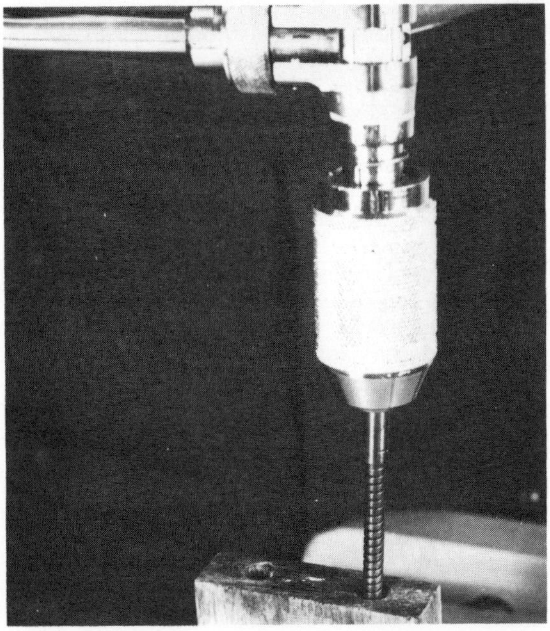

The Helicoil spring is inserted with a special tool held in the joiner's brace.

Square-threaded screws in surface cups are used to attach the rails to the stool sides.

EXAMINATION QUESTIONS

1

1. Design and make a child's wheelbarrow.
2. Make a sketch showing the general shape and explain how you would make a small tray suitable to hold four cups of tea.
   Your choice of materials would determine the type of finish you would use. (S)
3. Design a simple stand for a wrist watch for use on a bedside table, so that the time on a luminous watch face could be clearly seen from the bed. (S)
4. Design a cage suitable for keeping guinea pigs or white mice. List the points which your design must fulfil and then make a freehand sketch to show the form the cage will take. (S)
5. Design a portable nailbox suitable for a small quantity of 25, 38, 50 and 100 mm nails.
6. Show by a drawing and notes a design for a small pair of step ladders. *(a)* maximum height of four steps not more than 400 mm wide. *(b)* methods of jointing should be clearly shown. *(c)* the following materials may be used if necessary; resin glue, screw, nails, 50 mm back flap hinges, parana pine in boards 15 and 22 mm thick.
7. Design a coat-rack with three pegs, suitable for fixing to the wall. The backboard or frame should not be larger than 600×400 millimetres.
8. The synthetic resin powder shown below is mixed into a thin paste and can be kept in a jar ready for use—though it must not contact the hardener.
   Design and make a convenient carrier for the resin, hardener, brush and applicator—for workshop use.

9. Design and make a salad bowl 225 to 300 mm in diameter.
10. Give sketches showing the design and construction of a box to hold letters after they have been pushed through a slot in the door. Indicate the main measurements and state the finish. (WM)
11. By means of pictorial sketches and formal orthographic projections show the form and construction of a small hardwood box which will store 150 coloured slides 50×50 mm square and 3 mm thick. The top should have a hinged lid.
12. Design a letter box to be secured to a gate post at the end of a garden drive.
    It must be weatherproof, lockable and capable of taking envelopes 162×229 mm (C5). Name the finish. Materials in addition to wood may be used. (JMB)
13. Make preliminary sketches and then a full size working drawing of a box suitable for holding a set of draughtsmen each being 10 mm thick and 28 mm in diameter. Name the finish.
14. These shells are cemented to a piece of 6 mm plywood 250×100 mm.
    Make drawings to show the construction of a jewellery box for which this could form part of the lid.

15. Design a duet stool for a piano. It should be 500 mm high and must have some means whereby it can be easily moved. There must be some storage for sheet music, the size of which may be taken as 350×220 mm. (JMB)
16. Design a stool with a cork top for use in a bathroom, considering the following points:
    (i) The stool will be in a steamy atmosphere and will often get wet.
    (ii) A suitable height.
    (iii) How you would support and fix the cork top.
    Make as many preliminary sketches as you find necessary and then make a clear final freehand drawing of your design.
    (a) Give the main dimensions.
    (b) Name the joints you would use.
    (c) Show with a section how the cork top is fitted.
    (d) Name a suitable finish. (MET)

17. You are designing the layout of a boy's bedroom including a small table.

Give details of the construction of this table, the overall sizes, the timber sizes and state how you would finish it. (WM)

18. Design a table suitable for playing indoor games such as chess or cards.

There should be provision for storing the games when not in use.

Name the timber to be used. (JMB)

19. Design and make a wall rack suitable for holding books and for displaying pieces of pottery and other small objects. One shelf must be adjustable.

20. Screwdrivers are just one example of a group of handtools which are made and used in a large variety of shapes and sizes.

Select some common small tools, such as screwdrivers, bradawls, pliers and pincers, then design and make a simple rack for them. How would the rack be fitted onto a brick workshop wall, above the workbench?

21. Design a unit for fixing to the wall to take the radio shown below and a *Radio Times* (300× 250 mm).

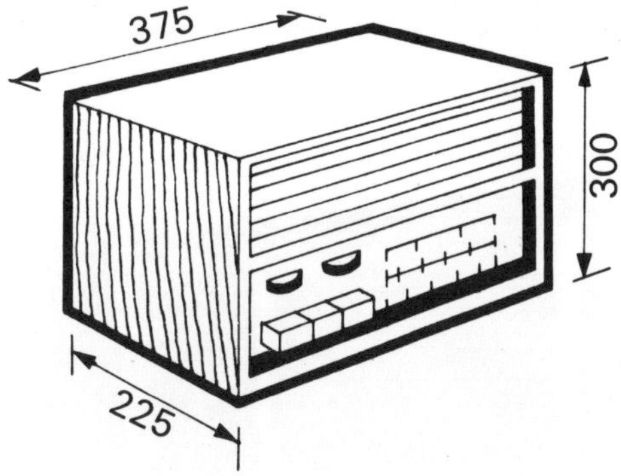

Consider the following points:

(i) The radio is heavy.

(ii) The *Radio Times* must be easy to get in and out.

(iii) The appearance of the unit will be improved if the method of fixing to the wall is hidden when the unit is in use.

Make as many sketches as you need to develop your ideas and then make a final freehand drawing of your design.

The following should be given:

(a) The main dimensions.

(b) The joints you would use.

22. The drawing shows the top of a small coffee table.

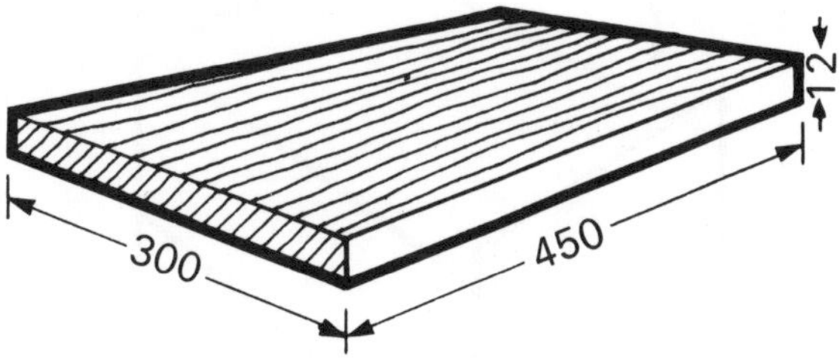

Make sketches showing details of:

(a) A complete suitable underframe to which the top can be attached.

(b) A sketch of one of the frame joints.

(c) A sketch of one method of fixing the top to the underframe.

(d) List the important points you would consider if asked to design the complete coffee table. (EM)

23. Design a framed hall mirror which is to be fixed to the wall. The mirror size is 300×250 mm. Your design should include a small shelf.

State the material and finish you would use and make a cutting list using finished sizes. (S)

24. Design a table to be used in your home to support the television set illustrated below. The cabinet is veneered in sapele mahogany and has a natural (not a highly polished) finish.

Your answer should include the main dimensions, details of the joints, the timber used and the finish. (S)

(c) A suitable timber.
(d) A suitable finish. (MET)

25. Using the basic idea and the dimensions given in the sketch design and construct a cabinet to store long playing records.

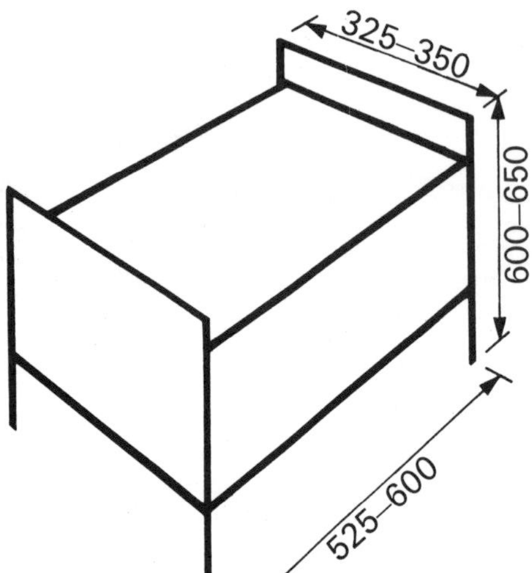

26. Design a gymnastic jumping stand. The sizes of the material, type of timber and the joints used are important. (S)

27. Design a hymn board to hang in a prominent position in a new school assembly hall to hold three numbered cards for one hymn. Each card measures 100×75×3 mm. State the materials and the finish you would use. (S)

28. The photograph shows a group of wood toys suitable for a baby (under one year old) to play with.

Make a study of the toys and games that you would expect an older child (select the age) to be interested in.

Design and make a constructional toy suitable for both boys and girls of that age and consider very carefully the safety aspects of your design.

29. (A) Give sketches showing the design and construction of a picnic table, approximately 750×450 mm, with folding legs. Add six further main measurements and state the finish you would use.
(B) Make out a cutting list for this table.
(C) Print neatly between two lines, 4 mm apart:
A FOLDING PICNIC TABLE. (W)

30. Make preliminary sketches of a table mounted show cabinet for displaying jewellery made in the school workshops.

The construction should keep the exhibits dust free and a suitable fastening must be selected and shown.

TABLE 1

a Fractions of an inch to millimetres
Wood Screw gauge
Imperial Standard wire gauge

INCHES FRACTIONS	MM.	WOOD SCREW GAUGE	IMPERIAL STANDARD WIRE GAUGE	INCHES FRACTIONS	MM.	WOOD SCREW GAUGE	IMPERIAL STANDARD WIRE GAUGE	INCHES FRACTIONS	MM.
			30			**9**			13·00
			29	3/16	4·762			33/64	13·09
			28			**10**	6	17/32	13·49
1/64	·3969				5·000			35/64	13·89
			27	13/64	5·159				14·00
			26				5	9/16	14·28
			25	7/32	5·556			37/64	14·68
			24			**12**			15·00
			23				4	19/32	15·08
			22	15/64	5·953			39/64	15·47
1/32	·7938				6·000			5/8	15·87
			21			**14**			16·00
			20	1/4	6·350			41/64	16·27
	1·000						3	21/32	16·66
			19	17/64	6·746				17·00
3/64	1·190				7·000			43/64	17·06
			18			**16**	2	11/16	17·46
			17	9/32	7·143			45/64	17·85
		0		19/64	7·540				18·00
1/16	1·587						1	23/32	18·25
			16			**18**		47/64	18·65
		1		5/16	7·937				19·00
			15		8·000			3/4	19·05
5/64	2·000						0	49/64	19·44
			14	21/64	8·334			25/32	19·84
		2				**20**			20·00
			13	11/32	8·731			51/64	20·24
3/32	2·381						2/0	13/16	20·63
		3			9·000				21·00
			12	23/64	9·128			53/64	21·03
		4				**22**		27/32	21·43
7/64	2·778						3/0	55/64	21·82
			11	3/8	9·525				22·00
	3·000			25/64	9·921			7/8	22·22
		5			10·000			57/64	22·62
1/8	3·175						4/0		23·00
			10	13/32	10·318			29/32	23·01
		6		27/64	10·715			59/64	23·41
9/64	3·571						5/0	15/16	23·81
			9		11·000				24·00
		7		7/16	11·112			61/64	24·20
5/32	3·968			29/64	11·509			31/32	24·60
	4·000						6/0	63/64	25·00
			8	15/32	11·906			1	25·40
		8			12·000				
11/64	4·365			31/64	12·303				
			7						

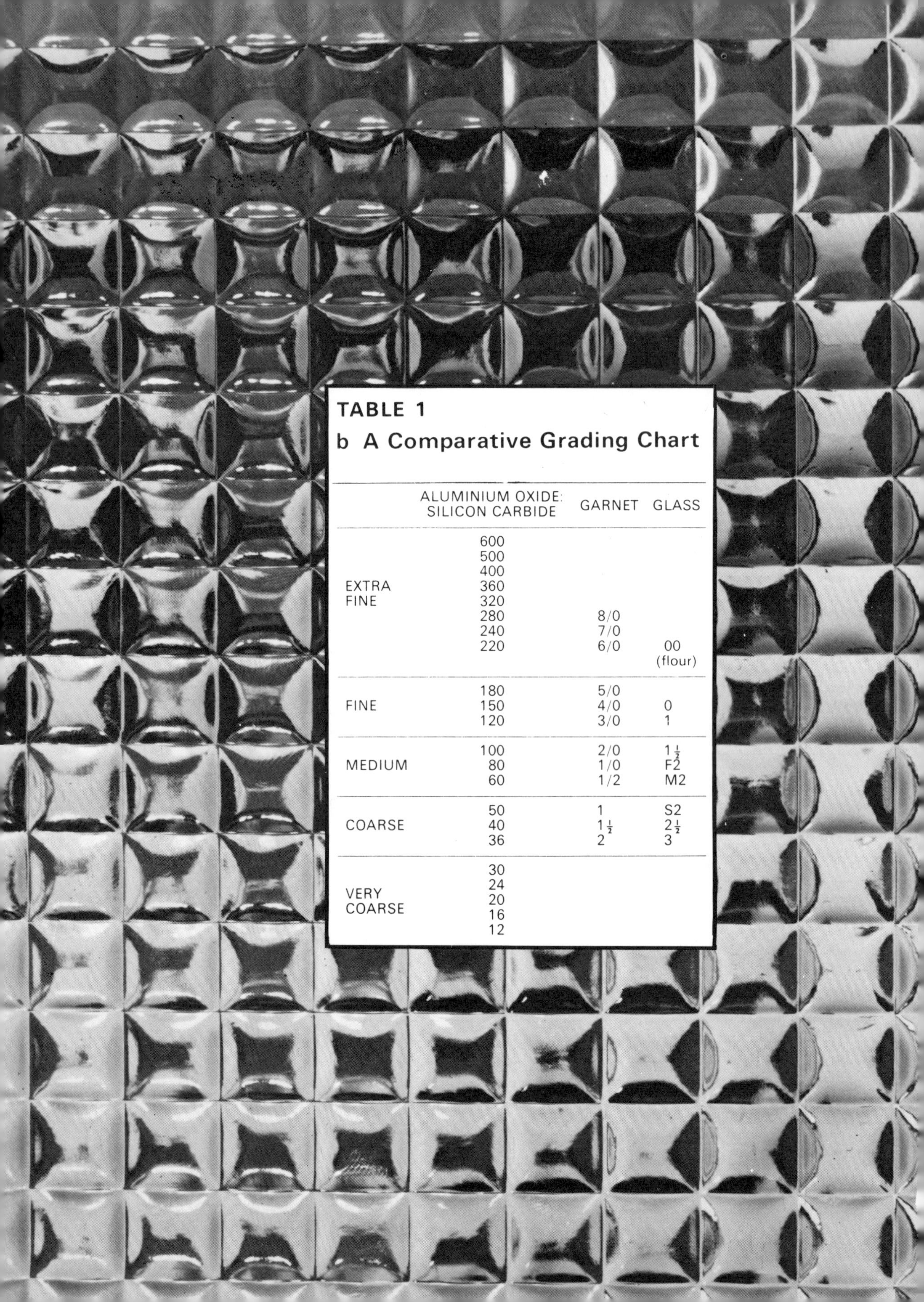

TABLE 1

b A Comparative Grading Chart

	ALUMINIUM OXIDE: SILICON CARBIDE	GARNET	GLASS
EXTRA FINE	600		
	500		
	400		
	360		
	320		
	280	8/0	
	240	7/0	
	220	6/0	00 (flour)
FINE	180	5/0	
	150	4/0	0
	120	3/0	1
MEDIUM	100	2/0	1½
	80	1/0	F2
	60	1/2	M2
COARSE	50	1	S2
	40	1½	2½
	36	2	3
VERY COARSE	30		
	24		
	20		
	16		
	12		

TABLE 2
Inches to Millimetres

Basis: 1 in = 25·4 mm (exactly)

inches	0	1	2	3	4	5	6	7	8	9	10	11
	millimetres											
—	—	25·400	50·800	76·200	101·600	127·000	152·400	177·800	203·200	228·600	254·000	279·400
$\frac{1}{32}$	0·794	26·194	51·594	76·994	102·394	127·794	153·194	178·594	203·994	229·394	254·794	280·194
$\frac{1}{16}$	1·588	26·988	52·388	77·788	103·188	128·588	153·988	179·388	204·788	230·188	255·588	280·988
$\frac{3}{32}$	2·381	27·781	53·181	78·581	103·981	129·381	154·781	180·181	205·581	230·981	256·381	281·781
$\frac{1}{8}$	3·175	28·575	53·975	79·375	104·775	130·175	155·575	180·975	206·375	231·775	257·175	282·575
$\frac{5}{32}$	3·969	29·369	54·769	80·169	105·569	130·969	156·369	181·769	207·169	232·569	257·969	283·369
$\frac{3}{16}$	4·762	30·162	55·562	80·962	106·362	131·762	157·162	182·562	207·962	233·362	258·762	284·162
$\frac{7}{32}$	5·556	30·956	56·356	81·756	107·156	132·556	157·956	183·356	208·756	234·156	259·556	284·956
$\frac{1}{4}$	6·350	31·750	57·150	82·550	107·950	133·350	158·750	184·150	209·550	234·950	260·350	285·750
$\frac{9}{32}$	7·144	32·544	57·944	83·344	108·744	134·144	159·544	184·944	210·344	235·744	261·144	286·544
$\frac{5}{16}$	7·938	33·338	58·738	84·138	109·538	134·938	160·338	185·738	211·138	236·538	261·938	287·338
$\frac{11}{32}$	8·731	34·131	59·531	84·931	110·331	135·731	161·131	186·531	211·931	237·331	262·731	288·131
$\frac{3}{8}$	9·525	34·925	60·325	85·725	111·125	136·525	161·925	187·325	212·725	238·125	263·525	288·925
$\frac{13}{32}$	10·319	35·719	61·119	86·519	111·919	137·319	162·719	188·119	213·519	238·919	264·319	289·719
$\frac{7}{16}$	11·112	36·512	61·912	87·312	112·712	138·112	163·512	188·912	214·312	239·712	265·112	290·512
$\frac{15}{32}$	11·906	37·306	62·706	88·106	113·506	138·906	164·306	189·706	215·106	240·506	265·906	291·306
$\frac{1}{2}$	12·700	38·100	63·500	88·900	114·300	139·700	165·100	190·500	215·900	241·300	266·700	292·100
$\frac{17}{32}$	13·494	38·894	64·294	89·694	115·094	140·494	165·894	191·294	216·694	242·094	267·494	292·894
$\frac{9}{16}$	14·288	39·688	65·088	90·488	115·888	141·288	166·688	192·088	217·488	242·888	268·288	293·688
$\frac{19}{32}$	15·081	40·481	65·881	91·281	116·681	142·081	167·481	192·881	218·281	243·681	269·081	294·481
$\frac{5}{8}$	15·875	41·275	66·675	92·075	117·475	142·875	168·275	193·675	219·075	244·475	269·875	295·275
$\frac{21}{32}$	16·669	42·069	67·469	92·869	118·269	143·669	169·069	194·469	219·869	245·269	270·669	296·069
$\frac{11}{16}$	17·462	42·862	68·262	93·662	119·062	144·462	169·862	195·262	220·662	246·062	271·462	296·862
$\frac{23}{32}$	18·256	43·656	69·056	94·456	119·856	145·256	170·656	196·056	221·456	246·856	272·256	297·656
$\frac{3}{4}$	19·050	44·450	69·850	95·250	120·650	146·050	171·450	196·850	222·250	247·650	273·050	298·450
$\frac{25}{32}$	19·844	45·244	70·644	96·044	121·444	146·844	172·244	197·644	223·044	248·444	273·844	299·244
$\frac{13}{16}$	20·638	46·038	71·438	96·836	122·238	147·638	173·038	198·438	223·838	249·238	274·638	300·038
$\frac{27}{32}$	21·431	46·831	72·231	97·631	123·031	148·431	173·831	199·231	224·631	250·031	275·431	300·831
$\frac{7}{8}$	22·225	47·625	73·025	98·425	123·825	149·225	174·625	200·025	225·425	250·825	276·225	301·625
$\frac{29}{32}$	23·019	48·419	73·819	99·219	124·619	150·019	175·419	200·819	226·219	251·619	277·019	302·419
$\frac{15}{16}$	23·812	49·212	74·612	100·012	125·412	150·812	176·212	201·612	227·012	252·412	277·812	303·212
$\frac{31}{32}$	24·606	50·006	75·406	100·806	126·206	151·606	177·006	202·406	227·806	253·206	278·606	304·006

TABLE 3
Feet to Metres

Basis: 1 ft = 0·3048 m (exactly)

feet	0	1	2	3	4	5	6	7	8	9
	metres									
0	—	0·3048	0·6096	0·9144	1·2192	1·5240	1·8288	2·1336	2·4384	2·7432
10	3·0480	3·3528	3·6576	3·9624	4·2672	4·5720	4·8768	5·1816	5·4864	5·7912
20	6·0960	6·4008	6·7056	7·0104	7·3152	7·6200	7·9248	8·2296	8·5344	8·8392
30	9·1440	9·4488	9·7536	10·0584	10·3632	10·6680	10·9728	11·2776	11·5824	11·8872
40	12·1920	12·4968	12·8016	13·1064	13·4112	13·7160	14·0208	14·3256	14·6304	14·9352
50	15·2400	15·5448	15·8496	16·1544	16·4592	16·7640	17·0688	17·3736	17·6784	17·9832
60	18·2880	18·5928	18·8976	19·2024	19·5072	19·8120	20·1168	20·4216	20·7264	21·0312
70	21·3360	21·6408	21·9456	22·2504	22·5552	22·8600	23·1648	23·4696	23·7744	24·0792
80	24·3840	24·6888	24·9936	25·2984	25·6032	25·9080	26·2128	26·5176	26·8224	27·1272
90	27·4320	27·7368	28·0416	28·3464	28·6512	28·9560	29·2608	29·5656	29·8704	30·1752

TABLE 4
Square Inches to Square Centimetres

Basis: 1 in² = 6·4516 cm² (exactly)

sq. in.	0	1	2	3	4	5	6	7	8	9
	square centimetres									
0	—	06·452	12·903	19·355	25·806	32·258	38·710	45·161	51·613	58·064
10	64·516	70·968	77·419	83·871	90·322	96·774	103·226	109·677	116·129	122·580
20	129·032	135·484	141·935	148·387	154·838	161·290	167·742	174·193	180·645	187·096
30	193·548	200·000	206·451	212·903	219·354	225·806	232·258	238·709	245·161	251·612
40	258·064	264·516	270·967	277·419	283·870	290·322	296·774	303·225	309·677	316·128
50	322·580	329·032	335·483	341·935	348·386	354·838	361·290	367·741	374·193	380·644
60	387·096	393·548	399·999	406·451	412·902	419·354	425·806	432·257	438·709	445·160
70	451·612	458·064	464·515	470·967	477·418	483·870	490·322	496·773	503·225	509·676
80	516·128	522·580	529·031	535·483	541·934	548·386	554·838	561·289	567·741	574·192
90	580·644	587·096	593·547	599·999	606·450	612·902	619·354	625·805	632·257	638·708
100	645·160	651·612	658·063	664·515	670·966	677·418	683·870	690·321	696·773	703·224
110	709·676	716·128	722·579	729·031	735·482	741·934	748·386	754·837	761·289	767·740
120	774·192	780·644	787·095	793·547	799·998	806·450	812·902	819·353	825·805	832·256
130	838·708	845·160	851·611	858·063	864·514	870·966	877·418	883·869	890·321	896·772
140	903·224	909·676	916·127	922·579	929·030	935·482	941·934	948·385	954·837	961·288
150	967·740	974·192	980·643	987·095	993·546	999·998	1006·45	1012·90	1019·35	1025·80
160	1032·26	1038·71	1045·16	1051·61	1058·06	1064·51	1070·97	1077·42	1083·87	1090·32
170	1096·77	1103·22	1109·68	1116·13	1122·58	1129·03	1135·48	1141·93	1148·38	1154·84
180	1161·29	1167·74	1174·19	1180·64	1187·09	1193·55	1200·00	1206·45	1212·90	1219·35
190	1225·80	1232·26	1238·71	1245·16	1251·61	1258·06	1264·51	1270·97	1277·42	1283·87
200	1290·32	1296·77	1303·22	1309·67	1316·13	1322·58	1329·03	1335·48	1341·93	1348·38
210	1354·84	1361·29	1367·74	1374·19	1380·64	1387·09	1393·55	1400·00	1406·45	1412·90
220	1419·35	1425·30	1432·26	1438·71	1445·16	1451·61	1458·06	1464·51	1470·96	1477·42
230	1483·87	1490·32	1496·77	1503·22	1509·67	1516·13	1522·58	1529·03	1535·48	1541·93
240	1548·38	1554·84	1561·29	1567·74	1574·19	1580·64	1587·09	1593·55	1600·00	1606·45

TABLE 5
Square Feet to Square Metres

Basis: 1 ft² = 0·092 903 04 m² (exactly)

sq. ft.	0	1	2	3	4	5	6	7	8	9
	square metres									
0	—	0·09290	0·18581	0·27871	0·37161	0·46452	0·55742	0·65032	0·74322	0·83613
10	0·92903	1·02193	1·11484	1·20774	1·30064	1·39355	1·48645	1·57935	1·67225	1·76516
20	1·85806	1·95096	2·04387	2·13677	2·22967	2·32258	2·41548	2·50838	2·60129	2·69419
30	2·78709	2·87999	2·97290	3·06580	3·15870	3·25161	3·34451	3·43741	3·53032	3·62322
40	3·71612	3·80902	3·90193	3·99483	4·08773	4·18064	4·27354	4·36644	4·45935	4·55225
50	4·64515	4·73806	4·83096	4·92386	5·01676	5·10967	5·20257	5·29547	5·38838	5·48128
60	5·57418	5·66709	5·75999	5·85289	5·94579	6·03870	6·13160	6·22450	6·31741	6·41031
70	6·50321	6·59612	6·68902	6·78192	6·87482	6·96773	7·06063	7·15353	7·24644	7·33934
80	7·43224	7·52515	7·61805	7·71095	7·80386	7·89676	7·98966	8·08256	8·17547	8·26837
90	8·36127	8·45418	8·54708	8·63998	8·73289	8·82579	8·91869	9·01159	9·10450	9·19740

TABLE 6
U.K. Fluid Ounces to Millilitres

Basis: 1 UK gal = 160 UK fl oz
= 4·545 96 litres

UK fl oz	0	1	2	3	4	5	6	7	8	9
	millilitres									
0	—	28·41	56·82	85·24	113·65	142·06	170·47	198·89	227·30	255·71
10	284·12	312·53	340·95	369·36	397·77	426·18	454·60	483·01	511·42	539·83
20	568·24	596·66	625·07	653·48	681·89	710·31	738·72	767·13	795·54	823·96
30	852·37	880·78	909·19	937·60	966·02	994·43	1022·84	1051·25	1079·67	1108·08
40	1136·49	1164·90	1193·31	1221·73	1250·14	1278·55	1306·96	1335·38	1363·79	1392·20
50	1420·61	1449·02	1477·44	1505·85	1534·26	1562·67	1591·09	1619·50	1647·91	1676·32
60	1704·73	1733·15	1761·56	1789·97	1818·38	1846·80	1875·21	1903·62	1932·03	1960·45
70	1988·86	2017·27	2045·68	2074·09	2102·51	2130·92	2159·33	2187·74	2216·16	2244·57
80	2272·98	2301·39	2329·80	2358·22	2386·63	2415·04	2443·45	2471·87	2500·28	2528·69
90	2557·10	2585·51	2613·93	2642·34	2670·75	2699·16	2727·58	2755·99	2784·40	2812·81
100	2841·22	—	—	—	—	—	—	—	—	—